"The authors have assembled data from 113,000 respondents—by far the most comprehensive random sample of detailed religious preferences ever collected in the United States."

KENNETH WOODWARD,
Newsweek

"The book indicates significant demographic changes that politicians, for example, will ignore at their peril. . . . One can understand little about the U.S. without understanding its religious diversity and how that plays in its national makeup and political decision making."

LAWRENCE GOODRICH,
Christian Science Monitor

"The study offers unique insight into America's religious scene. It includes . . . religious profiles of ethnic groups and the geographical distributions of religions in this country. It even ranks religions based on education, income, home ownership, and employment."

ROBIN EDWARDS,
National Catholic Reporter

"Most likely *One Nation Under God* will be cherished as much for its graphs, charts, and maps as anything else. . . . [It] includes a brilliant chapter on geography, the 'Who's Where' of American religion."

MARTIN MARTY,
Christian Century

For our wives,
Helen and Susan

ACKNOWLEDGMENTS

◆ ◆ ◆

It would not be feasible to thank by name the hundreds of people who, in one way or another, helped us in this endeavor. However, we would be remiss if we did not record our gratitude to the following persons whose advice and assistance proved invaluable in the course of the research and in the task of writing the text: Elliot Brackman, Deborah Bursztyn, Abigail A. Chesir, Richard Cimino, Michael J. Costelloe, John De Wolf, Barry Disman, John Fontana, Rita Foulk, Peter Guzzardi, Sarah Hamlin, Joseph C. Harris, Christy DeBoe Hicks, Arthur Hu, Dvora Inwood, Ariella Keysar, Dale Kulp, Valerie Kuscenko, Elliot I. Lachman, Rita Lefkort, Albert Menendez, James Monteith, Segundo Pantoja, Murray Polner, Jeffrey Scheckner, Nanette Shaw, Ira Sheskin, Anthony Stevens-Arroyo, and Kathy Sullivan.

CONTENTS

♦ ♦ ♦

1

INTRODUCTION

◆ ◆ ◆

Americans in general believe that there is a moral crisis in society. They fear that the family is in danger of losing its spiritual foundation when children grow up without faith in God, and without belief in the immortality of the soul. Today, 1 million Americans are in jail. America has higher rates of violence, drug addiction, and crime than other Western industrialized nations. Yet 80 million Americans attend worship services on any given weekend. What does all this mean? Do religion and worship impact at all on behavior? Is it possible that the situation would be worse if religion were not there?

The vast majority of Americans consider themselves to be religious and are not afraid to admit it. For most, *religion* means a personal affirmation of faith in God and an identification with a religious denomination, but it does not necessarily mean joining or being an active member of that particular group. It is more of a private commitment than a shared experience. This is one conclusion of the National Survey of Religious Identification (NSRI), conducted by the Graduate School of the City University of New York. The most extensive survey of religious identification in 20th-century America, the study reveals many insights but also raises numerous questions.

Our 1990 NSRI fills an information void. It reports the answers of a large, representative sample of American adults to the simple question "What is your religion?" The enormous popular-media interest that the NSRI generated at its release in April 1991 tells much about society. Front-page stories and feature articles appeared in hundreds of newspapers across the country, from New York to Los Angeles. Obviously, Americans hunger for the data, even though many, we learned, do not want government to collect them.

The survey reached a representative sample of 113,000 people across the continental United States by computer-generated telephone calls in a thirteen-month period, making it the largest and most comprehensive poll ever on religious loyalties, and the most accurate and detailed as to geographical distribution. (For a fuller description of our methodology, see the Appendix.) It examined religious identification in terms of state and region, as well as by seventeen other categories including age, marital status, and political-party affiliation. The study was undertaken because the United States did not have an adequate religious profile, principally due to the fact that the First Amendment to the Constitution, prohibiting an establishment of religion, has been interpreted as preventing the U.S. Census Bureau from asking any questions dealing with religious identification or belief.

The NSRI, which asked the question "What is your religion?" was not intended to gauge any individual's level of religious observance or commitment. The respondents, eighteen years of age or older, were not asked if they attended services regularly, contributed money to a religious organization, or had ever been baptized in a particular church. The results, then, cannot be construed to mean that those who identify themselves as Catholic, Methodist, or Baptist actually belong to the church of their denominational association. (For details on group variation in reporting and identification, see the Appendix.) According to the NSRI, many more Americans claim to be Catholic, Baptist, Methodist, Episcopalian, Lutheran, Presbyterian, or Unitarian-Universalist than the current membership figures of any of those churches reveal. This indicates that large numbers of Americans identify with a religious group but do not necessarily maintain regular contact with it. In contrast, the number of professed religious Jews, Muslims, Eastern Orthodox Christians, and members of other small minorities identified was lower than current institutional claims.

An overwhelming number of Americans (86.2%) consider themselves to be Christians. Roman Catholics are the largest Christian group, with 26.2%, followed by the Baptists, with 19.4%. Jews represent 2% of the population. Muslims represent 0.5%, only slightly more than Buddhists and Hindus. Those who said they had no religion numbered 7.5% nationally, with the western states such as Oregon (17%), Washington and Wyoming (14% each), and California (13%) registering the largest percentages in this category. A mere 2.3%, a remarkably low percentage, refused to answer, demonstrating that Americans are not at all reluctant to express their religious preference.

We Americans have difficulty with the idea that our life choices, family patterns, social habits, and characteristics can be described in statistical

Profile of Religious Identification
for U.S. Adult Population 1990

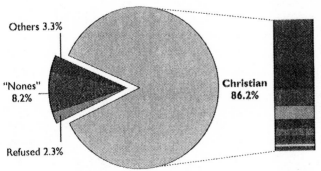

Others 3.3%

"Nones" 8.2%

Refused 2.3%

Christian 86.2%

Catholic 26.2%
Baptist 19.4%
'Protestant' 9.7%
Methodist 8%
Lutheran 5.2%
Christian 4.5%
Others 4.5%
Presbyterian 2.8%
Pentecostal 1.8%
Episcopalian 1.7%
Mormon 1.4%
Church of Christ 1%

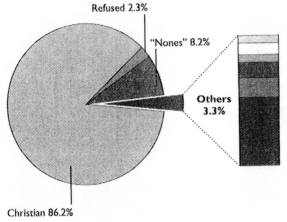

Refused 2.3%

"Nones" 8.2%

Others 3.3%

Christian 86.2%

Miscellaneous 0.1%
Unitarian 0.3%
Hindu 0.2%
Buddhist 0.4%
Muslim 0.5%
Jewish 1.8%

aggregates. In consequence, social statistics and demography—the description of human populations in terms of basic patterns, such as marriage, birth, death, migration, and employment—have remained largely of interest only to specialists. Yet the decennial U.S. Census of Population and Housing, which examines these very subjects, always generates considerable public attention due to its influence on congressional redistricting, funding of social programs, and other political hot potatoes.

Like the findings of the U.S. Census, most statistics reported by the media are official in the sense that they are produced by the government. Official statistics directly affect the everyday lives of millions when they trigger cost-of-living adjustments and determine qualifications for social programs. These official statistics do not merely hold a mirror to reality. They reflect presuppositions and theories about the nature of society. They are products of economic, social, and political interests. And yet, the absence of official government numbers concerning religion may also be telling. One of the key aspects of American life goes unrecorded: Despite the importance of religion as a social variable, the U.S. Census has never included a question on religion because of the high premium placed on the separation of church and state.

PAST ATTEMPTS AT COLLECTING RELIGIOUS STATISTICS

In the general absence of official and comprehensive information on religion, social scientists concerned with research relating to religious differentials have frequently had to rely on sample surveys of fewer than 2,000 persons to obtain their data. In most instances these surveys, such as the Gallup polls or the National Opinion Research Center (NORC) General Social Surveys, focus on the total population. Their samples, therefore, seldom include more than several hundred of the smaller religious denominations, and often considerably fewer, reflecting the fact that most religious groups constitute less than 2% of the total American population. These surveys can never provide a profile of groups such as Jehovah's Witnesses or Hindus.

Such general-population surveys are therefore not very useful for comprehensive analyses of subgroups. To overcome this problem, researchers have sometimes aggregated the data of several successive surveys, but this raises new problems related to comparability of information collected and to possible changes in attitudes and behavior in the intervals between surveys. Scholars and planners have had to improvise by using indirect measures to collect their own data on the size, distribution, composition, and vital processes of the various religious populations. A variety of sources has been used, each varying in the quality of data.

CHURCH-MEMBERSHIP STATISTICS

In Colonial times, church membership was a privilege restricted by demands of personal piety and moral purity; there were more regular churchgoers than communicants. It is estimated that the congregational size of churches in 1790 far exceeded the official membership, since only 10% of the population was actually church members. Today, more Americans claim to belong to a church than attend one regularly. A recent study sponsored by the Association of Statisticians of American Religious Bodies found that there were over 137 million church members in this country. Yet the ratio of the number of U.S. residents in 1990 (250 million) to the number of churches (over 255,000) is almost the same as it was in 1650. From this statistic we can conclude that organized religion is no weaker or stronger now than in the past.

Many social scientists consider church statistics to be unreliable, largely because membership means different things to different denominations. Some denominations have an extremely casual attitude toward membership data, while others are relatively meticulous. For Protestants, becoming a church member is a highly formal act. For Catholics, there is practically no formality at all; one is simply part of a parish because one lives in the parish area. Highly inclusive groups, such as the Catholic and Orthodox churches, contrast with very exclusive groups, such as the Jehovah's Witnesses and the Mennonites. Some of the more conservative, separatist/sectarian groups still maintain the Colonial tradition of severely restricting membership.

Statistical complications arise even when different denominations have the same criteria for membership. For example, Baptists and Catholics both restrict membership to those who have been baptized. But Catholics baptize and count infants, while Baptists baptize and count only adults. Comparing membership is, therefore, very difficult. Even groups that count only adults may have different definitions of who is an adult.

THE CENSUS OF RELIGIOUS BODIES: 1850–1936

What is often referred to as a national religious census—the official Census of Religious Bodies (CRB), conducted from 1850 to 1936—was not a census in the normal sense of the term. The CRB's data were not based on the regular U.S. Census, but were collected as part of a special poll that emphasized institutions, not individuals. The CRB enumerated the membership of the various religious groups, but it had only limited value for analytical purposes since it provided no information on the members' social and economic circumstances.

Between 1850 and 1890, the CRB obtained statistics on the number of churches, church membership, and the value of church structures by means of a special "social-statistics schedule" filled out by population-census takers who visited local churches. After 1890, the CRB switched to mid-decade. Multivolume reports appeared for 1906, 1916, 1926, and 1936, each edition based on special forms prepared by local church officials. The CRB asked each minister to report the number of members, number of church edifices, and edifice seating capacity, and then presented the collated data. Problems immediately arose as to membership criteria; the best census of religion took place in 1926, when a uniform method was used.

In 1936, the cooperation rate declined among conservative pastors and congregations, particularly of the Southern Baptist Convention, largely because of their antagonism to the liberal-leaning Federal Council of Churches of Christ in America (the forerunner of the National Council of the Churches of Christ in the U.S.A.), which at the time supported collection of church-membership statistics. The 20% noncooperation rate reduced the value of that year's data. In 1946, a governmental religious census was begun but never completed because Congress refused to allocate sufficient funds for the project. In 1956, the Eisenhower administration failed to recommend a census of religion, and no member of Congress was interested enough to raise the question.

According to the CRB information we do have, the pattern of church membership overall showed a rise, from 45% of the population in 1890 to 51% in 1906, 53% in 1916, 58% in 1926, but then a decline to 49% in 1936. Postwar Gallup surveys suggest that church membership reached its height in the 1950s and leveled off to around 62% in the 1990s.

THE MARCH 1957 POPULATION SURVEY

To many citizens, the idea of translating a matter of private conscience such as religious belief into national statistics implies subversion or hidden control. Thus, when a preliminary survey on religious affiliation was conducted by the Bureau of the Census in March 1957, only a partial report emerged. Opposition from Jews, Christian Scientists, liberal and civil-liberties organizations forced abandonment of the plan, and the data already collected were released only after demographers resorted to the Freedom of Information Act. No other government statistics have been secreted in this fashion. Usually all of the Census Bureau's data not pertaining to identifiable individuals is open to full public scrutiny.

In March 1957, the Census Bureau asked a question on religion in its monthly Current Population Survey. It could do so because the survey, unlike the U.S. Census, was voluntary. Anticipating a possible question on religion in the 1960 census, the bureau presented the item on religion to ascertain public reaction to such a question and to evaluate the quality of the answers to the specific wording of the question. But even before the first results of the survey were released in February 1958, the director of the Census Bureau announced that the 1960 census would not include any question on religion. The 1957 data, though obviously outdated now, constitute a unique set of information.

The 1957 Census Bureau survey asked all persons fourteen years of age and older in 35,000 households exactly the same question the NSRI eventually would: "What is your religion?" Ninety-six percent reported a religion, 3% stated they had no religion, and 1% did not answer. The report classified the population into Roman Catholic, Jewish, "Other Religion," "No Religion," "Religion Not Reported," and five categories of Protestantism: the four largest denominations—Baptist, Lutheran, Methodist, and Presbyterian—and the category "Other Protestant." The main finding was that 66.2% of the population was Protestant: 19.7% Baptist, 14% Methodist, 7.1% Lutheran, 5.6% Presbyterian, and 19.8% "Other Protestant." The non-Protestant minority consisted of Roman Catholics, 25.7%; Jews, 3.2%; "Other Religion," 1.3%; "No Religion," 2.7%; and "Religion Not Reported," 0.9%.

THE AIM OF THE NSRI

Just as collecting of statistics is an act of selection, so is producing information about these statistics. In designating the NSRI, our aim was not just to fill an information gap and contribute to human knowledge but to describe the societal implications of America's religious statistics to a wider audience.

This survey was a social experiment and a study in self-identification. The essence of our approach was an open-ended question posed to the adult civilian population of the forty-eight contiguous states. It provided a "bottom up" and grass-roots view of religion in America. Our objective was to capture the most spontaneous response to the question "What is your religion?" Obviously, the question generates a different order of meaning to different people, and the meanings vary. To the chagrin of some, those meanings are often more imprecise than the neat categories that would be so helpful to elegant analysis. However, since religion is a voluntary form of association in this society, we tried as far as possible to allow the answers we received to stand with as little relabeling as possible.

A study of subjective self-identity clearly does not purport to be a census of religious affiliation or denominational membership. It is different from the normative view provided by the religious institutions themselves. We did not intend to replicate the 1936 Census of Religious Bodies or to offer an alternative to church-membership statistics, but instead to provide a fuller replication of the March 1957 survey on religious demography.

Our book will sort out the analytical issues involving religious statistics and place them into a useful perspective. It will show that in 1990 the American public favored denominational and church names more than theological terms such as *fundamentalist*. In itself, this is an important finding for students of religious life and of American society. It will also be seen that the general public is somewhat confused by religious "brand names" and the complex world of church labeling. Clearly, many people do not understand the precision of theologians, nor do they always subscribe to the blandishments of denominational officialdom.

Categorizing religious groups is a complex and arcane art. The NSRI makes a significant contribution by presenting a large sample size reflecting the true richness of the country's religious tapestry, and the national coverage necessary to provide high-quality statistics on what is actually happening around us.

AMERICAN RELIGIOUS DISTINCTIVENESS

Over a decade ago, the Gallup Organization compared the religious beliefs of Americans to those of people living in other Western nations, many of which had either state-established churches or church-sponsored or religiously based political parties. The United States, with its separation of church and state, has in religious surveys conducted over many years consistently scored higher as to belief than other democratic nations. Furthermore, the Gallup results indicated that religious beliefs are lower in advanced industrial democratic nations, except in the United States, which went against the overall trend. The Gallup polls revealed that religious beliefs remained fairly constant in the United States while they apparently declined in the other Western democratic nations (see Table 1). This American peculiarity is acknowledged by the rest of the world; recently, the *Economist* recognized the uniqueness of religion in American life. In August 1992 it wrote that the "religious commitment" of the people of the United States "sets America apart from other modern democracies." In 1989 an international Gallup poll on the importance of religion among young adults aged eighteen to twenty-four found Americans ranked first, with 90% affirming religion's personal significance to them. They were ahead of Brazilians (80%) and significantly ahead of their peers in East Asian countries: Singapore (74%), Korea (68%), and, most especially, Japan (38%) and China (4%). The contrast could even be expanded to include Eastern European nations and their recent history, to which we can apply Dostoyevsky's warning that "without God everything is permitted."

TABLE 1-1

RELIGIOUS BELIEFS IN WESTERN NATIONS

COUNTRY	PERCENTAGE RESPONDING "RELIGION VERY IMPORTANT"	PERCENTAGE BELIEVING IN GOD OR UNIVERSAL SPIRIT	PERCENTAGE BELIEVING IN LIFE AFTER DEATH
United States	58	94	71
Italy	36	88	46
Canada	36	89	54
Benelux (Belgium, Netherlands, Luxembourg)	26	78	48
Australia	25	80	48
United Kingdom	23	76	43
France	22	72	39
West Germany	17	72	39
Scandinavia (Sweden, Denmark, Norway)	17	65	35

Source: George Gallup, "Religion at Home and Abroad," *Public Opinion*, March–May 1979, pp. 38–39.

Witness the murder of tens of millions of people by both Fascist and Communist governments in several major European countries in the 20th century after the state eliminated religion and took total control of society. It mattered little whether the totalitarian ideology seeking absolute control envisioned utopia or purgatory. It could be that a sense of the sacred sets some limits on human behavior, where its absence opens the gates to barbarism.

Another Gallup poll, taken in 1981, simply asked, "Are you affiliated with a church or religious organization?" As many as 57% of Americans answered yes, while only 4% of French respondents, 5% of Italians, 13% of West Germans, 15% of Spaniards, and 22% of the British answered affirmatively. The Czech Republic, considered by many to be the most democratic and Westernized of the former Communist nations of eastern Europe, had a poll taken of its citizens in 1993: It revealed that even though Catholics made up 39.2% of the population, citizens with "No religious affiliation" made up an even greater 39.7% of the population. What has transpired in American history that has led to differences between the basic religious beliefs of the people of the United States and those of other Western and Pacific Rim democratic nations, especially when so many other values and traditions are similar?

THE AMERICANIZATION OF RELIGION

While America may be among the most religiously diverse nations, one can observe a process of Americanization at work on all its religions. Catholics, Jews, and other groups in America have become more individualistic within their respective religions. Like Protestants, they are less reliant on authority and less submissive to a hierarchical structure than their forebears were. What effect this has on behavior is much more difficult to evaluate. Based upon data from a host of sources, one can only estimate that behavior that is sanctioned, and at times demanded, by traditional religious doctrine is not always the norm for those who say they are religious or affiliated with a particular religious group.

Indeed, today, minority religions—including Catholicism, Judaism, and Islam, among others—face the possibility of assimilation into a Protestant-ized American consensus. The free marketplace of ideas that American society emphasizes naturally benefits the majority Protestant religion and its values. This was most vividly portrayed in 1992 by the results of a Gallup survey revealing that American Catholics were moving away from their bishops' positions on some issues and closer to the views of a majority of their fellow citizens, who are Protestant. For example, a majority of American Catholics, in opposition to some of the canons supported by their bishops, favor ordaining women as priests, as well as the marriage of priests, and approve the use of condoms to prevent the spread of AIDS.

A vast majority of Catholic laypeople (87%) said that Catholics should "follow their consciences" on the use of artificial birth control. This is very similar to the thinking of Protestant laypeople on birth control. Even when it came to abortion, on which the U.S. Catholic bishops have spent hundreds of thousands of dollars publicizing their opposition, Catholic laypeople express differing viewpoints. While a slight majority of Catholics (52%) said abortion should be legal in "many" or "all" circumstances, a minority (41%) believed abortion to be a "morally acceptable choice" in most circumstances. Further, Voter Research and Surveys, a 1992 presidential-election polling consortium of the four major television networks (ABC, CBS, NBC, and CNN), revealed that voters who consider themselves Catholic had almost the same position on abortion as the general American population. According to this survey, a majority of Americans believe that abortion should be available, in most cases, even if they do not personally approve of it for themselves. The Reverend Otto Hentz, a theology professor at Georgetown University, noted that many Catholics "don't consider abortion moral, but they are unwilling to criminalize it." Indeed, 70% of American Catholics said they could in good conscience vote for candidates who support legal abortion. David Leege, a professor of government at the University of Notre Dame, has said that these surveys indicate how quickly "traditional generations of Catholics are passing on, giving way to the baby boomers of the 1940s and 1950s" whose thinking, especially for those under thirty-five, is similar to many Protestants on these issues. Sister Maureen Fiedler, a director of Catholics Speak Out, one of the groups that sponsored the Gallup poll, said that the findings demonstrated "a quiet but massive grass-roots revolution. . . . The people have developed a whole new consensus of opinion and behavior different from that of the bishops, but which they believe is morally acceptable to their consciences and faithful to the Catholic tradition."

It is important to note, however, that the officially recognized interpreters of that tradition, the National Conference of Catholic Bishops, vigorously disagree. Bishop Raymond J. Boland, communications director of the National Conference of Catholic Bishops, has responded to the survey by stating that "the church does not base its teachings or its practices on polls nor opinions nor votes," but rather on "thousands of years of traditional teaching based on the Scriptures. . . . We're not about to change it just because of polls that are extremely transient." However reflective it is of the American Catholic hierarchy and of traditional Catholics, this position is not necessarily the position of many Americans who identify themselves as Catholic. What is the significance of this growing dichotomy for the future of the American Catholic church? Will the bishops eventually win over the dissenting Catholic laypeople, or will the latter grow in their independence, resembling, more and more, Americans who identify themselves as Protestant?

Other religious minorities also feel this tension between clergy and laity on issues of importance. In the face of rising American Jewish interfaith marriages, for instance, Orthodox Jewish clergy and laypeople are as united in their opposition to the phenomenon as Reform Jewish clergy and laypeople are united in their acceptances. However, Conservative Jewish clergy are overwhelmingly opposed to interfaith marriages, while Conservative laypeople, similarly to Reform Jews, are accepting of interfaith marriages. What does this dichotomy portend for the future of Jewish life in the United States?

Our democratic society breeds the notion that if creeds can coexist, then they must be fundamentally similar. Daniel J. Boorstin finds that "religions are unimportant in American life; but religion is of enormous importance. To conform in the United States it is important to be a member of a church . . . which particular church is far less important. . . ." Presidents and would-be presidents in 20-century America, from Dwight Eisenhower to Ross Perot, have noted this growing religious commonality in the American people—an American civil religion—and have attempted to tap its power by identifying themselves with it.

Many Americans consider religion to be, as the sociologist Emile Durkheim suggested, important for the maintenance of the social order. Religion in late-20th-century America has become a unifying bond that cuts across ethnic, racial, and, to a certain extent, social divides. America is therefore almost unique, since in other parts of the world religious differences have generated great tensions, divisions, and, at times, open warfare. Religious conflicts, latent or violent, are found in varying degrees in contemporary Africa, Asia, Latin America, and Europe. Nigeria, India, Pakistan, Egypt, Lebanon, Yugoslavia, Ireland, Cyprus, and Sudan stand out as extreme examples of places where religious differences have ignited armed conflagrations.

The United States has always been a haven for members of religious minorities persecuted elsewhere in the world. The anomaly is that once these people arrive and acculturate to this society's majority values, their descendants frequently abandon their particular commitments and effectively become part of the majority Protestant culture. Thus, an impediment to the growth of minority religions in the United States—whether Catholic, Jewish, Muslim, Hindu, or Buddhist—is slow assimilation within America's popular institutional framework, whose major emphasis is on commonality. This may explain why the 1990 National Jewish Population Survey showed that the rate of interfaith marriage among American Jews in the late 1980s had grown to 52% (the survey also revealed that the most ethnic Jews were usually the most religious, with a lower rate of interfaith marriages). This may also explain why, except for Orthodox Jews, many more Jews observe Chanukah, which coincides with Christmas, and Passover, which coincides with Easter, than observe the equally important holidays of Sukkot (Tabernacles) and Shavuot (Pentecost), which do not coincide with any major Christian holidays. It may also partially explain the large number of Asian Americans and Arab Americans who are Christians.

Interestingly, while other religions on the American scene have become to some degree Protestantized, many if not most of the Protestant denominations—including the Methodists, Baptists, Disciples of Christ, and Pentecostals, among others—have been Americanized: re-created (or even created) in an American mold. The NSRI study reveals a dissonance between the mainline Protestant clergy and their congregants. The liberal social agenda of the church leadership, especially the National Council of the Churches of Christ, does not always relate to the social and political attitudes of its adherents, who tend to be white, middle-class, and suburban or rural, and who usually vote Republican. Further, the conflict between liberal and evangelical Protestant churches has intensified since World War II and is being played out in the media, the political arena, and the courts.

What is the significance of a growing evangelical Protestant population, now estimated to be one fourth of the U.S. population, within a secular society that stresses a unifying civil religion? This leads to another issue, which is the power of the American civil religion, with its own holidays, such as Thanksgiving, Memorial Day, and Independence Day, in which the secular and the sacred become intertwined. Protestant theologian H. Richard Niebuhr warned of the "chief rival to monotheism . . . that social faith which makes a finite society, whether cultural or religious, the object of trust and loyalty and which tends to subvert even officially monotheist institutions such as the church."

Would it be better if the culture recognized the distinct messages of the Baptists, Catholics, Jews, Methodists, Muslims, Lutherans, and others in order to critically evaluate the conduct of our American society and its civil religion, or could this lead to an erosion of a commonality of purpose in a pluralist society?

A corollary problem of contemporary American society is that despite his or her more frequent church attendance, the thoughts and values of the average churchgoer are less often derived from religious sources than from secular ones. Gerhard Lenski wrote that this is an example of "a transcendental faith . . . gradually being transformed into a cultural faith." A generation ago this was truer of Protestants than of members of other faiths, but Catholics and Jews are now moving in this direction too. What is there in American history and the American environment that propels this movement?

Despite the fact that ours is an increasingly secular society, a bewildering supermarket of religious options competes both actively and effectively for people's time, money, and loyalties. Why do religious groups flourish in the American milieu, and how do they contribute to the strength and vitality of the voluntary sector?

Max Weber wrote that Protestantism laid the foundation of the spirit of modern capitalism. For Calvinists and Puritans and, later, Methodists as well, work was to be seen not as a penance but as a means to glorify God, who demanded a unified system of life as a means to salvation. Weber believed that modern capitalism could not have come into existence without the Protestant Reformation. He thought that capitalism was a unique development in history since the driving force was not greed but a "dedication and commitment to work." How significant is it that American Protestants, Catholics, and Jews are almost indistinguishable in their dedication and commitment to the work ethic?

Finally, how significant is religious doctrine to the American man or woman of religious affiliation when studies cite the reasons for joining a particular church to be the friendliness of the congregation, the church's closeness to the individual's home, the desire to be needed and wanted, the personality of the clergyman, and, in last place, the worship service? Does this mean that religious organizations and houses of worship that provide opportunities for fellowship have a greater degree of success? What import, if any, does this have on religious faith, behavior, or dogma? Does the degree of involvement in a religious group have a major influence on an individual? Do regional, political, economic, educational, or class differences have religious significance in the United States?

More than a generation ago, the writer Will Herberg described how the numerous immigrants to these shores eventually became part of a tripartite Protestant, Catholic, and Jewish melting pot that defined their Americanism and shaped their future. Today, immigrants are more diverse and so are their religions, with all of them, old and new, still operating within the framework of a secular society that preaches a civil religion. The more-established religions have changed in the process of flourishing in an open and free marketplace of faiths and cultures. This has led to a widespread identification with religion on the part of individuals and a recognition of religion's unifying impact on American society. This phenomenon has roots in the First Amendment to the Constitution, which promotes the separation of church and state while demanding the free exercise of religion. It is no exaggeration to assert that, for all these reasons and more, the American experience with religion is unique among the nations of the world.

Religion counts in American society. It is linked to the voluntarism and individualism that was recognized by Alexis de Tocqueville over 150 years ago. This has led to an American exceptionalism. Religion in American society plays a number of roles, from organizing social authority to providing a sense of community and group solidarity. For these aspects of religious life, organizational identification and affiliation are most important. We have therefore focused on the social impact and importance of religion rather than on religious beliefs and behavior, which are much more difficult to evaluate. One cannot truly understand America without appreciating the various and diverse roles in which religion influences and shapes our shared lives. All of these issues and more will be raised and analyzed through the lens of the National Survey of Religious Identification. In the pages that follow, the reader may expect to find answers in whole or in part to the question of the unique place of religion in American life and society.

TABLE 1-2

SELF-DESCRIBED RELIGIOUS ADHERENCE OF U.S. ADULT POPULATION 1990

(Weighted Estimates)
Total U.S. Civilian Population Age 18 + in 48 states

RELIGIOUS DENOMINATION—CHRISTIAN	# OF RESPONDENTS	ESTIMATED ADULT POP.	EST. % OF ADULT POP.
Catholic	26,606	46,004,000	26.2
Baptist	19,370	33,964,000	19.4
Protestant (no denomination supplied)	12,009	17,065,000	9.7
Methodist	9,687	14,116,000	8.0
Lutheran	6,253	9,110,000	5.2
Christian (no denomination supplied)	5,112	7,921,000	4.5
Presbyterian	3,651	4,985,000	2.8
Pentecostal	1,660	3,116,000	1.8
Episcopalian	2,242	3,042,000	1.7
Mormon/Latter-Day Saints	1,742	2,487,000	1.4
Churches of Christ	1,009	1,608,000	1.0
Jehovah's Witnesses	720	1,381,000	0.8
Seventh-Day Adventist	357	668,000	
Assemblies of God	396	660,000	
Holiness/Holy	280	610,000	
Church of the Nazarene	385	549,000	
Church of God	332	531,000	
Orthodox (Eastern)	335	502,000	
Congregationalist	346	438,000	
Evangelical	205	242,000	
Mennonite	135	235,000	
Christian Science	146	214,000	
Church of the Brethren	161	206,000	
"Born Again"	176	204,000	
Nondenominational	127	195,000	
United Church of Christ	114	161,000	
Disciples of Christ	114	144,000	
Reformed/Dutch Reformed	106	161,000	

TABLE 1-2 (CONTINUED)

RELIGIOUS DENOMINATION—CHRISTIAN	# OF RESPONDENTS	ESTIMATED ADULT POP.	EST. % OF ADULT POP.
Apostolic/New Apostolic	63	117,000	
Charismatic	51	75,000	
Quaker	75	67,000	
Missionary/Mission	35	60,000	
Wesleyan	47	58,000	
Full Gospel	34	51,000	
Christian Reform	30	40,000	
Church of God in Christ	14	32,000	
Unity	18	31,000	
Foursquare Gospel	14	28,000	
"Fundamentalist"	22	27,000	
Worldwide Church of God	12	27,000	
Salvation Army	12	27,000	
Independent Christian Church	22	25,000	
Covenant	12	16,000	
Church of America	9	11,000	
Community Church	5	10,000	
Open Bible	4	4,000	
Total Christian	**97,255**	**151,225,000**	**86.2**

OTHER RELIGIONS	# OF RESPONDENTS	ESTIMATED ADULT POP.	EST. % OF ADULT POP.
Jewish	2,155	3,137,000	1.8(2.2)*
Muslim/Islamic	295	527,000	0.3(0.5)†
Unitarian Universalist	351	502,000	0.3
Buddhist	256	401,000	0.2(0.4)†
Hindu	142	227,000	0.1(0.2)†
Native American	51	47,000	
Scientologist	31	45,000	

TABLE 1-2 (CONTINUED)

OTHER RELIGIONS	# OF RESPONDENTS	ESTIMATED ADULT POP.	EST. % OF ADULT POP.
Baha'i	24	28,000	
Taoist	10	23,000	
New Age	12	20,000	
Eckankar	10	18,000	
Rastafarian	8	14,000	
Sikh	9	13,000	
Wiccan	6	8,000	
Shintoist	2	6,000	
Deity	5	6,000	
Other Unclassified	530	831,000	
Total Other Religions	**3,897**	**5,853,000**	**3.3**
RELIGIOUS "NONES"			
Agnostic	905	1,186,000	0.7
Humanist	14	29,000	
No Religion	8,980	13,116,000	7.5
Total Religious "Nones"	**9,899**	**14,331,000**	**8.2**
Refused	2,672	4,031,000	2.3
U.S. Total	**113,723**	**175,440,000**	**100.0**

* "Core" Jewish population including ethnic-cultural Jews.
† Adjusted for possible undercount.

RELIGION IN AMERICAN CULTURE: A HISTORICAL OVERVIEW

◆ ◆ ◆

RELIGIOUS MOTIVATIONS IN DISCOVERING AND SETTLING THE NEW WORLD

From a European perspective, American history is a tapestry of immigrants seeking a safe haven, a place, in part, to practice freely their different religions. Indeed, the history of America and its early settlement is rich with religious issues.

Some historians suggest that America's religious history began on October 12, 1492, when Christopher Columbus landed on and took possession of an island in the New World, which he named San Salvador (Holy Savior). His mission, besides acquiring wealth and power for himself and his patrons, King Ferdinand and Queen Isabella of Spain, was to convert the native population, whom he believed to be Indians. This population had been in America not only since before the birth of Jesus but even before the settlement of the first recorded town in the Western world, Jericho, founded thousands of years before the start of Christianity. With an optimism that later events hardly justified, Columbus declared, "I believe that they [the Native Americans] would easily be made Christians, as it appears that they have no religion." He wrote afterward that the stated purpose of his initial voyage and his subsequent explorations was not only to bring the unconverted to Christianity but also to raise funds in order to capture Jerusalem for Christendom, an event he hoped would usher in the Second Coming. Soon, the religious mission of the Spanish and Portuguese to spread the Christian gospel to what they called the "pagan" tribes of the New World was taken for granted by the other governments and peoples of Europe.

In the eyes of the approximately one million Native Americans who inhabited North America in the 16th century, when large numbers of Europeans first came to these shores, the "white-man problem" was viewed as an unconscionable takeover of lands populated by the spirits of their ancestors. In the eyes of the European immigrants the "Indian problem" was viewed as the need to convert the "savage tribes," either peacefully or by force. At the same time, the colonists sought to gain entry and live in the rich land of the New World through immediate settlement if the desired territory was empty, or through purchase or violence, if it was occupied. Many of the Native Americans eventually died through the disease, pestilence, and war that accompanied the Europeans' arrival. The remarkable thing was that there were men on both sides who dealt fairly and peacefully with one another. This group included William Penn, who reportedly treated Native Americans as sovereign owners of the land they occupied. Since Penn, as Roger Williams before him, believed that the land belonged to its native inhabitants, he was careful to see that they were reimbursed for it.

Significantly, the first Bible printed in America was in the Algonquin language. Tens of thousands of Native Americans adopted the Christian faith as their own although tens of thousands of others maintained their ancient nature and spirit beliefs, embodied by the shaman. Still other Native Americans attempted to synthesize the two antithetical religious systems.

Spanish Catholic missionaries began appearing as early as 1520 in what was to become the United States of America, first in Florida, then in the southwestern areas later known as New Mexico, California, and Texas. The religious motivation of these explorers from the Jesuit and, later, Franciscan and Dominican orders was obvious from the names they gave the missions and towns they founded: St. Augustine in Florida; Santa Fe in New Mexico; San Diego, San Francisco, and Los Angeles in California; Corpus Christi and San Antonio in Texas. Between the years 1680 and 1793, thirty missions were founded in Texas alone, five of them built along the San Antonio River. They were all designed to Christianize the natives. In the 17th and 18th centuries, French Jesuit missionaries and explorers set out from New Orleans and Canada to investigate the Mississippi Valley and Louisiana Territory and to convert the tribes of the prairies. The French, too, left the imprint of their religious faith on the map of the country at such sites as St. Louis, St. Paul, the St. Joseph River, and Lake St. Clair.

Many settlements, later to become cities, were carved out of the wilderness of the New World and were named after other biblical places and references. These towns and cities were founded by Protestants who came to these shores from England and other countries of western and northern Europe. These immigrants, frequently religious dissenters who sought to create a new "Israel" in America as they fled the religious persecution of the

"Egypts" of Europe, began coming to North America with their families in the 17th century, and greatly influenced the development of the American nation. They looked to their Bible as both spiritual guide and physical map, and the towns and cities they started resonated with biblical references: Bethlehem, Salem, Shiloh, Nazareth, Philadelphia, Providence, Lebanon, Canaan, Bethel, Eden, Zoar, and Zion.

Even before they arrived in the New World, John Winthrop (already elected governor of the Massachusetts Bay Colony) and his fellow Puritans aboard the flagship *Arbella* saw themselves as God's newly chosen people. The Puritans believed that man exists to exalt God and by doing God's will can receive future happiness. Puritans passionately strove to live righteous lives and to worship as they thought the early Christians had worshiped, approaching God without intermediaries. They felt that the Church of England was wrong to retain aspects of the hierarchy and ritual of the Roman Catholic church, that, in their view, were not authorized by Scripture. Puritans believed they were destined to create a "new covenant" with the Lord on their way to found a "city upon the hill," Boston, which they would attempt to make a "new Jerusalem." (Only one other modern nation, Israel, whose early history is recorded in the Bible, has ever looked to the Scriptures as a map of and justification for its existence.) Some Puritan leaders even suggested making Hebrew, rather than English, the language of Colonial America.

In their sermons, Puritan ministers extolled and sanctified their special interests. Since the Puritans believed that they had a covenant with God, their self-interest justified, they maintained, the building and expansion of the new nation. As a result, their impact on politics and economics in America was very great. They shaped the growth of religion in the United States as well as the development of the Protestant ethic. Their beliefs were eventually reinterpreted as the "American Way" and justified even into the 20th century by a long procession of evangelists from Billy Sunday and Aimee Semple McPherson to Billy Graham and Jerry Falwell. In the Bible the Puritans found precedence for the organization of their churches. This type of organization, in turn, provided a model for the town-meeting form of local government.

Although Puritan society faded as a way of life, its depiction of Americans as God's chosen people extended throughout the new nation. At the beginning of the 18th century, Cotton Mather's personal history of New England was read throughout the Colonies, spreading elements of the Puritan ideal to Colonial society as a whole. Even the prominent Deists of early America, such as Benjamin Franklin and Thomas Jefferson, recognized and appropriated biblical metaphors and symbolism into their liberal humanist rhetoric. Deists believed not in a personal God concerned with the problems of man but in a "prime mover" who had created the universe but subsequently had little to do with either nature or humankind. They rejected miracles and the omniscient Supreme Being revered by more traditional orthodox faiths. Deism appealed to many leading Colonial intellectuals, who considered it a "rational" religion in keeping with the then early scientific inquiry into the laws of nature.

In 1776, Benjamin Franklin proposed to the Continental Congress that the image of Moses leading the Israelites across the Red Sea should appear on the Great Seal of the United States. Thomas Jefferson also favored a symbol from the Israelites' Exodus from Egypt, but he wanted the new nation represented by an Israel led through the wilderness to the Holy Land by biblical clouds and fire. As president of the United States, Jefferson returned to this theme in his second inaugural address, in which he said, "I shall need, too, the favor of that Being in whose hands we are, who led our fathers as Israel of old, from their native land, and planted them in a country flowing with all the necessities and comforts of life."

RELIGION AND THE DEVELOPMENT OF CONSENSUS DEMOCRACY

The philosophy of many of these early American patriots, especially of the leading intellectuals of the American Revolution, was based not only on the teaching and imagery of the Bible but also on the texts of the great English thinkers of the 17th-century Commonwealth and the bloodless "Glorious Revolution" of 1688. Increasingly the Americans emphasized the importance of the individual and of individual rights and liberties. The Congregationalists of New England emphasized local church units and individual conscience; each Congregationalist church developed its own creed. This emphasis on the central place of the particular congregation in the life of the church distinguishes Congregationalism from other Protestant denominations. Congregationalism found its political counterweight in the New England town meeting, where participatory democracy operated at a high level. The followers of Roger Williams, who established the colony of Rhode Island and the American Baptist church, brought to America the concept of separation of church and state, and the right of the individual to be able to choose for him- or herself on all matters of religion. William Penn and the Quakers of Pennsylvania emphasized not only pacifism but an appreciation of religious pluralism and a deep-seated hatred of slavery that was to surface in a later generation.

Maryland was founded by Lord Baltimore and his aristocratic English Roman Catholic followers in 1632. Soon, however, Catholics became a minority of the colony's population as more non-Catholics, not only Anglicans but other Protestants as well, immigrated and settled there. Yet Maryland's Catholics continued to benefit from the religious toleration that they had legislated, although some in the new majority would have preferred to be intolerant. New York was also quite religiously diversified in the 17th century. Almost a generation after the English took control from the original Dutch rulers of New Amsterdam, in 1664, Governor Edmund Andros wrote, "No account can be given of children, births, or christenings. . . . There are religions of all sorts, one Church of England [Anglican/Episcopalian], several Presbyterians and Independents, Quakers and Anabaptists of several sects, some Jews." And Andros did not mention the considerable number of Dutch Reformed churches that continued to thrive under English governance.

Some southern colonies established as an official religion the Church of England, or Anglican Church (it later became the Episcopalian church), but the American version bore little or no resemblance to the established and monolithic Church of England in the mother country. If one wandered a few miles out of Charleston, South Carolina, for example, one would find English Quakers, French Huguenots, Anabaptists of different nationalities, and persons of no religion. Even in Virginia, where the Anglican establishment was strongest, it was not absolute, and diversity was growing.

An interesting aspect of the great diversity of religions in Colonial America was that they all developed a common image of the American nation. This brought about the extraordinary American development of a generalized religion integrating a society even while the nation had many religions. Within American society, the collective religion became America's civil religion, incorporating secular as well as religious values and emphasizing a national purpose. In its simplest form this identification of a generalized Protestant religion with America's national purpose cast America's "mission" as one of bringing the American way of life, democracy, and free enterprise to all parts of the globe. Eventually, the collective Americanized Protestant religion made its peace with other religions, such as Catholicism and Judaism, as long as they recognized the United States as being "different" from other lands and the spiritual descendant of biblical Israel.

References to America's "mission," "covenant," and "chosenness" continued through the 19th century, when during the trauma of the Civil War, President Abraham Lincoln, who defined himself as a "liberal" in religious belief, said that we "are almost a chosen people." The concept of chosenness and covenant tied to a national purpose remained prominent even in the 20th century. President Woodrow Wilson, the son of a Presbyterian minister, perceived the American mission to be "the liberation and salvation of the world." Even President Lyndon Johnson, master politician and pragmatist that he was, touched upon this symbolism in his 1965 inaugural address, when he spoke of "the exile and the stranger" who came as immigrants to the New World "to find a place where a man could be his own man. They made a covenant with this land [that] was meant one day to inspire the hopes of all mankind; and it binds us still. If we keep its terms we shall flourish." Soon, this civil religion developed its own special holy days for the American nation, including Thanksgiving, Memorial Day, Independence Day, and Presidential Inauguration Day. These tied sacred and secular symbols to the civil religion through the sadness, joy, and thanksgiving of the nation's history. President Ronald Reagan continued to express this theme when he said in his 1982 Thanksgiving address to the nation, "I have always believed that this anointed land was set apart in an uncommon way." Reagan's statement was but a secularized version of John Winthrop's statement aboard the *Arbella* in 1630: "The Lord will be our God and delight to dwell among us, as his own people, and . . . command a blessing upon us in all our ways."

THE AMERICANIZATION OF EUROPEAN RELIGIONS

The United States, the Western world's first new nation, had from the very start been a liberating place for the immigrants who came voluntarily to its shores. It had no feudal history as part of its national experience and therefore did not have to make the transition of the European countries from medieval society, with its corporate structure, state religion, and institutionalized status, to modern society, with its concepts of individual freedom and equality. Since it had no official national religion, all religions—in theory, at least—could enjoy full equality. In reality, however, the developing consensus democracy accepted the values of the prevailing majority Protestant religion, which became in the main, as we have discovered, thoroughly and characteristically American.

In the post-Revolutionary period, the principles of freedom for non-Protestant religions slowly gained ground. In George Washington's 1789 letter to the president of the Newport, Rhode Island, Hebrew congregation, he stated that "the Government of the United States gives to bigotry no sanction, to persecution no assistance." Despite such official sentiments, some of the established denominations in the former colonies strongly opposed complete disestablishment, preferring to depend on taxpayer support than on the voluntary contributions of church members. They soon realized that this would not be feasible because all religious groups wanted their own religious freedom, even if not all of them wanted religious freedom for everyone else. In order to avoid one religion becoming dominant, there was no safe way to continue but to create an unregulated free marketplace of religions. This notion was further aided by an unusual alliance that brought together freethinkers, rationalists, and Deists, many of whom were influential political figures who resented their taxes going to any religion, and the newly aggressive, upstart evangelical Protestant sects that did not want their taxes going to "false" religions. Furthermore—and this was crucial—even though five of the original thirteen states had government-supported churches, no one Protestant denomination had a sufficient national following to seek its own establishment as a state religion by the federal government. Freedom of religion was born of necessity. Yet many of the early religious organizations were not prepared to cope with these new conditions. The idea of voluntarily appealing for members was alien to organizations that had been accustomed to limiting the active involvement of laypeople (this was the case with many of the Episcopalian and Presbyterian churches, and even with some of the Congregationalists). Therefore, an opportunity was created for the spread of Evangelicalism, which brought about the growth of other Protestant denominations.

Some historians look upon the growth of denominations as a most significant development in Christianity. Eventually, a "denomination" was not seen by its adherents to be the sole or true church, because conscientious Christians understood that they could differ in their understanding of nonessential aspects of the Christian faith and still consider one another to be Christian. Early Americans soon came to realize that many of the Old World patterns could not be replicated in the New World, especially in a country that was building a new republic unlike any government in the rest of the world. This American form of Christianity, where everyone could make up their minds about what constituted religious faith and allegiance, fits in very well with the emergence of the new democracy.

Many of the older Protestant denominations had been feuding throughout Europe. Protestant immigrants came to America not only from England and Scotland but also from countries such as France, Netherlands, Germany, and Sweden to escape these battles and persecutions. In part to prevent the religious wars of Europe from entering the United States, Congress in 1789 adopted the First Amendment to the U.S. Constitution, forbidding the introduction of an established church in the New World. The relevant passage was: "Congress shall make no law respecting the establishment of religion or prohibiting the free exercise thereof." The amendment's author, James Madison, a Deist and a disciple of Thomas Jefferson, believed in complete separation between church and state. The members of the first U.S. Congress, which approved the first ten amendments (eventually known as the Bill of Rights), thought of America not as a completely disestablished nation, as Madison had wished, but rather as a society of multiple religious establishments in the different states. Many early Americans initially agreed with those congressmen. As late as the 1840s, Governor William Seward of New York, a Protestant, favored legislation to support Catholic schools as Protestant-controlled schools had previously been supported, though the bill was eventually defeated in the New York state legislature after a rancorous battle. (Some historians say that his support of the legislation is why Seward lost the 1860 Republican presidential nomination to Abraham Lincoln.) Our nation has slowly evolved in two hundred years from the concept of multiple establishment to disestablishment of religion, with elements of accommodation to America's own civil religion.

Eventually, other religious groups adopted the core civic religious values and language that grew out of the Americanized vision of Protestantism. It is interesting that even Isaac Mayer Wise, the early champion of Reform Judaism in America, used words that were similar to his Protestant colleagues' when he said that "America is our Zion and Washington is our Jerusalem." John Carroll of Baltimore, the first Catholic bishop appointed in the United States, was as much a patriot as his namesake cousin, the only Roman Catholic to sign the Declaration of Independence. Bishop Carroll was remarkably liberal in practical matters, favoring an English liturgy and expressing much dissatisfaction with political and ecclesiastical attitudes current in Rome in the latter half of the 18th century. Similarly, Wise was critical of traditional doctrine and liturgy in Judaism, and he attempted to develop a largely English service for 19th-century Reform Judaism. He also insisted on establishing the new Reform rabbinical seminary, the Hebrew Union College, in Cincinnati, Ohio, because he wanted it to be in the heartland of America. Beginning in the early 19th century and on into the 20th century, the major theme of American Jewish history has been the accommodation of Jewish Americans and their religion to American life and culture.

Understanding why some Western religions assumed their particular form in American life is essential to understanding what patterns exist today. There were at least two possible institutional patterns that could have developed: one that emerges out of the immediate environment and is produced through the consensus of a democratic society, and one that is brought into the immediate environment and is produced through the authority of a "higher tradition." Followers of the latter, known as traditionalists, have used religion's authoritative standards to evaluate and judge the natural creation of humankind, regardless of the particular society in which man temporarily finds himself. This attitude is not, however, typical of most religions in American society. As President Dwight Eisenhower once put it, "Our government makes no sense unless it is founded in a deeply felt religious faith—and I don't care what it is." The corollary of this is that it is not necessarily important to observe a particular religious *doctrine* so long as one believes in a *religion*.

The historian Henry Steele Commager has commented that even in the earliest days of the American republic, Americans believed in some form of religion that was generally optimistic, upbeat, and indifferent to doctrines. This pattern has continued in American life from the 18th century into the 20th century.

It is interesting to note that within the parameters of our distinctly American separation between church and state religion and religious affirmation have thrived—even more so than in Europe, where established churches existed for centuries. In this country, for instance, churches, church property, and church schools are exempt from paying taxes because, as the U.S. Supreme Court ruled in *Walz v. U.S. Tax Commission* (1970), they fulfill, among other things, a "moral" purpose. And although in the 20th century the Court has prevented any federal funds from going directly to church-supported institutions and church-supported schools (exceptions are made for children on a specific and categorical basis involving their health and welfare), each session of the Court is nevertheless opened by a prayer: "God save the United States and this honorable court." Meanwhile, religious chaplains—Protestant, Catholic, Jewish, and, in 1991, a Muslim—open with invocations each session of both houses of the U.S. Congress.

Alexis de Tocqueville noted, over 150 years ago, that religion in America's democratic society did not exist for the purpose of judgment and evaluation; rather, it has generally become the means of expression for a national consensus. He observed that instead of an emphasis on customs, ancient traditions, and the strength of memories, there existed in the United States a faith in the wisdom and good sense of humankind. America today, as then, has placed its trust in the egalitarian consensus of a democracy. Thus religion becomes an extension, an arm, of the national political institution. Indeed, de Tocqueville stated that American religion should be regarded as "the first of [America's] political institutions; for it does not impart a taste for freedom, it facilitates the use of it." He, along with other early-19th-century observers of the American scene, was also struck by the paradox that American churches, which received no direct support from the state, were able to exert a much greater conforming influence upon society than the established and state-supported churches of Europe. Insofar as they enforced an outer conformity to the popular religious tenets of their day, the American counterparts of these Old World institutions were more effective than their progenitors. However, seldom did this outer conformity question the basic values of the society from which it developed.

THE GROWTH OF PROTESTANT CHURCHES IN AMERICA

Prior to the American Revolution, a major event occurred in American Protestantism. It became known as the Great Awakening, and it led to a major revival of religion throughout the Colonies. Started in several northern colonies as early as the 1720s, by the 1740s the movement reached out to the other Colonies and to almost every Protestant group. A reaction against religious moderation, it resulted in divisions in denominations and the creation of new sects. A reaction against religious intellectualism as well, it brought to the fore several ministers who preached with deep emotion and fervor (one of its primary contributions to American religion was the institutionalization of revivalism). The key figures of the Great Awakening were Jonathan Edwards in New England, Theodore Frelinghuysen in the middle colonies, and William Tennent, Jr., and Gilbert Tennent among the Pennsylvania Presbyterians. Edwards, an eloquent orator who preached about the capacity of every person for holiness and communication with God, was the first great leader of the Great Awakening. He encouraged Calvinist belief in predestination and yet simultaneously spoke about the need for all people to act as if they were among the elect by avoiding sin and believing that they had been granted divine grace. The Englishman George Whitefield, who with John and Charles Wesley and James Hervey was a founder of Methodism, was inspired by Edwards and became an itinerant preacher, ministering in open fields to thousands of believers and curiosity seekers, many of whom later became part of the faithful.

The Great Awakening breathed new life into American Protestantism and gave it a distinctive mixture of fervor and pietism within a fundamentalist structure. It brought about the mass evangelism that perhaps more than any other factor shaped American Protestantism in the 19th and 20th centuries. Historian Franklin Littell states that the Great Awakening gave both sustenance and growth to "the revival churches"—the Baptists, Methodists, and Disciples of Christ. The Baptists, for example, were a small sect until the Great Awakening propelled the denomination into a major national movement with great strength in the South. The conversion of sinners was their objective, and the revival meeting, they found, was the best means to reach this goal. In the West, the revival meeting combined a religious experience with a social activity that alleviated the loneliness of the frontier. It also united many of the individualistic western settlers against the established religions of the East Coast, bringing the pioneers' nonconformism into their religious experience. Methodism, though begun in England, split off from Anglicanism and really came into its own in the New World as a result of the Great Awakening after the arrival in this country of George Whitefield. The Disciples of Christ began, grew, and flourished in America under the leadership of the dissident Presbyterian minister Thomas Campbell, who brought numerous Baptists, Methodists, and other dissenting Presbyterians into what soon became a new and distinctly American denomination.

All the new and basically American Protestant churches stressed not only revivalism but also voluntary association—something that the entrenched ecclesiastical establishments had particular difficulty dealing with as the 18th century gave way to the 19th century. Interestingly, a countervailing development in American Protestantism, especially in New England, brought about the emergence and development of Unitarianism, a liberal form of Protestantism with only marginal links to New England's Puritan past. Unitarianism was based upon the power of local congregations to make their own decisions in structure and theology; this encouraged some churches to move from Trinitarian Congregationalism to Unitarian Congregationalism. Unitarianism intertwined itself with America's unbounded confidence in its own future as well as a national belief in the ongoing improvement of human nature.

THE NUMBER OF CHURCHES IN EARLY AMERICA

Little documentation exists for the religious identification of Colonial settlers. We must surmise their religious preferences from the number and type of institutions they established. Thus, it is instructive to note the number of Colonial churches in 1660 and then, 120 years later, at the close of the American Revolution. In 1660 the largest denomination was the Congregationalists, with 75 churches, followed by the Anglicans, with 41. Then, further behind, came the Dutch Reformed, with 13 churches; Roman Catholics, with 12; Presbyterians, with 5; Lutherans and Baptists, with 4 each; and Jews, with one synagogue.

By 1780, there had been startling changes both quantitatively and qualitatively. The largest denomination was still the Congregationalists, with 749 churches. But there were three denominations vying for second place: the Presbyterians, who had 495 churches; the Baptists, with 457; and the Anglicans/Episcopalians, with 406. The German Reformed church, with 201 churches, and the Dutch Reformed church, with 127 churches, combine for a total of 328 Reformed churches. The Catholics and Jews had also grown, but at a slower pace: The Catholics had 56 churches, the Jews 6 synagogues.

The rise of Presbyterianism in 18th-century America, which was linked to Scotch and Scotch-Irish immigration, was of some political significance. During the Revolution, the influence of Presbyterianism, with its hostility toward bishops and aristocracy, was such that the uprising was referred to as the Presbyterian Rebellion by British Tories. The only clergyman to sign the Declaration of Independence was a prominent Scottish-born Presbyterian minister, New Jersey's John Witherspoon, the president of what would later become Princeton University.

At the time of the American Revolution, there were approximately 3.75 million people living in the thirteen colonies. Except for approximately

25,000 Catholics (15,000 of whom lived in Maryland) and 2,500 Jews (500 of whom lived in South Carolina), the inhabitants were all of different and various Protestant denominations. These included not only the British Protestant element, which made up 75% of the Colonies' 3 million whites, but also approximately 750,000 blacks, the vast majority of whom were slaves.

THE GROWTH OF AN AMERICANIZED CATHOLIC CHURCH

In the period following the Revolutionary War, the American Catholic population was somewhat homogeneous. It was primarily English, with some Irish, Germans, and French. (The Catholic population would have been predominantly French and under the jurisdiction of a French bishop if Quebec had supported the Revolution, but Quebec decided not to make common cause with the colonists, and the French missionary effort in northern New York and the Midwest—and the Spanish missions of California, Texas, and the Southwest as well—did not have a major impact on the Catholic church in the newborn United States.) Colonial Catholics had overwhelmingly supported General Washington and his cause, and they were as American as they were Catholic. Eventually, this distinctly American Catholic church was able to absorb and mold into its own form the vast number of Catholics, comprising many different ethnic and national groups, that soon began immigrating to these shores.

In general, American Catholics were not eager to have a bishop. Still, both priests and laity thought that if they *had* to have a bishop, they were better off with an "American," such as John Carroll, rather than the likely alternative, a Frenchman. However, they were concerned that if they got a bishop, they would antagonize their Protestant neighbors. They were therefore relieved when the Protestant Samuel Seabury (a Tory during the Revolution) went to Scotland in 1784 and had himself consecrated Episcopal bishop by three other bishops, and when the English archbishop of Canterbury consecrated Episcopal bishops for Pennsylvania and New York in 1787. Catholics anticipated a major negative reaction. When these appointments appeared to give Episcopalians new prestige in the United States, Catholics rightly interpreted it to mean that they too could have a bishop appointed without provoking a major storm. Only then did John Carroll and his fellow Catholics deem it appropriate for Carroll to go to Rome to be consecrated America's first Roman Catholic bishop. However, still concerned about the reaction from the Protestant majority, he made certain to have as his traveling companion the newly appointed Episcopal bishop of Virginia.

During the early 1800s, one of the great figures of the growing American Catholic church was Bishop John England of Charleston, South Carolina, considered by some of his co-religionists to be a dangerously democratic man. He wrote, "I do not know of any system more favorable to the security of religious rights and of church property than of the American law. . . . I prefer it to the law of almost every Catholic country with which I am acquainted." He then crafted the so-called Charleston Constitution, which some historians say headed off the creation of independent Catholic churches in his own and possibly other dioceses. He organized his diocese so that the authority of the bishop could not be challenged but would at the same time be aided by separate committees of laity and clergy who were to function in an advisory capacity. He created a Catholic seminary that he protected from French influence and where all students would be molded into what he called "the American spirit." Standing up courageously to the prejudices of the antebellum South, he established a school for black children in which he taught and for which he formed a special order of nuns. He preached incessantly throughout his diocese, took controversial political positions, and established a book society. He even started what many consider to be the first Catholic paper in America, the *United States Catholic Miscellany,* which some of his fellow bishops did not completely appreciate because of its progressive tone. Many of his ideas and programs were later adopted by other Catholic bishops and eventually led to a distinctly American Catholic hierarchy.

John Carroll saw the need for Catholic-sponsored higher education, and immediately after his appointment as bishop he opened St. Mary's Seminary in Baltimore in 1791. Georgetown University in Washington, a Jesuit-sponsored college, opened its doors that same year. The initial Catholic educational effort was primarily in the field of higher education because colleges were needed to supply men for the clergy. Earlier, different Protestant groups had established, for similar reasons, Harvard College and the Collegiate School, later Yale University (Congregationalist), King's College, later Columbia University and the College of William and Mary (Anglican), the College of Rhode Island, later Brown University (Baptist), the College of New Jersey, later Princeton University (Presbyterian), and Queen's College, later Rutgers University (Dutch Reformed).

Another interesting figure in the Catholic church of this period was Father Gabriel Richard of Detroit, who also established a paper, the *Michigan Essay or Impartial Observer,* which, unfortunately, was short-lived. He was also the first (and only) 19th-century Catholic priest to be elected to Congress, which had already witnessed the election of numerous Protestant ministers. Perhaps most interesting, in 1817 he cofounded the "Catholepistemiad," later to become the University of Michigan, of which he was vice president and the occupant of six different chairs. Another cofounder, a Protestant minister, was the president and the occupant of seven other chairs. Protestant-Catholic ecumenical endeavors were so rare in other nations of the world that this one could be considered almost unique to the American environment.

The successful "Americanization process" continued to affect the self-identity of the minority religions in the late 19th and early 20th centuries. Even though John Ireland, America's first archbishop, insisted that the Catholic church must be as thoroughly Catholic in America as it was in Rome, he also wrote that "as far as her garments assume color from local atmosphere, she must be American. That no one dare paint on her brow with a foreign tint, or pin to her mantle foreign linings."

RELIGION AND AFRICAN AMERICANS

When the Methodists and Baptists began their revival in the South, many slaves were attracted to this emotional type of religious worship, and soon after the Revolution, vast numbers of blacks came under the influence of revivalism and converted to the Methodist and Baptist churches. Previously, slave owners had been reluctant about spreading the whole gospel to their slaves. Some whites mistakenly believed that English common law prohibited the enslavement of Christians, while others were fearful that Christianized slaves would think of themselves as free and equal. But the Great Awakening was such a powerful religious force that blacks soon became the majority of worshipers in some evangelical churches. Their preachers, in emotional sermons, appealed to the poor and the outcast, and many blacks found hope in the belief in salvation as a means of escaping their earthly degradation.

Later these common religious beliefs and practices provided a new form of social cohesion in place of the old forms that had been destroyed when the slaves were seized in Africa and forcibly brought to America. Black churches brought about a distinctive culture and worldview that paralleled rather than replicated the culture of the land in which blacks resided involuntarily. Long before emancipation, black Christians had found strength and hope through their self-identification as God's chosen people and the new Israel. The key terms of their faith—salvation, freedom, and the Kingdom of God—were rooted in the black experience and expressed themselves in joy and jubilation tinged with mournfulness. Black preachers, like their white colleagues, also used the vivid imagery of the Bible—with one important difference. Blacks believed that they were still in Egypt waiting to be delivered and waiting to enter the Promised Land of the new Israel. The black religious experience was also different in degree and substance from the white religion. When he visited the South, W.E.B. Du Bois was impressed with what he called "the preacher, the music and the frenzy" of a southern black evangelical religious service. According to C. Eric Lincoln, freedom has always been the overriding theme of the "black sacred cosmos," and the message of the Church was, in whatever way it was articulated, that "God wants you free."

White Americans have looked upon freedom as an individual value, while African Americans have always emphasized the communal definition of the word. Dr. Martin Luther King, Jr.'s, eloquent peroration at the 1963 civil rights march on Washington—"Free at last, free at last, thank God Almighty, we are free at last"—reflected this theme.

One must also realize that the institution of slavery was different under the Spanish than as practiced by America's English and northern European colonists. Spanish Catholicism, while condoning slavery, held that slaves were humans, even though temporarily subjugated. Many slaves were therefore eventually freed under Spanish law, which held that a slave, as any other person, had basic social rights. In Texas, which was ruled by Spanish law under the control of Mexico, some of the first blacks in the state came as free settlers. The situation remained this way until Anglo-American immigrants arrived in large numbers after 1820. Then Texas assumed many of the characteristics of the surrounding southern states, and the "peculiar institution" of slavery began to grow there.

Black churches were among the most stable institutions to arise after the Civil War. Though many African Americans had been converted by the first Great Awakening, and by the second Great Awakening, which started on the frontier in the early 1800s, it was only after the Civil War and the destruction of slavery that black churches really came into their own. It is estimated that blacks comprised approximately half of the more than 5 million members of Southern Baptist and Methodist churches during Reconstruction. The sociologist E. Franklin Frazier referred to these black churches as a "nation within a nation" because not only did they give religious and cultural solace, but they also sponsored, and continue to sponsor to this day, housing developments, business organizations, and that most important means to upward mobility, schools. Even the first black publishing house was sponsored by a church—the African Methodist Episcopal church. The major economic role played by black churches gained momentum in the late 19th and early 20th centuries, especially under the leadership of Booker T. Washington, who assumed the mantle of leadership held by Frederick Douglass in an earlier period. Washington, deeply religious and an unofficial Baptist preacher, developed a strong following among black Baptists, and Tuskegee Institute, which he helped found, was considered, unofficially, a black Baptist school. Politically more conservative than Douglass, Washington preached solidarity—"Negro support of Negro business"—as the path toward economic progress. He felt this was the best means to social equality and political progress for African Americans. According to scholars C. Eric Lincoln and Lawrence H. Mamiya, Washington's economic views were similar to those of many black church leaders who wanted to participate in and gain from American capitalism. But the inner tension between the "racial pride, unity, and independence" of the black church tradition and the desire to be part of the American mainstream would continue into the 20th century.

It is also noteworthy that during Reconstruction, many black public officials came from the ministry, frequently using the church as a springboard to public office. After the Civil War, black religious leaders such as the Georgia bishop Henry Turner of the African Methodist Episcopal Church became elected political officials in their home states. This trend ended after Reconstruction but resumed in the mid-20th century, when African American ministers such as Martin Luther King, Jr., Adam Clayton Powell, Jr., Andrew Young, William H. Gray III, and Jesse Jackson became national political figures.

RELIGION GOES WEST

The period after the Revolution was, as one churchman described it, "the period of the lowest ebb of vitality in the history of American Christianity." He described the Eastern Seaboard as bad in terms of religion and morality, and the newly emerging West as worse. Those who went to the frontier did not go for religious freedom but, rather, for economic improvement. Their luggage was more likely to include liquor, guns, and knives than it was the Bible. The immorality of the frontiersmen soon became a major concern of missionaries and circuit-riding preachers. The backwoodsmen, however, were not influenced by the homilies of college-educated East Coast ministers. Rather, these lonely men, haunted by solitude, wild animals, and Indian raids, were affected by hellfire-and-brimstone preachers who offered everlasting peace and salvation and who themselves had gone west to redeem the wilderness. Frontier preachers were aided by the fact that even though there may have been few Bibles in the pioneers' backpacks, some westerners still personally recalled or remembered being told in their youth of the religious revival brought by the Great Awakening, which remained with them as a "still, small voice." Soon a new revivalism was targeted for the "sinful" frontiersmen.

The revival movement that began in the back country of North Carolina, Virginia, Pennsylvania, and Maryland soon moved west to Kentucky and Tennessee. One revival meeting in August 1801 at Cane Ridge in Bourbon County, Kentucky, brought 15,000 men, women, and children together for the largest and noisiest religious camp meeting that America had ever seen. Dozens of evangelical preachers (Methodists, Baptists, and even some Presbyterians) held this huge throng fascinated for almost an entire week. A youth who was later to become a Methodist preacher fearfully noted that "the vast sea of human beings seemed to be agitated as if by a storm."

The two churches that competed for dominance on the frontier were the Baptist and the Methodist, the Americanized churches of the poor and the workingman. They preached a democratic theology and eliminated elitist barriers between pastor and congregant. The Methodist preacher was funded to some extent by his church, and unlike his Baptist and Presbyterian colleagues, as long as he was unmarried he did not have to work a farm or teach in a classroom in order to make a living. He could ride his circuit for hundreds of miles in the open expanse of the wilderness, ministering to the life-and-death needs of his people. Baptist preachers had to earn their keep; frequently through farming, but even so they found time to bring great zeal and commitment to their religious tasks. Above all else, these circuit riders had a civilizing effect through their missionary activity in the growing nation. Not only did they spread the gospel and teach basic morality, but they were also influential in organizing hundreds of schools and colleges under the banners of their Protestant denominations.

By the mid-19th century, the Methodists had established thirty-four colleges, the Baptists twenty-five. Similarly, after 1865, black church groups established their own colleges in the South and Southwest in an attempt to create both a learned ministry and an educated citizenry. Missionaries also attempted to place a Bible in every Protestant home, and in 1816 the Protestant denominations collectively founded the American Bible Society, which served both educational and religious goals in distributing Bibles throughout the country.

RELIGIOUS PREJUDICE IN AMERICA

From the American West of the 19th century emerged a union of evangelical Protestantism and consensus democracy. But for a time there also emerged an antipathy to those who were different. Geographic diversity in religion was prevalent, but this was not true pluralism, which respects diversity. Through the mid-19th century, when evangelical Protestantism was strong in the United States, anti-Catholic, anti-Jewish, and even anti-Deist sentiments sprang up. As late as 1844, Joseph Story, associate justice of the U.S. Supreme Court, wrote in a decision that the United States was a "Christian [read 'Protestant'] country," and referred disparagingly to "Judaism or deism or any other form of Infidelity." Non-Christians were denied full citizenship rights in the state of New Hampshire as late as 1877, and it would be another several decades before the Supreme Court began interpreting the First Amendment in such a fashion as to enforce both its "no establishment" clause as well as its "free exercise" clause. That these two clauses protected all religious groups from state-endorsed religious practices as well as from excessive government entanglement in religious affairs was spelled out by the Court in *Lemon v. Kurtzman* (1971).

The mid-19th century witnessed the growth of Protestant-Catholic tensions, perhaps epitomized by the nativist cry of "America for Americans," meaning, actually, "America for Protestants." Although there had been relatively good Protestant-Catholic relations immediately after the Revolution, the Catholic population then was very small in number and English in background. During the course of the 19th century the picture began to change as large numbers of non-English Catholics entered the country. Between 1820 and 1865, almost 2 million Irish came to the United States, and the majority of them were Roman Catholic. In one decade alone, from 1840 to 1850, the Roman Catholic population in America grew from 650,000 to 1.6 million.

In the 1840s, New York State became a major battleground for Protestant-Catholic rivalries when new immigrants attempted to eliminate Protestant sectarian teachings from the public schools. A drive soon started to have the state support Catholic schools and their teachers in the same way that it already supported the Protestant teachers, permitting sectarian teachings in "public" schools, which were actually Protestant schools maintained by private, often Quaker-influenced associations. Not until the 20th century would Horace Mann's vision of a public school open to children of all creeds, social classes, and races be realized.

The new immigrants were led in their school plan by the Roman Catholic bishop John Hughes. Surprisingly, they were supported by a leading Protestant layman, New York's governor William Seward. The New York state legislature, torn between two religious communities and anxious to avoid polarization, passed legislation prohibiting the use of state funds for schools inculcating any "sectarian doctrine" in New York City, thus commencing a major movement from multiple establishment to disestablishment. In response, Archbishop John Ireland introduced the parochial-school system in the United States, a unique contribution of the American Catholic hierarchy. The disestablishment trend did not, however, decrease anti-Catholic sentiments, and anti-Catholic riots broke out in several American cities, including Philadelphia, Charleston, and St. Louis.

Two otherwise distinguished Americans, the Reverend Lyman Beecher and Samuel F. B. Morse, became leaders of the anti-Catholic nativist movement in the 1840s. Beecher was motivated by fears that the pope had designs on the Mississippi Valley. Morse went into a frenzy when, on a visit to Rome, his hat was knocked off during a religious procession. This fallen hat became something of a symbol of pervasive Catholic power to American nativists. Though Beecher and Morse expressed their opinions peaceably, the emotional effect of their writings sparked some unthinking Protestants into mob violence against Catholics.

Anti-Catholic feeling was fueled by the 1836 publication of *Awful Disclosures by Maria Monk*, a diatribe that propelled its author into notoriety when it was discovered that her story of horrors in Montreal's Hôtel Dieu convent was a complete hoax. Anti-Catholicism even became a leading principle of the pre–Civil War National American ("Know-Nothing") party, whose presidential candidate in 1856, former president Millard Fillmore, received more than one fourth of the national vote. Even after the Civil War and well into the 1890s, the American Protestant Association attempted to organize rural Protestants against urban Catholics.

It was perhaps predictable that when anti-Catholicism lessened at the end of the 19th century and large numbers of eastern European Jewish immigrants began to arrive here, anti-Semitism began to grow in this country. It was directed at poor and wealthy, native-born and foreign-born Jews alike. In June 1877, Joseph Seligman, one of America's wealthiest bankers, was excluded from the Grand Union Hotel in Saratoga Springs, New York, because he was a Jew. Many other hotels and clubs as well as businesses and corporations maintained anti-Semitic exclusionary policies. As more and more American Jews desired to go to college, universities developed silent quotas to keep Jewish student enrollment and tenured Jewish faculty to a minimum. Major human-rights organizations such as the Anti-Defamation League (ADL) of B'nai Brith and the American Jewish Committee (AJC) soon developed to fight bigotry and defend the rights of Jews and other Americans. The concept of a religiously and ethnically pluralist America was slow in developing in the 19th century, and entered our vocabulary and partial reality only in the 20th century, when anti-Catholicism and anti-Semitism both decreased markedly.

But neither the anti-Catholicism nor the anti-Semitism of this period could compare to the anti-Mormon hysteria of the latter half of the 19th century. It is noteworthy that this hostility was not directed at new immigrants or "outsiders": Joseph Smith, the founder of the Church of Jesus Christ of Latter-Day Saints, and almost all of the religion's other leaders were born on American soil. Mormonism, filled with American millennialism and utopian prophecy, initially drew its members from the dissatisfied, poor, and restless who were eager to find opportunities in a new native-born American faith. Mormonism began in 1820, when Joseph Smith, praying alone in a secluded area in upstate New York, was seized, he later reported, by a vision informing him that all existing religious beliefs were false and that he could not accept any of them. Seven years later, according to Smith's account, he found the plates from which the Book of Mormon was translated. This third testament, as the Mormons consider it, described an exodus of Israelites to pre-Columbian America, and claimed that these people were among the ancestors of the American Indians. The book, which takes its name from a man in it named Mormon, covers a period of approximately eight hundred years up to 400 A.D. and describes, among other events, a visit by Jesus to these people in North America.

Joseph Smith drew thousands of followers who soon considered him a prophet and the founder of the "only true church." Many thousands more considered him to be a dangerous heretic who was misleading gullible aco-lytes. Prophet or not, Joseph Smith was without favor in his own land. Moving from New York to Ohio, Missouri, and Illinois, Smith and his self-appointed apostles encountered much opposition based upon accusations of financial and moral improprieties. The rumors of polygamy among the Mormons sent many opponents into a frenzy that remained undiminished despite a blanket denial by the prophet's family. In Illinois, where the Mormons had established a large city, Nauvoo, major accusations were made against Smith's policies and actions. Soon, numerous civilians and even the Illinois militia organized against Smith and his followers. In an attempt to avoid major violence and because he had been promised a fair trial, Smith surrendered. He was subsequently murdered by a lynch mob that forcibly took him from jail.

After Smith's death, a bitter struggle for control of the Mormon church developed among his followers. A majority of the prophet's followers selected Brigham Young as Smith's successor. Young then ordered the Mormons to follow him on what proved to be a torturous and deadly exodus over the Rocky Mountains to the region of the Great Salt Lake, in what was then Mexican territory. Six thousand of these eighty thousand Mormon pioneers died in the attempt to reach their new permanent Zion. The first Mormons arrived in 1847, and the next year the United States acquired the area from Mexico. Congress refused the Mormons' petition for statehood for the new "State of Deseret," and the Utah Territory was established, of which Brigham Young was made governor. "Gentile" hostility in Washington toward Mor-mons continued. Altogether, six petitions for statehood were rejected before Utah was finally admitted to the Union in 1896. Hostility sparked up over polygamous practices, which the federal government sought to stamp out with fines, imprisonment, exile, and the seizure of church property. Finally, in 1890, the Mormon church yielded and renounced its most provocative institutions—plural marriage and the notion of a separate political "King-dom of God." These policy shifts were incorporated into Utah's state con-stitution. Still, the deep-seated emotions stirred by some Mormons' apparent challenge to Victorian notions of morality had already revealed the strong Puritan foundations of the national psyche.

Today, the abiding Americanism of the Mormon church is evidenced by its belief that when Jesus comes back to earth, he will return to the original Garden of Eden, which the church has determined to be sited close to Independence, Missouri.

THE ABOLITIONIST MOVEMENT

The greatest tragedy of American history is that the United States—the country that has been called "the nation with the soul of a church," a nation that in the 18th century embraced democratic ideas and ideals—was the nation that even as late as the mid-19th century had the world's largest slave system. This is one of history's greatest anomalies, compounded by the fact that the Founding Fathers—some of whom freed their own slaves—permitted slavery to exist while they espoused their democratic vision for the nation.

The rise of the abolitionist movement marked this nation's religious and moral encounter with a system that could have destroyed, if it had continued, the very foundations of the country. Eventually, the anti-slavery crusade had over two thousand chapters and 250,000 members. Abolitionist sentiment was deeply religious, imbued with Puritan concern for the moral behavior of all people throughout America. The anti-slavery crusade was just as strong, if not stronger, in the Midwest as it was in New England. The abolitionists believed that slavery was a mortal sin with a debilitating effect on the American conscience, and they spoke out with a fervor heard around the nation.

William Lloyd Garrison was running a small Baptist temperance journal in Massachusetts when a New Jersey Quaker, Benjamin Lundy, convinced him of the virtue of the anti-slavery cause. On January 1, 1831, the first issue of *The Liberator*, including an impassioned statement by Garrison, was published. He wrote, "I will be as harsh as truth, and as uncompromising as justice. On this subject [of slavery] I do not wish to think, or speak, or write with moderation. . . . I am in earnest—I will not equivocate—I will not excuse—I will not retreat a single inch—and I will be heard." And he was heard, as were many others, including James Russell Lowell, whose direct linkage of biblical themes and anti-slavery objectives gave what one critic described as "apocalyptic" meaning to his poem "The Present Crisis." During the Civil War, when the issue had finally been joined amid terrible suffering and destruction, Julia Ward Howe added her contribution to the nation's legacy. Future generations should not forget the meaning of her words behind the troubling rhythms of the "Battle Hymn of the Republic." Her eyes had seen the "glory of the coming of the Lord," and "a day of judgment was near."

In the black community, the African Methodist Episcopal Zion church was known as "the Freedom church" and counted among its members such outstanding abolitionist leaders as Frederick Douglass, Sojourner Truth, and Harriet Tubman. Douglass, who in 1838 escaped from slavery and found his dream of freedom, was a licensed deacon and preacher in the AME Zion church. He soon became a preeminent abolitionist and one of the major figures of mid-19th-century black America. Tubman, often called the Moses of her people, made nineteen trips to the South between 1850 and 1859 and led more than 350 slaves to freedom as the leading "conductor" of the

Underground Railroad. To Sojourner Truth (born Isabelle Bomefree), the abolitionist movement was "the secular counterpart of spiritual salvation." An outstanding orator, she was considered by many to be as eloquent as Frederick Douglass. Truth and Douglass, who was one of the leading feminists of his time, together provided the connecting link between abolitionism and the early women's suffrage movement.

Tragically, a great disparity developed between the North and the South concerning what was considered Christian with regard to slavery. Political, economic, and cultural factors had conditioned religious and ethical beliefs, especially when race was involved. As the abolitionist attacks continued to reach the antebellum South, controversy broke out, not on the evil of slavery but on the origins of the races, with the majority view in the South holding that there was a need to further Christianize and evangelize the slaves without necessarily freeing them. The major religious groups of the South—the Baptists, the Methodists, and the Presbyterians—soon split along regional lines, with other smaller religious groups following them. Some of these regional denominational schisms, which continued through the Civil War, took more than a century to mend. The Southern Baptist Convention, organized in 1845, would become the nation's largest Protestant denomination, and its cooperating churches exist today in all fifty states.

After the Civil War, Henry Ward Beecher condemned southern political and religious leaders for their errors, painting a very graphic and personal picture of the Last Judgment: "A day will come when God will reveal judgment and arraign these mighty miscreants." Others, such as clergyman Theodore Munger, spoke of regional responsibility. Still others, such as Munger's hero, clergyman Horace Bushnell, theologian Philip Schaff, an immigrant from Germany, and Abraham Lincoln, who grew up in the pro-slavery climate of Indiana and southern Illinois, took a broader picture of the Civil War, seeing it as a judgment for a centuries-long complicity of an entire nation in the sin of slavery. They also saw the Civil War as having prepared America to assume a great role as spokesperson for human freedom.

It was Abraham Lincoln, the liberal son of a conservative Baptist, who gave eloquent voice in both his Gettysburg and second inaugural addresses to the moral duty and religious destiny of an "almost chosen people." For at least a decade before the Civil War, Lincoln had spoken of slavery as "wrong," though he did not know how to end it. Lincoln agonized about slavery through the early years of the war, and then issued the Emancipation Proclamation in 1863, at which time the fog began to lift and Lincoln came to understand why the nation had been torn apart. In the spring of 1864 he wrote to a correspondent in Kentucky that after three years of immense suffering, "the nation's condition is not what either party or any man devised or expected. God alone can claim it. . . . If God now wills the removal of a great wrong, and wills also that we of the North as well as you of the South shall pay for our complicity in that wrong, impartial history will find therein new cause to attest and revere the justice and goodness of God." Lincoln was certain that there was a right and a wrong in the war but this was sometimes beyond human comprehension. "The Almighty has His own purposes," he said in his second inaugural address. Apparently an entire nation—in a supreme mystery—had been compelled to work out the will of Providence. Lincoln added, "If we shall suppose that American slavery is one of those offenses which, in the providence of God . . . He now wills to remove, and that He gives both North and South this terrible war, as the woe due to those by whom the offense came, shall we discern therein any departure from those divine attributes which the believers in a living God always ascribe to Him?" Shortly after his second swearing-in, Abraham Lincoln, whom many of his contemporaries referred to as a modern-day Moses, was assassinated, but his legacy of ennobling the American experiment and fulfilling the promise of liberty for all its people survived.

After the Civil War and Reconstruction, institutional segregation developed in the South and some border states; it would not be struck down until the U.S. Supreme Court decided in 1954 that the Reverend Oliver Brown had a right to an equal educational opportunity for his daughter Linda. Still, there were many progressive movements with a religious base in both the North and the South. An important religious development was the rise of the American Social Gospel movement, which began in the latter part of the 19th century and grew in the early 20th century. A major spokesman for the movement was Walter Rauschenbusch, who spelled out its meaning in his 1907 work, *Christianity and the Social Crisis,* a manifesto urging Americans to build upon nineteen centuries of Christian influence and rally sufficient religious and moral strength to destroy evil "and turn the present unparalleled economic and intellectual resources of humanity to the harmonious development of a true social life." The movement's moral message was that American capitalism needed "Christian modifications." In the South, the "Social Gospel" was largely a Methodist outgrowth of a "New South" movement that was expounded by Henry W. Grady and the Reverend (later Bishop) Atticus G. Haygood, president of Emory University. Haygood's 1880 Thanksgiving sermon, "The New South," was followed by his book *Our Brother in Black.* He asked southerners to forget the past and face their responsibilities to their "black brothers," working with them toward a better future. He also noted his gratitude that slavery was gone forever and that blacks and whites were beginning to learn the advantages of "work and thrift."

The American Social Gospel movement was but another phase of America's attempt to become a holy commonwealth and a better society for all its citizens. Its call for a "sanctified citizenry" that would make the American republic a model for the entire world was an up-to-date version of the Puritan belief in the "city upon the hill" that would create a new Zion in America. The movement depended upon a strong spirit of confidence in America's progress and world leadership that was temporarily slowed by World War I and the Great Depression but refueled again by the moral fervor generated by World War II and the social progress of the mid-20th century. The American Social Gospel movement, with its strong emphasis on social and economic reform motivated by its interpretation of the teachings of Jesus, had a major impact upon liberal Protestantism and its umbrella agency, the National Council of Churches of Christ. It colored an even wider canvas through the distinctive contribution of the American churches to the World Council of Churches and Protestant movements around the world.

THE AMERICANIZATION OF DIFFERENT RELIGIOUS AND ETHNIC GROUPS WITHIN A PROTESTANT CULTURE

Throughout the 19th century, huge waves of immigrants came to these shores from all parts of the globe. By the time the great hundred-year migration came to an end in 1924, when Congress passed restrictive immigration legislation, 35 million immigrants had arrived in the United States. As a result, the British Protestant elements of the population had been reduced to between one third and one half of the total population. America had become, by the start of the 20th century, the most ethnically, religiously, and linguistically diverse nation in the world. Nevertheless, the strength of the native culture was such that an assimilationist Americanization process started almost as soon as these immigrants reached their new nation. This process was reinforced by the public schools their children entered upon arrival. The schools' aim was to produce a new human type, "the American." The anthropologist Margaret Mead wrote as late as the mid-20th century that the immigrant child in America's public schools was to be taught "not the constancies of their parents' immediate past . . . but they must be taught to reject and usually despise their parents' values. They must learn those things which, to the extent that they make them Americans, will eliminate them forever from their parents, making them ancestorless, children of the future, cut off from the past."

The early success of the Americanization process is visible in the overwhelming cultural assimilation of pre-Revolution non-Protestant immigrants, both the Catholics and Jews, into the dominant Protestant religion. In 1954, when the American Jewish community celebrated the tercentenary of Jewish settlement in North America, it was discovered that the descendants of only one of the twenty-three Sephardic Jews (originally from Spain and Portugal) who in 1654 arrived in New Amsterdam from Recife, Brazil, were themselves Jewish; the other immigrants' descendants had all inter-married and assimilated into the Protestant majority. American Jews have obviously had great difficulty in maintaining and perpetuating their own values and religious commitments in the free marketplace of the New World. As early as 1783, Haym Salomon, the American patriot and early supporter of George Washington, wrote home to his family in Poland complaining that there was *"zer weining Yiddishkeit"* (very little Jewish life) in America.

In 1800, Samson Simson, who had just graduated from New York City's Columbia College (now University), gave a brief commencement address in Hebrew that had been written for him by a local rabbi. A survey of early-17th-century American Jewish history, it has been called the "first evidence of a communal self-consciousness among American Jews." Unfortunately, Simson's audience did not understand Hebrew and was therefore oblivious to the content of the address. This was not atypical of members of minority religions, at least until the mid-20th century. They could not be completely understood by many people, especially if they used languages such as Latin or Hebrew to express their beliefs and ideas. Some were made to feel different at a time when difference was not always accepted and thus they were quite susceptible to an Americanization process that eventually led to different degrees of assimilation into a majority of Protestant culture.

Similarly, many of the descendants of the early Catholics in the United States assimilated into the American mainstream by switching to one of the many Protestant denominations. (Note that only one of eight American presidents of Irish extraction, John F. Kennedy, was a Roman Catholic. Some were of Protestant Scotch-Irish descent, some came from families that converted to Protestantism, and some had taken the religion of a non-Catholic parent.) In the early 1950s, at about the same time as the American Jewish tercentenary, Dr. Henry P. Van Dusen, president of the Union Theological Seminary, reported on a nationwide survey revealing that even as late as the 1940s and 1950s, "about four times as many former Catholics have become Protestants as ex-Protestants have become Roman Catholics." One might add that along with this assimilation has come acceptance into mainstream America for both Catholics and Jews.

For Catholic Americans, a major change in how they were perceived by non-Catholics was Pope John XXIII's "opening of the doors and windows of the church" through Vatican Council II in 1962. Ironically, participatory and liturgical changes ordained by Rome in the wake of the council have brought about the greater Americanization of the Catholic church. The alterations have been immense, and not just in ecumenical affairs. One Catholic woman who remembers the days of Vatican II states, "Hearing the beautiful words of the mass spoken in English brought out their meaning instead of only reading it from my missal. By now the joy of being able to go to the altar, ascending the pulpit and doing the readings of the Old and New Testament in English, is truly what it means to be a Catholic woman. Now we can also visit a Protestant church or Jewish synagogue and share abundantly with our brethren."

A concomitant Americanization process was also at work within the dominant Protestant community: The Protestant denominations that had been brought from Europe, such as Episcopalianism and Presbyterianism, were being overwhelmed by the denominations that had taken root and grown in the United States, such as Baptist and Methodist sects. At the start of the American republic in 1776, the major church groups were the Episcopalians, the Presbyterians, and the Congregationalists. One hundred years later, their proportion of the total population had decreased dramatically, while the Methodists and Baptists had swept the country. Nonetheless, the Episcopalians and Presbyterians have remained quite strong within the American elite, as is clear from the large number of presidents from these religious faiths: Eighteen of America's 42 presidents have been either Episcopalian or Presbyterian. Of U.S. Supreme Court justices from 1789 to 1992, 55 of 112 have belonged to one of these two Protestant churches. It is also interesting to note that the only two blacks ever to serve on the U.S. Supreme Court, Thurgood Marshall and Clarence Thomas (who were from opposite ends of the political spectrum), belonged to Episcopalian churches when they were appointed to the nation's highest court.

For the first decades after the American Revolution, Congregationalists, Episcopalians, and Presbyterians comprised 55% of religiously affiliated Americans (the *overall* percentage of the population officially affiliated with churches was less than 20%). Within the next few generations, there was a great growth in religious affiliation. By the mid-19th century, the number of people who said they were affiliated with churches nearly doubled, to around 35%. But the religious affiliation of Americans had also *changed* quite dramatically. By 1850, the Baptists and Methodists comprised about 40% of those acknowledging a religious affiliation. The Congregationalists had lost strength, even in New England: In 1776, they could claim almost two thirds of New Englanders affiliated with churches, but by 1850 their share had dropped to a quarter in their historic heartland. During the 19th century, the Congregationalist proportion of the American population dropped very substantially, from 20% to 4%. The Episcopalians also dropped drastically, from 16% to 4%. The Presbyterians also declined, though not as much as the Episcopalians and the Congregationalists. The Presbyterian presence in the population dropped from 19% to 12%. The Baptists, on the other hand, rose from 17% to 21% of the population, and the Methodists had a phenomenal growth rate, from 3% to 34%. By 1900, Methodism had become one of the most successful denominations, appealing to the masses of Americans as they moved west and urbanized. Methodist preachers were winning adherents to their faith at the expense of other Protestant denominations.

THE GROWTH OF OTHER AMERICAN CHURCH GROUPS

In the early 19th century, a major movement was taking hold in New England. Unlike Methodism, which had mass support, this new school of philosophy had a great effect on the most creative minds of this era; it was called transcendentalism. It was an offshoot of Unitarianism, which many thought had become too conservative and orthodox, just as a century before Unitarianism had broken from Congregationalism because of the latter's supposed conservatism. The transcendentalists, many of whom were New England intellectuals, attempted to make direct contact between the individual soul and its Creator as was demanded by many of the evangelists. Transcendentalism is difficult to define but, basically, it is a search for meaning through spiritual intuition; what cannot be denied is the importance of both the movement and its members to American religious, social, and literary history. Without a definite creed, transcendentalism attempted to weave together a faith, a philosophy, an ethical code, and an emphasis on a moral way of life. It tended to reinforce the "republican virtues" of an American civil religion, and advanced the secularization of intellectual life. Outstanding writers and thinkers such as Ralph Waldo Emerson and Henry David Thoreau were leading transcendentalists. In contrast to transcendentalism, this period also produced nonrational sectarian movements, including Christian Science, a quintessentially native American religion. Christian Science maintains that health is spiritual and therefore eternal, and that disease and illness are delusions of the human mind and can therefore be destroyed by prayer. Christian Science has become quite controversial because its basic teachings reject medical treatment, and lawsuits have occasionally been filed when children of Christian Scientists are denied health care that medical authorities deem necessary. Christian Scientists attending colleges and other schools ask for and usually receive exemptions from medical testing and treatment, even for what might be considered by others to be medical emergencies.

Christian Science was founded by an American woman, Mary Baker Eddy. Christian Scientists believe that Eddy's book *Science and Health with Key to the Scriptures* contains the "complete" spiritual meaning of the Bible; it emphasizes prayer as a means to cure spiritual as well as physical problems. There is no official minister in a Christian Science seminar: Lay leaders use the King James Version of the Bible and Mrs. Eddy's book in religious sessions. A public practitioner (one who prays for those who ask his or her prayers on their behalf) must be approved by the Mother Church, the First Church of Christ, Scientist, in Boston, after instruction and proof of successful healing of those in need. Christian Scientists put enormous effort into evangelizing through publications and reading rooms placed in central locations in many cities. One offshoot is a highly respected American newspaper, *The Christian Science Monitor,* which is circulated and read around the world.

Another sect with an emphasis on health and nutrition, as well as a strict life-style, that emerged in this period was the Seventh-Day Adventist church. This new American church was also largely the outgrowth of the writings of a woman (Ellen Harmon White, a disciple of the doomsday prophet William Miller, who wrote *Testimonies for the Church* in 1855) and slowly branched out westward from New England. Its origins lie in the Great Disappointment of October 22, 1844, when the Second Advent (that is, the Second Coming of Christ) failed to occur in conformity with Millerite prophecies.

THE GROWTH OF CATHOLICISM AND JUDAISM IN AMERICA

From the time of the American Revolution to the turn of the current century, the American Catholic church grew from less than 2% of the church-affiliated population to nearly 15%. This growth was fueled by mass immigration from Ireland and Germany and, later, by large migrations from Italy, Austria, Hungary, Poland, and other nations in central and eastern Europe. American Catholicism became the epitome of the immigrant church, an anchor of familiarity in a strange environment.

James Gibbons was elevated to the position of cardinal in 1886 and served until his death in 1921. For some, this was the "Golden Age" of the Catholic church in America. As one writer commented, the history of the American Catholic church from 1870 to 1921 "is largely a biography of [Gibbons's] episcopate." The Catholic population in the United States during this period grew from 7 million to almost 20 million. The number of priests increased from 7,000 to 20,000, the number of bishoprics from 55 to over 100. Cardinal Gibbons presided over the Americanization of the Catholic church. He believed that part of his mission was to make good Americans out of the Catholic immigrants and to show non-Catholic Americans that the Roman Catholic church was not a "foreign" institution, but American as well as universal.

Similar growth occurred in the American Jewish population. German Jewish migration to the United States from the 1840s to the 1870s swelled the Jewish population to over 300,000, even before the large migration of eastern European Jews. This latter migration, which began in the 1880s and continued through 1924, brought millions, including religious leaders who reinvigorated the Conservative and Orthodox Jewish movements and who stressed Jewish traditions and Hebrew liturgy. Unlike the German Jews of a previous generation who had brought Reform Judaism to America, the eastern European immigrants, such as Rabbis Jacob Joseph, Bernard Revel, and Solomon Schechter, attempted, each in his own way, to maintain European Jewish tradition in America. Rabbi Joseph, the first and last chief rabbi of New York, emphasized an intensive Jewish education patterned after the Orthodox yeshivas of eastern Europe. Rabbi Revel was instrumental in developing Yeshiva University, with its Judaic and secular studies, and helped it become the flagship of modern Orthodoxy. Rabbi Schechter reinvigorated the Jewish Theological Seminary and made it the world center of Conservative Judaism.

The Orthodox leaders immediately stressed the need for Hebrew day schools to preserve Jewish tradition in America. A half century later, conservative leaders developed their own Hebrew day-school network. By then, the Orthodox community, under the leadership of Rabbi Aaron Kotler, had developed graduate Jewish study programs in advanced Talmudic seminaries called *kolels*. This return to tradition by an active minority within Judaism is often attributed to the two momentous events that affected world Jewry in the mid-20th century: the Holocaust, which saw the deaths of 6 million Jews (one out of three Jews in the world), and the re-creation of a national Jewish commonwealth after two thousand years of exile: the State of Israel.

Entering the 20th Century

Total membership in all religious groups (except the Quakers, the Unitarians, and the Universalists) grew by leaps and bounds during the 20th century as the general population increased threefold. The anomaly, according to historian Henry Steele Commager, was that religion prospered while theology went bankrupt. There were 42 million churchgoers by 1916, 55 million by 1926, and 72 million by 1942. And despite the existence of so many different religious groups and sects, many groups were becoming more and more alike, even in the disparate areas of ritual and church architecture (this was not always true, however, of some American religions, such as the Mormons, Christian Scientists, and Seventh-Day Adventists, or of fundamentalist Protestants, Orthodox Jews, and traditional Catholics).

Post–World War II immigrants to these shores from the Caribbean and Latin America, Asia, the Middle East, and Africa have also come under the influence of the assimilationist process, either from self-selection before coming to these shores or shortly after their arrival. Most of the Asian Americans who responded to the 1990 NSRI said that they were not members of Asian-based religions, such as Hinduism, Buddhism, or Islam, but that they were Catholics and Protestants. Indeed, the religious affiliation of Asian

Americans in the 1990s is basically the same as that of other Americans: Catholics and Baptists are the largest groups. Similarly, most Arab Americans polled in 1990 were Christian, not Muslim. As the American Muslim population is becoming more ethnically and racially diversified, it is also becoming more attuned to the American civil religion. On April 2, 1993, the Islamic Center of New England held a ground-breaking ceremony for their new mosque in Sharon, Massachusetts. The growth of the Muslim population in metropolitan Boston necessitated the decision to move from their original location in Quincy to Sharon, a city whose very name resonates with biblical allusion. Addressing a large ecumenical audience of Protestants, Catholics, and Jews, as well as Muslims, Imam Talal Eid, echoing the words of American religious leaders of past centuries, said "Welcome to Sharon—the new Jerusalem."

Today, the Protestantization of minority religions in America continues, which may explain why many Catholics who go to mass on a regular basis hardly differ with Protestants in their acceptance of intermarriage, divorce, and birth control. It also explains to some degree why adherents of smaller non-Christian religions like Judaism are intermarrying at a very rapid rate, conforming to the majority value structure of a Protestant/secular-American society. However, the total picture is more complex. Difference exists alongside commonality. There are distinctions as well as similarities among members of various religious groups in the areas of education, income, political affiliation, geographic location, and social values. These will be examined in later chapters.

In the early 1950s, when a polling group asked a small sample of Americans to identify themselves in terms of religious "preference," 95% of the respondents declared themselves to be Protestants, Catholics, or Jews. Sixty-eight percent said that they were Protestant, 23% said that they were Catholic, and 4% said that they were Jewish. In his book *Protestant, Catholic, Jew,* Will Herberg writes about the paradox "of pervasive secularism and mounting religiosity," a mind-set involving thinking and living within a broad framework of reality that is far from one's professed religious beliefs. This paradox still exists with us today because it is, as we have seen, part of our American cultural tradition.

Coexisting with this paradox is the ongoing link through our history, in joy and in tragedy, between religion, in the broad sense, and the American experiment. The American political experiment, in its hope for the future and its memory of the past, keeps on reverting to divine Providence. John Adams described the American political experiment two hundred years ago as a "grand scheme and design in Providence" for the liberation of mankind. Protestant thinkers and believers have written and spoken on this theme endlessly. In a similar vein, the Jewish congregation of Newport, Rhode

Island, expressing to President Washington their joy in their newfound freedom, declared that "this so ample and extensive Federal Union" must be "the work of the great God, who rules the armies of the heavens and among the inhabitants of the earth." Almost a century later the American Catholic bishops echoed Abraham Lincoln when they declared, "We believe that our country's heroes were the instruments of the God of Nations in establishing this home of freedom," adding that America is "a work of special Providence, its framers 'building wiser than they knew.' "

Reinhold Neibuhr, one of 20th-century America's leading Protestant theologians, observed almost a half century ago that Americans are "at once the most religious and the most secular of nations. How shall we explain this paradox? Could it be that we are most religious partly in consequence of being the most secular culture? . . . Perhaps we are so religious because religion has two forms among us. One challenges the gospel of prosperity, success and achievement of heaven on earth. The other claims to furnish religious instruments for the attainment of these objectives."

In the end, the resolution of this paradox could rest on the belief that although anyone can be a good American, the ultimate guarantee of an American's freedom is his or her belief that America is a religious nation and that Americans are a religious people. Seen in this light, it is also a good way for understanding how and why individual Americans identify and behave as they do.

3

GEOGRAPHY IS DESTINY

◆ ◆ ◆

A SENSE OF PLACE

Anyone who travels across the vast continent of North America will encounter an amazing diversity of physical and social environments that reflect wide differences in climate, topography, land use, and architecture. Places of worship also reflect changes in the natural environment: an adobe chapel in the southwestern desert, a towering Gothic cathedral in a crowded city, a white clapboard steeple on Church Street, Smalltown, U.S.A. Christmas in Boston is very different from Christmas in Los Angeles, in a myriad ways. The media's nostalgic image of that which is typically American, whether on television or the cover of *Life* magazine, is often an austere white New England Congregationalist parish church on the town green. For the present-day foreign traveler, that image may well be the stark geometric architecture of an evangelical or Pentecostal church surrounded by fleets of yellow school buses close to an interstate highway. Geography and scenery create a sense of place that pervades our perception of religion. Different settings resonate in the mind. America, a land of few holy sites, has nonetheless accommodated a rich assortment of religious cultures and has created holy images throughout its sundry terrains.

Climate and the inexorable change of the seasons affect our view of the world and the forces that shape it. Limitless plains or congested urban streets, incessant rain or inevitable sun, sudden tornadoes or unpredictable earthquakes, influence our personal sense of place in the natural order of things. The connection between nature and spirituality can be traced back to the dawn of Western history and its Greek, Celtic, and Teutonic pagan roots. It could surely be said that the three great monotheistic religions of the world—Judaism, Christianity, and Islam—were influenced by their desert origins. Abraham, Moses, Jesus, and Muhammad were all inspired by their sojourns in the wilderness.

We would not claim to explain the spiritual disposition of the inhabitants of a locale in terms of their natural environment. Yet it must have some impact. The geographic diversity of the United States may in some way be reflected in religious preferences. Surely a relationship exists between the particular local environment and the regional differences in religious preference among the Pacific Coast, the Rocky Mountain states, the South, the Northeast, and the Midwest. A warm climate and plentiful supplies of surface water in lakes and rivers undoubtedly encourages the practice of adult baptism by immersion in the southern states. Can it be an accident that one third of American-based cults are headquartered in California, or that the airwaves of the South are full of gospel country music? A 1991 Gallup Youth Survey showed that 94% of teenagers living in the American Midwest believe in Heaven, compared with only 84% in the East. Teens living in the South are more likely to read the Bible (55%) than those in the eastern (31%) or western (45%) United States.

When we refer to the geography of American religion, we are really speaking about social rather than physical scenery. Certain locations and habitats attract certain types of people, and religion is an activity practiced in groups. Elements of fashion and camaraderie are present in the practice of religion in a specific time and place, and this reinforces a cultural status quo. The cultural milieu attracts and repels different sorts of people in a dynamic and migratory society like the contemporary United States. People literally search for compatible life-styles, and so a sorting process operates as to where people live and with whom they mix. As the figures mentioned above show, peer-group influences are important, especially on the young. The peer group perpetuates tradition and reinforces majoritarian tendencies, which in turn produce the regional religious cultures we will describe.

In any given community, churches and religious organizations may exist for some faiths and not for others. Because it requires less effort to choose within the existing religious infrastructure than to establish new forms of religious organization, the institutional inheritance factor serves to bolster established religions. The most obvious symbol of a religion is its house of worship. The mere physical presence of a chapel, church, or synagogue on the landscape is a form of advertising for potential members. Houses of worship are testimonies to faith, not merely symbols of belief, and they are statements about the place of their congregants in the local environment.

We will examine differences in degree of devotion and type of affiliation with regard to specific states, particular religions, rural-urban classification, and Colonial and immigrant settlement patterns. This chapter will attempt analysis on the basis of social and community geography, viewing religion as a group phenomenon that reflects a population's social environment. There are obviously gaps between religious affiliation and daily conduct, yet a certain linkage between religious preference and some aspects of personal conduct is demonstrable. Religious preference does not operate very accurately as a predictor of behavior on the individual level, but it becomes important when it influences norms of group behavior. Religious preference will be seen to have an effect on delinquency and drug or alcohol abuse for individuals who are part of a circle of people acting according to a defined value system. It also has a noticeable effect on politics and social beliefs. For example, the NSRI shows that Nebraska contains greater than average proportions of Catholics, Methodists, Lutherans, Presbyterians, and Episcopalians. As a columnist in the *Lincoln Journal-Star* concluded, "Just knowing that much about Nebraska would safely lead social analysts to fairly perceptive descriptions of this state's popular mass character, its social preferences and its brand of politics." And Nebraska can be seen as a Republican, patriotic, God-fearing, socially conservative middle-American state with traditionally defined male and female roles and a belief in the validity of old-fashioned family values. This type of information, which the NSRI made available to church leaders, academics, and product marketers on a state-by-state basis, was regarded by the *National Catholic Reporter* as "the greatest contribution" of our study when it first appeared. In this chapter we will go further and reveal even more valuable data specific to particular regions, metropolitan areas, and various religious denominations.

REGIONAL RELIGIOUS PATTERNS

The NSRI is particularly valuable because it conclusively confirms previously scattered data on the geography of American religion. One of the more significant findings was confirmation of the existence of homogeneous religious subcultures within the nation and their persistence over the last hundred years. Though the geographical unity of Colonial times could not be maintained as evangelists persuaded, colonies united, immigrants arrived, frontiers expanded, and pioneers migrated, distinctive heartlands still persist, especially for four religious families: Baptists in the South, Lutherans in the Upper Midwest farm belt, Roman Catholics in the Northeast, and Mormons in Utah and the other Rocky Mountain states. To some extent this finding belies conventional wisdom, which suggests that American society as a whole has become more socially uniform and thereby religiously integrated under the influence of a pervasive mass culture and high mobility.

BAPTISTS OF THE SOUTH

The concentrated strength of the Baptists, the nation's largest Protestant denomination, in the American South contrasts with their relative lack of significance in other regions. They are the largest religious group in fourteen states (nearly all of those are in the South) and in the District of Columbia. Baptists comprise more than half the residents of Mississippi, Alabama, and Georgia. Almost one third of American Baptists reside in Texas (11%), North Carolina (7%), Georgia (7%), and California (6%). That Baptists dominate the South is of enormous cultural significance to the nation. As we have seen, Baptists come in many varieties and are split by race into black and white groups; nevertheless, they form a formidable cultural force in shaping the outlook of the populace and social institutions of the region. The most influential organization is the 17-million-strong Southern Baptist Convention. Few readers will fail to notice that the darker areas of Map 1A, which comprise those states where Baptists currently exceed 25% of the population, almost replicate the former Confederate States of America. More-

1A. Percentage of each state's population that is Baptist

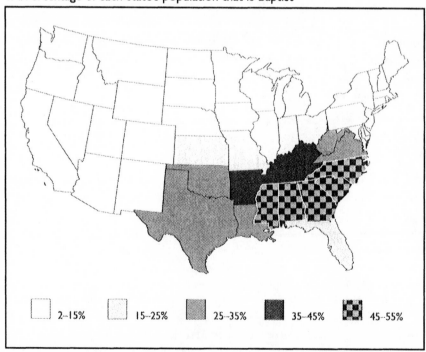

2–15%	15–25%	25–35%	35–45%	45–55%

over, the bloc of states in which more than 45% of the population is Baptist is clearly the territory known as the Deep South.

Sheer concentration of numbers and the lack of significant rivals to their religious outlook allow the Baptist churches to enforce traditional group values in a way that contrasts with religious beliefs and practices elsewhere. In regions that have greater diversification and more widespread religious pluralism, beliefs and practices are less public, more individually chosen. NSRI results show that in every southern state, the percentage of people with no religion was lower than the 7.5% national average. Such findings may explain the region's "Bible Belt" nickname, a pejorative 20th-century term invented by the iconoclast Baltimore journalist H. L. Mencken. The region's ostensible religious obsession has been depicted by other artists, including the modern American composer Carlisle Floyd in his portrait of hypocritical religious elders in the Tennessee Valley, where he set his opera *Susannah*.

Southern Christianity is a relatively stable, distinct religion based upon an evangelistic and fundamentalist heritage that involves inerrancy, which means the acceptance of a literal interpretation of the Bible, as well as an emphasis on an experience of personal conversion. Southern Christianity is

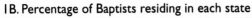

1B. Percentage of Baptists residing in each state

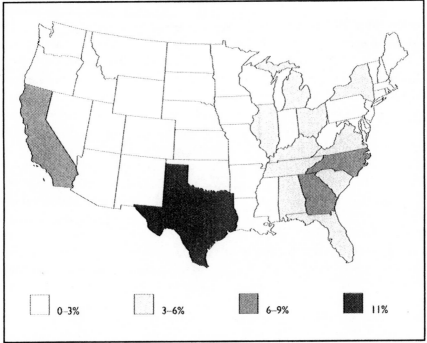

0–3%   3–6%   6–9%   11%

emotional, Jesus-centered, and contains a strict moral code, but it is also expressed through southern gospel music, Christian country music, and televangelists, as well as through local secular laws against alcohol and obscenity.

Why should the South be so religiously unique? The answer lies in its history, for nowhere else in the nation is history taken so seriously or evoked so often. Many scholars suggest that the dominance of the Baptist faith in the South can only be explained in terms of the "captive region thesis," that is, the Baptist religion is a faith of a subordinate people struggling against their conquerors. After the South's defeat in the Civil War, the Baptist church was one of the few institutions that remained under southern control. It assuaged the white populace's feelings of resentment against northern military occupation. With the old planter aristocracy destroyed, the clergy became the defenders of southern morals and values, of the "southern way of life."

Irrespective of race, the Baptist clergy in their writing and preaching have been more influential in community and political affairs in the South than in any other American region. In part this is because the individualistic morality of the Baptists necessitates a close personal relationship between the pastor and the congregant. For the poor white majority and the even more oppressed African Americans, the evangelical focus of the church, with its emphasis on the conversion experience, allowed them to deal with their grinding poverty. The African American Baptist and Methodist churches, centers of black social and political life, were the only institutions over which African Americans held any control.

Until the 1960s, the South was the region most removed from the mainstream of American industrial society. Unlike in the West, few newcomers entered the South, and immigrants from overseas with religious influence were few and far between in the region. "Baptist culture was almost palpable," as the University of Chicago religious scholar Martin Marty has aptly stated. In the early part of this century, the First Baptist Church in a southern community often owned the town's swimming pool and other recreation facilities. The Baptist student union dominated the campus life of the colleges. Huge evangelistic rallies competed for attendance with high-school football. Remarkably, the emergence of the "New South" over the last few decades has not altered things very much, as residents of the South are still more church-oriented than people in other sections of the country. Billy Graham, a Southern Baptist preacher from North Carolina, seems just as potent in the age of videos and universal car ownership as he was in an earlier time. The same is true for the clergy from other denominations in the southern evangelical Protestant tradition, such as the Assemblies of God, the Baptist Missionary Association of America, the Church of God (Cleveland, Tennessee), and the Pentecostal Holiness church. In fact, the most important visible contemporary development in American religion has been a resurgence of the revivalist, theologically conservative Protestantism associated with the South and the growing influence of "old-time" religion in other regions. A symbol of this nationalization of southern religion was the election in 1976 of Georgia's Jimmy Carter, the first self-professed born-again Christian and Southern Baptist to become president of the United States.

CATHOLICISM: STRONGEST IN THE NORTHEAST

In some ways, the geographical distribution of the country's Catholics is an inversion of the Baptist situation. Instead of being in the South, the heartland of Catholicism lies in the Northeast, particularly New England. States with a numerical majority of Catholics include Rhode Island, Connecticut, and Massachusetts. Unlike Baptists, who are numerically dominant only regionally, Catholics constitute a significant percentage of forty-eight states (see Map 2A). Nevertheless, 55% of Catholics reside in the Northeast and Midwest. The arrival of Catholics from Europe, mainly between 1840 and

2A. Percentage of each state's population that is Catholic

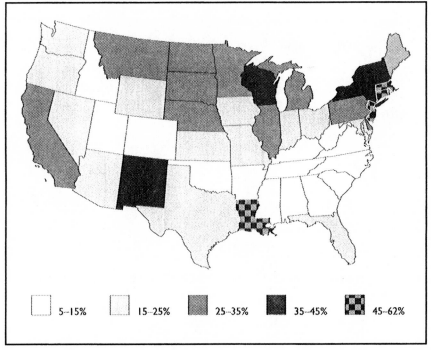

| | 5–15% | | 15–25% | | 25–35% | | 35–45% | | 45–62% |

1924, and the more recent entry of Latin Americans built up American Catholicism and created its geographic map. The numerical distribution shows the effect of recent westward migration as well as immigration, factors of little importance to the Baptist churches. In the Northeast, Catholics constitute more than one third of the population in New Jersey, New York, New Hampshire, and Vermont. Successive waves of immigration caused the amazing transformation of Massachusetts from a Puritan stronghold to a Catholic-majority state. In the heavily Catholic states of Wisconsin, New Mexico, and Louisiana, Catholic distribution reflects the presence of typically Catholic ethnic groups such as the South Germans, Chicanos and Cajuns. In terms of Catholic population distribution by states, more than one third of American Catholics live in four states: New York (12%), California (13%), Pennsylvania (6%), and Texas (6%).

The mobility and sheer size of the Catholic population has hindered that church's own community monitoring. Still, the close correlation of our figures, based on a telephone survey, to the Catholic data, based on local parish collections of demographic events such as baptisms and funerals, legitimizes both sets of figures. Joseph C. Harris, a Catholic layman and

2B. Percentage of Catholics residing in each state

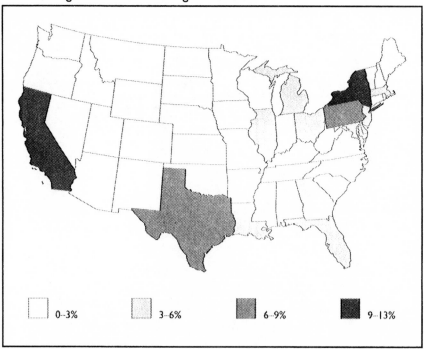

statistical consultant from Seattle, reported to us that his calculations of variations by states between NSRI figures and an annual publication, P. J. Kenedy & Sons' *The Official Catholic Directory,* produce a very impressive correlation coefficient of .9621. This finding has bolstered the reputation of the *Directory*'s statistical appendices, the accuracy of which had been regarded skeptically in many Catholic circles.

According to a noted sociologist, Georg Simmel, the size of a particular group is an important determinant of its members' behavior. From this perspective, we might deduce that the greater the size of the group, the greater will be the variation in religious practice, and the more freedom for individual deviance that will exist because of the difficulty of enforcing social discipline among large numbers of people. This scenario has proven particularly true for America's 46 million adult Catholics, who are widely dispersed across the nation. Many have become "nominal" baptized Catholics, who identify themselves as Catholic in surveys but do not currently have contact with parishes (and who account for around 4% of the NSRI's Catholic identifiers). As we might have predicted, nonaffiliates tend to be young adults and migrants. The discrepancy in terms of real numbers between our higher counts and Catholic records is most noticeable in the Northeast, where Catholicism is numerically strongest.

Migration is also detrimental to church affiliation. Hence, the NSRI results for Catholics in the fast-growing state of North Carolina, which received considerable immigration from the North during the 1980s, produced a figure of 5.9%, whereas the local Catholic churches' membership rolls suggested 2.5%. (The difference is around 250,000 people.) A spokesman for the Raleigh diocese did not question our findings but merely stated, "We've been saying for some time that for every person who registers with our church there is at least one out there who is Catholic or claims to be Catholic but doesn't register." He went on to suggest, rather pragmatically, "I don't know that a measure of being religious is whether or not you register." Other states with much higher numbers of Catholics according to the NSRI than according to church records are Florida, Virginia, Washington, Colorado, and New Hampshire, all of which grew rapidly through migration during the last decade. Most of these states lack a history of Catholic settlement and are weak areas organizationally for the church.

The relationship of America's two largest religious groups, the Catholics and Baptists, who hold the loyalties of nearly half the country's population, is important to everyone. The social distance between the two faiths is wide. This gap is perhaps best symbolized by the contrast between the fiercely independent local Baptist church in its plain chapel, whose congregation hires its own pastor, and the ornate cathedral run by a clerical hierarchy owing ultimate allegiance overseas. Both organizationally and personally,

Catholic-Baptist relationships are marked by caution and reserve. There is little interaction because of their different theologies, governance systems, religious life-styles, and, above all, geographic locations. Aside from their significant numbers in such traditionally Catholic areas as southern Louisiana, South Texas, and South Florida, Catholics are underrepresented in southern states, particularly in Arkansas, Alabama, and Tennessee, where they total less than 5% of the population. Catholic newcomers to the South are faced with the fact that they are a small minority there and that there is still anti-Catholic sentiment, especially outside the cities. Southern Catholics do not have much political clout, and there are not enough funds for parochial schools, church programs, or personnel. This has meant that southern Catholicism has maintained a less communitarian flavor but has become more ecumenical, innovative, and, to some extent, adaptive to local culture. One of the largest American Catholic television ministries is Mother Angelica's Eternal Word Network, based in Birmingham, Alabama.

The pattern of religious loyalties in Louisiana is unique: The state is 46.8% Catholic and 29.2% Baptist. The religious divisions are geographical and cut as well across the state's racial divide (Louisiana is one-third black). The southern half of the state, including the cities of New Orleans, Baton Rouge, and Lake Charles, as well as the bayou country and the Gulf coast, has been historically Catholic almost since the region was first settled by Europeans in 1718. This area has the highest percentage of Roman Catholics and the lowest percentage of unchurched, of any area in the United States. In contrast, the parishes, as Louisianans call their counties, in the north of the state around Shreveport are a stronghold of Protestant fundamentalism. The unique Louisiana mixture of Cajuns, Creoles, and poor whites seems to make for an explosive political mixture, as the careers of Huey Long and David Duke have shown. An intriguing question, though, is why Louisiana's sharp religious differences do not create the same sort of political and social tensions as its racial differences do.

LUTHERANISM IN THE UPPER MIDWEST

The Upper Midwest, the old Northwest Territory, is the heartland of the third major regional religious culture, the Lutherans. There have been three waves of Lutheran immigration in American history: First, in 1638, New Sweden was founded in the Delaware Valley. Later, in the 18th century, 60,000 Germans left the Rhineland for Pennsylvania. Then, in the late 19th century, a large Scandinavian settlement arrived in the country's northern-tier farmlands.

In the countries of northern Europe, Lutheranism was typically the state-established church. Lutheran immigrants tended to reproduce their national

3A. Percentage of each state's population that is Lutheran

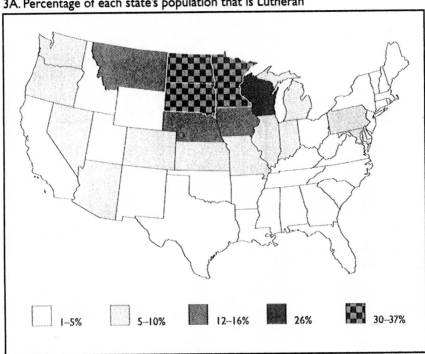

divisions in the New World. Separate ethnic churches representing Sweden, Denmark, Finland, Iceland, and others were established. Even these later split on doctrinal grounds: By 1900, there were twenty-four separate Lutheran church organizations in America. The 20th century has found Lutherans attempting to submerge ethnic differences and merge their churches.

Today, the main divisions arise from the ideological and theological differences between the liberally inclined Evangelical Lutheran Church in America and the conservative Lutheran Church–Missouri Synod. Among the populace, Lutheranism is viewed broadly, as an ethnic or community church: Very few of our Lutheran respondents qualified their reply by specifying their particular denomination.

In this country, Lutheranism remains geographically concentrated. More than one third of the population of Minnesota and the Dakotas is Lutheran. Close behind is Wisconsin, with 26%. Montana, Nebraska, and Iowa each have three times the national proportion of Lutherans, which is 5.2%. No doubt this geographical clustering helped consolidate the group and prevented switching of denominations. However, migration from rural areas

3B. Percentage of Lutherans residing in each state

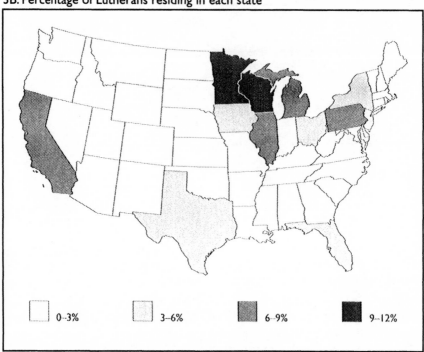

and farm states during this century has transformed the overall distribution. Altogether, as Map 3B shows, almost half the nation's Lutherans live in five states—Minnesota (12%), Wisconsin (10%), California (9%), Pennsylvania (8%), and Illinois (7%).

It is difficult to separate what is Lutheran from what is northern European ethnic in the character of the Upper Midwest. In part this is because the region's physical environment of forests, lakes, and severe winters is very close to its population's ancestral homeland in the Nordic countries. This may help to explain why there is so much similarity between the cultural and social environments of the region's rural areas and those of northern Europe.

Lutheranism is a moderate, formalistic Christian denomination not given to religious innovation or demonstrativeness. Lutheranism produces a sober, serious, industrious people, relatively tolerant but supportive of the political status quo (official statistics also reveal that the states with a high proportion of Lutherans have a low rate of legal abortions). Lutherans take pride in their civic virtues and their strong sense of community, which their religion promotes.

MORMONS: THE ESTABLISHMENT OF A PROMISED LAND

The Church of Jesus Christ of Latter-Day Saints, the only truly successful religious group experiment in the American West, constitutes our fourth major religious geographic concentration. Today 69% of the population of Utah and 31% of neighboring Idaho are Mormon. The essentially western settlement pattern of the group is such that no state east of the Rocky Mountains is even 2% Mormon. Mormons exhibit a high degree of what geographers refer to as spatial congruence, which is to say that they tend to live where they are numerically dominant. Mormons dominate Utah more than any other denomination dominates a state. They are the most clustered religious group in the nation: More than two thirds live in four states—Utah (34%), California (19%), Idaho (9%), and Arizona (5%).

Mormons are the most geographically isolated and uniquely distributed religious group in the nation. Thus they stand highest of any religious group on the index of dissimilarity. This index measures the social distance between any two groups, on a scale of 0 to 100, according to the percentage of each group that would have to change its state of residence for the two groups to be distributed in an exactly similar way. The "I values" for American

4A. Percentage of each state's population that is Mormon

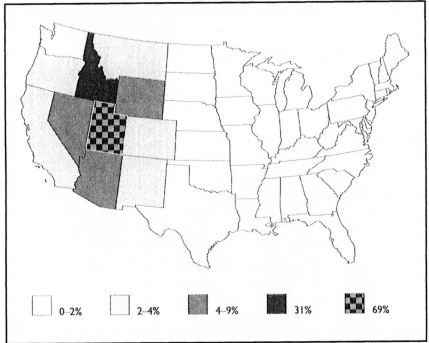

4B. Percentage of Mormons residing in each state

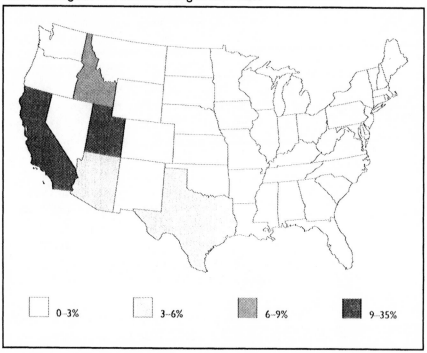

Mormons in Table 3-3A show that 56.1% of them would have to move so that their geographic distribution would mirror that of Presbyterians, the closest religious group to them on the index. For Mormons to mirror Baptists, 68% would have to migrate. In contrast, the lower the index, the closer the two groups are in geographic space, and the closer their social distance. For instance, 29.3% of American Jews would have to move for Jews to be geographically distributed like Catholics, and only 18.0% of American Methodists would have to move for Methodists to be distributed like Pentecostals.

In Chapter 2 we saw that the Church of Jesus Christ of Latter-Day Saints is a history-centered, "this-worldly" religion. In their early years, the Mormons were distinguished from their neighbors by their communal effort, religious vision, explicit ideology, and a value system that conflicted with other frontiersmen's emphasis on nuclear families seeking purely personal goals. The Mormons' migration westward was an attempt to find a "Promised Land" and to establish "a new Zion," that is, to ingrain the "rule of God" on earth for a people with a heritage going back to ancient Israel and archaic America. Moreover, the Mormon leadership, so designated by personal commitment and talent rather than by education or social position, wanted to found a socioeconomic as well as a religious community that would be ruled by revealed principles and run by the priestly servants of God. Their social organization had an egalitarian, co-operative, and communitarian impulse inspired by the Mormon interpretation of the prophet Isaiah's vision of the desert blooming as a rose (Isaiah 35:1–2). In fact, the Mormons were the only millennial and utopian movement of 19th-century America to survive and flourish. Undoubtedly their geographical isolation and concentration in the Great Basin assisted in their success in building in unpopulated Utah a home for their persecuted group free from the constraints of "Gentile" influences. Converts were warned to flee the world and "gather" with the Saints to await the Second Coming.

The Mormons have always placed an emphasis on recruitment and spreading their message. In the 19th century, a great deal of the Mormon community's limited resources was applied to the costly task of bringing 85,000 European converts to Utah through the Perpetual Emigrating Fund. This importation policy ceased around 1896, when the Mormon church began the slow process of accommodation to the American mainstream, and was replaced by a massive program of taking Zion to the unconverted and building a network of wards and stakes (that is, bishoprics) all over the world: These consist of meetinghouses, welfare storehouses, social-service offices, and temples, established wherever groups of Mormons are located. The faint echo of the traditional communitarian norms can be seen in these practices of social welfare based on an efficient tithing system. However, the NSRI data suggest that resistance to the message of the Mormons still persists in the American East. The 40,000 young male Mormon missionaries who are estimated at any given time to be evangelizing during a two-year commitment to the church still appear to be making a significant numerical impact in the United States only west of the Rockies and in Texas. However, despite their abstinence from tobacco, alcohol, tea, and coffee, the Mormons of Salt Lake City are no longer perceived as being on the cutting edge of religious and social experimentation in the 1990s.

METHODISM AND PROTESTANT DENOMINATIONS WITHOUT SPECIFIC REGIONAL BASES

One large religious group that does not have a strong regional bias is the Methodists, so they can claim a real national following. Thus the index of dissimilarity between the total U.S. population and Methodists is quite low (see Table 3-3D). As stated earlier, the term *Methodist* covers a de-

5A. Percentage of each state's population that is Methodist

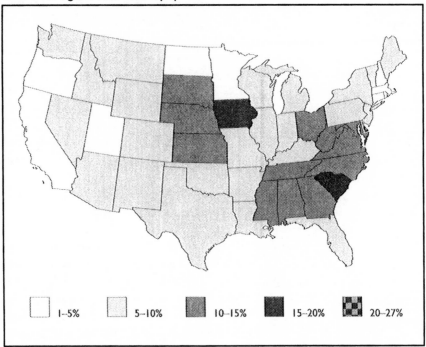

| | 1–5% | | 5–10% | | 10–15% | | 15–20% | | 20–27% |

nominational family, so our relevant figures reflect not just adherents of the large United Methodist church but also some smaller bodies and the three historically African American Methodist churches. Methodists form a moderate percentage of the population of most states, although because they are only 8% of the U.S. population, their overall percentages are lower than those of Catholics or Baptists. Only in Delaware do Methodists exceed 20% of the population. Except for their significant presence in Texas and California, Methodists are most likely to be found east of the Mississippi River, particularly in rural areas. That Methodists are typically American is not surprising, as their denomination is essentially an American invention.

The Methodists, and the other religious denominations that were dominant in the Colonial period, tend to be well distributed now across most of the states. The indices of dissimilarity with the national population are also low for other WASP-dominated denominations, such as Presbyterians and Episcopalians. Low index scores apply to the Pentecostals as well as the Jehovah's Witnesses. The mainline Presbyterian church (U.S.A.), formed in 1983, united the northern and southern branches of the denominations,

5B. Percentage of Methodists residing in each state

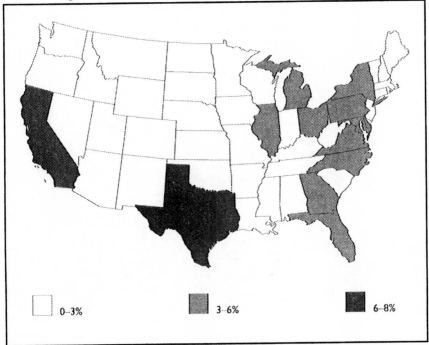

□ 0–3%   ▨ 3–6%   ■ 6–8%

which had been estranged since the Civil War. Partly motivated by its hope to transcend North-South divisions, the church moved its headquarters from New York to Louisville, Kentucky, a small, ostensibly noncosmopolitan city in a border state. Though a new denomination, dating only from 1917, the Jehovah's Witnesses are very actively disseminating their publications nationwide in order to develop a national rather than specifically regional following. The Pentecostal percentage of each state (see Map 6A) has a spatial pattern that resembles in some way the Mormon distribution, though at a lower level of concentration. Pentecostalism is a denominational family with a considerable African American—and, hence, southern—membership. It is overrepresented in a circle of states in the western section of the South centered on Arkansas.

THE JEWISH DISTRIBUTION

People defining themselves as Jewish by religion (as opposed to by culture or ethnicity) are geographically clustered in the Middle Atlantic states, Florida, and California. They also are the most urbanized; 90% live in

6A. Percentage of each state's population that is Pentecostal

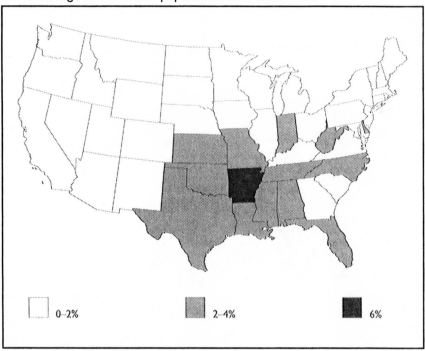

0–2%   2–4%   6%

metropolitan areas. Nevertheless, Jewish population distribution is now much closer to the U.S. population as a whole than it was even forty years ago. Forty percent of America's Jews by religion now live in the southern and western regions of the country (the figure was only 12% in 1930). There has been a considerable movement of Jews out of the heartland of the country and toward the two coasts. Jews are much more mobile than any other religious group of the country. Eighty-five percent are living in a different city or town from the one in which they were born, and a quarter of the adult Jewish population moved to a new city or town during the period 1985–90. The migration of Jews is very much linked to their impressive socioeconomic success and increasing social acceptance, which in recent years have provided them with greater freedom in selecting a place of residence. Areas of the country associated with "post-industrial high-tech economy" have seen the largest Jewish population growth rates in recent decades. As we will document later, the Jewish population, both male and female, is particularly well educated, and its occupation structure is highly skewed toward professional, technical, and managerial roles, and toward economic centers related to government, academic, and health sec-

6B. Percentage of Pentecostals residing in each state

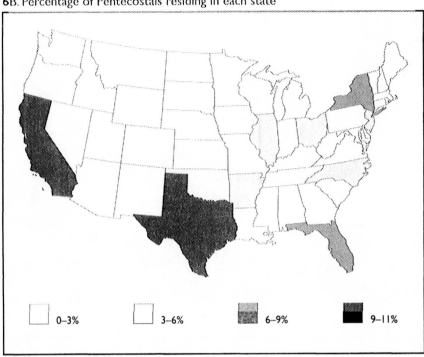

| | 0–3% | | 3–6% | | 6–9% | | 9–11% |

tors. Studies have shown a clearer and stronger relationship between population distribution and economic growth for the Jewish population than for the nation as a whole. Their migration has led to the demise of many Jewish communities in small market towns, especially in the High Plains and in the rural South, and the growth of new centers of Jewish population in areas such as Silicon Valley in northern California, and the university and scientific centers of New England. In addition, the migration of elderly Jews to the Sunbelt has meant that a large proportion of adherents of this ancient religious tradition reside in new communities and worship in newly built religious structures.

The pattern of clustering found among Jews is duplicated by adherents of many other smaller religious groups, including Hindus, Mennonites, Congregationalists, and the Churches of Christ, the Churches of God, and the Holiness churches. It is only by having a critical mass in any one area that most small groups can maintain their viability over the generations. Unless there is geographical rootedness, the prospects for long-term survival of these small minority groups are dim.

7A. Percentage of each state's population that is Presbyterian

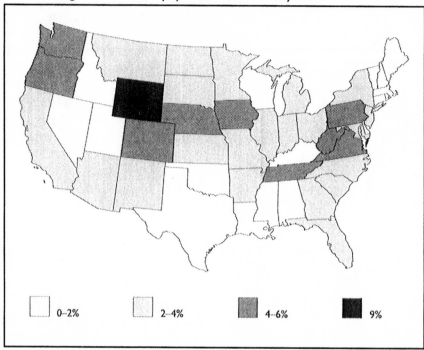

0–2%   2–4%   4–6%   9%

DENOMINATIONAL CLUSTERING
AND SOCIAL DISTANCE

When we examine relationships among the religious groups in geographic space and so in social distance (see Tables 3-3A, 3-3B, 3-3C, and 3-3D), the clustered denominations mentioned directly above and the Mormons seem most deviant from the overall national pattern. In contrast, we learn that the generic replies to the NSRI—"Protestant," "Christian," and even "Refused"—are less geographically specific and therefore more widespread and national than we might have imagined. These tables provide interesting pairings of similarity in geographical distribution, some of which, like Pentecostal–Baptist and Methodist–Presbyterian, would surprise few observers. On the other hand, the Eastern Orthodox Christian–Muslim and Jehovah's Witness–Episcopalian indices are perhaps smaller than might have been expected, and demonstrate that these populations overlap geographically.

In terms of maximum social distance, we might not be surprised by the high index of dissimilarity between groups with very little in common (Mor-

7B. Percentage of Presbyterians residing in each state

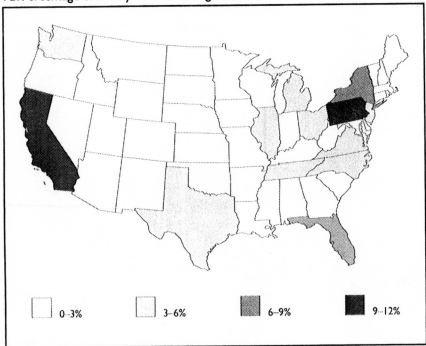

0–3% 3–6% 6–9% 9–12%

mons and Hindus, for example), but why certain Protestant denominations are so highly segregated *is* surprising. Why the Holiness and Born Again/Evangelical respondents should be so far apart geographically is not easily explained. There is also a high index of dissimilarity between Holiness respondents and followers of the Church of the Nazarene, showing that the two responses refer to different populations. The former are concentrated in the South, while the latter, members of a major component of the conservative wing of the Holiness movement, are mainly concentrated in the center of the country. The very high level of dissimilarity ("I value" of 70.3) between Congregationalists and respondents identifying with the Churches of Christ is also a significant finding. This evidence seems to suggest that "Congregationalist" is still a very specifically New England self-identification.

RELIGION IN RURAL AREAS

In modern Western societies there is no doubt that rural residents are more religious, in their belief and behavior, than urban dwellers. Aside from

8A. Percentage of each state's population that is Episcopalian

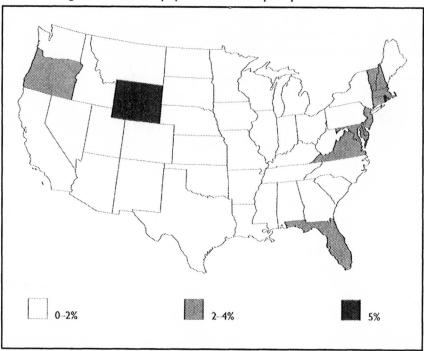

differences in education and class, the explanation often given is that rural people are simply more in touch with nature, or "real life." In contrast, life in industrial cities, with its accompanying fixation on material goals, tends to deprive people of the capacity for contemplation of world and self that leads to wonder and amazement. Modern technology, more prevalent in cities, gives the impression, or at least fosters the illusion, that people are not fundamentally dependent on powers outside or above themselves. The NSRI figures bear this out. As Table 3-4 shows, our respondents in urban areas were slightly more likely (8.6%) than those in rural areas (7.1%) to report that they had no religion or were agnostics. Conversely, rural residents were more inclined from the outset to answer our question on their religion, with fewer than 2% of them refusing. Our lowest refusal rates were in states with low levels of urbanization: Mississippi (0.6%), Vermont (0.7%), and South Dakota (1.0%).

Rural America, or what the Bureau of the Census defines as nonmetropolitan areas, contains just under a quarter of the nation's population. Rural communities, more culturally homogeneous than urban America, have distinctive cultural values, folkways, customs, and traditions. County fairs,

8B. Percentage of Episcopalians residing in each state

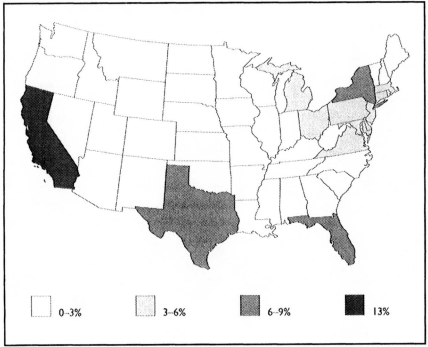

agricultural shows, and rodeos dot the rural landscape. Today, a single denomination still dominates many rural counties. Historically, church participation is higher in rural areas, particularly where there otherwise is social deprivation combined with religious and ethnic homogeneity. Going to church on Sunday is the highlight of the hardworking farm family's week, especially the poor family that cannot afford any other social outlets. Rural religion reflects America's historical settlement patterns of the previous century, and it has been shielded from the recent influx of immigrants from non-Western societies. More than 91% of rural Americans are Christians; three quarters of them are Protestants.

The rural and agricultural nature of religious enthusiasm in America goes back to the first half of the 19th century. Older religious traditions seem to survive better in the countryside. For instance, the urbanization of both whites and blacks in this century has weakened Methodism. Our evidence for this is that Methodists are proportionately almost twice as common in the countryside (11.5%) as in the cities (6.5%) and suburbs (7.4%). Other groups that are currently overrepresented in rural areas are the Church of the Nazarene, the Churches of Christ, the Churches of God, the Brethren, the

9A. Percentage of each state's population that is Jewish

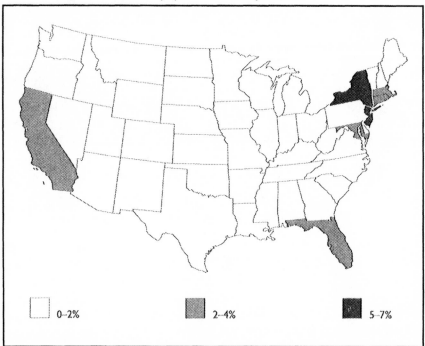

Assemblies of God, and the Holiness churches. These religious preferences reflect a conservative temperament that inevitably has social outcomes in terms of the political atmosphere and life-styles of many rural communities, which are typically resistant to changing fads and fashions.

Another example of a religion best suited to rural areas is the Old Order Amish faith of Lancaster County, Pennsylvania. These extreme traditionalists among the Mennonites, descended from Swiss Anabaptists, are famous for their photogenic horse-and-buggy mode of transportation. Those who are searching for the primitive or counterculture often see in these simple farmers a model of low energy consumption. They have resisted modern plumbing and electricity in their homes, as well as automobiles, tractors, and other self-propelled farm machinery. Their only apparent compromises with industrial civilization are gasoline-powered units (nevertheless pulled by horses) that operate various modern farm implements, electric lights on their carriages, and other devices operated by 12-volt batteries. They have no poor or neglected people. Their core value of *"Gelassenheit,"* composure through submission to a higher authority, embraces a doctrine of nonresistance and the rejection of oath taking. This and their German dialect, distinctiveness

9B. Percentage of Jews residing in each state

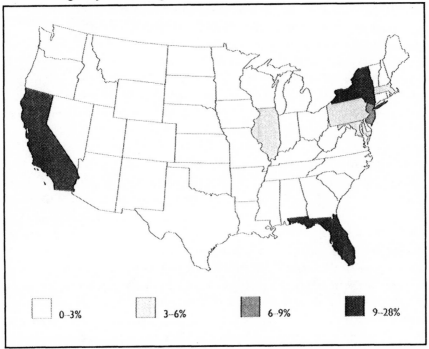

| | 0–3% | | 3–6% | | 6–9% | | 9–28% |

of manner and dress, and behavioral patterns that include gerontocracy, patriarchy, and religious congregationalism comprise a life-style that appears to be viable only in a rural environment and farm economy.

PROTESTANTISM AND RURAL GUN OWNERSHIP

There is a clear correlation between religious faith and civilian gun ownership, a vestige of traditional rural life. Even in the context of a variety of control variables, data from the National Opinion Research Center (NORC) General Social Survey show that Protestants in general are more likely to own guns than those of other faiths or those with no religious preference. One explanation for this disproportionate tendency could be that religious fundamentalism motivates self-protection because it places substantial emphasis on individual salvation. Fundamentalism's individualistic orientation holds each person responsible for his or her own fate and, hence, his or her own protection. Defense of property is often used as a justification for gun ownership. (As will be discussed in greater detail later, Protestant denominations with large rural followings also have the highest rates of home ownership in the nation.)

Another explanation for the gun ownership/Protestantism correlation may lie in history. The Baptists in the South and the Methodists in the West adopted proselytizing strategies, suited to the life-style and spirit of the frontier, that appealed to the disenfranchised segments of society that peopled it. Masses of frontiersmen converted to Protestantism while simultaneously establishing a tradition of gun ownership. Moreover, most immigrants who came to the United States prior to 1850 were Protestants who settled in rural areas where hunting was common.

Robert L. Young of the University of Southern Mississippi has proposed a convincing cultural explanation as to why the "Protestant heritage" and "the spirit of gun ownership" persist today. Protestants, he suggests, are no more likely than others to own guns; it is just that Protestants are more likely to hunt than people of other faiths because farming areas are Protestant and hunting is popular in such areas. How then, though, can we explain why, among nonhunters, Protestants are nevertheless still more likely than non-Protestants to own guns (44% versus 27%)? Rural and even urban Protestants, Young explains, are more likely to have been socialized into a subculture where guns are part of everyday life. This is because, irrespective of current residence, the average Protestant has a rural childhood background or ties to kin in rural areas. Catholics, in contrast, comprise 29% of urban dwellers but only 15% of rural residents. As late as 1960, less than a quarter of white Protestants lived in cities of 250,000 residents or more, whereas half the Catholics did. Today, when they meet as neighbors in the suburbs, it is likely that a former urban Catholic lives alongside a Protestant who moved in from outside a metropolitan area. These findings might seem to be of interest only to a few academics and the National Rifle Association, but they have real impact on the streets when, as in New York State, the urban Catholic and Jewish communities' concern for curbing escalating violence clashes with the cultural values of Protestant upstate citizens over gun-control legislation. It also has national implications when apocalyptic sects such as the Branch Davidians of Waco, Texas, amass vast quantities of heavy weapons.

RELIGION IN NORTHERN CITIES

The cities of the North have experienced considerable social and demographic change in recent decades as new immigrants settled and older established residents moved to the suburbs or the Sunbelt. However, the NSRI indicates that from a religious perspective the changes are smaller than one might have expected. Certainly the data in Table 3-4 show that the religious profiles of cities with populations of more than 250,000 are remarkably consistent with those of suburban and smaller metropolitan areas. Nationally, the real contrast is between these two types of urban settings and rural America. Undoubtedly, most of the nation believes that the crisis of urban America as regards crime and declining educational and family standards is due to an observable deterioration in moral conduct in its great cities. However, this trend cannot be associated with major changes in the religious loyalties of city dwellers. Change in urban religion nowadays is more notable as regards declining practice than ideological or theological innovation.

Recent developments in society have made the city even more anonymous than it was earlier in the century: Urban dwellers do not congregate as much as they once did anywhere, let alone in church. Yet it is churches that provide some of the most important and impressive buildings in the modern northern city, even after urban renewal. These church buildings do not reflect the reality of the religious profiles of Chicago, Philadelphia, and New York (see Table 3-5) but mirror instead a history of religious loyalties. Philadelphia's most impressive churches tend to be Episcopal or Quaker meetinghouses rather than Baptist ones. In New York, the best buildings tend to be owned by the Episcopal church, which represents only 2 percent of the population. Episcopal holdings include the well-endowed, pink stone Trinity Church in Lower Manhattan, which still holds extensive real estate in the Wall Street vicinity under grants from England's 18th-century monarch Queen Anne; the Gothic-style Grace Church in Greenwich Village; the Byzantine-style St. Bartholomew's Church in Midtown; and the massive Gothic Cathedral Church of St. John the Divine in Morningside Heights. Catholic New York (with 43% of the city's population) has only one place of worship in this class: St. Patrick's Cathedral on Fifth Avenue, home to New York's feisty archbishop, John Cardinal O'Connor. It is situated cheek by jowl with Saks Fifth Avenue department store and Rockefeller Center. Aside from Reform Judaism's impressive Temple Emanu-El, New York City's Jews have relatively modest houses of worship; they seem to make their communal architectural statement through the massive hospitals they have built: Beth Israel, Mount Sinai, Maimonides, Montefiore, and, in the nearby suburbs, Long Island Jewish.

The NSRI data in Table 3-5 on the central city, the core political unit of the metropolis, deal with three of the four largest cities in the United States. The data for these northern cities dispute some commonly held views of big-city dwellers, who are shown to be no more likely to refuse to answer religious questions than other people; furthermore, they have only average proportions of religious "Nones." New York is the most Catholic city of the three, and, conversely, it has the lowest percentage of Baptists. It is one quarter non-Christian (twice as much so as Philadelphia). The Big Apple is more religiously diverse and has many more Jews, Muslims, Hindus, and Buddhists

than any other American city. In the past, New York served as the national
headquarters of most American Christian denominations, performing a similar function in religion to that of Madison Avenue in advertising or Wall
Street in finance. It still houses the offices of the National Council of the
Churches of Christ. Yet it is unique in that 16% of its citizenry favors non-
Christian religions. In fact, Judaism, with 11% of the population, is the city's
overall second preference. Using a wider ethnic/cultural definition, 14%, or
over 1 million New Yorkers, identify themselves as Jews, making New York
City the largest Jewish population center in the world, surpassing even Israel's
major cities. The city is also home to major national Jewish organizations,
rabbinical seminaries, and cultural institutions. The Judaic religious undercount can be explained in part by the reluctance of wary European-born Jews
to reveal their faith and also because many New York Jews identify themselves
as part of a cultural rather than a religious tradition. The latter fact has serious
implications for organized religious Judaism. When a December 1991 Gallup
survey of more than 1,000 New Yorkers asked "How important is religion to
your life?" the lowest score was provided by Jews. Only 34% answered that
it was very important, compared with 47% of white Protestants, 57% of both
white Catholics and Hispanics, and 74% of blacks.

The results of this Gallup survey, which showed that New Yorkers in
general rated the importance of religion in their lives about as highly as did
Middle Americans, led *New York Newsday* to proclaim in a headline: "We're
a Long Way from Sin City." The newspaper editorialized that "New York is
hardly a godless den of iniquity—it's a city where most people pray every day
and large majorities believe in heaven, hell and life after death." The Gallup
poll corroborated our NSRI finding that 90% of New Yorkers identify with
a religious group and believe in God. One third of the city's residents attend
a public worship service in any given week. Surprisingly, religious belief and
practice was much more prevalent in high-crime areas such as Brooklyn and
the Bronx than in Manhattan. One commentator from the American Baptist
Churches suggested that prayer was a natural reaction in a setting where
people "live under a canopy of fear and concern for their safety." This could
explain why organized religion continues to function despite the obvious
evidence of the breakdown in civilized society in our great cities and high
levels of interpersonal violence, drug addiction, and child abuse.

Undoubtedly there is some exaggeration in the picture we get because our
attention is constantly drawn to the negative aspects of life by our 24-hour-
a-day news media. The truth is that the overwhelming majority of urban
dwellers are decent, God-fearing people who do not commit crimes but are
increasingly victims of a small but vicious minority that does. The American
city of today is the type of anarchic environment described by the 17th-
century English philosopher Thomas Hobbes, a place where "life is nasty,

brutish and short." Yet it is not religion and the clergy that have failed the cities of America, but civil society, its politicians, and the criminal-justice system; for in no other urban environments in the world are the criminals so well armed with guns, nor is any legal system so assiduous as ours in protecting the rights of malefactors.

RELIGIOUS DIVERSITY IN THE MAJOR SUNBELT STATES

The NSRI produces valuable insights into the contemporary religious character of the America of shopping malls, condominium developments, and freeways that has emerged in recent decades in the Sunbelt states. As people, and with them political and economic power, have migrated south and west, American religion has followed. This was imperative for religious organizations because the Sunbelt states contain disproportionately large numbers of children, who are the future of religion in America.

CALIFORNIA

If we wish to understand what is happening and will happen culturally in the United States in the 1990s and beyond, we cannot ignore developments in California. The 1990 U.S. Census revealed that the state had a population of nearly 30 million, or nearly 12% of the country's inhabitants. No one state has ever before had such a large share of the total population of the nation. This demographic fact was translated into political power by the congressional redistricting that followed the 1990 census. California also has undue cultural influence over the nation and large sections of the world by means of the economic domination of Hollywood over the entertainment industry, particularly television and motion pictures. This industry is based in Los Angeles County, an area whose population is exceeded by only a handful of states. The NSRI had over 10,000 respondents in California, so we are in a position to reveal the fine texture of similarities and differences in religious identification among the state's key metropolitan regions.

First we must investigate how California developed its religious profile. Like the inhabitants of all western states except Utah, 19th-century Californians demonstrated a low level of religious interest compared to other Americans of the period. According to the religious historian Sandra Sizer Frankiel, they also tended to reject mainline Protestantism and to favor alternative religious traditions such as Unitarianism, Spiritualism, Adventism, Christian Science, and Theosophy. These radical religions had in common spirituality that could be practiced on an individual basis. This appealed to independent-minded Californians separated from family and traditional communities by hundreds of miles of wilderness and thousands of miles of sea. Though such groups accounted for only 5% of the population, according to the 1906 Census of Religious Bodies, their presence tended to challenge and undermine the traditional Protestant denominations. This prevented the creation of a religious establishment in any cultural or political sense and so laid the basis for a more secular local society. In 1872, California officially became a secular society when the state legislature overthrew the restrictions on Sunday business, the so-called Sabbath laws.

Understanding the state's history, we can now analyze the contemporary religious scene in California. As any child of the 1960s knows, the Golden State is America's center of unconventional religious movements and unorthodox religions. In the 1970s it elected as governor an ex-Jesuit seminarian, Edmund G. (Jerry) Brown, Jr., whose attraction to Buddhist practices was well publicized. Though the NSRI found surprisingly few explicitly New Age devotees, Scientologists, or followers of Eckankar, those we did find tended to be overconcentrated in California. The numbers are not as important as their very existence, which demonstrates the general acceptance of mysticism, occultism, and other spiritual alternatives by the general population. Surveys conducted by the sociologist Phillip E. Hammond and reported in 1989 found that nearly one third of Californians believed in reincarnation and that over 20% practiced meditation. Californians were also more likely to adopt the "new morality," and were less likely to belong to a church or a synagogue, to pray, or to read the Bible.

Other surveys have also established a particular Californian preference for autonomy, spiritualism, and the practice of personal piety over involvement in religious institutions. However, in the absence of responsibility to a community, some people become psychologically vulnerable to fanatics of various descriptions. These have ranged from the radical Jim Jones, notorious for his instigation of the 1978 Jonestown, Guyana, massacre, to Terry Cole Whitaker of the Church of Religious Science, as well as many gurus, so-called spiritual healers, and outright charlatans made wealthy by the generosity of their flocks. The most tragic outcome of California's freewheeling religious attitude was Jonestown. An unusual mixture of classical Pentecostalism's redemptive message laced with multiracial idealism and Marxist socialism, Jim Jones's "religion of the disinherited," as he preached it at his People's Temple, attracted many poor San Francisco Bay Area African Americans and a few young middle-class whites. In the cult's settlement in the jungles of Guyana, hero worship turned to unquestioning obedience as Jones's followers participated in their own oppression even before 900 of them committed mass suicide. It is therefore not surprising that even David Koresh, who perished with over 70 of his followers in a Waco, Texas, inferno in April 1993, actively began his recruitment of members for the Branch Davidian sect in southern California.

This Californian tendency to seek out leadership has also favored highly conservative Protestant preachers with very socially conformist messages. This group includes Phineas Bresee, who founded the Church of the Nazarene in Los Angeles in 1895 in order to preserve the Methodist tradition "in purity, sobriety and in honor," and Aimee Semple McPherson, who established the International Church of the Foursquare Gospel in the same city in 1927.

It would be wrong to generalize about the religious culture of any area as large and varied as modern-day California. We are fortunate that the large scale of the NSRI allows us to look in some detail at the regional differences that occur in the state's religious profile. Most attention is usually focused on the divide between the northern and southern sections of the state, between the area dominated by San Francisco and that dominated by Los Angeles. However, both these metropolitan areas are now so populous that there is even variation within them in terms of local popular religious culture.

San Francisco, which dominates the Bay Area, is actually only a small city of 700,000 inhabitants. Nevertheless, its history and cultural assets make it the regional capital. This old port city has long seen itself as cosmopolitan, an American hybrid of Paris and Singapore. In terms of sophistication, tolerance, and liberalism it can be pictured as the New Orleans of the West. The West Bay metropolitan area, which includes suburban Marin and San Mateo counties along with the city itself, has the lowest proportion of Christian identifiers of any area in the country, at just 70% (see Table 3-6). As one might expect of a city with a large homosexual population following a life-style antithetical to traditional religion, there is a relatively high proportion of nonbelievers (20.1%) and members of faiths known for their liberal outlook, such as Reform Judaism (4.1%), Unitarianism (0.4%), and Episcopalianism (3%). By the same token, San Francisco and its environs have fewer Baptists (6.4%) than most other urban areas. Nevertheless, with a greater-than-state or -national average of Catholics (33.5%) and Muslims (0.7%), there is a sufficient natural constituency of those one would expect to be morally critical of so-called alternative life-styles and gay rights. What we learn from the figures is that denominational identification does not translate directly into cultural hegemony. It is only one influence that must be factored into an equation that also includes commitment to official doctrinal beliefs and actual church membership. Moreover, as we shall see later, conservative-liberal tensions on social issues tend to cut both across and among denominations. It is, therefore, quite likely that Presbyterians in San Francisco are very much more accepting of homosexual relationships than Presbyterians in Kentucky.

For some readers, the surprising feature here might be the relative insignificance of Eastern religions (1.1%) in an area where those of Asian descent are the largest part of the ethnic-minority population. Eastern religions have clearly not made as much headway in numbers of adherents as has been claimed; in reality, most Asian Americans tend to be either Christians of some sort or "Nones."

Is there variation, then, within the Bay Area? The data for the East Bay, which is centered on Oakland, show some differences. Overall, this district is slightly more Christian than the city of San Francisco. It has relatively fewer Catholics and Jews, and more Baptists and Mormons. It also contains more unclassified groups and was the source of more refusals to our questions than any other area of the country. Unfortunately, our data do not reveal whether or not these refusals all came from Berkeley, a city often considered to be radical.

When we examine the southern California metropolitan areas, we notice immediately that they have 7% to 9% more respondents in Christian denominations and fewer with no religion than in the north. We also find that Angelenos, with only a 1.3% refusal rate, are more willing to answer as to their religion than respondents in the East Bay area (3.8% refused). If it were not for its large Hispanic population, southern California would probably be heavily Protestant. The generic answer "Christian" is also very popular in southern California. This may be associated with the fact that the smaller Protestant bodies seem stronger in that area than elsewhere in the country.

Orange County is a unique island of conservatism in California, while Los Angeles County is the most cosmopolitan, and San Diego County contains more mainline Protestants. During the 1970s and 1980s, Orange County was regarded as "Reagan country" because of its strong support for their "favorite son" during his gubernatorial and presidential races. The religious profile of this socially and politically conservative stronghold is thus of interest to many analysts. NSRI data show that Orange County has fewer Baptists but more Lutherans, Presbyterians, and Mormons than other places in the state. It also has more diversity among its Protestants. This suggests the presence of small cohesive denominations and sects with a high intensity of religious practice that maintain their individuality rather than blend into a dominant church ethos, as one sometimes finds elsewhere. Orange County is also home to one of the largest Muslim populations of Middle Eastern origin in the country; the newly established Islamic Resource Center, one of a number of burgeoning Muslim organizations, has its headquarters in Tustin. It would be interesting to inquire whether conservative Protestants and Muslims of Orange County perceive themselves as dissenters from the dominant secular and hedonist culture of southern California—as typified by what is popularly referred to as "the People's Republic of Santa Monica"—and so identify themselves as mainstream Americans. Or do they instead also protest the "decadent" religion of "back East"?

TEXAS

When we consider contemporary religious culture, we cannot ignore that other powerhouse of the Sunbelt, the Lone Star State, with its over 16 million inhabitants. Texas is no longer the rural society made familiar by history and Hollywood. It is not simply the cotton fields of East Texas, with its black and white Baptist farmers, nor the stereotypical irreligious Anglo cowboys and Mexican Catholic peons out on the plains and in the Rio Grande Valley. Though many Texans still wear ten-gallon hats and cowboy boots to the office and even to church on Sunday, Texas is largely a modern urban society dominated by two great metropolitan centers.

Houston is now the fourth largest city by population in the United States, and Dallas stands seventh. In terms of 1990 metropolitan-area populations, the Dallas–Fort Worth "Metroplex" is number eight in the nation, and Houston is number ten. Texas can be described as both a southern and a western state, and this is reflected in its religious profile. Dallas, which claims to be "America's City," is of course known to the world through the television series as a modern, gaudy, booming oil center, while its close neighbor Fort Worth, "Cow Town," represents the ranching side of the local economy. Table 3-7 demonstrates that the "Metroplex" area can also rightfully claim the title "the buckle on the Bible Belt," since almost 75% of its residents identify with Protestant denominations, and nearly 49% identify with just two denominational families, the Baptists and the Methodists. One indication of the bedrock conservatism of the area is that the fundamentalist Churches of Christ have more identifiers locally than the Presbyterian, Episcopalian, or Lutheran denominations, or any particular non-Christian group. This fact might have been anticipated for an urban sprawl that coincidentally grew up on the prairie around the banks of the Trinity River and contains seven denominational colleges, the two most prominent of which are Texas Christian University (affiliated with the Disciples of Christ) and Southern Methodist University.

Houston is one of the world's largest ports and a major manufacturing center as well as the hub of the oil industry. The makeup of the city's local economy and the work force it has attracted may explain why its religious profile seems a little more cosmopolitan and national, according to Table 3-7, than that of the "Metroplex." Houston has more Catholics and fewer adherents of the smaller Protestant denominations; in part, this is probably due to its much larger proportion of ethnic minorities, particularly Hispanics. Yet specific local religio-cultural patterns persist. As mentioned earlier, Pentecostal churches flourish in the south central region of the nation, so, in common with Dallas, Houston has three times the national average percentage of Pentecostal adherents.

FLORIDA

The two states with a religious profile that most closely approximates that of the total United States are Missouri and Florida. In some ways, we might have expected this. The "Show Me" State's diversity relates to its central location on the borders of the South and the Midwest. In contrast, Florida has achieved its national resemblance through the migration there of people from many areas of the country. It has been the fastest-growing state in recent decades and epitomizes the realignment of the U.S. population toward the Sunbelt. As Florida's population increased from less than 2.8 million in 1950 to 13 million in 1990, it became the fourth most-populous state in the Union. A magnet for retirees from the Northeast and Midwest, it also attracted other people, including immigrants from overseas. The relocation of the elderly and the new trend of seasonal migration have had an impact on both sending and receiving states, transforming Florida in particular from a typical southern agricultural state to a more urban one with a national character.

If we really want to see how rapid growth has changed the religious character of large metropolitan areas of the South, we should turn our attention to Miami. Table 3-7 shows that Protestants of all denominations account for under half the city's population, and Christians altogether for less than 80%. Miami is not quite a Havana–cum–New York City annex, as is sometimes claimed, but such influences are very noticeable. The proportion of religious "Nones" and refusals is certainly much higher than in Texas. Whereas only 13% of respondents in Dallas identified as Jews and Catholics, nearly 45% did so in Miami. The actual Jewish component may be somewhat higher since, as was noted earlier, many Jews are reluctant to state their religion to an interviewer. This may account for the relatively high proportion of refusals (2.5%) in the Greater Miami metropolitan area.

IRRELIGION AND THE FRONTIER PHENOMENON

Social scientists explain rates of political participation, crime, suicide, and divorce in terms of the social, demographic, and economic profiles of the people living in a particular locality. In any society, the dominant religion acts as a social control mechanism. However, the variety of dominant religions in the United States produces a variety of regional cultures. Thus it is of social as well as statistical significance that there are marked regional and state variations in the proportion of people who disclaim a religious preference, the "Nones." There is also a high correlation between the geographical distribution of our "No Religion" respondents and those who refused to answer or stated that they were agnostics. Map 10 shows quite clearly that irreligion is a regional phenomenon characteristic of the western states. East of the Rockies, only the population of Vermont is over 10% irreligious. This

10A. Percentage of each state's population that is of no religion

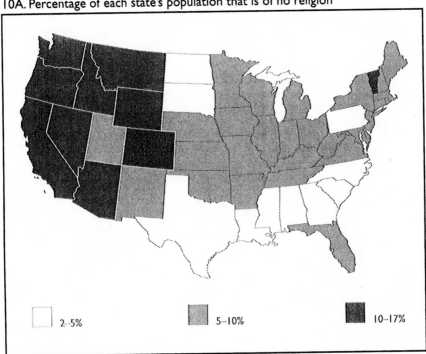

2–5%   5–10%   10–17%

cultural oddity may account for the fact that Vermont sent a Socialist, Bernard Sanders, to Congress in 1990. In contrast, Pennsylvania has an above-average rate, for a northeastern state, of respondents identifying with a religion. This explains why Pennsylvania is known to be socially conservative on social and educational issues such as abortion and government tuition vouchers for parochial-school children.

The West is the fastest-growing section of the country, and so we should investigate the manner in which it is different from the rest of the country and whether its difference portends future trends for the nation. The NSRI findings received more attention in the West, and particularly the Pacific Northwest, than in any other region, because Oregon and Washington State led the "No Religion" column. Commentators asked, "Is Oregon Atheist?" The *Seattle Post-Intelligencer* reported that "the Pacific Northwest may be God's country, but no region in the nation is less religious." Some local ministers described the area as "militantly anti-religious" and were surprised that the figures were not worse (from their point of view). The NSRI findings only confirmed on a more authoritative basis what had been known for many years—that the area was the most unchurched region of the United States.

The western states lead in religious diversity as well as "No Religion"

10B. Percentage of people with no religion residing in each state

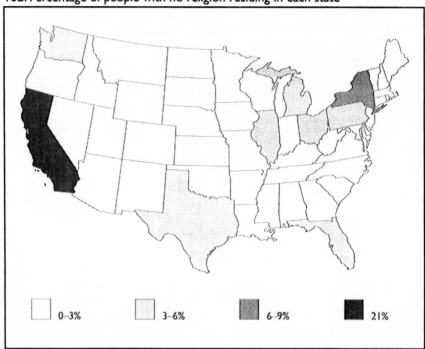

0–3%   3–6%   6–9%   21%

responses. It seems that religious diversity and high levels of irreligion go hand in hand. The Pacific Northwest and Rocky Mountain regions contain the seven most religiously diverse states in the Union. Wyoming, Washington, Oregon, Nevada, Arizona, Colorado, and Montana all average under 60% of their population belonging to the four largest religious groups of the state. They are also among the top ten nationally with regard to "No Religion" response rates. Discounting Montana and Colorado, the remaining five states constitute five of the six highest-scoring "No Religion" states.

Our explanation for this phenomenon stresses two points: mobility (that is, migration creates people without ties) and the natural environment. This line of thinking links to the "frontier" concept, to the effect of land and space on people. Historically, people have moved to the open West to explore new life-styles and flee from tradition. Washington State's radical heritage attracted political mavericks and social freethinkers who rejected connections to established institutions (e.g., churches). That the major denominations, such as the Catholic and Baptist churches, are weak in the region, and that the smaller denominations are stronger, follows logically.

Nature and a more pristine environment also act as a distraction from organized religion. Many young adults get more personal satisfaction from climbing Mount Rainier or the Cascades, or canoeing on the Columbia River, than from Sunday services. Religious leaders in the area admit that the rich surroundings mean that in the summer their churches are empty as members flock to the mountains or to Puget Sound to enjoy recreational activities. The spiritual satisfactions from the scenery and nature outweigh church services, which lose out in the battle for people's limited leisure time.

The process of migration has a disorienting effect on the individual, which often leads to a reassessment of religious loyalties. Americans have usually migrated for economic reasons, whether to California during the 1849 gold rush, to the prairies for free land in the 1880s, or to Detroit for car-production jobs in the 1950s. The effects of this movement reach out beyond the economic system. In their hometowns, the future migrants were less likely to face new people, so they were less exposed and challenged. Moving forces the individual to cut established ties with family and neighbors, and to create new ones with strangers. High levels of migration break down cultural traditions by mixing people from different backgrounds. This process also makes difficult the creation of new traditions. By disrupting social networks, migration undermines religious affiliations and outlook. It severs what Peter Berger has described as "the thin thread of conversation" that links the individual to the religious group. We see here the secularizing influences of pluralism as people switch loyalties in their new community. In new or growing centers of population, religious organizations are constantly trying to recruit and retain new members. They cannot rely on stable social ties of friendship and kinship to integrate new members. Survey evidence shows that interregional migrants are the people most likely to switch religious groups or to become nonaffiliated as they become exposed to new commitments and "alternative legitimations." Thus we would expect the growing regions to have the greatest proportion of religion changers, and the facts bear out this expectation. The Pacific region has the highest proportion of religious switchers (36.5%), while New England has the lowest (14.9%). In today's society, well-educated males in high-prestige occupations are most likely to migrate and switch religious affiliation.

The religious "Nones," who are regarded by sociologists of religion as innovators, are considered unusual in a society like the United States, where, as the NSRI has revealed, nearly everyone has a religious identity. Most "Nones" are migrants, and appear to have been raised with religion. Some give up their religious identity to please significant others, such as a spouse. If nonreligious behavior is deviant in America, then we can appreciate that such behavior is more likely to go unnoticed or uncommented-upon in the West than elsewhere. As we have seen, the residents of the Pacific Northwest are convinced that the area of the last frontier has a culture more tolerant of change and deviance. Some would suggest that the local environment is so heavily influenced by countercultural values that dissent expands to actually encourage the discarding of established religious identities. We ask, from a different perspective: Why do the largely unchurched residents in the western states still cling to a religious identity if they do not affiliate with a religious group? Why are there so few religious "Nones"?

American history confirms that the result of migration is a lower level of religious participation. In 1850, when today's religious heartland was the frontier, the states on the west bank of the Mississippi River—Minnesota, Iowa, Missouri, Arkansas, and Louisiana—and Texas had the lowest rates of religious adherence. At that time, saloons and brothels were more numerous and popular in those states than churches. The reason was not too hard to find: Single young men have always been much more likely to migrate than other people.

THE WEST AND NEW RELIGIOUS MOVEMENTS

The relative lack of older people also explains why the frontier served as the breeding ground for the religious experimentation we saw was a particular feature of California. As the sociologists Stark and Bainbridge have stated, the West is "especially hospitable to novel and exotic religions." The West has cults, or, more politely perhaps, "New Religious Movements" (NRMs), while the South and Midwest have sects, enthusiastic offshoots of established churches. As some would see it, eccentrics of all description go west. Although their numbers were not large enough to appear in NSRI results, we know that Idaho and the Pacific Northwest are home to far-rightists, including white supremacist "Identity Christians" and "Christian Constitutionalists" obsessed with a theological vision of a Promised Land free from the impurity of the rest of the country.

One example of the NRM-frontier phenomenon in recent Oregon history was Rajneeshpuram. Based upon the teachings of the guru Bhagwan Shree Rajneesh, this movement revolved around a mixture of Indian mystical ontology, Western psychotherapy, and New Age psychology. It attracted social experimenters working on self-improvement. Its devotees were mainly baby boomers born around 1950, who by 1980 could be described as veterans of the hippie generation. They arrived in Wasco County, in northern Oregon, when the guru's foundation purchased land and moved his headquarters from Poona, India. The guru was determined to create a utopian self-sustaining community on the Big Muddy Ranch. His ashram Rajneeshpuram, aimed at creating an agricultural paradise to answer the social and ecological crises of contemporary society, soon accommodated 2,500 residents, or *sanyassins*. Temporary accommodation was arranged for an additional 15,000 devotees expected for the ashram's summer festivals. Businesses were quickly established, and, at least at first, the commune seemed idyllic, pulsating with joy and contentment.

The first signs of trouble occurred in 1984, when representatives of the ranch began to recruit thousands of transients from sixteen metropolitan areas under their "Share-a-Home" program. Billed as a humanitarian effort aimed at demonstrating how the movement's philosophy could alleviate a major American social problem, it soon became clear that the recruitment was a ploy by Ma Anand Sheela, the Bhagwan's personal secretary, to swing the November Wasco County elections. Local ranchers and public officials with the support of *The Oregonian* newspaper turned public opinion sharply against the mystic and his devotees. Stories emerged of the guru's ninety-three Rolls-Royces and his other odd compulsions; these discredited the whole enterprise. Anti-cult writers had a field day when internal friction on the ranch led to quarrels and charges of intent to murder among the disintegrating leadership. The end came with the dissolution of the commune in 1985 and the arrest and deportation of the Bhagwan.

In true western-frontier fashion, the guru and his followers were run out of town. There was a limit to the tolerance of deviant and exotic behavior. There are some historical similarities, of course, between this story and that of the early Mormons. The major difference is in the outcome. Somehow the Mormons became an established and respected part of American society, though it took them a century and a half and the disavowal of some of their extremist behavior, such as collectivism and polygamy. Perhaps a similar fate awaits some of the countercultural religious movements of today's West.

Thus our review of the interplay between religious identity and geography in contemporary American society finds that religion is still very much an integral part of local society and culture. It is influential almost everywhere, buttressed by either historic communal ties, the search for spiritual autonomy, or concern for a loved one's safety; reasons vary with locality. In the regions where one denomination is dominant, the pressures to conform to particular community values and norms of behavior still operate to produce a distinctive social milieu with measurable social and political consequences. It is the differing patterns of religious identification that account for much of the diversity in America by helping to give different regions their individual character.

TABLE 3-1

RELIGIOUS COMPOSITION OF STATE POPULATIONS, 1990 (In Percent)

STATE	ROMAN CATHOLIC	BAPTIST	METHODIST	LUTH-ERAN	PRESBY-TERIAN	PENTE-COSTAL	JEWISH	EPISCO-PALIAN	MORMON	NONE
Alabama	4.5	51.4	10.4	0.6	1.8	2.6	0.1	0.7	0.2	3.9
Arizona	23.9	11.6	6.6	5.7	2.9	1.3	1.6	1.4	4.9	12.2
Arkansas	4.9	42.4	8.8	1.7	2.4	5.9	0.1	0.7	0.4	5.8
California	28.9	10.0	4.0	3.7	2.8	1.5	2.3	1.8	2.2	13.0
Colorado	25.1	10.0	7.7	7.3	4.4	1.0	1.8	1.8	2.4	11.4
Connecticut	50.4	5.0	3.9	2.3	0.7	1.4	2.4	4.4	0.0	5.8
Delaware	26.4	9.2	26.5	2.4	3.4	3.4	1.4	3.0	0.0	7.2
D.C.	16.1	46.8	6.8	0.2	2.0	0.0	2.3	4.5	0.0	6.3
Florida	23.2	22.2	8.2	3.3	3.6	2.4	3.6	2.4	0.6	7.2
Georgia	6.3	50.8	11.5	0.9	2.2	1.8	0.5	1.6	0.4	4.6
Idaho	11.5	3.9	5.8	4.1	2.0	0.4	0.0	1.0	30.5	11.9
Illinois	33.1	14.8	7.8	7.6	2.6	1.4	1.5	0.9	0.2	7.0
Indiana	19.5	16.5	9.9	5.1	2.2	2.1	0.3	0.7	0.7	7.4
Iowa	21.5	6.1	15.7	15.4	4.5	0.5	0.0	0.8	0.8	5.9
Kansas	17.3	16.4	14.7	5.4	3.7	2.5	0.3	1.3	0.7	5.7
Kentucky	13.3	42.5	7.2	1.3	1.9	2.0	0.2	1.0	0.2	6.5
Louisiana	46.8	29.2	5.2	0.8	0.5	2.3	0.2	0.6	0.2	2.9
Maine	31.2	11.9	7.5	0.5	0.4	2.0	0.4	2.0	0.8	10.0
Maryland	24.9	17.4	13.8	6.0	3.0	1.7	2.8	2.7	0.3	7.2
Massachusetts	54.3	4.3	2.4	1.2	0.8	0.4	3.5	2.8	0.2	7.3
Michigan	29.2	15.7	6.8	8.3	2.6	1.3	0.8	1.4	0.3	8.7
Minnesota	29.2	3.5	4.3	33.9	3.1	1.0	0.8	1.0	0.3	5.6
Mississippi	7.0	55.0	11.4	1.3	1.6	3.9	0.6	1.4	0.3	2.8
Missouri	20.3	24.9	7.1	5.9	2.4	2.4	0.6	0.8	1.1	6.5

STATE	ROMAN CATHOLIC	BAPTIST	METHODIST	LUTH-ERAN	PRESBY-TERIAN	PENTE-COSTAL	JEWISH	EPISCO-PALIAN	MORMON	NONE
Montana	27.6	4.1	9.4	12.2	2.4	1.6	0.0	2.0	2.6	10.2
Nebraska	29.4	4.4	11.0	16.3	4.4	0.6	0.5	2.0	0.8	7.0
N. Hampshire	41.3	9.2	11.3	0.3	2.0	0.0	0.9	2.2	0.0	8.1
Nevada	23.6	7.5	6.2	5.5	1.2	1.0	1.0	2.7	8.7	13.4
New Jersey	45.9	10.2	6.7	3.1	3.2	1.9	4.3	2.3	0.1	5.5
New Mexico	37.3	11.8	7.3	3.2	2.6	0.8	0.7	0.8	2.7	10.0
New York	44.3	8.3	6.1	2.7	2.4	1.5	6.9	2.0	0.2	6.4
North Carolina	5.9	47.1	12.7	2.4	3.6	2.1	0.5	1.0	0.7	4.8
North Dakota	30.1	3.9	3.5	36.5	2.8	0.0	0.4	0.0	0.4	1.6
Ohio	24.2	15.3	10.4	4.4	2.4	1.7	0.7	1.2	0.2	7.4
Oklahoma	8.0	32.6	9.2	2.2	1.4	2.9	0.2	1.2	0.3	6.5
Oregon	15.3	8.7	4.9	6.7	4.2	1.2	0.4	2.2	2.4	17.2
Pennsylvania	33.2	9.9	8.7	8.6	5.3	1.1	1.7	1.7	0.1	4.9
Rhode Island	61.7	6.3	1.4	0.7	0.8	0.0	1.6	5.1	0.0	6.0
South Carolina	5.7	46.5	15.6	2.5	3.5	2.0	0.3	2.0	0.6	3.2
South Dakota	25.7	6.1	10.5	30.3	2.9	0.8	0.2	1.4	1.0	2.5
Tennessee	4.7	43.0	10.7	1.0	4.3	2.6	0.3	1.1	0.4	6.0
Texas	23.2	32.0	9.2	2.4	1.8	2.9	0.7	1.9	0.7	4.9
Utah	6.0	2.4	1.2	1.2	1.0	0.4	0.7	0.5	69.2	7.8
Vermont	36.7	5.3	5.6	1.3	2.0	0.4	1.1	3.5	0.0	11.4
Virginia	12.2	31.2	13.1	2.3	4.1	2.0	1.1	3.2	0.7	6.4
Washington	19.0	7.2	6.2	7.8	4.6	1.5	0.4	1.8	1.9	14.0
West Virginia	5.9	29.3	14.9	0.9	4.3	3.2	0.1	0.8	0.6	8.0
Wisconsin	38.6	4.0	6.4	26.2	1.7	1.0	0.4	0.9	0.4	6.1
Wyoming	18.0	8.6	9.9	5.0	8.7	1.2	0.0	5.2	8.8	13.5
U.S. Total	26.2	19.4	8.0	5.2	2.8	1.8	1.8	1.7	1.4	7.5

TABLE 3-1 CONTINUED

RELIGIOUS COMPOSITION OF STATE POPULATIONS, 1990 (IN PERCENT)

STATE	CHURCH OF CHRIST	JEHOVAH'S WITNESS	7TH-DAY ADVENTIST	ASSEMBLIES OF GOD	HOLINESS/ HOLY	BORN AGAIN/ EVANGELICAL	NAZARENE	MUSLIM	ORTHODOX CHRISTIAN	UNITARIAN
Alabama	3.4	0.4	0.6	1.2	1.5	0.4	0.9	0.2	0.2	0.1
Arizona	0.6	1.0	0.4	0.4	0.0	0.4	0.5	0.2	0.1	0.2
Arkansas	4.5	0.3	0.1	1.5	0.2	0.0	0.3	0.0	0.0	0.2
California	0.3	1.1	0.8	0.3	0.1	0.3	0.2	0.6	0.4	0.4
Colorado	0.7	0.4	0.2	0.3	0.0	0.4	0.3	0.0	0.1	0.7
Connecticut	0.4	0.3	0.0	0.0	0.3	0.1	0.0	0.1	0.6	0.3
Delaware	0.0	0.9	0.0	0.0	1.4	0.0	0.0	0.0	0.0	0.0
D.C.	0.0	0.8	0.0	0.0	2.1	0.0	0.0	0.6	0.2	0.0
Florida	0.7	0.9	0.8	0.4	0.8	0.2	0.3	0.1	0.2	0.3
Georgia	0.7	0.9	0.1	0.3	1.4	0.2	0.2	0.3	0.0	0.1
Idaho	0.5	1.2	0.3	0.6	0.0	0.2	0.5	0.0	0.1	0.4
Illinois	0.8	0.6	0.1	0.2	0.0	0.7	0.3	0.4	0.5	0.4
Indiana	1.8	0.5	0.2	0.4	0.1	0.2	1.3	0.1	0.2	0.1
Iowa	0.6	1.0	0.3	0.6	0.0	0.8	0.4	0.0	0.0	0.1
Kansas	1.1	0.6	0.3	1.0	0.6	0.1	0.9	0.1	0.2	0.4
Kentucky	2.1	0.5	0.3	0.3	0.4	0.1	0.3	0.0	0.0	0.2
Louisiana	0.3	0.7	0.1	0.7	0.5	0.1	0.0	0.1	0.1	0.0
Maine	0.4	0.3	0.1	0.0	0.1	0.1	1.1	0.0	0.3	0.6
Maryland	0.3	0.9	0.5	0.1	0.9	0.2	0.1	0.2	0.4	0.3
Massachusetts	0.2	0.6	0.1	0.1	0.0	0.4	0.1	0.4	0.6	0.8
Michigan	0.6	0.9	0.3	0.2	0.0	0.4	0.1	0.3	0.6	0.3
Minnesota	0.4	0.4	0.2	0.1	0.0	0.9	0.2	0.1	0.2	0.4
Mississippi	1.8	1.0	0.1	0.3	0.4	0.0	0.2	0.0	0.0	0.0
Missouri	1.3	0.5	0.3	0.8	0.0	0.7	0.5	0.0	0.0	0.2

STATE	CHURCH OF CHRIST	JEHOVAH'S WITNESS	7TH-DAY ADVENTIST	ASSEMBLIES OF GOD	HOLINESS/ HOLY	BORN AGAIN/ EVANGELICAL	NAZARENE	MUSLIM	ORTHODOX CHRISTIAN	UNITARIAN
Montana	0.4	0.8	0.1	1.0	0.0	1.1	0.0	0.0	0.0	0.3
Nebraska	1.4	0.2	0.2	0.2	0.1	0.6	0.3	0.0	0.4	0.5
N. Hampshire	0.7	1.9	0.0	0.6	0.0	0.7	0.0	0.0	0.9	0.9
Nevada	0.5	0.7	0.0	0.0	0.0	0.2	0.5	0.2	0.2	0.2
New Jersey	0.1	0.9	0.1	0.1	0.2	0.1	0.1	0.6	0.9	0.1
New Mexico	1.2	1.2	0.1	0.1	0.0	0.1	0.2	0.0	0.2	0.3
New York	0.2	1.0	0.4	0.1	0.0	0.3	0.1	0.8	0.7	0.3
North Carolina	0.4	0.8	0.2	0.3	1.7	0.0	0.1	0.2	0.0	0.1
North Dakota	0.4	0.1	0.0	0.2	0.0	1.5	0.2	0.0	0.0	0.0
Ohio	1.9	0.9	0.3	0.2	0.2	0.3	0.9	0.4	0.3	0.1
Oklahoma	4.7	0.6	0.4	1.7	0.3	0.1	0.8	0.0	0.1	0.1
Oregon	0.4	1.1	1.1	0.3	0.0	0.4	0.3	0.1	0.2	0.4
Pennsylvania	1.0	0.6	0.3	0.2	0.1	0.6	0.2	0.3	0.4	0.1
Rhode Island	0.0	0.4	0.1	0.1	0.0	0.2	0.0	0.4	0.3	0.4
South Carolina	0.4	0.8	0.3	0.3	2.6	0.0	0.2	0.2	0.1	0.0
South Dakota	0.5	0.3	0.0	0.2	0.0	0.7	0.0	0.3	0.2	0.3
Tennessee	5.4	0.6	0.7	0.3	0.5	0.0	0.5	0.1	0.0	0.1
Texas	2.1	0.6	0.2	0.6	0.1	0.1	0.3	0.2	0.1	0.2
Utah	0.2	0.2	0.0	0.2	0.0	0.3	0.0	0.0	0.3	0.1
Vermont	0.0	0.6	1.2	0.0	0.0	0.2	0.4	0.0	0.6	1.1
Virginia	0.7	0.6	0.4	0.2	1.1	0.1	0.2	0.2	0.2	0.2
Washington	0.6	1.4	0.9	0.9	0.1	0.4	0.5	0.0	0.1	0.5
West Virginia	1.6	0.6	0.5	0.2	1.0	0.3	1.1	0.1	0.2	0.1
Wisconsin	1.1	0.2	0.2	0.2	0.0	0.5	0.1	0.2	0.2	0.2
Wyoming	0.3	0.7	0.5	0.5	0.0	0.2	0.7	0.0	0.0	0.0
U.S. Total	1.0	0.8	0.4	0.4	0.3	0.3	0.3	0.3	0.3	0.3

TABLE 3-1 CONTINUED

RELIGIOUS COMPOSITION OF STATE POPULATIONS, 1990 (In Percent)

STATE	CHURCH OF GOD	CONGREGA-TIONALIST	BUD-DHIST	MENNO-NITE	HINDU	AGNOSTIC	CHRISTIAN	PROTES-TANT	REFUSED	OTHER	TOTAL
Alabama	1.2	0.0	0.0	0.0	0.1	0.2	2.4	8.9	1.3	0.8	100.0%
Arizona	0.1	0.3	0.1	0.2	0.0	1.1	6.4	10.8	2.8	2.3	100.0%
Arkansas	0.8	0.0	0.2	0.0	0.0	0.2	5.3	9.6	3.2	0.7	100.0%
California	0.1	0.2	0.7	0.1	0.1	1.2	7.5	10.7	2.8	1.9	100.0%
Colorado	0.2	0.3	0.1	0.2	0.2	1.1	5.2	11.9	2.8	2.0	100.0%
Connecticut	0.1	1.9	0.2	0.0	0.1	0.5	2.2	11.4	3.9	1.3	101.0%
Delaware	0.8	0.0	0.0	0.3	0.0	0.0	1.6	6.1	5.7	0.3	100.0%
D.C.	0.0	0.0	0.3	0.0	0.0	0.5	1.8	4.0	2.2	2.5	100.0%
Florida	0.3	0.2	0.1	0.1	0.1	1.0	4.1	9.3	2.1	1.3	100.0%
Georgia	0.4	0.0	0.1	0.2	0.2	0.3	3.9	7.3	1.4	1.4	100.0%
Idaho	0.2	0.0	0.2	1.3	0.0	1.1	6.9	10.9	3.1	1.4	100.0%
Illinois	0.2	0.2	0.1	0.1	0.2	0.6	4.9	8.6	2.8	1.4	100.0%
Indiana	0.6	0.0	0.1	0.9	0.0	0.3	9.7	14.9	2.3	1.9	100.0%
Iowa	0.1	0.6	0.0	0.2	0.1	1.1	6.5	12.9	1.5	2.0	100.0%
Kansas	0.0	0.2	0.3	0.6	0.1	0.6	7.7	14.6	1.7	0.9	100.0%
Kentucky	0.4	0.0	0.1	0.1	0.0	0.3	7.3	8.6	1.7	1.2	100.0%
Louisiana	0.1	0.1	0.1	0.0	0.0	0.0	2.0	4.4	1.2	0.8	100.0%
Maine	0.0	2.8	0.1	0.0	0.1	0.9	3.1	20.3	2.2	0.8	100.0%
Maryland	0.3	0.1	0.1	0.1	0.2	0.7	2.8	8.3	2.3	1.4	100.0%
Massachusetts	0.0	1.9	0.4	0.0	0.1	1.0	2.2	9.7	3.1	1.1	100.0%
Michigan	0.3	0.4	0.1	0.1	0.2	0.5	3.5	12.0	2.1	2.3	100.0%
Minnesota	0.0	0.4	0.1	0.2	0.1	0.6	2.8	7.4	2.2	0.8	100.0%
Mississippi	0.6	0.0	0.0	0.1	0.0	0.5	2.1	5.3	0.6	1.3	100.0%
Missouri	0.5	0.0	0.1	0.0	0.0	0.4	7.1	12.1	2.2	1.3	100.0%

STATE	CHURCH OF GOD	CONGREGA-TIONALIST	BUD-DHIST	MENNO-NITE	HINDU	AGNOSTIC	CHRISTIAN	PROTES-TANT	REFUSED	OTHER	TOTAL
Montana	0.0	2.2	0.0	0.3	0.0	0.6	8.4	8.8	2.7	1.2	100.0%
Nebraska	0.1	0.6	0.1	0.0	0.2	0.1	4.0	11.4	1.7	1.5	100.0%
N. Hampshire	0.0	1.4	0.4	0.0	0.0	0.9	4.0	9.0	2.0	1.3	100.0%
Nevada	0.2	0.2	0.5	0.0	0.0	1.2	8.0	11.4	2.5	2.7	100.0%
New Jersey	0.1	0.1	0.1	0.1	0.3	0.6	2.5	6.3	2.7	0.8	100.0%
New Mexico	0.1	0.0	0.1	0.4	0.0	1.0	7.1	8.0	1.6	1.1	100.0%
New York	0.0	0.2	0.2	0.1	0.6	0.6	2.3	6.9	2.9	1.5	100.0%
North Carolina	0.3	0.0	0.1	0.1	0.0	0.3	3.2	8.0	1.7	1.7	100.0%
North Dakota	0.5	1.5	0.0	0.0	0.0	0.4	3.0	9.9	2.5	0.6	100.0%
Ohio	0.3	0.1	0.1	0.4	0.1	0.5	5.2	15.3	2.2	2.4	100.0%
Oklahoma	0.2	0.0	0.2	0.3	0.1	0.4	7.0	12.2	4.2	2.1	100.0%
Oregon	0.0	0.1	0.5	0.2	0.0	1.2	11.7	14.7	2.4	1.7	100.0%
Pennsylvania	0.1	0.0	0.1	0.3	0.1	0.7	2.9	12.6	1.9	2.3	100.0%
Rhode Island	0.0	0.8	0.0	0.3	0.0	0.5	2.3	7.0	2.9	0.7	100.0%
South Carolina	0.9	0.0	0.1	0.0	0.0	0.2	2.3	6.7	1.8	1.2	100.0%
South Dakota	0.2	1.0	0.0	0.3	0.0	1.0	1.0	10.9	1.0	0.7	100.0%
Tennessee	1.3	0.0	0.1	0.0	0.0	0.2	4.0	9.5	1.6	1.0	100.0%
Texas	0.2	0.0	0.2	0.0	0.0	0.6	4.1	7.5	1.6	1.6	100.0%
Utah	0.0	0.0	0.1	0.1	0.0	0.9	2.5	1.9	2.9	0.0	100.0%
Vermont	1.2	4.1	0.0	0.2	0.0	1.2	3.0	17.3	0.7	0.9	100.0%
Virginia	0.2	0.1	0.4	0.3	0.1	0.6	4.7	9.8	1.9	1.7	100.0%
Washington	0.0	0.2	0.5	0.1	0.1	1.4	8.0	13.9	3.3	2.7	100.0%
West Virginia	1.8	0.0	0.1	0.1	0.1	0.2	3.4	15.8	1.9	2.9	100.0%
Wisconsin	0.0	0.3	0.3	0.1	0.0	0.3	1.8	6.3	1.5	0.8	100.0%
Wyoming	0.0	0.9	0.0	0.1	0.2	0.5	7.3	5.3	3.3	0.6	100.0%
U.S. Total	0.3	0.2	0.2	0.2	0.1	0.7	4.6	9.8	2.3	1.4	100.0%

TABLE 3-2
GEOGRAPHIC DISTRIBUTION OF RELIGIOUS GROUPS (In Percent)

STATES	ROMAN CATHOLIC	BAPTIST	METHODIST	LUTHERAN	PRESBYTERIAN	PENTECOSTAL	JEWISH	EPISCOPALIAN	MORMON	NONE
Alabama	0.28	4.33	2.13	0.19	1.05	2.36	0.09	0.67	0.23	0.85
Arizona	1.35	0.89	1.22	1.63	1.54	1.07	1.32	1.22	5.19	2.41
Arkansas	0.18	2.07	1.05	0.31	0.82	3.12	0.05	0.39	0.27	0.74
California	13.29	6.21	6.02	8.57	12.05	10.04	15.39	12.75	18.93	20.88
Colorado	1.28	0.69	1.28	1.87	2.10	0.74	1.33	1.41	2.29	2.03
Connecticut	2.56	0.40	0.65	0.59	0.33	1.03	1.77	3.44	0.00	1.03
Delaware	0.27	0.13	0.89	0.12	0.33	0.51	0.21	0.48	0.00	0.26
D.C.	0.15	0.59	0.21	0.01	0.18	0.00	0.31	0.65	0.00	0.21
Florida	4.64	5.99	5.37	3.32	6.73	6.98	10.47	7.39	2.24	5.03
Georgia	0.63	6.87	3.77	0.45	2.06	2.62	0.73	2.47	0.75	1.61
Idaho	0.18	0.08	0.30	0.32	0.29	0.09	0.00	0.24	8.88	0.65
Illinois	5.85	3.53	4.51	6.76	4.30	3.60	3.86	2.45	0.66	4.32
Indiana	1.67	1.91	2.78	2.20	1.76	2.62	0.37	0.92	1.12	2.21
Iowa	0.92	0.35	2.21	3.33	1.81	0.31	0.00	0.53	0.64	0.88
Kansas	0.66	0.85	1.84	1.04	1.33	1.39	0.17	0.77	0.50	0.76
Kentucky	0.76	3.27	1.34	0.37	1.01	1.66	0.17	0.88	0.21	1.29
Louisiana	3.05	2.57	1.11	0.26	0.31	2.18	0.19	0.60	0.24	0.66
Maine	0.59	0.30	0.47	0.05	0.07	0.55	0.11	0.58	0.28	0.66
Maryland	1.84	1.74	3.34	2.23	2.07	1.83	3.01	3.07	0.41	1.86
Massachusetts	5.05	0.54	0.73	0.56	0.70	0.54	4.73	4.01	0.35	2.37
Michigan	4.19	3.04	3.20	6.01	3.49	2.72	1.67	3.10	0.81	4.36
Minnesota	1.97	0.32	0.95	11.54	1.96	0.98	0.79	1.04	0.38	1.32
Mississippi	0.28	2.95	1.48	0.26	0.60	2.26	0.35	0.86	0.52	0.39
Missouri	1.60	2.66	1.84	2.35	1.78	2.76	0.69	0.97	1.63	1.80

STATES	ROMAN CATHOLIC	BAPTIST	METHO-DIST	LUTH-ERAN	PRESBY-TERIAN	PENTE-COSTAL	JEWISH	EPISCO-PALIAN	MORMON	NONE
Montana	0.34	0.07	0.38	0.76	0.28	0.29	0.00	0.38	0.60	0.44
Nebraska	0.72	0.14	0.88	2.00	1.00	0.21	0.18	0.75	0.36	0.60
N. Hampshire	0.71	0.21	0.63	0.03	0.32	0.00	0.22	0.58	0.00	0.48
Nevada	0.44	0.18	0.42	0.48	0.17	0.54	0.24	0.52	1.53	0.86
New Jersey	5.48	1.65	2.62	1.87	3.58	3.30	7.47	4.23	0.22	2.29
New Mexico	0.87	0.37	0.56	0.38	0.57	0.27	0.24	0.29	1.18	0.82
New York	12.31	3.12	5.55	3.78	6.24	6.07	27.91	8.57	1.04	6.21
N. Carolina	0.60	6.51	4.26	1.24	3.45	3.13	0.75	1.58	1.34	1.72
N. Dakota	0.30	0.05	0.11	1.82	0.26	0.00	0.06	0.00	0.07	0.06
Ohio	4.06	3.46	5.71	3.72	3.76	4.15	1.71	3.10	0.63	4.33
Oklahoma	0.39	2.14	1.46	0.54	0.64	2.05	0.14	0.90	0.27	1.10
Oregon	0.67	0.52	0.70	1.48	1.73	0.77	0.26	1.49	1.97	2.64
Pennsylvania	6.09	2.45	5.23	7.95	9.10	2.94	4.54	4.81	0.34	3.14
Rhode Island	0.96	0.13	0.07	0.05	0.12	0.00	0.36	1.22	0.00	0.32
S. Carolina	0.31	3.38	2.75	0.68	1.76	1.57	0.24	1.66	0.60	0.60
S. Dakota	0.28	0.09	0.37	1.64	0.29	0.13	0.03	0.23	0.20	0.09
Tennessee	0.35	4.38	2.64	0.38	3.03	2.85	0.33	1.28	0.56	1.58
Texas	6.09	11.34	7.91	3.17	4.42	11.08	2.67	7.68	3.44	4.49
Utah	0.16	0.09	0.10	0.16	0.25	0.15	0.27	0.21	34.47	0.73
Vermont	0.32	0.06	0.16	0.06	0.16	0.05	0.14	0.47	0.00	0.35
Virginia	1.17	4.03	4.10	1.11	3.67	2.78	1.53	4.71	1.25	2.14
Washington	1.43	0.73	1.53	2.96	3.24	1.64	0.44	2.09	2.67	3.68
W. Virginia	0.16	1.10	1.35	0.13	1.11	1.29	0.04	0.34	0.31	0.77
Wisconsin	2.92	0.41	1.58	9.98	1.20	1.10	0.44	1.05	0.57	1.61
Wyoming	0.13	0.08	0.23	0.18	0.57	0.12	0.00	0.56	1.16	0.33
U.S. Total	100%	100%	100%	100%	100%	100%	100%	100%	100%	100%

TABLE 3-2 CONTINUED

GEOGRAPHIC DISTRIBUTION OF RELIGIOUS GROUPS (In Percent)

STATES	CHURCH OF CHRIST	JEHOVAH'S WITNESS	7TH-DAY ADVENTIST	ASSEMBLIES OF GOD	HOLINESS/HOLY	BORN AGAIN/EVANGELICAL	NAZARENE	MUSLIM	ORTHODOX CHRISTIAN	UNITARIAN
Alabama	5.53	0.85	2.62	5.62	7.32	2.14	4.73	1.12	1.14	0.62
Arizona	0.88	1.92	1.59	1.70	0.00	1.94	2.39	1.02	0.52	1.13
Arkansas	4.26	0.37	0.25	4.09	0.57	0.00	0.92	0.00	0.00	0.73
California	3.59	17.13	25.75	10.35	3.60	11.83	7.75	24.77	16.73	18.37
Colorado	0.93	0.69	0.71	1.15	0.00	1.75	1.29	0.00	0.46	3.56
Connecticut	0.53	0.52	0.00	0.00	1.19	0.44	0.00	0.46	2.77	1.52
Delaware	0.00	0.31	0.00	0.00	1.13	0.00	0.00	0.00	0.00	0.00
D.C.	0.00	0.25	0.00	0.00	1.54	0.00	0.00	0.51	0.17	0.00
Florida	3.64	6.09	11.20	6.00	12.51	3.43	5.05	1.79	3.64	5.99
Georgia	1.82	3.05	0.70	2.25	10.96	1.72	1.69	2.70	0.00	1.00
Idaho	0.20	0.63	0.33	0.70	0.00	0.27	0.66	0.00	0.14	0.62
Illinois	3.68	3.59	1.24	2.65	0.00	10.61	4.46	6.34	8.03	7.06
Indiana	4.01	1.45	1.20	2.57	0.67	1.47	9.38	0.77	1.56	0.86
Iowa	0.67	1.45	0.90	1.93	0.00	2.94	1.45	0.00	0.00	0.43
Kansas	1.10	0.78	0.80	2.87	1.80	0.33	2.90	0.34	0.70	1.53
Kentucky	3.11	0.96	1.20	1.28	1.78	0.49	1.44	0.00	0.00	1.14
Louisiana	0.51	1.55	0.46	3.42	2.55	0.56	0.00	0.59	0.59	0.00
Maine	0.20	0.19	0.13	0.00	0.15	0.16	1.76	0.00	0.52	1.14
Maryland	0.58	2.25	2.59	0.55	5.20	1.27	0.62	1.33	2.69	2.21
Massachusetts	0.48	1.89	0.65	0.70	0.00	3.19	0.78	3.34	5.07	7.43
Michigan	2.24	4.38	3.02	2.16	0.00	4.93	2.42	3.87	2.61	4.30
Minnesota	0.70	0.92	0.95	0.51	0.00	5.22	0.57	0.61	0.62	2.70
Mississippi	1.86	1.35	0.28	0.89	1.24	0.00	0.67	0.00	0.00	0.00
Missouri	2.68	1.34	1.66	4.75	0.00	4.75	3.33	0.00	0.00	1.58

STATES	CHURCH OF CHRIST	JEHOVAH'S WITNESS	7TH-DAY ADVENTIST	ASSEMBLIES OF GOD	HOLINESS/ HOLY	BORN AGAIN/ EVANGELICAL	NAZARENE	MUSLIM	ORTHODOX CHRISTIAN	UNITARIAN
Montana	0.13	0.33	0.09	0.93	0.00	1.16	0.00	0.00	0.00	0.37
Nebraska	0.89	0.17	0.34	0.37	0.19	1.25	0.62	0.00	0.89	1.22
N. Hampshire	0.31	1.10	0.00	0.77	0.00	1.03	0.00	0.00	1.40	1.54
Nevada	0.24	0.44	0.00	0.00	0.00	0.32	0.78	0.33	0.34	0.37
New Jersey	0.31	3.64	0.84	0.90	1.87	1.02	1.01	6.43	9.78	1.19
New Mexico	0.73	0.95	0.16	0.18	0.00	0.20	0.39	0.00	0.43	0.70
New York	1.45	9.42	7.78	2.09	0.00	7.15	2.34	19.97	17.70	8.33
N. Carolina	1.07	2.78	1.43	2.31	13.62	0.00	0.86	1.84	0.00	1.02
N. Dakota	0.10	0.03	0.00	0.15	0.00	1.27	0.17	0.00	0.00	0.00
Ohio	8.29	5.11	3.52	2.51	2.62	4.31	12.71	6.02	4.57	1.67
Oklahoma	5.95	0.99	1.36	6.20	1.14	0.42	3.28	0.00	0.44	0.49
Oregon	0.46	1.64	3.38	0.99	0.00	1.51	1.11	0.39	0.80	1.75
Pennsylvania	4.78	3.73	3.86	2.75	1.44	9.45	3.09	4.95	6.68	1.83
Rhode Island	0.00	0.21	0.11	0.12	0.00	0.27	0.00	0.56	0.42	0.62
S. Carolina	0.56	1.46	1.13	1.21	10.95	0.00	0.91	0.97	0.49	0.00
S. Dakota	0.14	0.11	0.00	0.16	0.00	0.65	0.00	0.29	0.20	0.32
Tennessee	10.59	1.53	3.69	1.70	2.95	0.00	3.17	0.68	0.00	0.75
Texas	14.35	5.33	3.67	11.82	2.05	2.25	6.63	4.71	2.39	5.24
Utah	0.14	0.18	0.00	0.40	0.00	0.69	0.00	0.00	0.73	0.27
Vermont	0.00	0.18	0.73	0.00	0.00	0.15	0.29	0.00	0.47	0.96
Virginia	1.74	1.94	2.68	1.43	8.22	0.82	1.61	1.72	1.74	1.91
Washington	1.17	3.57	4.74	5.08	0.59	2.58	3.17	0.00	0.68	3.75
W. Virginia	1.15	0.56	0.97	0.42	2.17	0.71	2.57	0.25	0.50	0.28
Wisconsin	2.16	0.51	1.06	1.13	0.00	3.24	0.64	1.36	1.38	1.51
Wyoming	0.05	0.17	0.25	0.26	0.00	0.12	0.41	0.00	0.00	0.00
U.S. Total	100.00	100.00	100.00	100.00	100.00	100.00	100.00	100.00	100.00	100.00

TABLE 3-2 CONTINUED

GEOGRAPHIC DISTRIBUTION OF RELIGIOUS GROUPS (In Percent)

STATES	CHURCH OF GOD	CONGRE-GATIONALIST	BUDDHIST	MENNONITE	HINDU	AGNOSTIC	CHRISTIAN	PROTESTANT	REFUSED	OTHER	TOTAL
Alabama	7.92	0.00	0.00	0.00	1.30	0.49	0.85	1.48	0.93	0.83	1.64
Arizona	0.60	1.80	0.67	1.99	0.00	2.42	2.06	1.63	1.81	2.16	1.48
Arkansas	3.07	0.00	0.86	0.00	0.00	0.28	1.09	0.93	1.33	0.42	0.95
California	4.86	9.75	38.04	8.07	9.56	21.47	19.58	13.12	14.70	14.46	12.05
Colorado	1.08	1.62	0.60	1.79	2.12	2.18	1.50	1.61	1.63	1.68	1.33
Connecticut	0.54	10.23	1.20	0.00	1.06	0.99	0.63	1.54	2.26	1.09	1.34
Delaware	0.87	0.00	0.00	0.54	0.00	0.00	0.09	0.17	0.67	0.05	0.27
D.C.	0.00	0.00	0.33	0.00	0.00	0.18	0.10	0.10	0.24	0.39	0.25
Florida	6.34	4.24	2.36	3.51	4.16	7.78	4.65	4.96	4.79	4.30	5.24
Georgia	4.23	0.00	1.18	3.51	4.16	1.17	2.22	1.95	1.60	2.32	2.62
Idaho	0.33	0.00	0.37	3.55	0.00	0.67	0.61	0.45	0.55	0.36	0.41
Illinois	3.73	3.75	2.09	3.10	7.34	4.12	4.91	4.05	5.65	4.09	4.63
Indiana	5.43	0.00	1.01	13.52	0.00	1.00	4.72	3.40	2.25	2.69	2.24
Iowa	0.45	2.73	0.00	1.51	0.89	1.84	1.58	1.48	0.73	1.42	1.12
Kansas	0.00	0.81	1.36	4.03	0.80	0.89	1.67	1.49	0.74	0.57	1.00
Kentucky	2.41	0.00	0.67	1.00	0.00	0.66	2.36	1.31	1.11	1.13	1.49
Louisiana	0.69	0.69	0.77	0.00	0.00	0.00	0.74	0.76	0.89	0.86	1.64
Maine	0.00	5.63	0.22	0.00	0.39	0.66	0.33	1.03	0.48	0.25	0.50
Maryland	2.34	0.78	0.87	1.30	3.07	2.01	1.17	1.63	1.94	1.71	1.94
Massachusetts	0.00	18.73	4.39	0.00	1.93	3.62	1.16	2.40	3.29	1.69	2.44
Michigan	4.55	6.09	1.70	2.52	5.97	2.79	2.85	4.60	3.44	5.47	3.76
Minnesota	0.00	2.87	0.80	2.37	1.41	1.58	1.07	1.33	1.70	0.89	1.77
Mississippi	2.52	0.00	0.00	0.70	0.00	0.77	0.47	0.56	0.27	0.86	1.04
Missouri	4.18	0.00	0.93	0.00	0.00	1.23	3.19	2.55	1.99	1.70	2.07

STATES	CHURCH OF GOD	CONGRE-GATIONALIST	BUDDHIST	MENNONITE	HINDU	AGNOSTIC	CHRISTIAN	PROTESTANT	REFUSED	OTHER	TOTAL
Montana	0.00	2.88	0.00	0.65	0.00	0.29	0.59	0.29	0.38	0.25	0.32
Nebraska	0.26	1.55	0.29	0.00	1.01	0.09	0.55	0.74	0.47	0.61	0.64
N. Hampshire	0.00	2.54	0.81	0.00	0.00	0.60	0.39	0.41	0.39	0.37	0.45
Nevada	0.39	0.39	1.10	0.00	0.00	0.87	0.84	0.56	0.53	0.83	0.49
New Jersey	1.26	1.27	1.41	2.10	7.45	2.79	1.70	2.01	3.68	1.58	3.13
New Mexico	0.25	0.00	0.28	1.64	0.00	0.91	0.94	0.50	0.43	0.43	0.61
New York	0.00	5.90	6.57	4.88	34.67	6.49	3.63	5.11	9.20	6.90	7.28
N. Carolina	3.25	0.00	1.21	1.80	0.00	1.20	1.86	2.18	1.99	2.88	2.68
N. Dakota	0.52	1.57	0.00	0.00	0.00	0.15	0.17	0.26	0.28	0.10	0.26
Ohio	5.31	1.78	1.98	11.76	3.48	3.26	4.95	6.84	4.21	6.66	4.39
Oklahoma	1.03	0.00	1.15	2.56	1.01	0.76	1.93	1.58	2.33	1.69	1.27
Oregon	0.00	0.47	2.59	1.54	0.00	2.05	2.92	1.72	1.20	1.24	1.15
Pennsylvania	1.94	0.00	2.17	9.66	3.82	5.00	3.02	6.17	3.98	6.99	4.81
Rhode Island	0.00	1.31	0.00	0.82	0.00	0.30	0.20	0.29	0.51	0.18	0.41
S. Carolina	5.12	0.00	0.64	0.00	0.00	0.42	0.70	0.96	1.11	1.07	1.41
S. Dakota	0.23	1.14	0.00	0.57	0.00	0.42	0.06	0.31	0.12	0.12	0.28
Tennessee	10.35	0.00	0.89	0.00	0.00	0.59	1.71	1.91	1.38	1.25	1.97
Texas	5.55	0.00	6.20	0.00	0.00	6.13	6.11	5.25	4.79	6.95	6.88
Utah	0.00	0.00	0.31	0.47	0.00	0.93	0.38	0.13	0.88	0.04	0.70
Vermont	1.10	3.78	0.00	0.31	0.00	0.41	0.15	0.40	0.07	0.13	0.23
Virginia	2.02	1.01	4.52	5.03	1.99	2.23	2.55	2.50	2.07	2.69	2.50
Washington	0.00	1.59	4.44	1.32	1.56	4.10	3.42	2.79	2.83	3.36	1.97
W. Virginia	5.27	0.00	0.33	0.49	0.58	0.22	0.53	1.17	0.60	1.33	0.73
Wisconsin	0.00	2.40	2.68	1.33	0.00	0.88	0.77	1.27	1.29	1.00	1.98
Wyoming	0.00	0.67	0.00	0.12	0.29	0.14	0.29	0.10	0.26	0.07	0.18
U.S. Total	100.00	100.00	100.00	100.00	100.00	100.00	100.00	100.00	100.00	100.00	100.00

100

TABLE 3-3A 1
INDICES OF DISSIMILARITY

	ROMAN CATHOLIC	BAPTIST	METHODIST	LUTHERAN	PRESBYTERIAN	PENTECOSTAL	JEWISH	EPISCOPALIAN	MORMON	NONE	CHURCH OF CHRIST	JEHOVAHS WITNESS	7TH-DAY ADVENTIST	ASSEMBLIES OF GOD	HOLINESS/HOLY	BORN AGAIN/EVANGELICAL
Roman Catholic	0.0	45.2	32.2	34.6	26.5	32.6	29.3	21.1	59.9	25.1	49.2	23.3	38.3	43.0	70.5	28.2
Baptist	45.2	0.0	22.7	50.8	33.3	18.6	57.3	36.6	68.9	40.0	30.6	35.2	42.2	29.1	40.6	52.2
Methodist	32.2	22.7	0.0	38.2	19.5	18.0	49.0	24.5	65.4	27.6	33.1	24.7	36.2	32.2	48.2	38.3
Lutheran	34.6	50.8	38.2	0.0	30.5	43.4	53.5	42.2	61.5	35.7	51.8	39.4	45.8	46.9	73.8	25.0
Presbyterian	26.5	33.3	19.5	30.5	0.0	21.4	40.9	20.7	56.1	19.9	43.4	19.0	27.2	33.7	56.7	27.1
Pentecostal	32.6	18.6	18.0	43.4	21.4	0.0	45.8	24.2	63.0	27.3	30.7	23.7	32.2	22.7	51.1	41.1
Jewish	29.3	57.3	49.0	53.5	40.9	45.8	0.0	32.0	64.1	39.3	64.1	35.0	39.9	56.8	67.8	47.5
Episcopalian	21.1	36.6	24.5	42.2	20.7	24.2	32.0	0.0	57.6	24.1	47.3	19.4	29.6	36.7	56.9	36.2
Mormon	59.9	68.9	65.4	61.5	56.1	63.0	64.1	57.6	0.0	47.2	70.0	52.1	52.8	59.5	82.1	61.3
No Religion	25.1	40.0	27.6	35.7	19.9	27.3	39.3	24.1	47.2	0.0	45.4	14.9	21.7	35.6	64.4	30.5
Church of Christ	49.2	30.6	33.1	51.8	43.4	30.7	64.1	47.3	70.0	45.4	0.0	46.1	50.2	29.1	62.5	51.6
Jehovah's Witness	23.3	35.2	24.7	39.4	19.0	23.7	35.0	19.4	52.1	14.9	46.1	0.0	24.5	33.6	59.4	33.3
7th-Day Adventist	38.3	42.2	36.2	45.8	27.2	32.2	39.9	29.6	52.8	21.7	50.2	24.5	0.0	38.8	57.5	41.4
Assemblies of God	43.0	29.1	32.2	46.9	33.7	22.7	56.8	36.7	59.5	35.6	29.1	33.6	38.8	0.0	58.3	43.1
Holiness/Holy	70.5	40.6	48.2	73.8	56.7	51.1	67.8	56.9	82.1	64.4	62.5	59.4	57.5	58.3	0.0	75.4
Born Again/Evang.	28.2	52.2	38.3	25.0	27.1	41.1	47.5	36.2	61.3	30.5	51.6	33.3	41.4	43.1	75.4	0.0
Nazarene	44.2	35.9	29.8	45.0	34.2	31.6	58.1	41.2	61.6	33.8	31.0	36.7	41.0	28.4	61.5	44.6
Muslim	28.9	53.6	43.2	50.2	38.9	43.3	28.4	34.6	63.0	31.0	57.4	29.2	35.9	55.3	73.5	41.8
Orthodox	21.6	56.1	43.7	45.6	37.5	44.2	24.0	31.8	64.2	33.6	58.1	31.5	42.0	56.3	73.5	34.1
Church of God	54.1	29.2	33.1	56.1	42.4	33.4	64.2	48.5	73.9	46.2	31.7	41.8	50.3	41.0	45.7	55.6
Unitarian	24.6	48.4	38.1	39.0	28.6	37.2	36.9	26.4	51.9	19.5	54.4	22.7	30.6	42.5	69.8	32.0
Congregationalist	43.9	67.2	56.6	48.7	52.4	57.7	56.8	48.4	72.7	49.3	70.3	53.1	60.6	61.4	83.7	43.5
Buddhist	38.9	51.5	44.9	51.8	39.8	42.5	46.7	33.1	54.5	27.2	57.1	33.8	29.4	46.2	69.9	46.3
Mennonite	46.0	50.9	37.0	43.5	35.0	43.6	58.7	42.8	65.4	42.0	50.1	42.2	51.2	48.6	68.4	41.8

TABLE 3-3A 1 CONTINUED

INDICES OF DISSIMILARITY

	ROMAN CATHOLIC	BAPTIST	METHODIST	LUTHERAN	PRESBYTERIAN	PENTECOSTAL	JEWISH	EPISCOPALIAN	MORMON	NONE	CHURCH OF CHRIST	JEHOVAH'S WITNESS	7TH-DAY ADVENTIST	ASSEMBLIES OF GOD	HOLINESS/HOLY	BORN AGAIN/EVANGELICAL
Hindu	37.0	57.0	46.6	49.2	43.7	47.7	27.5	41.8	75.1	43.8	64.3	40.6	51.7	60.0	71.4	43.6
Agnostic	24.7	44.1	31.6	37.9	21.8	31.0	33.5	20.2	48.1	12.3	50.0	18.0	22.5	38.2	66.3	33.0
Christian	31.6	35.2	26.4	37.4	23.9	26.1	45.7	28.9	48.2	12.8	38.7	18.9	26.7	29.2	63.5	35.1
Protestant	23.2	34.9	19.5	31.9	15.9	22.6	41.9	22.2	55.4	15.2	36.1	18.4	29.8	31.3	60.8	27.5
Other	24.5	35.1	20.9	33.0	17.4	23.4	41.1	21.4	54.2	16.4	39.0	15.5	29.0	32.7	62.3	28.3
Refused	17.3	37.7	25.6	34.8	18.8	23.9	33.7	17.7	53.5	13.6	43.6	14.6	28.2	34.0	63.6	28.2
Total	18.9	30.4	16.2	34.3	15.0	16.8	38.9	16.7	57.4	15.8	37.8	15.2	29.7	29.8	57.4	27.5

TABLE 3-3A 2

INDICES OF DISSIMILARITY

	NAZARENE	MUSLIM	ORTHODOX CHRISTIAN	UNITARIAN	CHURCH OF GOD	CONGREGATIONALIST	BUDDHIST	MENNONITE	HINDU	AGNOSTIC	CHRISTIAN	PROTESTANT	REFUSED	OTHER	TOTAL
Roman Catholic	44.2	28.9	21.6	24.6	54.1	43.9	38.9	46.0	37.0	24.7	31.6	23.2	17.3	24.5	18.9
Baptist	35.9	53.6	56.1	48.4	29.2	67.2	51.5	50.9	57.0	44.1	35.2	34.9	37.7	35.1	30.4
Methodist	29.8	43.2	43.7	38.1	33.1	56.6	44.9	37.0	46.6	31.6	26.4	19.5	25.6	20.9	16.2
Lutheran	45.0	50.2	45.6	39.0	56.1	48.7	51.8	43.5	49.2	37.9	37.4	31.9	34.8	33.0	34.3
Presbyterian	34.2	38.9	37.5	28.6	42.4	52.4	39.8	35.0	43.7	21.8	23.9	15.9	18.8	17.4	15.0
Pentecostal	31.6	43.3	44.2	37.2	33.4	57.7	42.5	43.6	47.7	31.0	26.1	22.6	23.9	23.4	16.8
Jewish	58.1	28.4	24.0	36.9	64.2	56.8	46.7	58.7	27.5	33.5	45.7	41.9	33.7	41.1	38.9
Episcopalian	41.2	34.6	31.8	26.4	48.5	48.4	33.1	42.8	41.8	20.2	28.9	22.2	17.7	21.4	16.7
Mormon	61.6	63.0	64.2	51.9	73.9	72.7	54.5	65.4	75.1	48.1	48.2	55.4	53.5	54.2	57.4
No Religion	33.8	31.0	33.6	19.5	46.2	49.3	27.2	42.0	43.8	12.3	12.8	15.2	13.6	16.4	15.8
Church of Christ	31.0	57.4	58.1	54.4	31.7	70.3	57.1	50.1	64.3	50.0	38.7	36.1	43.6	39.0	37.8

102

TABLE 3-3A 2 CONTINUED

INDICES OF DISSIMILARITY

	NAZERENE	MUSLIM	ORTHODOX CHRISTIAN	UNITARIAN	CHURCH OF GOD	CONGRE-GATIONALIST	BUDDHIST	MENNONITE	HINDU	AGNOSTIC	CHRISTIAN	PROTES-TANT	REFUSED	OTHER	TOTAL
Jehovah's Witness	36.7	29.2	31.5	22.7	41.8	53.1	33.8	42.2	40.6	18.0	18.9	18.4	14.6	15.5	15.2
7th-Day Adventist	41.0	35.9	42.0	30.6	50.3	60.6	29.4	51.2	51.7	22.5	26.7	29.8	28.2	29.0	29.7
Assemblies of God	28.4	55.3	56.3	42.5	41.0	61.4	46.2	48.6	60.0	38.2	29.2	31.3	34.0	32.7	29.8
Holiness/Holy	61.5	73.5	73.5	69.8	45.7	83.7	69.9	68.4	71.4	66.3	63.5	60.8	63.6	62.3	57.4
Born Again/Evangelical	44.6	41.8	34.1	32.0	55.6	43.5	46.3	41.8	43.6	33.0	35.1	27.5	28.2	28.3	27.5
Nazarene	0.0	53.8	54.5	43.6	37.3	62.1	50.8	33.4	57.3	38.8	26.0	26.4	34.3	30.0	31.3
Muslim	53.8	0.0	22.1	35.8	59.0	60.8	37.1	53.5	34.3	31.6	36.6	35.7	29.4	33.9	33.7
Orthodox	54.5	22.1	0.0	31.6	63.0	52.0	43.8	52.0	31.2	33.5	40.0	35.5	27.4	35.1	33.6
Unitarian	43.6	35.8	31.6	0.0	53.6	41.7	30.8	50.8	44.7	19.7	26.7	25.9	21.5	28.1	26.3
Church of God	37.3	59.0	63.0	53.6	0.0	71.9	63.0	56.5	62.3	52.9	41.2	39.4	45.7	42.3	39.9
Congregationalist	62.1	60.8	52.0	41.7	71.9	0.0	58.0	59.4	54.9	52.9	55.7	48.6	45.7	50.8	49.1
Buddhist	50.8	37.1	43.8	30.8	63.0	58.0	0.0	55.8	59.5	50.1	31.1	36.6	48.5	34.6	36.0
Mennonite	33.4	53.5	52.0	50.8	56.5	59.4	55.8	0.0	53.9	26.4	38.6	34.1	34.4	36.4	39.1
Hindu	57.3	34.3	31.2	44.7	62.3	54.9	59.5	53.9	0.0	43.4	50.1	44.3	40.9	43.3	40.6
Agnostic	38.8	31.6	33.5	19.7	52.9	50.1	26.4	43.4	46.1	46.1	19.5	21.8	38.8	21.0	20.7
Christian	26.0	36.6	40.0	26.7	41.2	55.7	31.1	38.6	50.1	0.0	0.0	16.2	19.7	17.8	20.0
Protestant	26.4	35.7	35.5	25.9	39.4	48.6	36.6	34.1	44.3	19.5	16.2	0.0	19.1	10.4	11.9
Other	30.0	33.9	35.1	28.1	42.3	50.8	34.6	36.4	43.3	21.8	17.8	10.4	14.9	0.0	13.8
Refused	34.3	29.4	27.4	21.5	45.7	48.5	34.4	40.9	38.8	21.0	19.1	14.9	15.9	15.9	12.0
Total	31.3	33.7	33.6	26.3	39.9	49.1	36.0	39.1	40.6	19.7	19.1	11.9	0.0	13.8	0.0

TABLE 3-3B

INDICES OF DISSIMILARITY	
SOCIAL DISTANCE BETWEEN RELIGIOUS GROUPS	
NO MORE THAN 25% OF ONE GROUP WOULD HAVE TO CHANGE THEIR STATE OF RESIDENCE TO BE DISTRIBUTED GEOGRAPHICALLY AS IS THE OTHER GROUP	
RELIGIOUS GROUP DYAD	TOTAL
No Religion-Agnostic	12.3
Jehovah's Witness-No Religion	14.9
Methodist-Pentecostal	18.0
Baptist-Pentecostal	18.6
Jehovah's Witness-Presbyterian	19.0
Jehovah's Witness-Episcopalian	19.4
Presbyterian-Methodist	19.5
Presbyterian-No Religion	19.9
Episcopalian-Presbyterian	20.7
Roman Catholic-Episcopalian	21.1
Pentecostal-Presbyterian	21.4
Roman Catholic-Orthodox Christian	21.6
7th-Day Adventist-No Religion	21.7
Orthodox Christian-Muslim	22.1
Unitarian-Jehovah's Witness	22.7
Baptist-Methodist	22.7
Assemblies of God-Pentecostal	22.7
Jehovah's Witness-Pentecostal	23.7
Orthodox Christian-Jewish	24.0
Episcopalian-No Religion	24.1

Table 3-3B

INDICES OF DISSIMILARITY
SOCIAL DISTANCE BETWEEN RELIGIOUS GROUPS

NO MORE THAN 25% OF ONE GROUP WOULD HAVE TO CHANGE THEIR STATE
OF RESIDENCE TO BE DISTRIBUTED GEOGRAPHICALLY AS IS THE OTHER GROUP

RELIGIOUS GROUP DYAD	TOTAL
Episcopalian-Pentecostal	24.2
7th-Day Adventist-Jehovah's Witness	24.5
Roman Catholic-Unitarian	24.6
Jehovah's Witness-Methodist	24.7
Born Again/Evangelical-Lutheran	25.0
GENERAL CATEGORIES	
Christian-No Religion	12.8
Refused-No Religion	13.6
Protestant-Refused	14.9
Protestant-Christian	16.2

TABLE 3-3C

INDICES OF DISSIMILARITY

SOCIAL DISTANCE BETWEEN RELIGIOUS GROUPS
—MORE THAN 64% OF ONE GROUP WOULD HAVE TO CHANGE THEIR STATE OF RESIDENCE TO BE DISTRIBUTED GEOGRAPHICALLY AS IS THE OTHER GROUP

RELIGIOUS GROUP DYAD	TOTAL
Jewish-Church of Christ	64.1
Mormon-Jewish	64.1
Jewish-Church of God	64.2
Mormon-Orthodox Christian	64.2
Church of Christ-Hindu	64.3
Mormon-Mennonite	65.4
Mormon-Methodist	65.4
Baptist-Congregational	67.2
Jewish-Holiness/Holy	67.8
Holiness/Holy-Mennonite	68.4
Mormon-Baptist	68.9
Holiness/Holy-Unitarian	69.8
Holiness/Holy-Buddhist	69.9
Mormon-Church of Christ	70.0
Church of Christ-Congregationalist	70.3
Roman Catholic-Holiness/Holy	70.5
Holiness/Holy-Hindu	71.4
Church of God-Congregational	71.9
Mormon-Congregational	72.7
Holiness/Holy-Orthodox Christian	73.5
Holiness/Holy-Muslim	73.5
Mormon-Church of God	73.9

106

TABLE 3-3C CONTINUED

INDICES OF DISSIMILARITY
SOCIAL DISTANCE BETWEEN RELIGIOUS GROUPS —MORE THAN 64% OF ONE GROUP WOULD HAVE TO CHANGE THEIR STATE OF RESIDENCE TO BE DISTRIBUTED GEOGRAPHICALLY AS IS THE OTHER GROUP

RELIGIOUS GROUP DYAD	TOTAL
Mormon-Hindu	75.1
Holiness/Holy-Born Again/Evangelical	75.4
Holiness/Holy-Congregational	83.7

TABLE 3-3D

INDICES OF DISSIMILARITY	
DEGREE OF CLUSTERING OF EACH RELIGIOUS GROUP GEOGRAPHICALLY DISTRIBUTED AS IN THE AMERICAN POPULATION AS A WHOLE = 0.0	
RELIGIOUS GROUP	TOTAL
Protestant	11.9
Christian	11.9
Refused	12.0
Presbyterian	15.0
Jehovah's Witness	15.2
No Religion	15.8
Methodist	16.2
Episcopalian	16.7
Pentecostal	16.8
Roman Catholic	18.9
Christian	20.0
Agnostic	20.7
Unitarian	26.3
Born Again/Evangelical	27.5
7th-Day Adventist	29.7
Assemblies of God	29.8
Baptist	30.4
Nazarene	31.3
Orthodox Christian	33.6
Muslim	33.7
Lutheran	34.3
Buddhist	36.0
Church of Christ	37.8
Jewish	38.9

TABLE 3-3D CONTINUED

INDICES OF DISSIMILARITY	
DEGREE OF CLUSTERING OF EACH RELIGIOUS GROUP	
RELIGIOUS GROUP	TOTAL
Mennonite	39.1
Church of God	39.9
Hindu	40.6
Congregationalist	49.1
Holiness/Holy	57.4
Mormon	57.4

TABLE 3-4

RELIGIOUS IDENTIFICATION BY TYPE OF RESIDENTIAL LOCATION			
(METROPOLITAN STATUS CODE)			
	URBAN	SUBURBAN	RURAL
% of U.S. Population	32.2	40.5	23.3
	%	%	%
Catholic	29.4	29.8	15.1
Baptist	18.9	15.4	26.9
Methodist	6.5	7.4	11.5
Lutheran	4.3	5.6	5.9
Presbyterian	2.6	3.2	2.6
Pentecostal*	2.0	1.9	2.9
Episcopalian	1.9	1.9	1.1
Jehovah's Witness	0.8	0.8	0.7
Other Protestants	12.2	13.3	16.3
Mormon	1.2	1.4	1.9
Orthodox	0.3	0.4	0.1
Christian	4.5	4.4	5.1
Total Christian	(84.6)	(85.5)	(90.1)
Jewish	2.5	2.0	0.3
Muslim	0.5	0.3	0.0
Eastern Religions	0.5	0.4	0.1
Alternative Religions	0.1	0.1	0.0
Unitarian	0.3	0.3	0.2
Unclassified	0.5	0.5	0.5
No Religion/Agnostic	8.6	8.4	7.1
Refused	2.4	2.4	1.7
	100.0	100.0	100.0

*Includes Assemblies of God

TABLE 3-5

RELIGIOUS PROFILES OF SELECTED CITIES BY PERCENTAGE			
	NEW YORK CITY	CHICAGO	PHILADELPHIA
1990 Population	7.3 M	2.8 M	1.6 M
	%	%	%
Catholic	43.4	38.6	37.1
Baptist	10.7	24.7	25.9
Methodist	2.9	3.5	4.3
Lutheran	1.3	2.9	2.5
Presbyterian	1.2	1.0	2.1
Pentecostal*	2.3	1.4	2.2
Episcopalian	2.2	1.0	1.4
Jehovah's Witness	1.1	0.7	1.3
Other Protestants	6.8	6.5	8.0
Mormon	0.2	0.2	0.2
Orthodox	0.8	0.6	0.1
Christian	2.5	3.6	2.9
Total Christian	(75.4)	(84.7)	(88.0)
Jewish	10.9	2.6	3.7
Muslim	1.5	1.0	1.2
Eastern Religions	1.4	0.5	0.1
Alternative Religions	0.1	0.0	0.1
Unitarian	0.4	0.2	0.1
Unclassified	1.0	1.0	0.3
No Religion/Agnostic	7.4	7.9	4.8
Refused	1.9	2.2	1.7
	100.0	100.0	100.0

*Includes Assemblies of God

TABLE 3-6

RELIGIOUS PROFILES OF SELECTED CALIFORNIAN METROPOLITAN AREAS					
	LOS ANGELES COUNTY (PMSA)	ORANGE COUNTY (PMSA)	SAN DIEGO COUNTY (MSA)	SAN FRANCISCO–MARIN–SAN MATEO (PMSA)	ALAMEDA–CONTRA COSTA (OAKLAND–PMSA)
1990 Population	8.9 M	2.4 M	2.5 M	1.6 M	2.1M
	%	%	%	%	%
Catholic	31.5	29.3	27.6	33.5	26.1
Baptist	11.9	6.2	9.9	6.4	11.7
Methodist	3.1	4.1	6.9	3.7	2.4
Lutheran	3.5	5.0	4.1	2.8	3.5
Presbyterian	2.2	4.6	2.9	3.5	3.1
Pentecostal*	1.3	0.7	1.6	0.7	3.2
Episcopalian	1.7	1.4	2.9	3.0	2.1
Jehovah's Witness	0.7	0.4	0.8	1.0	0.9
Other Protestants	10.9	15.6	14.2	11.6	11.7
Mormon	1.8	3.2	1.7	0.8	3.3
Orthodox	0.5	0.3	0.2	0.7	0.3
Christian	9.6	8.8	6.9	2.7	4.7
Total Christian	(78.7)	(79.6)	(79.7)	(70.4)	(73.0)
Jewish	3.9	2.7	1.9	4.1	2.3
Muslim	0.8	1.5	0.5	0.7	0.5
Eastern Religions	1.3	0.8	0.5	1.1	1.1
Alternative Religions	0.3	0.5	0.5	0.3	0.2
Unitarian	0.4	0.4	0.7	0.4	0.6
Unclassified	0.5	0.3	0.3	0.2	1.0
No Religion/Agnostic	12.8	11.6	12.9	20.1	17.5
Refused	1.3	2.6	3.0	2.7	3.8
	100.0	100.0	100.0	100.0	100.0
Ethnic Minority	59	35	35	43	42

*Includes Assemblies of God

112

TABLE 3-7

RELIGIOUS PROFILES OF SELECTED METROPOLITAN AREAS IN TEXAS & FLORIDA BY PERCENTAGE			
	DALLAS–FORT WORTH (CMSA)	HOUSTON (CMSA)	MIAMI–FT. LAUDERDALE (CMSA)
1990 Population	3.9 M	3.7 M	3.2 M
	%	%	%
Catholic	12.6	23.6	34.0
Baptist	38.1	34.7	16.2
Methodist	10.6	8.9	5.0
Lutheran	1.8	3.1	2.2
Presbyterian	2.1	1.4	2.8
Pentecostal*	4.3	4.2	2.6
Episcopalian	1.5	2.7	1.9
Jehovah's Witness	0.8	0.5	0.9
Church of Christ	2.8	1.3	0.2
Other Protestants	13.2	7.0	8.8
Mormon	0.6	0.2	0.2
Orthodox	0.1	—	0.2
Christian	3.6	3.8	4.4
Total Christian	(91.1)	(91.4)	(79.4)
Jewish	0.6	0.9	9.5
Muslim	0.2	0.6	0.1
Eastern Religions	0.4	0.4	0.3
Alternative Religions	0.1	0.1	0.3
Unitarian	0.3	0.2	0.2
Unclassified	0.5	0.2	0.4
No Religion/Agnostic	5.8	5.4	7.3
Refused	1.0	0.8	2.5
	100.0	100.0	100.0

* Includes Assemblies of God

TABLE 3-7 CONTINUED

RELIGIOUS PROFILES OF SELECTED METROPOLITAN AREAS IN TEXAS & FLORIDA BY PERCENTAGE			
	DALLAS–FORT WORTH (CMSA)	HOUSTON (CMSA)	MIAMI–FT. LAUDERDALE (CMSA)
Race	%	%	%
White, Non-Hispanic	67	56	50
Black	12	19	16
Hispanic	6	21	33
Asian/Other	5	4	1

FROM THE ETHNIC FACTOR TO THE NEW AGE

◆ ◆ ◆

Race and ethnicity are "hot buttons" in today's America; they are "the American obsession," as Studs Terkel aptly subtitled his recent book *Race*. An extremely sensitive topic at this time, race and ethnicity wield formidable power in defining individual identity and imposing rules on social intercourse and political debate. Many social commentators automatically assume that the growth of minority populations and their increasing assertiveness foster religious pluralism in the nation. They associate ethnic differences with religious differences and characterize ethnicity and religious loyalty as part of the same cultural identity. As a result, stereotypes emerge, so that being a Korean Presbyterian or a Cherokee Baptist is regarded as a strange and inauthentic phenomenon, almost disloyal to the particular cultural heritage. From this perspective, the maintenance of social difference is now widely regarded as a positive end in itself, a view that is inimical to the claims of universalist missionary religions.

This chapter will help to dispel the myths that confuse particular religious identification with particular ethnic groups in contemporary America. To do this, we will examine religious profiles of white (non-Hispanic), black, Hispanic, Asian, and Native Americans. We will show how religious groups, such as the American Catholic church, are trying to cope with the challenge of new ethnic patterns.

The attraction of the exotic and concern for the survival of minority cultures have led to the adoption of new religions by some white Americans. Similarly, non-Western religious traditions have infiltrated the mainstream of American society through New Age beliefs and ecological concerns. This in turn leads us to the issue of cultural conflict when re-emergent pagan ideas confront monotheism.

Since the founding of the republic, the federal government has never been reluctant to inquire into the race or ancestry of Americans in either the U.S. Census or other official data collections. Nevertheless, terms such as *race* and *ethnic group* are somewhat nebulous and have given rise to considerable debate, mostly in liberal circles outside the United States, about whether any system of racial or ethnic classification is intellectually or morally defensible. Yet, ironically, it is the most liberal or radical elements in the United States who are most zealous about dividing up the citizenry along skin-color lines. In an age of affirmative action and competing group demands for public attention and access to limited resources, there is a premium on claims for special status. Today, multiculturalism and diversity are the acceptable guiding principles in education and social policy. This leads to the affirmation of "roots" and ancestry and sometimes, in the extreme, to an overemphasis of the differences between groups of people without equal attention to the common denominators that bind together all Americans and, indeed, the entire human race.

Religion has reduced utility as an organizing principle in this social atmosphere, since most religions claim universal and eternal truths applicable to people regardless of their background. There is an obvious tension here. Bluntly speaking, religion—particularly the three Abrahamic faiths—is basically hostile to the cultural relativism that now pervades large areas of American culture. Christians, Jews, and Muslims are expected to believe and behave in certain ways regardless of whether they reside in Ethiopia, Uzbekistan, or Illinois, and irrespective of whether they are black, brown, or white, or speak African, Asian, or European languages. In fact, they do, since all three faiths teach that an individual's moral worth is not related to arbitrary characteristics such as race or station at birth. However, if, as is sometimes now claimed on many American college campuses, literature written by "dead white males" is inherently irrelevant, then, to put it quite starkly, the nation's largest religious group, the Catholic church, has a very serious problem. Indeed, by such reasoning all three great monotheistic faiths could be dismissed as alien, since their leading figures, Moses, Saint Paul, and Muhammad, are all dead Semitic males.

BREAKING THE MYTHS OF
RELIGIOUS AFFILIATION

In no area of American social life are stereotypes so far from the truth as in the relationship of religion and ethnic origin. As we shall see, growing ethnic diversity has not led to religious fragmentation. On the contrary, religious identification and belief tend to crosscut racial and ethnic divisions among Americans and to provide a largely unappreciated level of social cohesion and consensus on core values. In fact, for many new immigrants the church rather than the public school is the new melting pot aiding their acculturation into their new society.

The power of stereotype was evident in media reaction to the findings of the NSRI on religious identification by ethnic origin. That most Americans who claim Irish or French descent are not Catholic, that most Asian Americans are Christian, and that not only are most Arab Americans not Muslim but most American Muslims are not Arabs appears strange to those not fully aware of the country's religious and immigration history. Although these findings are not necessarily new, the NSRI provides them with an overwhelming weight of statistical evidence.

As history tells us, immigrants to a new society are hardly ever representative of the population in their country of origin. There is a process of self-selection even before they migrate. Clearly, the Pilgrim Fathers were not average Englishmen of their time, or they would not have felt the need to sail away to seek religious freedom. This pattern of dissimilarity has been the case for most groups. Most early French immigrants to these shores were Huguenots, members of the Protestant Reformed church, who sought refuge from religious persecution by Catholics in their native land. Hence, more Americans of French origin are Protestant than are Catholic. Only a small proportion of the millions of immigrants to the country from Russia, either of the Czarist empire or the defunct U.S.S.R., have been adherents of the Russian Orthodox church. Instead, they have been, overwhelmingly, members of religious minorities: Jews, Armenian Christians, Mennonites, and, more recently, Pentecostals, 30,000 of whom sought refuge in the United States between 1989 and 1991.

THE RACIAL AND ETHNIC PATTERNS OF RELIGIOUS IDENTITY

The question of religious identification among the different races is of considerable importance because of the way religion and ethnic culture affect each other. As we have noted, counting people is not just a statistical exercise but a political one as well. The U.S. Census Bureau results for 1990 report subtotals of the population for five "races": whites, blacks, Asians and Pacific Islanders, Native Americans, and "Others." Hispanics are reported independently by means of a separate question, and all the official figures state that "Hispanics can be of any race." In the 1990 census, slightly more than half of all Hispanics identified themselves as white, 3% as black, 1.5% as Asian (mostly Filipino), and the rest stated that they were of "other race." From a strictly biological stance, most Hispanics are actually either Native Americans from Latin American countries or mestizos, those of mixed European and Native American ancestry, a category that the official U.S. classification system does not recognize.

When we decided to collect data on race for the NSRI, we adopted a simpler system of categorization more easily adapted to telephone interviewing. First we asked if the respondent was Hispanic. All those who answered negatively were then asked their race, and these answers were categorized into white, black, or "other." Thus for all the NSRI data in the charts and tables relating to this chapter, the terms *white* and *black* mean non-Hispanic white and non-Hispanic black. The NSRI classification of "other" race means mostly Asian Americans and Native Americans. Our system reflects the common usage of the term *minority,* that is, to include the Hispanics, blacks, Asian Americans, and Native Americans who together comprise 20% of the total American population of 250 million; and our *whites* are the nearly 200-million-strong majority group of non-Hispanic whites. However, as we shall see, some people, such as those of Middle Eastern or North African origin, are still not quite sure where to place themselves under either classification system, although the Census Bureau regards them as white. In addition, some other respondents in both the census and the NSRI report themselves into what might be regarded as the wrong category—but that is their privilege, at least under our system. Even so, among our sample of nearly 114,000 people, we had as many refusals to answer as to race as to religion (not a large number in either case). This is perhaps unsurprising, given the complications of self-reporting and the complexities of the racial-classification process. Nevertheless, once we divide up the population on the basis of race we find that the majority and the various minorities have very different religious profiles. Non-Hispanic whites, who account for four out of every five Americans today, are an overwhelmingly Christian population in their religious identification, as Chart 4-1 shows. All told, around 58% of non-Hispanic whites identify with Protestant churches. Among non-Hispanic whites, the largest groups of non-Christians are religious "Nones" (9%) and Jews (2%). Most of the tiny proportion of "Other Religion" respondents recorded in the religious-denomination column identify with smaller Eastern religions, as well as theosophical and other newer religious offerings.

The ethnic mix of Catholics is roughly proportionate to that of America in general. Eighty percent of American Catholics are non-Hispanic whites, and the remainder are blacks, Hispanics, and members of other races. Glancing across the various charts and tables relating to the religious identification of

Chart 4-1

Religious Profile of White Non-Hispanics
(1990 NSRI)

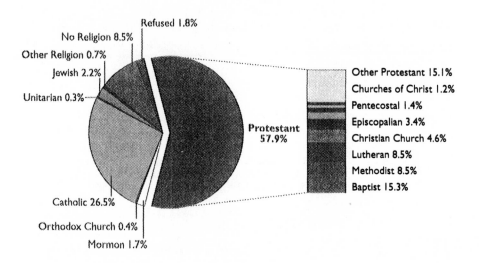

the racial groups provides quick evidence of the extent to which the other religious groups are, or are not, reflective of the racial composition of the nation as a whole. Knowing the historical origins of the various religious groups renders the actual figures predictable. Among the Lutheran churches, which originate from northern Europe, we find that 97% of their adherents are non-Hispanic whites. This Lutheran proportion is just ahead of the Mormons, with 94%; Jews and Presbyterians, with 93% each; and Episcopalians, with 90%. Among the other main groups, the Methodists are 86% non-Hispanic white, the Baptists 69% and the Pentecostals 68%. Among the larger churches, only the Jehovah's Witnesses have a minority majority, with 48% of their population identifying themselves as non-Hispanic whites.

We do not mean to suggest that religion in America today is an inherited attribute. Indeed, the pattern of inheritance is increasingly less common with every passing year. Yet most people still acquire their religious identity from their family upbringing and an ethnic community tradition. In fact, some sociologists, such as the Reverend Andrew Greeley, assert that churches in America have survived because of their ability to go beyond purely associational ties and play a communal or "quasi-ethnic" role in American society. The very impersonality of much of modern society creates in individuals a need for communal ties broader than the family but narrower than the total public. For immigrants to America of earlier generations, religion had a social function in helping to decide "who one was." One by-product of this was that religion sustained many communities, such as the Polish and Irish Catholics, and the Swedish and Norwegian Lutherans, until the middle of this century.

THE MELTDOWN OF ANCESTRAL DIVISIONS AMONG WHITE AMERICANS

By the 1950s, white ethnics started to move out of their linguistic or country-of-origin groups and to amalgamate. This postwar generation of Americans sought a sense of belonging within the enlarged boundaries of three main religio-ethnic groups, creating a new tripartite America of Protestant, Catholic, and Jew from what had been numerous smaller ethnic-origin groups. Czech, Polish, Italian, and Irish Catholics intermarried, as did Finnish and Danish Lutherans, and Polish and Hungarian Jews. Institutional change began to reflect this new reality as, for instance, the various national Lutheran churches combined and replaced their old European-language liturgies with English versions. American Catholicism held steadfast, though the abandonment of Latin by the Catholic church in the 1970s came too late to revitalize many of its old national parishes in the immigrant neighborhoods of industrial cities. Nevertheless, by the 1970s the loss of immigrant languages and the processes of migration to the suburbs and ethnic intermarriage were too widespread to reverse among third-generation Catholic Americans from southern and eastern Europe.

The process that dissolved the historical ethnic antagonisms of the Old World was regarded as the great glory of the United States only a few decades ago. There is strong evidence that as white Americans become increasingly distant from their immigrant forebears, they increasingly tend to forget, distort, or remember selectively their ethnic origins. Professor Stanley Lieberson of Harvard University has described this new reality as "ethnic groups in flux." This process has gone further among those of older northwest European background, some of whom can trace their genealogy back more than ten generations in this country, and consists of a recognition of being white but a lack of any clear-cut identification with any specific European origin. These Americans, currently 6% of the population but likely to increase, are "unhyphenated whites," and they are increasingly floating voters where religious identity is concerned. Without any connection to the cultural traditions of their ancestors, they are ripe for religious switching; so far the evidence suggests that they are attracted to evangelical Protestantism.

"Unhyphenated whites" are a small minority, but their existence teaches us an important lesson: We cannot view ethnic and racial categories as a given; they are continually evolving. The ethnic identifications and roots that people report in surveys are more fluid than is generally realized because most American whites have a menu of ethnic origins from which they can choose. The U.S. Census Bureau asks the subsample of householders who receive the bureaus long form a separate ancestry or ethnicity question beyond the one on race. This question allows these respondents to provide a single, double, or triple ancestry, or none at all. As a result, the total number of ancestries reported by the census adds up to more than 100% of the U.S. population. The main European ancestries for whites in 1980 were English and German, each with 22% of all Americans; Irish, with 18%; French, with 6%; Italian, with 5%; Scotch and Polish, with 4% each; Dutch, with 3%; and Swedish, with 2%. Once we had decided to carry out a religious survey, we were curious to learn how the U.S. Census data on ancestry would correlate with religious identification. As we noted earlier, we asked all our respondents a race question, but limited resources prevented us from asking everyone an ancestry question. Midway through the project, however, we decided to ask the ancestry question of a limited sample large enough to allow us to say something about the major ethnic-origin groups. We used the very same question as the 1990 U.S. Census, but our analysis was different. We allowed to be coded as an ancestry the answer "Jewish," which the U.S. Census does not allow because it considers "Jewish" a religious-group answer.

The data in Table 4-1 present the results we obtained for the most common ethnic ancestries or nationality groups among non-Hispanic whites. While the religious identification data were limited and relate only to the larger denominations, this information is still very valuable. The long-established groups from the old Protestant nations of northern Europe (the Dutch, the English, and the Scandinavians) are still about two-thirds Protestant, but a considerable portion report themselves as Catholic, and slightly more said they were of no religion, agnostic, or identified with some new religious offering. The more recently arrived Poles and Italians were about three-fourths Catholic, but there were already as many Protestants as persons of no religion among them. The Protestant segments among these two ancestry groups are presumably the result of intermarriage and religious switching. The considerable number of American Jews of Polish origin obviously affects the Polish figures and lowers the Catholic score here. French Americans have a slight Protestant plurality, but there is a clear Protestant majority among German Americans, as the history of their immigration would predict.

TABLE 4-1

WHITE NON-HISPANICS: SELECTED ANCESTRY OR ETHNIC ORIGIN BY RELIGION

RELIGIOUS IDENTIFICATION

ETHNIC ORIGIN	CHRISTIAN (SO STATED)	CATHOLIC	PROTESTANT	JEWISH	ALL OTHERS*	TOTAL
Dutch	6	10	64	0	15	100
English	6	12	63	1	19	100
French	3	39	47	1	11	100
German	7	26	51	1	16	100
Irish	3	33	51	0	13	100
Italian	2	72	14	0	12	100
Jewish	1	5	6	66	22	100
Middle Eastern**	10	44	13	0	33	100
Polish	2	73	11	5	12	100
Scandinavian	3	22	61	0	14	100

* Includes religious "Nones," other non-Christian religions, and some small Christian denominations
** Small sample

Given the debate about recording Jewish ethnicity in both governmental and Jewish communal circles, it is not surprising that Jews by religion, who are 2.2% of the white population, were split between those who identified with a national origin and those who self-reported as "Jews." Among those who reported themselves as being of Jewish ethnic origin rather than of the nationality of the country from which their ancestors originated, only two thirds reported Judaism as their current religion. In fact, it appears that around 12% of Americans of Jewish descent are Christians. This high level of religious assimilation should not surprise those who read Chapter 2. On the other hand, the Jewish ethnic group showed a large proportion, 22% in the "No Religion" and "Miscellaneous" columns. This finding suggests that secularization has progressed furthest among Americans of Jewish ancestry. This was confirmed by the 1990 National Jewish Population Survey, which reported that there was one secular or cultural Jew for every four religious Jews in America.

Other confirmation was provided by the *Bergen Record* newspaper, which carried out a survey on religious topics in its readership area in Passaic and

Bergen counties in northern New Jersey during December 1991. The *Record* asked the ancestry question along with the religious-identification question among a largely white suburban sample, and found that 73% of their respondents who claimed Polish ancestry were Catholic, that 8% each were Protestant or Jewish, and that 11% were religious "Nones." The German Americans were almost equally split between Catholics and Protestants, 42% and 43% respectively; 3% were Jewish. Among the *Record*'s Jewish ethnic-origin sample, 75% said that they were Jewish by religion, 15% claimed no religion, 6% said that they were Catholic, and 4% said that they were Protestant. The Irish American respondents were 71% Catholic, 20% Protestant, 2% Jewish, and 7% religious "Nones." Even though the sample size for each separate ethnic group in the *Record* poll was quite small, these local figures were remarkably similar to those found nationally by the NSRI. This is valuable supportive knowledge because it contains some surprises. Typically, New Jerseyans' roots are closer generationally to Europe than are most white Americans'. In addition, New Jerseyans are twice as likely to adhere to Catholicism or Judaism as are average white Americans, so we should expect the Irish and Jewish ancestry groups to be less assimilated in that state.

The New Jersey figures clearly corroborate the NSRI finding that religious and denominational diversity is growing among the old nationality groups of white ethnic America as intermarriage and religious switching increases in momentum. We can presume from this that diversity is also growing within most American families to the extent that we can no longer automatically assume that surnames such as O'Reilly, Schmidt, Vanderzee, Cohen, Colombo, Kowalsky, or Thatcher indicate a person's religion. This makes for a more complicated world, but it has its positive side. A by-product of greater variety of religious expression among extended family members should be greater toleration of religious differences. In such an atmosphere, we also predict that religious identification will increasingly come to be viewed much more as a personal than as a family or group characteristic. Such individualism, for good or ill, contributes to the Protestantization of all religion in America.

IRISH AMERICANS: SOME SURPRISING FINDINGS

The news arising from Table 4-1 that was reported from Detroit to Dublin and Boston to Belfast was the finding about the religious loyalties of Irish Americans. The very narrow majority of Protestants among them was, apparently, surprising news. In fact, National Opinion Research Center

(NORC) data from the 1970s, which also cross-tabulated those claiming Irish ancestry by their current religious identification, found that only 39% of Irish Americans were Catholic. So the NSRI figure, relating to 1990, of 33% Catholic should not have been so shocking. The gap between the perception and the reality has a number of roots.

Many Americans, particularly in the South, claim Irish descent but are actually of Scotch-Irish origin. Their ancestors were Presbyterians who emigrated in the late 18th and early 19th centuries, mostly from northern Ireland. Many of these land-hungry settlers went through the Cumberland Gap to open up the frontier in Kentucky and Tennessee. Their progeny would include Davy Crockett, Sam Houston, and Andrew Jackson. In Ireland, the Protestant gentry (particularly the Presbyterian yeoman farmers), inspired by the American and French revolutions, agitated for independence from England and the founding of a republic. The defeat of the United Irishmen in the rebellion led by the Protestant patriot Wolfe Tone in 1798 followed by the Act of Union with Britain fueled a stream of emigration. Thus the original Irish immigrants to reach these shores were mostly Presbyterians seeking freedom and farmland in a Protestant republic. It was they who led the first Saint Patrick's Day parades in New York. Only when members of the Irish Catholic majority began to arrive as immigrants after 1840 did the religious complexion of Irish Americans begin to change. It is important to remember that historically, a quarter of Ireland's population has been not Catholics but Protestants or religious "Nones," and this includes such famous Irish figures as Robert Emmet, Edmund Burke, Charles Parnell, Roger Casement, Maud Gonne, and the writers William Butler Yeats and Samuel Beckett.

The strong non-Catholic strain in the Irish American ancestry population is demonstrated by the religious profiles of the U.S. presidents of Irish American stock. Whereas Andrew Jackson, James Buchanan, Chester Arthur, William McKinley, Woodrow Wilson, Richard Nixon, and Ronald Reagan were Protestants, only John F. Kennedy was a Catholic. In his 1972 book, *That Most Distressful Nation*, Andrew Greeley carefully teased out from census data the socioeconomic success of the "Bog Irish" Catholic population compared to the lesser fortunes of the Scotch-Irish Protestants, and showed how the status of the two Irish-origin religious groups had reversed in America.

Our data suggest that outside the larger cities of the Northeast and Midwest, intermarriage of Irish people with those of other origins often leads to the adoption of Irish self-identification but the loss of Catholicism in the next generation. For instance, former president Ronald Reagan's biography records that his father was Catholic but that he himself was raised in his mother's Protestant church in a small Illinois town.

Most Americans associate Irishness with Saint Patrick's Day on March 17. This is an unofficial national holiday, especially popular with young people, that involves wearing green, parading, and partying. The holiday accounts for some of the enthusiasm with which Irish origin is claimed. This phenomenon is an excellent example of sociologist Herbert Gans's concept of "symbolic ethnicity," which he regards as particularly appealing to the middle classes. In Gans's view, this modern American ethnicity is expressed in terms of interest in selected cultural aspects of one's roots. It does not need to be supported by institutions like language or residential proximity or, we would add, religious behavior.

Saint Patrick, the patron saint of Ireland and of the New York Catholic archdiocese, is nowadays particularly associated with the New York Catholic Irish. For over a century the New York City parade, the world's largest and most famous, has been organized by the Ancient Order of Hibernians, a private Catholic fraternal organization sworn to uphold the religious tenets of their faith that has also, historically, taken the lead in advocating the Irish nationalist cause against the Protestant ascendancy and British presence in Northern Ireland. However, in the 1990s it has been the Hibernians' religious values that have brought it into public prominence and dispute with the city's political establishment and Human Rights Commission. The group has been accused by the *New York Times* of engaging in "hateful discrimination" for its refusal to allow an Irish gay and lesbian group to march in the parade. Probably much to their surprise, the Hibernians have been supported by the American Civil Liberties Union in their right as a private organization to control the content of their parade. Obviously the Hibernians, with their strong ties to the Catholic hierarchy under the socially conservative leadership of Archbishop John Cardinal O'Connor, cannot endorse any sexual practice of any kind except among heterosexual couples joined by the Catholic sacrament of holy matrimony. On the other hand, the Hibernians cannot still claim to represent all Irish Americans. This is very much a dispute for our times, as it involves conflicting values and identities, as well as constitutional issues of assembly and free speech, and battles over what differentiates private from public activity.

The close association of "Irish" and "Catholic" in the minds of most Americans is also due to the fact that the first large population of Catholics to enter the country came from Ireland. The historical evidence suggests that American Irish Catholics were far more diligent in their religious devotions and church attendance than their cousins who migrated to England or Australia. Moreover, as a politically astute and English-speaking population, they quickly gained control of the curial and administrative positions in the American Catholic church and have never really relinquished them, with the result that they have been much more prominent in the ecclesiastical leadership than any other ethnic-origin group of Catholics. Since the 1870s, every bishop of Baltimore, Boston, and New York, save one, has been of Irish origin. The Irish have also supplied the vast majority of America's cardinals. Until recently, the only nationality group to rival them was the German Catholic population, but that ethnic group's effectiveness in America was seriously undermined by the advent of World War I. Moreover, a high rate of German-Irish intermarriage among Catholics tended to reduce the conflict and merge the groups.

POLISH AND ITALIAN CATHOLICS

The other two large nationality groups among white Catholics, the Poles and Italians, arrived later than the Irish and Germans. The Italians tended to demonstrate lower levels of piety and be less loyal to the organizational church. Yet they were more easily assimilated by the Irish Catholic structure. The Poles were more of a political problem for the Irish because they are much more fiercely loyal Catholics. Nevertheless, they were socially disadvantaged linguistically and economically in any competition for positions of power and influence in the American Catholic church, and they have continued to be less socially mobile than the other groups. They tended to found their own array of religious and fraternal organizations as well as separate schools, hospitals, orphanages, and cemeteries.

ARAB AMERICANS: MORE CHRISTIAN THAN MUSLIM

In addition to noting the erosion of many historic and formerly cohesive ethno-religious groups, the NSRI also highlighted some surprising facts about the nation's 1.5 million Arab Americans, who are officially considered part of the white population. Our subsample of respondents of Middle Eastern and North African origin was small, as was to be expected, given that the 1990 U.S. Census confirmed that only 1,067,000 Americans, less than four out of every thousand, reported their ancestry as "Arab" or provided a more specific Arab national ethnicity. Nevertheless, the overwhelmingly Christian nature of the NSRI Arab American responses is a consequential finding. It appears that only around 30% of Arab Americans are Muslim, though this may be a slight underestimate since this segment of the population probably contains recent immigrants unable to respond to our survey. Statistics indicate that the majority of Arabs who emigrated to the United States in the hundred-year period ending in 1965 were Christians from Lebanon or Syria, primarily from the Maronite or Syrian and Greek Catholic church traditions. Yet it seems that the newest immigrants from Egypt, Jordan, and Iraq are also disproportionately Christian.

From a sociological perspective we should expect the most Westernized populations from these Arab countries—the urban Christian populations, often educated in French or English, for example—to be most attracted to settle in the United States. Arab Christians, such as the Lebanese Maronites, Egyptian Copts, and Iraqi Chaldeans and Assyrians, have long suffered an identity crisis in the increasingly strife-torn Middle East. Moreover, the past decade has seen the rise of strict forms of Muslim fundamentalism determined to impose Islamic discipline on religious minorities. In September 1991, the *Economist* magazine noted that "Christianity is dying in the land of its birth. Christians are leaving Palestine and Lebanon in such numbers that local churches fear for their future." Though we do not have exact statistics, we believe that a similar pattern exists within the recent Iranian immigration to the United States, so that the religious minorities of Iran, such as Christians, Jews, Baha'i, and agnostics, are strongly represented among the 236,000 Americans of Iranian descent. It stands to reason that few strict believers in the Shiite Muslim faith would want to flee the "cleansed" revolutionary environment of Islamic Iran to dwell in what the Ayatollah Khomeini described as "the Great Satan."

NEW MINORITY GROUPS AND THE CATHOLIC CHURCH

Faced by an increasingly homogenized white population, the main pastoral concern of the American Catholic church in the area of ethnicity is no longer the minority populations. According to a persuasive recent book by Richard Alba, *Ethnic Identity: The Transformation of White America,* we are witnessing "the twilight of ethnicity." In its place a new white group with political overtones, so-called European Americans, can be seen emerging. A socially conservative middle-class grouping known to political pollsters as white Catholics has developed, and, its origins lie in rapid Catholic gains in education and income in recent decades. The net result is a more Americanized population in outlook and behavior and one less accepting of religious authority. The tangible symbol of this change can be seen in working-class ethnic inner-city parishes. These have mostly disappeared, and as a result Catholic churches and parochial schools have been forced to close. Often, as in Detroit and Chicago, this process has generated much local anger and anguish among the parishioners who have remained in the "old neighborhood" and withstood "white flight." Nevertheless, the urban parish priest still tends to concentrate on his traditional area of success, caring for the spiritual and social needs of immigrants and the urban poor, most of whom are not ethnic whites but nonwhites.

This new development has led to curiosity about the ratio of white to nonwhite Catholics and, especially, about the level of minority support for the faith. As we observed earlier, the NSRI indicates that around 20% of American Catholics are minority-group members. Just over 5% are blacks, a figure that is higher than previously supposed and that represents 9% of the total U.S. black population. The rise in the number of black Catholics is probably due to two causes. The first factor is immigration: Large proportions of recent African and Caribbean (particularly Trinidadian and Haitian) immigrants are Catholic. In addition, as we shall discuss at length later, the opportunity for educational success offered to inner-city black residents by the Catholic parochial schools has now begun to pay evangelizing dividends among the families of this new generation of parochial-school children. As early as 1971, a black public-school principal in Detroit told *Newsweek* that "most black people join the Catholic Church so their kids can attend parochial school." The combination of immigration and missionizing has raised the number of black Catholics in New York State to over 500,000, or more than 7% of the total New York Catholic population. Black Catholics remain a significant proportion of the Catholic community in their historical enclaves of Louisiana (15%) and Maryland (13%).

Catholic leaders tend to underestimate their success with the fast-growing Asian American population. Most Filipino and many Vietnamese immigrants are Catholics. The NSRI suggests that currently, more than 2% of America's Catholics are Asian. This might seem a minor detail, but the concentrated geographical distribution of this population means that Asian Americans comprise more than 7% of Californian Catholics, and more than 6% of Catholics in Washington State.

In contrast, the Catholic church tends to *exaggerate* the size and importance of the Hispanic Catholic population; in fact, only two thirds of Hispanics identify as Catholic. Church spokesmen have claimed that up to a quarter of all Catholics are Hispanic, but NSRI figures suggest that only 14% of the people who identify themselves as Catholic are Hispanic. Our figure may well be a slight underestimate because of language barriers and problems associated with polling undocumented aliens. Obviously, Hispanics are an important and growing constituency for the church, but their impact varies geographically. Over half of Catholic Texans and New Mexicans are Hispanic, as are just over one third of Catholic Californians. Hispanics are also a significant component of the Catholic populations of Arizona (30%), Colorado (24%), and Florida (21%). In contrast, they comprise less than 2% of the Catholic populations of Ohio, Minnesota, and Missouri.

The geographical distribution of the minority populations means that Catholic dioceses are very unevenly affected by minority populations and their concerns. Spanish-language services and Spanish-speaking priests are a necessity in some states but a minor consideration in others. The presence of minorities has political ramifications both within and without the Catholic church. Texan and Californian bishops, for whom 60% and 45%, respectively, of their flocks are minority-group members, have different social agendas than midwestern and New England bishops in states such as Ohio, Wisconsin, Minnesota, Missouri, Connecticut, Rhode Island, and New Hampshire, where more than 95% of their parishioners are white. The former pursue basic issues relating to immigration, poverty, welfare, and migrant labor, while the latter are more concerned with social questions such as higher education, aging, homosexuality, and the role of women in the church.

MULTICULTURALISM AND THE CATHOLIC CHURCH

The Catholic church has been cautious about accommodating the new emphasis on ethnic-minority affirmation. Its present policy is largely confined to offering the mass in several languages, providing headset translation for the sermon, or using tambourines, drums, and percussion instruments in addition to the organ and piano. The Catholic church has been at the fulcrum of Western political and cultural history since the time of the Roman emperor Constantine the Great over 1650 years ago. Its very essence, as well as its important role in this country's educational system at primary, secondary, and college levels, make it a prime target for multiculturalists intent on changing traditional educational norms. Moreover, most of the extremists proclaiming a cultural politics of liberation are strident secularists who advocate worldviews that are anathema to Catholic teachings. For its part, the church demonstrates skepticism toward attempts to divide its flock in the interests of "cultural empowerment" and so divert its followers' attention away from the church's own religious agenda.

This does not mean that there have not been clashes. The reevaluation of Christopher Columbus became a major controversy during the 1992 quincentennial commemoration of his voyage. The classic Catholic depiction of Columbus is as a religious hero and agent of divine grace, as he was portrayed in surrealist painter Salvador Dalí's evocative and passionate masterwork *The Discovery of America by Christopher Columbus*. But in May 1990, the liberal National Council of Churches of Christ passed a resolution stating, "For the descendants of the survivors of the subsequent invasion, genocide and slavery

. . . a celebration is not an appropriate observance." Some anti-Colombians, angry over the passing away of "Mother Earth and Native America," even went so far as to declare Columbus's arrival in the New World a major disaster. The attack on a historic figure revered by earlier generations of Americans for his courage, faith, and sense of adventure went beyond the fact that the behavior of the 15th-century sailor and his attitudes toward women, racial minorities, and non-Christians did not meet "politically correct" modern standards. Instead, the anti-Colombians tried to promote consciousness-raising among the Native American and Hispanic American populations. They were more successful with Native Americans than with Hispanics, perhaps because the latter resisted the pigeonholing of those holding to simplistic views of identity in the postmodern world. Hispanics comprise a population in which miscegenation has inextricably blended the conquered and conquerors, the exploited and the exploiters, the victims and the oppressors.

The Catholic church has had problems with black militancy and separatism among a small minority of African Americans. Black Catholics have long been a vital part of southern Catholicism, and historically the church had a good record of forming societies, like the all-black community that the Oblate Sisters of Providence founded in Baltimore in 1829, and providing schooling even before emancipation. Historian Albert Raboteau has suggested that slaves found Catholicism's feast days, incense, relics, and libations "more akin to the spirit of African piety than [was] the sparseness of Puritan America." Yet the church's perceived authoritarianism led to its abandonment by many blacks after emancipation.

The race issue emerged in the early 1970s, when there was a call for black nuns to resign from white parochial schools and to go to predominantly black ones. This was followed by calls for black community control of parochial schools in inner-city areas. The church tried to meet demands for a different style of Catholicism by introducing a new hymnal for black parishioners and establishing a new national office and national newspaper for black Catholics. Nevertheless, most of the clergy and sisters serving black Catholics are white. There are only some 300 black priests among the 57,000 Catholic priests in the country, and only 11 black bishops.

This situation perturbed the Reverend George Stallings, Jr., who created an uproar with his announcement in 1989 that he hoped to create an African American rite within the Catholic church that would include its own liturgy, canon law, and clergy. When his request was rejected by Washington, D.C.'s James Cardinal Hickey, Stallings defected and set up the Imani Temple ("*Imani*" is the Swahili word for faith). In May 1990, he severed allegiance to the authority of the pope and had himself consecrated a bishop by the Old Catholic church.

Excommunicated by the Vatican, he then established an African American Catholic church, which, as of 1992, claimed nearly 4,000 members organized into seven temples in Washington, D.C., Philadelphia, Richmond, Baltimore, New Orleans, and Los Angeles. Stallings now claims that his former church is a racist and Eurocentric yoke around the necks of blacks. He also asserts that Jesus was black and that he and his followers will destroy "every image of a white Jesus we can find." His new church's links to Catholic teaching and tradition were severely eroded when Stallings announced that his church would ordain women and married men and permit divorced and remarried members to receive communion. Such revolutionary changes allow us to predict that his movement will not lead to mass apostasy among the nation's more than 2.5 million black Catholics. Most perceive the new separatism as a betrayal of the black Catholic tradition. Most black Catholics recognize that the Catholic religious approach to race is neither secular nor American. Catholicism's attraction is its internationalism and its claim to be a church for all peoples.

RELIGION IN THE AFRICAN AMERICAN COMMUNITY

The Stallings saga highlights the most significant ethnic factor in American religion: the historical tradition of a separatist and racially aware black church. Numbering nearly 30 million, the African American population is the nation's largest and, historically, its most important minority. Today it comprises almost 12% of the total U.S. population, a decrease from 20% in 1800. We have already described how the experience of slavery and emancipation affected its religious development and how, with other avenues of social expression closed, the church became the most important black community institution. In their classic 1990 work, *The Black Church in the African American Experience,* C. Eric Lincoln and Lawrence H. Mamiya state categorically that "the church is the key to understanding this entire subculture" of black life in America. The church is also the tangible symbol of the black community's presence. During the political struggle for civil rights, in the years 1962–65, at least ninety-three southern black churches were bombed or burned because they led the way in voter registration and racial integration.

National polls about religion have long shown that African Americans are more religious in thought and behavior than other Americans. Recent Gallup polls have reported that 82% of blacks say that religion is very important in their lives, compared with 55% of whites. In 1990, 80% of blacks claimed to be church members, compared with 67% of whites, and 55% of blacks said that they had attended services the previous week, compared with 44% of whites. Moreover, blacks gave a more positive vote of confidence in the church: 71% held it in esteem, compared with 56% of whites. It was no surprise to us, then, when the NSRI showed a lower-than-average refusal rate among blacks (1.2%) on the religious-identification question, and that religious "Nones" and agnostics combined comprised less than 6% of the black population, compared with nearly 9% for whites and just over 19% for Asian Americans.

The general religious profile of blacks is well known, but details about recent changes have been hard to quantify. In the 1940s, it was thought that around two thirds of blacks identified with the Baptist churches and 20% with the various Methodist denominations. The NSRI results provided in Chart 4-2 show that the Baptists have fallen to a bare majority and that the Methodists have been reduced to only half the proportion of a generation ago. The rise of black Catholicism was remarked upon earlier. The other major trend is the rise of Pentecostalism, especially the Church of God in Christ, and the Holiness sects known among African Americans as the

Chart 4-2

Religious Profile of African Americans
(NSRI "Black" Respondents)

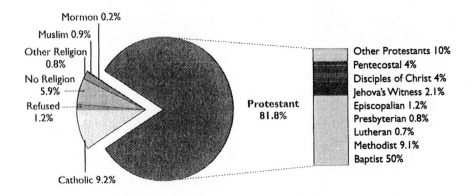

Mormon 0.2%
Muslim 0.9%
Other Religion 0.8%
No Religion 5.9%
Refused 1.2%
Catholic 9.2%
Protestant 81.8%

Other Protestants 10%
Pentecostal 4%
Disciples of Christ 4%
Jehova's Witness 2.1%
Episcopalian 1.2%
Presbyterian 0.8%
Lutheran 0.7%
Methodist 9.1%
Baptist 50%

Sanctified church. Overall, more than 90% of blacks identified as Christians of some kind, and nearly 82% with Protestant denominations.

Skeptics immediately seized upon the NSRI's findings about the relatively high numbers of black Catholics and low numbers of Methodists and, especially, Muslims. We were fortunate, therefore, to be contacted by the College Board, which provided us with evidence confirming our own findings. The College Board, headquartered in New York City, administers the Scholastic Aptitude Tests, the famous SATs, which aspiring college-bound high-school seniors take. In order to monitor the changing nature of the population, the College Board asks voluntary questions regarding the race and religion of those taking the tests. More than 942,000 students took the examination in 1990 in twenty-four states, mostly in the East and the Southwest, including New York, Florida, Texas, and California, where the SATs are the prime means of college entrance selection. Among the students were nearly 93,000 black high-school seniors. Though not a totally representative sample, geographically or, presumably, in terms of social class, these students do include a very large number of young African Americans. The high-school students' religious preferences as compiled by the College Board were remarkably similar to our NSRI results. As one always finds with people of this age, the refusal, or noncooperation, rate (7.2%) was higher than in the general population, as was the percentage in the "No Religion" category (7.2%). If one factors in a 10% upward adjustment to allow for the overall lower student scores for all the religious groups, then the differences between the NSRI and College Board results in the percentage figures for all "Christians" and the aggregate "Protestants," as well as for the Baptist category, are all less than 4 percentage points. Moreover, the discrepancy for Methodists is only 1% and for Catholics only 1.2%. Even more heartening to us was the finding that the two Muslim figures were exceedingly close, since polls tend to be much more inaccurate with small groups, or what we refer to as rare populations, than with much larger segments of the population.

The Baptist faith has attracted a majority of African Americans for a number of reasons. After the Civil War, Baptist ministers in both the North and the South were very enthusiastic about missionizing former slaves. The ministers' preaching placed particular emphasis on freedom and the egalitarian structure of the Baptist congregation, which dispensed with bishops and other hierarchy and assured the latitude in worship and creed that ex-slaves demanded. Some commentators have also noted the appeal of baptism by immersion, linking this rite to African tribal custom. Attempts at interdenominational black church dialogue, such as the National Congress of Black Churches, attest to the importance of baptism. The congress's meetings have reflected deep emotional and theological divisions along the line between the immersing Baptists and the "sprinklers" from Methodist denominations, which divisions have hindered the groups' ability to work together.

Black Baptists began to flock to independent and segregated congregations during the Reconstruction era, a period of particularly bad race relations. These autonomous local churches came together in 1880 and formed the National Baptist Convention. This organization split in 1915, and a further division in 1961 resulted in the present three national bodies: the National Baptist Convention of the U.S.A., the National Baptist Convention of America, and the Progressive National Baptist Convention. Unlike the mainline white denominations or the even more efficient operations of the Church of the Nazarene or the Church of Jesus Christ of the Latter-Day Saints, none of these denominations has a large central headquarters or extensive bureaucracy.

With its 33,000 member congregations, the National Baptist Convention of the U.S.A., headquartered in Nashville, Tennessee, is the largest Baptist grouping and the nation's third-largest Protestant denomination. It supports black colleges, operates a religious publishing house, and sponsors overseas missionary work. Yet it has a tradition of being publicity-shy and socially and politically conservative. This tradition was particularly noticeable during the presidency (1953–82) of Reverend Joseph H. Jackson. The organization's reluctance to engage in nonspiritual issues led to the defection of the social-activist element headed by Dr. Martin Luther King, Jr., and the subsequent formation in 1961 of the Progressive National Baptist Convention. Since then, the National Baptist Convention of the U.S.A. has become a little more outspoken and visible in the National Council of Churches of Christ under the current leadership of the Louisiana minister Dr. Theodore J. Jemison. He has been president since 1982.

Part of the reason for the lack of coordination and cohesion of the black churches is their dearth of resources and their isolation from one another. Most maintain the power to govern, finance, and program at the local level. It is easy to see why there is a lack of infrastructure. Their congregants are mostly working-class or poor people. Furthermore, even into the 1980s the majority of these churches' pastors were functioning without benefit of formal theological education. In *The Black Church in the African American Experience*, C. Eric Lincoln and Lawrence J. Mamiya report that two thirds of the black clergy had no college training, and that more than 80% had not completed seminary degrees. Most have modest incomes, and a sizable minority hold down second jobs. They lack the staff and financial resources to maintain membership files and statistics or long-range programs, and so they deal with their ministry on a day-to-day basis. Such pastors have tended to adhere to a nearly literal interpretation of Scripture, and that makes them (and their congregations) suspicious of any kind of revisionism or new innovations such as female or gay ministers. Generally, there is a strong emphasis on tradition in the black church.

Black churches manage to enroll a high percentage of the people who self-identify with those churches. Recent research by Hart Nelsen of Pennsylvania State University has shown that around 92% of rural African Americans residing in the South belong to a church. Undoubtedly, this more-traditional setting produces strong social pressure to belong. The rate of affiliation is lower in southern cities (81%), lower still in suburbs in both the North and South (70%), and lowest in metropolitan cities outside the South (49%), where the greatest social problems of black America exist.

Since the 1992 riots in Los Angeles, the negative social trends that have affected the African American community to a disproportionate extent since the 1960s have come to haunt the entire nation. Widespread unemployment, eroding family structures (resulting in growing numbers of single-parent families, teenage parents, and impoverished seniors), escalating violence, crime and drug abuse, homelessness, deteriorating health statistics, the AIDS pandemic, and ineffective systems of public education have all hit the inner cities hardest. And in those inner-city neighborhoods, the only strong institution left is the local black church. It is one of the few local sources of hope in the face of a mounting social crisis. Such churches are increasingly called upon to provide day care for the elderly, emergency food distribution, literacy programs, and housing renovation. Yet the local congregation may not be equal to this enormous challenge. On average, it is small, having only 250 members, and is 70% female. Moreover, the NSRI shows that the only significant group of religious "Nones" in the African American population exists among young urban males. This population feels alienated not only from white society and mainstream American culture but also from the black church.

The religious groups that do appeal to inner-city young black males tend to be the extreme varieties of black religious expression associated with black nationalism. This phenomenon can be observed in the career of Hulon Mitchell, Jr., the son of a Pentecostal minister from a small town in Oklahoma. In the 1960s, Mitchell emerged as Hulon Shah, a Black Muslim preacher in Chicago, and later as Father Michel of the Protestant Modern Christian Church in Atlanta. In 1979, he turned up in Miami as Yahweh ben Yahweh, an "Original Jew" with a fervent racial and ostensibly religiously based hatred of white Jews. During his wanderings he had formed the conviction that God and Moses were black and that whites are "the devil, Satan, serpent, and beast." Thanks to donations, proselytizing by followers, and municipal subcontracts, his movement acquired $8 million worth of property holdings and stores before Yahweh was arrested on racketeering charges in 1992 and some of his sect's followers were jailed for murder.

Among the best-known of these black nationalist religious movements is the Lost Found Nation of Islam in the Wilderness of North America, founded in 1933 in Detroit. It was led to prominence in the 1960s by Elijah Muhammad (né Poole), the son of a Baptist minister from Sandersville, Georgia. Its theology involved an unequivocal rejection of white America and its symbols, including Christianity, "slave names," and even foods. It asked the African American community to turn inward and engage in economic nationalism. Its economic accomplishments were dissipated in internal quarrels that often turned violent. The most famous dissension led to the defection of Malcolm X (originally Malcolm Little), who converted to Sunni Islam and was subsequently assassinated. In recent years, the foremost leader of the successor organizations has been Nation of Islam minister Louis Farrakhan. He has placed particular emphasis on antiwhite and anti-Semitic rhetoric in his emotional appeal. On the practical level, his ministry has sought out converts in prisons and among former drug addicts and turned them into a disciplined following, including a substantial bow-tie-and-suit-wearing security organization. Farrakhan's organization has about 30,000 members nationwide, but its influence as role models in the inner city is more widespread, due to the publicity it has received by appearing in Spike Lee films and from rap groups such as Public Enemy.

Undoubtedly, the mainstream black Christian denominations, with their respectable outlook, have been somewhat reluctant to address directly the issues of the underclass. Certainly, they have not put the emphasis on prison mission work that large numbers of incarcerated young black males might suggest. Their limited overtures left a vacuum into which others have moved. Like the Nation of Islam, the Three Percenters, Ahmaddiya, and fringe groups, mainstream Sunni Muslims have also seen prisons as a fertile missionizing area, although most of these prison conversions are temporary.

Still, informal reports suggest that several hundred thousand black prison inmates identify as Muslims. The NSRI results suggest that around 40% of America's 1.5 million Muslims are African Americans. Our figures show that among blacks, only Muslims have a majority of male identifiers and that most of these are young urban dwellers. For different reasons, both our NSRI data and the College Board data in Chart 4-3 probably underreport the number of African American Muslims. The total is probably closer to 2% rather than 1% of the black population. Obviously, our telephone sampling method could not reach prison inmates or youth on the streets. Furthermore, such populations are very unlikely to take the SAT examinations.

Two features of Chart 4-3 are worthy of note. Though the Jehovah's Witnesses have a large body of black adherents, they do not appear among the student population. That is because this sect discourages higher education for its members in the same way that it frowns upon other elements of modern life, such as political involvement and blood transfusions. The Col-

Chart 4-3

Religious Preference of African American
1990 High School Seniors ("Black" Respondents)

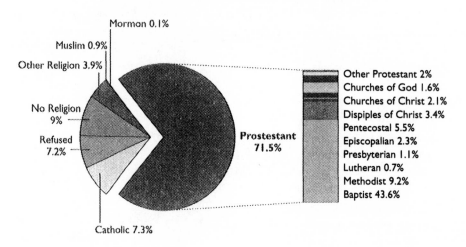

Mormon 0.1%

Muslim 0.9%

Other Religion 3.9%

No Religion 9%

Refused 7.2%

Prostestant 71.5%

Catholic 7.3%

Other Protestant 2%
Churches of God 1.6%
Churches of Christ 2.1%
Dispiples of Christ 3.4%
Pentecostal 5.5%
Episcopalian 2.3%
Presbyterian 1.1%
Lutheran 0.7%
Methodist 9.2%
Baptist 43.6%

lege Board provides a list of religious groups from which to choose, so it is more likely to receive more "other religion" responses from people who cannot find their particular group on the list of seventy or so major religious bodies. This may account for the fact that the largely white midwestern fundamentalist Churches of Christ scored so well among the black students. This denomination was probably mistaken for the black Pentecostal Church of God in Christ, which does not appear on the list. In contrast, all the historic black Methodist denominations are listed by the College Board.

Islam is a patriarchal religion that emphasizes the division of sex roles and female modesty. Its appeal to male black Americans seems to lie in the boost it gives to self-respect. Yet it is also demanding of its followers, with its thrice-daily prayers and abstinence from alcohol. Most of the recent growth in the number of Sunni Muslims is due to the leadership of Wallace Deen Muhammad, the son of Elijah Muhammad. He, not Minister Farrakhan, is the real leader of the vast majority of Muslim blacks. During the 1970s and 1980s, W. D. Muhammad, as he is known, slowly dispensed with the racist rhetoric of his sect's past and led his followers toward orthodox Koranic Islam. This has meant a growing emphasis on classes in Arabic and on the hajj, the pilgrimage to Mecca. The change in outlook is evident in the content of Muhammad's weekly newspaper, *The Muslim Journal,* which supports conservative causes like the free market, hard work, personal responsibility, and family values. It also endorsed George Bush for president in 1988 and supported the 1991 Gulf War. This clearly demonstrates the separation of orthodox Muslim political views from those of the majority of African Americans as well as those held by the leadership of the black churches.

We conclude that African American society incorporates an overtly religious culture and articulates a religious vocabulary. This is because this community continues to clearly express an allegiance to denominations with a traditional theological and social outlook. Yet, the impact is somewhat different from that found among whites with similar religious loyalties.

RELIGION IN THE HISPANIC COMMUNITY

From a religious perspective, the nation's other large minority, the fast-growing 22-million-strong Hispanic or Latino population, stands in stark

Chart 4-4

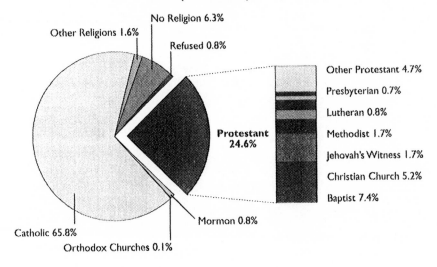

Religious Profile of Hispanic Americans (1990 NSRI)

No Religion 6.3%

Other Religions 1.6%

Refused 0.8%

Other Protestant 4.7%

Presbyterian 0.7%

Lutheran 0.8%

Protestant 24.6%

Methodist 1.7%

Jehovah's Witness 1.7%

Christian Church 5.2%

Baptist 7.4%

Catholic 65.8%

Mormon 0.8%

Orthodox Churches 0.1%

contrast to African Americans. There is no tradition of a separatist or auton-omous Hispanic church. Yet Hispanics' strong family tradition and social con-servatism make them a naturally religious population. Our NSRI results show that exactly two thirds of Hispanics identify as Roman Catholics and 23% as Protestants. Only 4% of Hispanics are adherents of non-Christian religions, and only 6% are of no religion. The movement toward Protestantism, mostly to fundamentalist, Pentecostal, and charismatic sects, has been quite recent, and is surprising given the virtual assimilation of Catholicism into Hispanic culture. Charts 4-5—4-7 provide the religious profiles for high-school students for the three main subgroups among the Hispanic population. Charts 4-5 and 4-6 show that Protestantism has grown most among the Puerto Rican and Central American subgroups. In contrast, Protestantism has made few inroads among Mexican Americans, except in Texas (Chart 4-7). The conservative Catholic nature of the Mexican American approach to religion can be seen in the approach of the theologian Virgil Elizondo, who suggests that in multi-cultural settings it is important to stress that "Christianity breaks down the barriers of separation" and unites the faith community.

The major challenge for the Catholic church has been the low level of prac-tice among Hispanic Catholics. According to Roberto Gonzalez and Michael

Chart 4-5

Religious Preference of Puerto Rican Origin 1990 High School Seniors

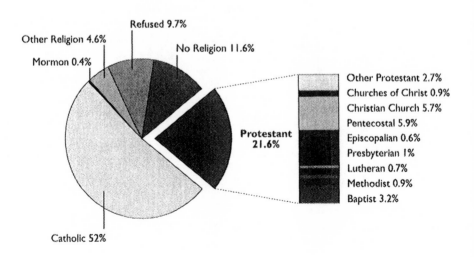

Other Religion 4.6%
Mormon 0.4%
Refused 9.7%
No Religion 11.6%

Protestant 21.6%

Other Protestant 2.7%
Churches of Christ 0.9%
Christian Church 5.7%
Pentecostal 5.9%
Episcopalian 0.6%
Presbyterian 1%
Lutheran 0.7%
Methodist 0.9%
Baptist 3.2%

Catholic 52%

Chart 4-6

Religious Preference of Latin American Origin High School Seniors

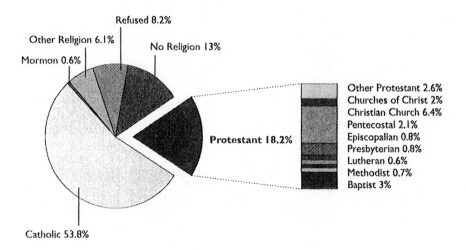

LaVelle in their book *The Hispanic Catholic in the U.S.*, only 23% of Hispanic Catholics are practicing. It was probably this concern that prompted the Vatican to place three cities with significant Hispanic populations—Miami, San Antonio, and Los Angeles—on the itinerary of Pope John Paul II's second visit to the United States in 1987. The church has probably overestimated the ease with which Hispanics would be assimilated into North American Catholicism. The Latin American Catholic church has been much less affected by Vatican II and is now very different from its U.S. counterpart; as a result, the U.S. Catholic church feels foreign to many immigrants. This feeling of estrangement has been reinforced by a shortage of Hispanic priests, who comprise only 4% of the national total of priests, whereas Hispanic Catholic believers are 14% of all U.S. Catholics. The church's rigorous entrance examinations and long preparation time are undoubtedly barriers to entry into the priesthood for low-income Hispanics. In contrast, Protestant denominations place less stress on academic requirements and more emphasis on spiritual anointing. Consequently, about three times as many Hispanics are enrolled in Protestant seminaries and schools of theology as in Catholic seminaries.

The lack of Hispanic Catholic personnel forms the main obstacle to the U.S.

Chart 4-7

Religious Preference of Mexican
Origin 1990 High School Seniors

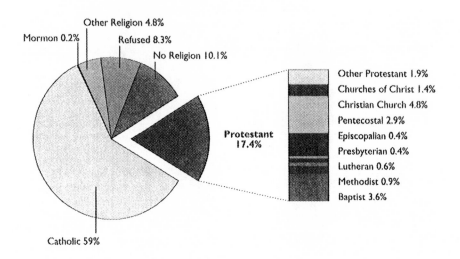

Other Religion 4.8%

Mormon 0.2%   Refused 8.3%

No Religion 10.1%

Other Protestant 1.9%
Churches of Christ 1.4%
Christian Church 4.8%
Pentecostal 2.9%
Protestant 17.4%   Episcopalian 0.4%
Presbyterian 0.4%
Lutheran 0.6%
Methodist 0.9%
Baptist 3.6%

Catholic 59%

Catholic church's National Pastoral Plan for Hispanic Ministry, a strategy aimed at making parish life more intimate and inviting to American Hispanics. Moreover, the rise of a new Hispanic Protestant clergy has caused tensions between Catholics and evangelicals, as the former accuse the latter of poaching souls. A sociological analysis suggests that Protestant success with Hispanics is largely due to the upheaval of the immigration process itself. The image of a technologically advanced, prosperous America that beckons the Latin American villager is also that of a *Protestant* America. Many Hispanic immigrants have been pre-evangelized in Latin America, which is experiencing a Protestant explosion of its own. Once in the United States, many nominally Catholic immigrants find they are in a milieu of change: new neighborhood, new language, new jobs—all of which, along with fear and anxiety, lead them either to question their traditional religious beliefs or to be open to new ones. The evangelical churches stress intimacy on both the divine and human levels—a personal relationship with God and the fellowship of believers. The unrestricted freedom provided by the tradition of congregational autonomy to preach and pray in a style true to their cultural background is another feature of Protestantism that Hispanics find appealing.

Studies in the 1980s by the National Opinion Research Center (NORC), as well as the information provided by David Martin in his book *Tongues of Fire: The Explosion of Protestantism in Latin America,* claimed a strong correlation between Protestantism and the rise of a new Hispanic middle class that sees itself becoming respectable and responsible members of American society. We tested this hypothesis with our NSRI data and found no supportive evidence among our large sample of 4,867 Hispanic respondents. In fact, there were no statistically significant social-class differences evident between Catholics and Protestants. They both exhibited almost the same household-income profiles and exactly the same patterns in the distribution of their educational attainment. Since Protestantism has advanced most among the longer-established Puerto Rican population and the newer and poorer Central American immigrants, we believe that our NSRI finding—that Protestants are just average Hispanics—makes sense in the 1990s. It may well be that over time the Protestant adherents will become socially mobile. However, we should caution against the belief that "Protestant" equals "middle-class," since among the white non-Hispanic population, as will be shown in a later chapter, Catholics have a higher socioeconomic status than the members of the Baptist, Pentecostal, and other evangelical and fundamentalist denominations that are currently making inroads among Hispanics.

Undoubtedly we should expect the Protestantization trend among Hispanic Americans to continue, especially as a new generation of American-born English-speaking Hispanics emerges. It is also likely that white, or "Anglo," Protestant churches will begin to attract this younger population, who are receptive to more lenient views of gender, sexual, and economic equality than are the members of the immigrant churches.

The Mexican tradition of freewheeling religiosity, which includes devotions and altars in the home for patron saints, arose in priest-poor rural areas. However, such features do not pose unusual difficulty for the Catholic church. In contrast, Caribbean Hispanics have a religious tradition that is more controversial. Their tradition has a syncretic, that is, mixed flavor that includes elements of the sacred drawn from pre-Christian and non-Western sources, with strong African ingredients. While voodoo as practiced in the United States has had a Catholic overlay, this veneer is dissipating. Voodoo features elaborate initiation rituals, ritual meals, and a clergy of men and women who combine the skills of priest, social worker, herbalist, and psychotherapist. Yet it is still a secret cult, and few adherents openly admit their membership. Instead, they pass as Catholics.

Santeria (the name derives from the Spanish *"santero,"* a seller of religious images), a secretive folk religion often linked with voodoo, probably has several hundred thousand followers across the country, approximately 70,000 of them around Miami. No longer confined to black Hispanics, Santeria began when slaves gave the names of saints to African gods in order to hide vestiges of their tribal religions, which had been banned by their Spanish Catholic masters. The image of the Virgin of Caridad del Cobre, the patron saint of Cuba, for instance, can be found on altars in many homes and businesses, draped in a golden cape with yellow candles burning at her feet. She is actually a symbol of Oshun, the goddess of love in Santeria. She rules romance, rivers, money, the color yellow, and sweet desserts. The first open Santeria congregation, the Church of Lukumi Bubalu Aye, was established in Hialeah, Florida, which is 90% Hispanic and known locally as the "northernmost city in Latin America." In 1987, the Haileah city council banned animal sacrifice, a central ceremonial role in Santeria, when the church announced its intention to sacrifice chickens, doves, pigeons, sheep, and turtles. The church sued the city on the grounds that the ban violated their First Amendment right to free exercise of religion. The case went to the U.S. Supreme Court in 1992 after a federal district judge ruled that the ban was directed at "conduct" rather than "belief." In June, 1993, the Supreme Court ruled in favor of the *Santeros*. However, even before a final decision, controversy over Santeria sacrifices figured in a bitter local election in 1991, when one candidate accused another of being a *santero,* that is, a Santeria priest. Then supporters of rival candidates began receiving cow's tongues at their office doors and fish heads in their mailboxes. A severed and muzzled goat's head was discovered in the police-department parking lot. Animal sacrifice became a potent symbol for non-Hispanics angry over continued Hispanic immigration and a source of embarrassment to many Hispanic Americans. To others, the opposition complaints were seen as racial prejudice. Most Santeria devotees claim that they also venerate Jesus, and they deny any links to human sacrifice (sacrificial-style killings by drug runners in northern Mexico in 1989 were said to be Santeria-inspired). Catholic church teachings cannot accommodate animal sacrifices and their attendant gore and rituals, nor the belief in spirit possessions also associated with Santeria.

The growing Hispanic population is seen as an attractive market for evangelizers. This competitive situation has provoked the Catholic church to undertake a concerted defensive strategy aimed at maintaining its cultural dominance among Hispanic communities. This dynamic is a prime example of the social and religious reality all religious bodies have to acknowledge: There are no guaranteed religious monopolies in the United States.

THE RETURN TO TRIBAL ROOTS AMONG NATIVE AMERICANS

The Native American population, numbering 1.8 million people according to the 1990 U.S. census race question, is also believed to be re-embracing its

Chart 4-8

Religious Preference of "American Indian" 1990 High School Seniors

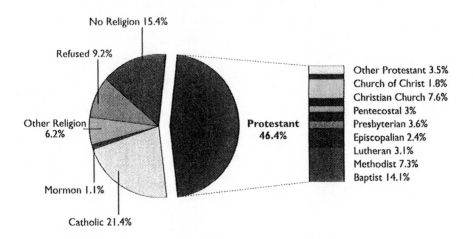

No Religion 15.4%

Refused 9.2%

Other Religion
6.2%

Mormon 1.1%

Catholic 21.4%

Protestant
46.4%

Other Protestant 3.5%
Church of Christ 1.8%
Christian Church 7.6%
Pentecostal 3%
Presbyterian 3.6%
Episcopalian 2.4%
Lutheran 3.1%
Methodist 7.3%
Baptist 14.1%

ancestral tribal religions. Although the NSRI did not deal specifically with Native Americans some respondents stated "Native American" or "Indian" as their religious identity. These results suggest that around 47,000 American adults maintain such beliefs.

The best source available for the Native American religious profile is the College Board statistics presented in Chart 4-8. These figures show that in terms of religious identification, Native Americans resemble white Americans more than they do any other minority group: 21% are Catholic, and nearly half identify with other Christian denominations. Nevertheless, 28% of these young Native Americans identified with no religion or some undefined religion, or refused to answer. This is a comparatively large proportion, even for a teenage population. This trend toward irreligion, however, makes these youths typical westerners.

The real problem with our high-school sample may be one of definition as to who *is* a Native American. Claims to native heritage have already begun to complicate the lives of college-entrance and affirmative-action officers. Moreover, the tribes themselves vary in their rules about the amount of native blood they require for membership. The Navaho demand one fourth,

but other tribes, especially in the East, will recognize people who are one
sixteenth Native American.

For U.S. Census purposes, a Native American is anyone who claims to be
one. The result between 1980 and 1990 was a 38% increase in the official
Native American population. In Alabama, the number rose by 118%; in
New Jersey, by 78%. In addition, more than 7 million white Americans
report a tribal ancestry in answer to the ancestry question of the census form.
The Census Bureau terms such people "Wannabes." It is now more socially
acceptable to be a Native American, and many whites no longer hide their
native origins. Films like *Dances with Wolves* have surely advanced this trend.
What, then, is the importance of this to American religion? The significance
of the trend lies in the rapidly growing number of Americans who identify
with native cultures.

The relatively high proportion of Catholics among Native Americans
might be seen as surprising, given that the largest state of Native American
residence is Oklahoma, whose Catholic population is only 8%. And yet,
during the 19th century, the Catholic church was the most active in missionizing among the Plains and southwestern tribes, such as the Choctaw,
Sioux, Blackfeet, Flatheads, Navaho, Hopi, and Apache, as well as among
the tribes in California. From 1819 on, the annual congressional appropri-
ation for Indian education and agriculture directly funded mission schools,
hospitals, and orphanages. In fact, it was not until well into this century that
U.S. government aid to mission schools ended, but by then Catholicism was
well rooted among many tribes.

During the late 1980s, the Catholic church appointed two new Native
American bishops. The church attempted to accommodate traditional native
ways in response to pressure from the Native American Catholic organization, the Tekakwitha Conference. In Native American congregations, peace
pipes are now passed during the mass as a sign of reconciliation, and church
walls are decorated with murals depicting ancestral spirits. A new assertiveness led some Native Americans to protest when the Spanish missionary
pioneer Junípero Serra was proposed for canonization; they charged that he
had been guilty of "extreme brutality."

The Protestant denominations, such as the Baptists, Methodists, and
Churches of Christ, have placed much more emphasis on their traditional
temperance work among Native Americans since alcohol abuse has been a
serious problem on the reservations.

In general, the success of Christianity among the Native American population is impressive given the problems that hindered missionary work: the
linguistic and religious diversity, geographical spread, and high mobility of
the tribes.

Undoubtedly, part of the European hostility to this continent's prior inhabitants was rooted in religious attitudes. Whites made negative judgments about Native American spirituality. They asserted that the natives either had no religion or were slaves to superstition. Unquestionably, the Algonquian and Iroquois tribes, whom the whites first encountered in the East, had a sincere belief in witchcraft; they thought that suffering and misfortune were caused by spirits invoked for destructive ends by evil-intentioned persons. Associating colonization's terrible effects, especially catastrophic epidemics, with white settlers, the natives believed that Christians practiced witchcraft against them. In turn, the settlers believed that the native shamans, the so-called medicine men, were sorcerers and that their religious practices were forms of devil worship. Modern ethno-history has revealed the pervasive power of Native American religion in shaping the tribes' response to contact with whites. The primary documents on native uprisings are full of references to creator gods, prophets, magic, and settlers' charges of primitive "fanaticism." From a historical perspective, the encounter between Native Americans and Europeans seems to have been a clash of almost irreconcilable cultures in which differing religious outlooks played a significant role.

The popular influence of Native American spirituality and philosophy, which relates to its harmony with many New Age ideas, began in the 1960s. Indian tribal religions varied, but they provided an enticing menu for flower children. One of the first native rituals to attract wide attention was the Navaho "chant," a ceremony that lasts several days and nights, requiring many people for its execution. The chant is designed to reorder one's relationship with the powers of creation. Ritual drumming and the "talking stick" have also attracted imitation. Recently, the appeal of Native American religion has become increasingly associated with concerns about the degradation of this country's natural environment. This is not a new sentiment. The 18th-century rationalist philosopher Jean-Jacques Rousseau represented the aboriginal American as "the noble savage"—a picture of man before the fall into corrupting civilization.

Historically, most tribal religions held that time was cyclical rather than chronological; earthly events were interpreted through a template of sacred stories. Traditional initiation ceremonies involved withdrawal to the woods, fasting, consuming purifying beverages, and dancing as part of an overall ritual of cleansing and world renewal. (Recently, these rituals have been blended with mysticism to form the underpinning for the new men's movement led by Robert Bly, which has attracted wide publicity for its attempt to recover pride in masculinity.) These religious features demonstrate a collective relationship to nature; a key Native American belief is that the land and many animals—especially the bald eagle—are sacred.

Above all, the tribal prophecies about the disappearance of the buffalo and other ecological disasters seem to resonate today. This has, however, led to some fanciful developments. Some in the "green lobby" have made much of Chief Seattle's 1854 allegedly visionary speech on environmental problems, which is said to have claimed, "We are part of the Earth and it is part of us." This text has appeared in children's books and Earth Day mailings. In reality, Chief Seattle was a baptized Roman Catholic, and his original speech mentioned nothing about whites ravaging the environment. The distortion of the historical record was revealed in an exposé in the *New York Times* in April 1992. Most of Chief Seattle's "speech" appears to have been based on a 1971 script for an ecology film that ran on network television and was produced, as it happened, by the Southern Baptist Radio and Television Commission.

Nevertheless, such thinking relates to a contrast that is often drawn between the attitude of the Judeo-Christian tradition to the natural environment and that of the Native Indian religion. That Genesis 1:28–29 states that mankind is given "dominion" over the planet's fauna and flora is regarded by the book's detractors as the cause of Western civilization's supposedly aggressive insensitivity to nature and ecological concerns. These critics tend to ignore the counterargument: that the Bible also teaches man stewardship and to be a partner in the ongoing work of creation, and that it incorporates positive ecological laws, like those against the destruction of trees and for leaving fields fallow.

This primacy-of-nature attitude echoes deep within the majority of Americans, for nature worship bares some resemblance to Hellenistic and Celtic druidic worship and other pagan pre-Christian European beliefs. The Judeo-Christian tradition itself replaced the pagan view that regarded creation as the product of mythical struggles between gods. In this primordial thinking, nature is infused with the power of the divine, and the gods are personifications of the forces of nature. People are dwarfed by nature and submissive to its power in the pagan view, and in order to seek harmony with it they worship idols, animals, trees, the earth, the sun, and the moon. The current ecological view—that the well-being of our planet, the biosphere, is the supreme ethical concern and that human claims to a unique status are arrogant, unfounded, and absurd—is the stepchild of pagan thinking, and irreconcilable with monotheism. American mainstream religions maintain that human beings are not just organisms. Monotheists dignify and empower humanity, and in this theistic world view, people bow in submission only to a transcendent Creator. This essentially theological debate pits those who espouse a pagan view against followers of the three Abrahamic faiths—Christianity, Judaism, and Islam.

DIVERSITY OF ASIAN AMERICAN
RELIGIOUS AFFILIATION

The nation's Asian-origin population exploded during the 1980s. The total doubled to more than 7.2 million, or 2.9% of the U.S. population, by 1990. The countries of origin of this burgeoning minority also diversified while their numbers grew. In 1960, half of all Asian Americans were Japanese, but by 1990 the Japanese accounted for only 12% of the total. Today, the largest groups are the Chinese, with 23% and the Filipinos, with 19%. Koreans and East Indians, each with 11%, now approach the Japanese in numbers. We thus have a varied and fast-changing population, in which many of the newcomers have little cultural connection to earlier Asian immigrants.

Because they come from across the Pacific, Asian immigrants tend to settle in the West: 35% of Asian Americans, some 2.4 million, live in California; 9% live in Hawaii. In the East, the largest number of Asian Americans live in New York State, with 9% of the national total. Given their diverse origins and western settlement pattern, we would expect of Asian Americans a more diverse pattern of religious identification than that of other racial groups. Charts 4-9 and 4-10 show that this is indeed the case. It seems that around half are Christian, which may surprise those who would expect far fewer Asian American Christians. Here we must once again emphasize the self-selection process of American immigration. People decide to immigrate who find American society compatible with their life-style and aspirations. This automatically creates a Christian bias among immigrants, since the baptized elements of Asian societies and those who attended Christian mission schools tend to be the most Westernized. It also appears that one in four or five Asian Americans is Catholic. Again, this should not surprise us, as many Filipinos, as well as many among the ethnic Chinese and Vietnamese communities who fled from persecution in Communist Vietnam, are Catholic.

The Catholic component of the Asian population is not as noteworthy as the high level of Protestantism. Between one in three and one in four Asian Americans identifies with a Protestant denomination. The most well re-searched group for understanding this social phenomenon is the ambitious and commercially successful Korean community, which has founded over 2,000 local churches. Around half of Koreans are Presbyterian, but the community also supports 500 Southern Baptist and 250 United Methodist churches. Though over 90% of Koreans entered this country after 1965, the first recorded group arrived in Hawaii in 1902. They had been encouraged to emigrate by missionaries, and most had converted before or soon after their arrival. This pattern persists. Recent surveys in Korea reveal that 24% of the population is Buddhist, and 21% is Christian. However, surveys among Korean immigrants in Los Angeles and Chicago conducted by Won

Chart 4-9

Religious Profile of Asian Americans
(NSRI "Other Race" Respondents)

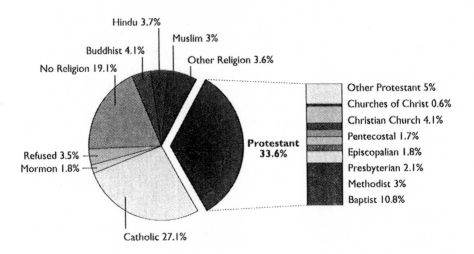

Moo Hurh and Kwang Chung Kim have shown that whereas over 70% are actually affiliated with a Christian denomination, only 3% said that they were Buddhists. Indeed, Korean Americans are seriously religious. Church participation, incorporating frequent prayer meetings and tithing, was found to be a way of life for most immigrants regardless of age, sex, education, or length of residence, with over 80% of affiliates attending weekly worship services. With their emphasis on hard work, a respectable middle-class life-style, and attention to their children's educational accomplishments, they are modern exemplars of the Protestant ethic. They are also generally more conservative and evangelistic than their non-Korean counterparts in the mainline denominations.

Christianity grew in Korea as a nationalist reaction to Chinese and Japanese cultural pressures. Receptivity to Christianity rose after the country became a Japanese colony in 1900. In his book *Early Buddhism and Christianity in Korea,* James Huntley Grayson wrote, "Patriotism and Protestantism became linked in the Conspiracy Trials of 1912, the Independence Movement of 1919, and Protestant resistance to worship at Shinto shrines." There is some continuity with this tradition in contemporary America. The Korean

Chart 4-10

Religious Preference of Asian American
1990 High School Seniors

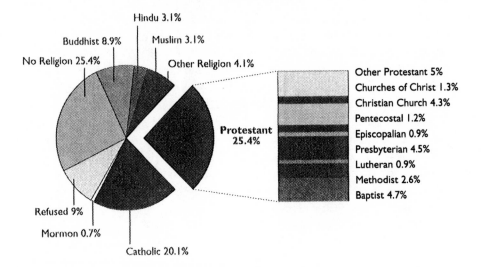

Hindu 3.1%

Buddhist 8.9%   Muslim 3.1%

No Religion 25.4%

Other Religion 4.1%

Protestant
25.4%

Other Protestant 5%

Churches of Christ 1.3%

Christian Church 4.3%

Pentecostal 1.2%

Episcopalian 0.9%

Presbyterian 4.5%

Lutheran 0.9%

Methodist 2.6%

Baptist 4.7%

Refused 9%

Mormon 0.7%

Catholic 20.1%

ethnic church provides the religious and ethnic fellowship that many immigrants crave. Additionally, it attempts to keep Korean nationalism alive. Therefore, most Korean churches also teach their American-born congregants the Korean language, history, and culture alongside their religious curriculum.

The Korean church is the heart of the community, and church leaders are community leaders and channels of communication. Undoubtedly this social organizational structure provides the ethnic cohesion that has supported remarkably rapid economic success. Yet it operates in nonpolitical and noneconomic areas, too. When a scientific research group at Philadelphia's Fox Chase Cancer Center wanted to introduce a program of serological testing for hepatitis-B virus in 1982, the local church leaders and Korean doctors were able to provide 2,300 individuals from eighteen churches for screening.

The Korean experience is not unique among Asians. There are also many Chinese immigrant or ethnic churches. These, too, are a focus for Chinese cultural identity, and they act as a social and psychological bridge facilitating personal adjustment and identification to America. These churches have many new converts, and thus membership in them involves exposure to a new belief system and a new worldview for many immigrants. Doubtless, these churches' appeal goes beyond purely religious motivations. For some newcomers, the church fills the social gap created by the absence of extended family, while others attend the churches for the express purpose of learning English. This demonstrates the social emphasis in the Asian American communities on adjusting to the present rather than on maintaining continuity with the past. Asian Americans, who suffered considerable discrimination and hostility only a few decades ago, are now regarded as a model minority. They are certainly the most successful minority in terms of income, educational attainment, and residential integration. The outstanding achievements of their young people in scientific subjects and mathematics within the nation's troubled public-school system demonstrate the positive effects that secure home and family lives can have. The mix of ethnic cohesion, firm family ties, and strong world-affirming religious behavior seems to mirror the Jewish community's successful formula earlier this century. Jews also concentrated on educational investment for escaping poverty and overcoming prejudice and, thereby, achieving the American dream.

And yet, a balanced assessment of the NSRI and College Board data in Charts 4-9 and 4-10 suggests that Asian Americans are characterized by a high proportion of religious "Nones." This is not surprising in view of the cultural history of the majority of Asian Americans. East Asia has never been a center of religious enthusiasm on the level of West Asia—the birthplace of Judaism, Christianity, Islam, Hinduism, Buddhism, Bahaism, and Sikhism. Furthermore, younger Asian Americans are particularly well educated, especially in scientific subjects, and high levels of education among young middle-class adults are associated with irreligion in present-day America. We noted earlier that the country's most Asian city, San Francisco, was also its most irreligious. Again, the Asian American pattern follows that of the well-educated Jewish community (as we also mentioned earlier, the Jewish American community has the highest proportion of irreligious and secular members of any white ethnic group). It is also worth noting that the Asian American proportion of religious "Nones," at around one in five, is just above the general level for the western states where most of them reside, further evidence of their fast integration into the mainstream of society.

Another influence for lower levels of religious identification among Asian Americans could be the nature of Eastern religions themselves. The 19th-century French sociologist Emile Durkheim cited Buddhism to bolster his claim that gods or spirits are not essential to religion, since Buddhism has no meaningful gods or spirits. Although many would disagree with Durkheim's thesis that Buddhism is an "atheistic religion," it is certainly the case that Buddhism is not oriented toward the supernatural or divinity. Data show that Buddhism attracts less than 9% of Asian Americans and so is much weaker than might have been expected. It appears that in American society many former Buddhist adherents are lost to Christianity, atheism, and secular humanism.

The number of Asian Americans who identify with Islam or Hinduism is also unexpectedly low. The NSRI figures suggest that neither religion seems to have much more than 3% of the Asian American total. Most South Asian immigrants, of course, are not drawn from the ranks of the deeply religious rural masses of the Indian subcontinent. Most are well-educated, scientifically-trained professionals with a modern Western or secularized outlook, and they are also well dispersed around the country, so it is difficult to establish a mass of adherents. As a result, most of the 450,000 American Hindus tend to worship and perform their rituals at gatherings in home settings. The common language is often English, and the texts and the ritual patterns are those identified with ecumenical Hinduism and the All-India Sanskrit tradition. When temples *are* established, the community tends to split into regional and sectarian groups. This situation makes difficult the religious socialization of the younger generation from Hindu families, particularly because they are well educated, English-speaking, and reasonably well integrated into American suburban society.

The NSRI numbers have proven hard for religious elders to accept. We received complaints from both the Sikh and Baha'i communities that they had been undercounted. Unfortunately, we did not provide separate Sikh figures in our interim report. A reassessment of the "miscellaneous" replies showed that we had 8 Sikh respondents, which suggests a population of, at most, around 30,000. However, we received letters from Sikh organizations containing extravagant claims of ten times that number. In reply we explained that according to the 1990 U.S. Census, the total population of East Indian origin was less than 1 million, and we suggested that it was very unlikely that one third of these were Sikhs, since that religion accounted for less than 2% of India's native population.

The Sikhs, as our encounter with them may suggest, are very assertive, and they have gallantly attempted to establish a vibrant community structure in cities, such as Houston, where they have concentrated. They also hold a colorful annual parade in New York City that features floats and men in traditional robes and turbans. Nevertheless, the NSRI and College Board data have a clear message, and that is that Eastern religions face a very arduous task simply maintaining the loyalty of their traditional Asian adherents in America.

EASTERN RELIGIONS IN THE UNITED STATES

An assessment of Eastern religions outlines the difference between visibility and actual statistics. Undoubtedly, Eastern religions have established a beachhead in American culture, not just through immigration but also through the conversion of many white Americans, especially in California. This pattern of growth accelerated once the 1965 Immigration Act allowed the entry of more Asians, especially religious teachers. As American society has become more tolerant of difference in general, it has become more accepting of religious difference and innovation. This has assisted the Eastern religions and all the esoteric philosophies that float on the margins of society. New Thought metaphysical churches, Spiritualism, and new religious movements such as Scientology and Eckankar are similar to Eastern religions in some ways. The major difference between Eastern and Western religions is that the latter are revelatory, centering upon a specific revelation of divine truth. In contrast, Eastern religions invite people to participate in a common search for spiritual truth guided by a teacher—the proverbial guru. In the West, revelation is cognitive, known, and demands conformity. In Eastern religions such as Hinduism and Buddhism, truth is known as it is experienced, and the adherent continually strives to approach it more closely. This approach provides ample opportunity for charismatic leadership, and the 1960s and 1970s saw American youth migrating to ashrams in India to follow one or another of the now largely discredited gurus like the Bhagwan Shree Rajneesh and Swami Nityananda. Still, subtle Hindu ideas like "self-realization" find their way into mainstream America via the health and vegetarian movement, the New Age movement, and the ecumenical movement. Tens of thousands of middle-class white Americans have passed through the International Society for Krishna Consciousness, better known as Hare Krishna, since it arrived in this country in 1966. It is an authoritarian and conservative movement, structured on a four-caste system, emphasizing religious enthusiasm. Members assume Hindu customs and dress, and are often seen in public places with shaven heads, chanting and soliciting contributions or selling publications. The chanting is held to purify the believer, who is banned from gambling, alcohol, eating meat, and engaging in out-of-wedlock sex.

Buddhism has been relatively successful in attracting American-born lifetime converts. Yet Buddhism is a very diverse pluralistic religion with many different ethnic variations and branches of the faith. There are Theravadins from Southeast Asia, Zen Buddhists from China, Korea, Japan, and Vietnam, Vajrayana Buddhists from Tibet and Mongolia, and the authoritarian and separatist Nichiren Shoshsu Soka Gakkai from Japan. The last group, which claims to work miracles in people's lives, such as curing their diseases and finding them better jobs, has attracted many Americans seeking success, including entertainers Tina Turner and Herbie Hancock.

In 1988, an American Buddhist Congress in Los Angeles, seeking a unified voice on religious and social issues, included representatives from forty-seven separate organizations. American Buddhism tends to be a do-it-yourself religion that plays down a strong role for the traditional hierarchy of celibate Buddhist monks, who lead austere lives. Instead, Americans have created a largely lay-centered, democratic faith more amenable to feminists. Yet without the social controls provided by the protective cloak of monasticism and the accompanying cultural traditions, the future of Buddhism in America may be troubled. Certainly, there were setbacks in the 1980s due to scandals involving alcoholism, financial abuses, and casual sexual relations between teachers and acolytes in Buddhist communities across America.

The popularity of meditation has been associated with Zen Buddhism, but only about 20% of America's Zen centers are actually headed by Asians. Nevertheless, the only contemporary Buddhist teacher who claims to be the living Buddha is the Taiwanese Grandmaster Lu. Currently residing in Seattle, he has a devoted following of tens of thousands of ethnic Chinese Buddhists around the Pacific Rim, from Hong Kong to Vancouver, who believe his claims to read minds, perform miraculous healing, and give good fortune, prosperity, and ensure happy marriages.

Surely the Eastern religions have prepared the ground for New Age and Gnostic ideas to flourish in contemporary American culture. An inevitable friendship has developed between the New Age followers and the adherents of smaller pre-Christian European religious traditions, the neopagans and the Wiccans, or witches. Defining the New Age by clear-cut teachings is problematic. New Age ideas grew out of Theosophy, which is the teachings of a movement devoted to mystical speculation about the origins of the universe derived from Hindu and Buddhist ideas, and the counterculture of the 1960s. Such ideas were "swirling through the culture," the popular media, education, and even business during the 1980s, according to Richard John Neuhaus, who also claims that there are "a lot of people in the Christian category that flirt with New Age and other esoterica." This syncretic quality, which enables the New Age and new religious movements to incorporate elements from diverse religious traditions, probably accounts for their low number of hard-core partisan adherents in our survey.

Facing what Peter Berger has called "the crisis of modernity," New Age devotees, mainly young, well-educated single adults, seek spiritual renewal in Third World, pre-enlightenment thought that takes seriously the supernatural and the paranormal. These beliefs have in common an appeal to "lost truths," "ancient wisdom," and spiritual practices derived from the non-Western world. Certainly these beliefs are non-Christian, since they emphasize processes rather than goals. New Age thought features "transformation of the self" through spiritual evolution and harmonization of the individual with the flow of the "Ultimate," rather than a goal such as salvation through approval and acceptance of a deity. The list of New Age, New Thought, and New Alternative philosophies, as the publishers categorize them in a large inventory of self-help books, takes in a vast and eclectic range of beliefs and practices, including nature religion, Satanism and the occult, psychic phenomena and clairvoyance, alchemy, astrology, the channeling of spiritual energy, faith healing, yoga, fire walking, crystals, holistic health, "brain machines," the Gaia theory, which asserts that the earth acts with a sense of purpose in maintaining its functions, as well as out-of-body experiences and UFO abductions.

THE NEW AGE MOVEMENTS

Though New Age belief is not so much a religion as a creedless philosophy, it can be envisaged as part of the larger societal 1980s trend toward individualism, narcissism, withdrawal, and self-absorption. Such criticism is close to the traditional European censure of Eastern religion, which, it has been claimed, leads to political and social apathy because it tends to tranquilize the populace. Another criticism of New Age belief is that it makes such a fad of physical and mental health that it tends to view disabled people as having a "bad karma" from a past life. Despite such critiques, some mainstream groups have made accommodations to it. Goddess religions, which revere matriarchy and regard the Earth as a goddess, are increasingly important in some feminist circles. The Unitarian Universalists have welcomed organized groups, or covens, of such goddess worshipers from the modern pagan movement. Wicca priestesses have been accepted into Unitarian seminaries and gained academic credibility as a result. In 1989, William F. Schultz, the president of the Unitarian Universalist Association, stated that compatibility with pagans "fits very neatly with our tradition. . . . For us, a religion grounded in nature is part and parcel of our heritage. . . . We have gone too far on this side of rationalism." The Christian *New Generation Press,* which publishes on ecology and spirituality, launched projects in an attempt to provide a "biblical rooting of new age spirituality . . . so that Christians can adopt a more sacred understanding of spiritually distant social currents." Matthew Fox, who had been a priest in the Dominican order for a quarter of a century, has developed the idea of "creation spirituality," which links Eastern mysticism with Christianity in a New Age–style view of the sacredness of nature. And a group at the Reconstructionist Rabbinical College was reported to have organized a New Age *havurah* (that is, prayer group), where these rabbinical students "in experiencing their own Judaism . . . use breath, dance and music to feel as proof of their energy within some sense of God's presence." Of course in this climate we should expect neo-paganism to take the opportunity to reclaim some of the popular celebrations that Christianity appropriated. A good example is Halloween, originally Samhain Eve, the Celtic New Year, a day when the Druids believe the walls between the worlds are thinnest and thoughts turn to ancestors on the other side.

Today, our religious organizations are in competition for followers, and, as we have seen, some are willing to adapt their offerings to the fashions of the time or the cultural needs of potential congregants. Minority groups are seen by many denominations as the fastest-growing and most-likely source of new members. Thus "ethnic inclusiveness" is not just a fashionable and worthy idea but a marketing device. Still, it is the liberal mainstream denominations, which discuss the matter most, that pass the resolutions that appear to be losing in the marketplace. In 1988, the United Methodist church, which has numerical goals for minorities in its leadership, reported that it had lost more than 140,000 black members since the racially segregated central jurisdiction of the denomination was abolished in 1968.

Indeed, conservative denominations, such as the Mennonites, Southern Baptists, and Mormons, which place much less emphasis on social integration as a means of promoting harmony among people of diverse backgrounds, have launched successful recruitment drives among minorities. In contrast, New York City's 2,200-member Upper West Side Riverside Church, a multiracial congregation with a long-standing liberal and interdenominational tradition, was reported as being in "turmoil" in 1992. The cause was changes introduced into worship, sermons, liturgical music, and day-to-day operations following the appointment of an innovative and liberal black pastor, the Reverend James A. Forbes, Jr. According to the *New York Times,* "The divisions at Riverside have grown so deep that a professional mediator has been called in."

Historically, religious worship has been one of the most segregated activities in American life. Admitting this does not invalidate our earlier statement that theological consensuses often cut across different ethnic groups. Nor is worshiping separately only a matter of black and white. Swiss- and Scotch-origin Presbyterians, and Jews of German and Spanish origin, still pray in different congregations, but they share common loyalties and religious beliefs. This situation reflects a society where many, especially among ethnic minorities, are most comfortable living among those most like themselves. Moreover, congregations are essentially local, and even in these days of widespread car ownership, they draw on the neighborhood for support; change will come only slowly. Therefore we can expect the ethnic factor to continue to affect local congregational life well into the 21st century. Nevertheless, religion will not add to the much-feared "disuniting of America" predicted by historian Arthur Schlesinger, Jr. Religion will continue to be a binding element in our diverse society because prevalent religious thinking in America challenges the notion that people of various ethnicities, races, classes, or genders do not have anything meaningful to say to one another or to their Maker, and it asserts that the Scriptures can speak directly to hugely diverse groups of people irrespective of their origins and that these texts transcend time, place, and background in their ability to uphold our common values.

There is a tension between ethnicity and religion in American society. Ethnicity tends to take a historical, backward-looking view, whereas religion deals more with the future and the promise of individual salvation. Concern for ethnicity is essentially a concern about the point of origin, whereas religion is essentially about the point of destination.

THE POLITICS OF RELIGION AND THE RELIGION OF POLITICS

♦ ♦ ♦

The relationship between politics and religion has developed much differently in the United States than in leading nations of Europe. Christian Democratic political parties sponsored by church organizations and religious groups have played major roles in Italy, Germany, Belgium, and the Netherlands since the end of World War II. Recently, former Communist states like Hungary and Poland have witnessed similar phenomena. These Christian-based political parties have produced major national figures—German chancellors Konrad Adenauer and Helmut Kohl, Italian prime ministers Alcide De Gasperi and Giulio Andreotti, French prime minister (later foreign minister) Robert Schuman, and Poland's president Lech Walesa.

Although Great Britain has had its Anglican church since King Henry VIII split with Rome in 1529, appeals to religious loyalties and use of religious rhetoric have largely disappeared from national political debate in that country. In fact, during the 1970s, Lord Hailsham—a leading Anglican churchman, Conservative party politician, and cabinet minister—attacked the mixing of religion and politics. The former home secretary and lord chancellor stated that "the introduction of religious passion into politics is the end of honest politics, and the introduction of politics into religion is the prostitution of religion."

Without either an established church as in Britain or church-organized political parties as in much of the rest of Europe, America and its political landscape have nonetheless resonated with religious rhetoric. And this in a country that prides itself on separating church and state. One need only look at the 1992 presidential election to witness religious expression almost unique within the democratic world's political arena.

THE 1992 PRESIDENTIAL CAMPAIGN

The political commentator and linguist William Safire observed, "Never has the name of God been so frequently invoked, and never has this or any other nation been so thoroughly and systematically blessed, as in the 1992 campaign."

President George Bush opened his reelection campaign in the last week of January 1992. Speaking before 1600 delegates at a convention of the National Religious Broadcasters, a Christian television and radio group, he said, "I want to thank you for helping America, as Christ ordained, to be a light upon the world. . . . One cannot be America's president without a belief in God, without a belief in prayer." Bush called for a constitutional amendment to allow organized prayer in the nation's public schools, describing prayer as "the ultimate value that sustains America." He also talked of "religious values" and said, "The first value is not simply American but universal . . . I refer to the sanctity of life. I will stand on the side of choosing life." He then cited the teachings of Jesus Christ as the moral force behind the previous year's Persian Gulf War. Indeed, in June 1991, shortly after the war ended, Bush, an Episcopalian, flew to Atlanta for the annual meeting of the nation's largest Protestant group, the Southern Baptist Convention. As tears filled his eyes, he recalled how he had prayed fervently at Camp David before ordering the start of the Gulf War. Similarly, in December 1992, after losing the presidential election to Arkansas governor Bill Clinton, George Bush used religious imagery when he explained his decision to send American troops on a Christmas rescue operation—Operation Restore Hope—to feed the starving population of Somalia. In a nationwide television address, he said he was sending American soldiers on a mission to do "God's work."

Former senator and presidential candidate Eugene McCarthy, asserting that Bush talked too much about prayer during the election campaign, commented, "I read where Barbara said she and George pray out loud. It seems like discrimination. If I have to read George Bush's lips, why does he speak out loud for the Lord?"

During the 1992 presidential primaries, Pat Buchanan, a self-styled "traditional" Roman Catholic, tried to appeal to Republican conservatives, many of whom are fundamentalist and evangelical Protestants, in a failed attempt to wrest the nomination from the incumbent president. Buchanan advocated an America based on Christian culture, rejected cultural pluralism, and called for a "new world order" emphasizing "America first." He accused the

Bush administration and the National Endowment for the Arts of "investing tax dollars in pornographic and blasphemous art" and having "perverted the image of Jesus Christ." Fighting back, Bush sought to wrap himself in the supportive mantle of leading Protestant evangelicals like Pat Robertson and Jerry Falwell. As the *New York Times* commented, "Somewhere between [the primaries in] New Hampshire and Georgia, the economy dropped off the screen and was replaced by good, old-fashioned Christian values." Many conservative evangelicals, desiring to build a Christian-based political movement for the future, nevertheless were unsure that a Roman Catholic, even one on the political right, should be the person to head such a movement. They therefore did not give Buchanan large-scale support in 1992. Furthermore, Pat Robertson, Jerry Falwell, and other leading evangelicals had already committed themselves to Bush, some more reluctantly than others, primarily because of his support of school prayer, school choice, and "traditional" family values, and because of his opposition to abortion, except in cases of rape or incest or to save the life of the mother.

Buchanan came under serious attack from some politically moderate Catholics, especially after his address at the Republican National Convention that practically called for a holy war against those with nontraditional values. They accused the professional journalist, television commentator, and one-time presidential speech writer (for Nixon and Reagan) of disregarding the Roman Catholic church's opinions on major social issues. Paul Elie, a writer for both the liberal Catholic publication *Commonweal* and *The New Republic*, stated, "Pat Buchanan is profoundly at odds with the teaching of his church on a host of social issues from the role of women to the role of the church in society. . . . One can see that Buchanan has rejected or ignored the full counsels of his faith." Elie went even further, commenting that Buchanan's deriding the church's "gospel of social action" as having been "picked up in the vestibule of the First Church of Christ Socialist" puts him "in conflict not only with the post–Vatican II church, but with its reading of the whole Christian tradition," including the "social encyclicals" of Pope John Paul II. Buchanan's attitude toward the Catholic church's "gospel of social action" did not become a major issue because he never won a state primary against President Bush. Many of Buchanan's ardent supporters hoped that he could set the stage for a major challenge to capture the Republican presidential nomination in 1996. However, if Pat Buchanan were to become a major factor in the 1996 race, it is likely that many in the Catholic church would oppose him, for some of his extreme positions, just as many Protestant groups opposed conservative Republican Barry Goldwater in 1964.

But the use of "Christian values" and themes was not limited to Republican candidates attempting to win over a conservative audience. They were also used by leading Democratic candidates who were fighting for moderate

and progressive voters. Bill Clinton, a Southern Baptist, said, "I pray virtually every day, usually at night, and I read the Bible every week. . . . I
also believe in a lot of the old-fashioned things like the constancy of sin, the
possibility of forgiveness [and] the reality of redemption." In October 1991,
shortly after declaring for the Democratic presidential nomination, Clinton
went to the heart of the nation's "spiritual problems" in a speech at his alma
mater, Georgetown University, and proposed a "new covenant" between the
"people and their government [that would] restore a sense of community to
this great nation."

In his acceptance address at the July 1992 Democratic National Convention, Clinton led the hall in the Pledge of Allegiance and used the term "new
covenant" more than a dozen times. He also quoted from the Bible and made
frequent reference to the Almighty; one commentator said that Clinton was
obviously reaching out for the votes of evangelical and fundamentalist Protestants who had not voted Democratic in recent presidential elections. But
the words were not uncharacteristic for this Southern Baptist whose vice-
presidential nominee, Senator Al Gore, was not only a Southern Baptist but
also a former graduate student in religion at the divinity school of Vanderbilt
University. The 1992 Clinton-Gore campaign marked the first time that
either of the two major political parties had nominated Southern Baptists for
both president and vice president of the United States. And this ticket, as
Bill Clinton mentioned on several occasions, was on a "great crusade" to
change and cleanse the government. Several conservative Christian evangelists who supported President Bush's reelection campaign, particularly Pat
Robertson and Jerry Falwell, were taken aback by a Democratic presidential
candidate using biblical imagery in his campaign (such rhetoric was certainly
not typical of the northern liberals who had recently been Democratic presidential nominees, who also did not speak of "family values" or conserving
"basic values" or leading a "great crusade," the way the moderate southern
governor did on a continual basis throughout the campaign). Robertson and
Falwell accused Clinton of "misquoting and manipulating Holy Scripture for
political purposes." Robertson, speaking on his television program, *The 700
Club,* labeled Clinton's rallying cry of a "new covenant" extremely dangerous
and "pseudo-Christianity," noting that the term had been used by Jesus at
the Last Supper. Clinton responded in an address at the University of Notre
Dame, stating, "America does not need a religious war. . . . It needs a
reaffirmation of the values that are rooted in our religious faith."

Clinton's religious themes were also challenged by the incumbent president, but in a more subtle manner. In an address before the national convention of the Knights of Columbus in August 1992, Bush proclaimed,
"America is still the most religious nation on earth," and added, "our
fundamental moral standards were established by Almighty God." In his

renomination acceptance address at the Republican National Convention, he said, "I believe that America will always have a special place in God's heart, as long as He has a special place in ours." He attempted to make "religion and morality" one of the major issues in his reelection campaign. As the *New York Times* commented, "President Bush . . . put religion and morality at the heart of his effort to undermine public trust in Gov. Bill Clinton, suggesting that the Democratic nominee lacks the moral fiber to be president." This accusation was echoed and reechoed by Bush throughout the campaign, and it became a central issue in his bid for reelection. He frequently said, "If you are looking to restore America's moral fiber, why buy a synthetic when you can get real cotton?" While addressing a conference of evangelicals, he cited the pro-life, pro–school prayer, and pro–school choice Republican party platform, which also included references to "the Judeo-Christian heritage that informs our culture" and the party's belief in the American people as "free men and women with faith in God." He then attacked the Democratic party platform, which, he said, left out three simple letters: "G.O.D." Responding, Clinton declared that "the implications that [Bush] has made, that Democrats are somehow godless, are deeply offensive to me and to all of us who cherish our religious convictions but also respect America's tradition of religious diversity." The Democratic candidate never muted his religious rhetoric, but attempted to give it an inclusive message with enough room for saints and sinners and those of all religious beliefs. He also attempted to portray Republicans like Pat Robertson and, especially, Pat Buchanan as preaching a "negative" message of "religious war" that excluded many Americans. However, Buchanan insisted that he had been fighting to protect America's "Judeo-Christian values" in his combative address at the 1992 Republican National Convention.

Throughout the campaign, Clinton skillfully used religious phrases to describe his political problems and opportunities. At least one observer noted that Clinton worked an audience like a "preacher." Commenting on an October presidential debate, a reporter noted that Clinton "had the empathy and confidence of a television evangelist." Earlier in the campaign, at a Memphis worship service in March 1992, Clinton had stated, "The Scripture says let him who is without sin cast the first stone. . . . All I can say is in the last month I met a lot of perfect people." In appearances in Protestant churches, Clinton frequently used the themes of spiritual redemption and forgiveness, alluding to his past indiscretions and fallibility. It made little difference whether the congregants were white or black. Indeed, *Newsweek* commented, "Clinton can move an African-American audience with the cadence of a Baptist preacher." The same publication later noted, "As [all] candidates enter the Bible Belt, God suddenly became their co–campaign manager." But this was true of some candidates even outside the Bible Belt.

On a Sunday morning before the Illinois primary, Clinton told his over-whelmingly black audience in a Chicago Baptist church: "When your pastor said I was not perfect, I started to say 'Amen' and stand up and lead a shout. This is a place not for saints but for sinners." No person, he continued, should be asked to meet a standard of perfection. Hillary Rodham Clinton felt almost equally at home speaking in churches, albeit Methodist ones rather than Baptist. After surprising her Methodist Republican parents by telling them that she was marrying a Baptist Democrat, Hillary Clinton studied religion so intensively that she was eventually able to lecture around the state of Arkansas on "what it means to be a Methodist."

One of the political reporters covering the 1992 campaign observed that Clinton enjoyed campaigning in churches so much that he seemed to be interested in "a calling more spiritual than political." Some members of the campaign press corps began calling Clinton "Reverend Bill." However, this was not a laughing matter for religious minorities, such as Catholics, who began to note a double standard for what majority Protestants can do and members of other religious groups cannot do in America's multireligious society. Thus *The Tablet*, the official newspaper of the Roman Catholic diocese of Brooklyn, admitted in an editorial to being "uneasy" about the Arkansas governor's use of Protestant church pulpits in the campaign. *Tablet* editor Ed Wilkinson noted that at a Sunday service, Bill Clinton "used the pulpit of a local Brooklyn [Protestant] church . . . to make a campaign speech" and quoted from Scripture "at least a dozen times," eventually receiving the endorsement of the minister. Wilkinson asked, "Why the double standard? . . . If a Catholic church had been used, there would have been a resurgence of cries to strip the Church of its nonprofit status." If, Wilkinson added, "Bill Clinton had asked to speak from the pulpit of a Catholic church anywhere in New York City, [he] would have been flatly denied the opportunity." In a show of even-handedness, however, Wilkinson also noted, "Some people are still burning [about] the way Christ the King High School was used in 1988 by candidate George Bush to make a speech in support of capital punishment, a stand diametrically opposed by the national bishops." The editorial recommended that the Catholic church "find a way to be involved in the [electoral] process without falling into the trap of endorsing candidates." Unlike, that is, numerous Protestant churches and ministers.

The impact of religion and the importance of a spiritual message in a presidential election was also made obvious by the primary campaign of former senator Paul Tsongas of Massachusetts, who is of the Greek Orthodox faith. *The New Republic* called him "the Puritan" during his unsuccessful campaign for the Democratic nomination. Political reporter Sidney Blumen-thal cited him as a son of Greek immigrants "who assumed the mantle of the

Yankee legacy and became the true Puritan." Political writers referred to him as "Saint Paul," a nickname first applied to him by a political rival in Massachusetts who had accused him of sanctimoniousness. Tsongas frequently cited his battle with cancer as "the crucible" that transformed his political ambitions and led to personal existentialism and "spirituality." After his early primary win in New Hampshire, Tsongas promised the voters that with their support he and they would ascend to a higher level of "spirituality." When he finally withdrew from the race after losing the Illinois and Michigan primaries, the *Economist* headed its article with the caption "Good Bye St. Paul." It stated that he was "self-righteous in the way that true saints are not."

The only Democratic candidate who fought Bill Clinton through the last primary and on to the floor of the Democratic National Convention was former California governor Edmund G. Brown, Jr., universally known as Jerry. Brown, as we mentioned earlier, is a former Jesuit seminarian who spent several years studying Zen Buddhism. He worked with Mother Teresa after losing a bid for the United States Senate and retiring as governor. During the 1992 presidential campaign, he informed the media that he had spent many weeks meditating in a Trappist monastery and searching his soul for "purity of intention" before making the actual decision to run for the Democratic nomination. California state senator Tom Hayden, a radical leader of the 1960s, said that Jerry Brown's "life is about trying to reconcile spirituality and politics. . . . He is more like a combination of the Dalai Lama and [the Czech Republic's President, the former playwright] Václav Havel than George McGovern and Gary Hart." Mervin Field, the director of the California Poll, called him "a real seminarian. He wants to save souls." During the campaign, Brown would discuss his political goals, as one reporter noted, "with the mixture of religion and introspection" that has come to personify him. It was not surprising that Brown's major support came from voters in the western states, where his emphasis on environmental issues, "airy spiritualism and blue-sky technology" were most acceptable.

During the 1992 campaign, George Bush frequently made reference to religious schools as an option in schools of choice. This was particularly important to evangelical Protestants, Roman Catholics, and Orthodox Jews, who stress religious schools as alternatives to public schools. It was a popular issue that differentiated George Bush from Bill Clinton. Bush would have given parents the choice of using a voucher to send children to public, religious, or private schools, whereas Bill Clinton advocated choice only within the public-school system. During the campaign, Bush declared, "Every parent should have the power to choose which school is best for his child—public, private, or religious." What was not adequately discussed,

Clinton retorted, was the economic cost and its ultimate effect on the nation's public-school systems.

The George Bush–Dan Quayle Republican ticket in 1992 attempted to shore up conservative political and traditional religious support by emphasizing not only a belief in school vouchers but also an anti-abortion position, which differentiated them from the Bill Clinton–Al Gore Democratic ticket. Vice President Quayle also went on the campaign trail with attacks on "the cultural elite" he saw in Hollywood, New York, and university faculty halls. Throughout the campaign Quayle wrapped himself in all the trappings of a conservative soldier embattled in what *Newsweek* called a "genuine cultural war." Quayle pointed his weapons at social activists, especially those in the entertainment establishment, portraying them as the vanguard of an American "life-style liberalism." He also criticized television sitcoms, such as *Murphy Brown,* that he said glorify alternative "life-style choices" by mocking the importance of fathers and by endorsing single parenthood. Quayle's was a concerted attempt to make "family values" and "traditional values" a campaign issue that could aid the Republicans. It soon became obvious, however, that this tactic produced as much opposition as support.

Bill Clinton also took a calculated risk during the summer of 1992, when he provoked a symbolic confrontation with the Reverend Jesse Jackson during a national meeting of Jackson's Rainbow Coalition in Washington, D.C., a confrontation that only exacerbated the already difficult and, at times, stormy relationship between the two men. Clinton publicly criticized a previous speaker at the conference, the rap performer Sister Souljah (Lisa Williamson), calling her a racist for having said, in a recorded interview published in the *Washington Post* in the aftermath of the Los Angeles riots, "If black people kill black people every day, why not have a week and kill white people?" Clinton compared the performer to Louisiana's racist politician David Duke, and stated that whites and blacks should be equally condemned if they make racist statements. Sister Souljah claimed that she had been quoted out of context, and Jackson averred that Clinton had exposed a "character flaw" in himself in attempting to embarrass Jackson by staging a "sneak attack" at the conference. Though taken aback by the imbroglio, most Democratic officials, including several leading black politicians such as Representative Mike Espy of Mississippi and Ron Brown, chairman of the Democratic National Committee and a leading Jackson supporter in 1988, supported Clinton (Clinton later named both to his cabinet). Other black leaders, such as Representative Charles Rangel of New York and Roger Wilkins, supported Jackson.

The problem between Jackson and Clinton went much deeper than their fight over a rapper's comments. Clinton, unlike most recent national Democratic leaders, had decided not to use Jackson as a conduit to the nation's black voters. Instead, he had decided, early in his campaign, to reach out directly to blacks via one of their most important institutions—the church. Black Baptists welcomed his liberal social-welfare philosophy combined with familiar religious rhetoric. In the summer of 1992, Clinton spoke to 2,500 mostly black churchgoers in the West Angeles Church of God in Christ, close to the scorched storefronts of the Los Angeles riots. To the approval of the congregants, he said, "Justice should be color-blind. When someone breaks the law, they ought to be punished whether they are African American, Hispanic, Asian, or white, and whether they are in or out of uniform. . . . The people at the top of the totem pole, they should be responsible too." After his talk, Clinton received the warm public endorsement of the church's pastor, Bishop Charles E. Blake. It was, therefore, not surprising that on the day of his inauguration, January 20, 1993, Bill Clinton became the first president in American history to select an overwhelmingly black church, the Washington Metropolitan African Methodist Episcopal Church, as the location for the inaugural prayer service.

After the 1992 presidential election, sociologist Orlando Patterson of Harvard University, writing in the *New York Times,* stated, "African-Americans are strongly drawn" to Bill Clinton, especially because of his frequently stated theme of "the Puritan ideal of America as a covenanted society." Indeed, Clinton had spoken and would speak continually of a new spirit of community, a sense that Americans are working together toward a just society premised upon, as Patterson expressed it, the "evangelical doctrine of equality before God." Patterson expressed hope that a moderate southern leader could undo the damage of "our southern 'fathers' who first shattered the northern vision of a covenanted society."

Despite Bill Clinton's education at Georgetown, Yale and Oxford, and Al Gore's schooling at St. Albans, an Episcopalian school, and, later, Vanderbilt and Harvard universities, many Southern Baptists could still identify with the Democratic nominees. According to Dr. Richard D. Land, executive director of the Southern Baptist Convention's Christian Life Commission (which opposed the Clinton-Gore ticket), Southern Baptists "recognize these guys. These are their kind of folk in the way they talk, how they sound." Professor Leonard of Samford University in Birmingham, Alabama, described Clinton's cadence as reminiscent of Southern Baptist and African American preaching. Sam Hill of the University of Florida allowed that the two candidates were "men of substantial faith" but added that they "don't speak the language of Zion." He said that they speak "the language of Georgetown, Vanderbilt, Harvard, Oxford and Yale." (This was probably truer of Gore than of Clinton.)

Unlike John F. Kennedy, who emphasized humanist values and de-emphasized his Catholicism in the 1960 presidential campaign, Bill Clinton had no hesitancy in using the rhetoric of his religious beliefs, those of a moderate Southern Baptist, during his quest for the presidency. But he did this in an inclusive and nonthreatening manner. There was room in his message for members of all faiths and for nonbelievers. He was able to blend together the universalist and particularist aspects of his values. In a campaign address at the University of Notre Dame he reminded his audience that if elected, he would be the first American president to have graduated from a Catholic college (Clinton received his degree from Georgetown University; Kennedy, the nation's only Catholic president, graduated from Harvard University). Interviewed on VISN, an interdenominational religious cable network, Clinton professed, "My faith tells me that all of us are sinners, and each of us has gone in our own way and fallen short of the glory of God. Religious faith has permitted me to believe in my continuing possibility of becoming a better person every day. If I didn't believe in God, if I weren't in my view . . . a Christian, if I didn't believe ultimately in the perfection of life after death, my life would have been that much more different." But just as Kennedy in 1960 sought to allay some Americans' fears that the Vatican would control a Kennedy White House, Clinton made clear his position on the separation of church and state in the VISN interview: "That I have a deep faith in God and a sense of mission to try to do the right thing every day should be reassuring to the American people. But I don't expect to get any marching orders from the fact that I was raised in the Baptist church."

In a national poll taken just weeks before the 1992 election, 10% of those responding said that religion would be the determining factor in their vote, while 74% said that a candidate's economic plan would determine their votes. Among those who attend church regularly, 26% said that religion would be the determining factor in their vote, as against 50% who cited the economy. Examining not only this poll but, even more important, the actual religious breakdown of the 1992 election results, one understands why Fred Barnes wrote in *The New Republic* just prior to the election: "Religion is the stealth issue of the presidential race. It will probably have more influence on the outcome than any issue except the economy." And it would appear that it did.

THE ROSS PEROT PHENOMENON

Ross Perot's 1992 independent presidential candidacy stimulated much more voter interest than any other in recent history, including George Wallace's in 1968 and John Anderson's in 1980. By the end of May 1992, only three months after he had announced on CNN's *Larry King Live!* that he could be induced by the will of the people to run for president, Perot surpassed both Bush and Clinton in a *Time* magazine/CNN public-opinion poll. In June he was receiving between 30% and 35% in numerous polls, often running ahead of both party candidates. Michael Kelly of the *New York Times* wrote that Perot, never having held any elected office, had nevertheless traveled in a few months from "oddity to viability, exclusively on the strength of mass media exposure. . . . He is the nation's first pure media presidential candidate." Perot's neighbors in Texarkana, Texas, referred to him as "a good Christian man." Many Americans referred to him as a "folk hero," "a can-do self-made millionaire," and, probably most important during a season of antipolitical feelings, as a "nonpolitician." Theodore J. Lowi, president of the American Political Science Association, noted that the Perot phenomenon "is not apathy. [It] is antipathy," Lowi asserted, to the Democratic and Republican parties and their presidential candidates.

Perot achieved fame as a very successful businessman in the computer-software industry with a reputation for direct action, whether that involved rescuing employees held hostage in pre-Khomeini Iran or conducting on-the-spot searches for Vietnam MIAs. Lawrence Wright, a political commentator and writer for the *New York Times Magazine* (and one of Perot's fellow Texans), called Perot an eclectic figure with support from both Democrats and Republicans. Further, Wright noted, "he's an advocate of traditional family values who is for abortion," a "billionaire populist," and "a Presbyterian who supports Catholic schools and has a predilection for hiring Mormons." Wright also reported that Perot had been greatly influenced by his deeply religious Methodist mother. Although Perot had headed task forces on improving the schools in his home state and preventing drug trafficking, very little was known of his viewpoints on a host of social, economic, and political issues. In television appearances, he frequently recommended *On Wings of Eagles,* the book he had selected novelist Ken Follett to write about his Iranian rescue mission, as a means of finding out "who I am and what I believe in." When asked on the NBC-TV *Today* show how he felt about the Los Angeles riots, he said that America needed to rebuild and strengthen the family structure, and he cited "the church" as the most important institution for maintaining family stability. Echoing the civil religion of former president Dwight Eisenhower, he said, "It doesn't matter what the religion is; they all teach the same things."

As *New York* magazine political reporter Joe Klein observed, the important thing about Perot's independent candidacy was not the candidate but his "constituency," which seemed to be an independent and frustrated middle class that had come to disdain not only the two major political parties but also the compromises of public life. The disaffected were, as the *Economist* noted, "ready to turn for salvation to a self-made businessman who has never run for office." A Perot organizer in North Carolina stated, "We need a change in this country. . . . We want our dignity, our respect as a nation back. . . . We know our strength comes from above. With His help we will save our country."

Eventually, Ross Perot learned in 1992 what John Anderson had learned in 1980, what George Wallace had learned in 1968, and what both Henry Wallace and Strom Thurmond had learned in 1948: The bloom of spring does not always last through the heat of the summer for a third-party/ independent candidate for president. John Anderson, for example, had the support of 24% of potential voters in a May 1980 poll and received only 6.7% of the vote in the November election. George Wallace saw his numbers drop from a spring 1968 figure of 24% to an actual vote of 14%. Perot's figures dropped from a high of 35% in June 1992, when he actually led Bush and Clinton in some polls, to an actual vote of 19%. But this was after a roller-coaster campaign that saw him withdraw in July and then re-emerge as a candidate in October.

The Perot vote was overwhelmingly white Protestant. His highest percentages were in those states where the black vote was below the national average of 12%; in those states he received almost 23% of the total vote. Where the black population was above average, as in most of the South, Perot received only 13% of the vote. However, the total Perot vote of 19% was notably higher than John Anderson's 6.6% in 1980 and George Wallace's 13.6% in 1968. It was also higher than Progressive Party candidate Robert La Follette who had managed in 1924, to win 17% of the national vote. Only former president Theodore Roosevelt had a higher percentage of the vote as a third-party candidate. Running on the Progressive ("Bull Moose") party ticket in 1912, Roosevelt took more than 27% of the national vote, polling better than the incumbent president, Republican William Howard Taft, who received 23% of the vote, and possibly tilting the election to Democrat Woodrow Wilson, who won with 42%.

POLITICS AND RELIGION: TWO CASE STUDIES

To understand the issue of religion and national politics today, it is important to use two salient case studies: the 1960 and, especially, the 1964 presidential election campaigns. Even more than the former, the 1964 campaign polarized the Protestant community and set the tone and many parameters for religion and politics in future campaigns.

In 1960, there was a great deal of talk about the "religious issue." After the Democratic party nominated John F. Kennedy, the media constantly emphasized that Kennedy was the first Roman Catholic to seriously seek the presidency since New York governor Al Smith lost in 1928. The question posed was: Can a president adhering to the Roman Catholic faith remain true to the constitutional principle of separation of church and state? The question was made more newsworthy by popular feeling that Al Smith's defeat had been due, primarily, to the religious issue. Historian Richard Hofstadter, writing in *The Reporter* at the start of the 1960 campaign, attempted to put Al Smith's defeat in another perspective by pointing to Smith's other political handicaps, such as his opposition to Prohibition, his Tammany Hall background, and Herbert Hoover's pre-Depression popularity.

The strongest attack on John F. Kennedy came in the fall of 1960 from a group of more than 100 traditional Protestant clergymen and lay leaders, including the editor of the *Christian Herald,* Daniel Poling; the editor of the conservative publication *Christianity Today,* L. Nelson Bell, father-in-law of evangelist Billy Graham; and the Reverend Norman Vincent Peale, author of *The Power of Positive Thinking.* The group issued a statement arguing that no Catholic president could turn away from the Roman Catholic church's "efforts . . . to breach the wall of separation of church and state." Peale later withdrew from the group after other leading Protestants, including the eminent theologian Reinhold Niebuhr and John C. Bennett, dean of faculty at Union Theological Seminary, publicly opposed this conservative group's position. Another group, Protestants and Other Americans United for Separation of Church and State, issued a statement condemning prejudice and praising Kennedy because he did not support some of the well-known policies of the Catholic church, including aid to nonpublic schools and opposition to birth control.

Many more liberal and mainline Protestant leaders publicly supported Kennedy after he delivered a major address on September 12, 1960, before hundreds of members and guests of the Greater Houston (Texas) Ministerial Association. In this speech he stated, "I believe in an America where the separation of church and state is absolute—where no Catholic prelate would tell [a Catholic] president how to act and no Protestant minister would tell his parishioners for whom to vote—where no church or church school is granted any public funds or political preference—and where no man is denied public office merely because his religion differs from the president who might appoint him or the people who might elect him." He went on to say, to the chagrin of some in the Catholic hierarchy, that "whatever issue may come before me as president, if I should be elected—on birth control, divorce, censorship, gambling, or any other subject—I will make my decision in accordance . . . with what my conscience tells me to be in the national interest, and without regard to outside religious pressure or dictates. And no power or threat of punishment could cause me to do otherwise." Following his address, *The Christian Century,* the leading interdenominational Protestant publication of moderate opinion, changed from opposition to neutrality in the election, and the liberal nondenominational *Christianity and Crisis* became even more fervently pro-Kennedy. Still, most Protestant publications would not support him. Nonetheless, polls showed that Kennedy gained votes from moderate Protestants, who were still in control of major mainline churches. Also, Jewish voters were relieved by his remarks, and most voted for him in the general election.

In the end, the University of Michigan Survey Research Center noted that Kennedy, winning one of the closest elections in the 20th century, had probably lost more Protestant Democrats than he had gained in achieving the support of Catholic Republicans and independents. He lost numerous Bible Belt border states and western states to Richard Nixon. Yet he did get the support of 40% of white Protestants and of the vast majority of Jews and black Protestants. As Lawrence Fuchs, a professor of American civilization at Brandeis University, observed, "He had won many converts to his view that Catholics could believe in, give expression to, and direct the future of the American Zion conceived and nurtured by Protestants more than two hundred years before." Kennedy was an articulate, Harvard-educated, Catholic politician, assimilated into the nation's Protestantized culture, who had adapted America's civil religion to express his vision of the country's special mission.

The election of John F. Kennedy in 1960 broke the "unwritten law" that only a white Protestant could be president of the United States. The question remains, however, could Kennedy have been elected had his professed opinions reflected more closely those of the majority of American Catholics regarding, for example, federal aid to education going directly to parochial as well as public schools? Also, what would have happened if he had not taken a strong secular-humanist position at the newsworthy Houston Ministerial Association meeting? Kennedy's stand may have changed the entire tenor of the campaign. Religion scholar Martin Marty commented at the time that Kennedy had revealed himself to be "spiritually rootless and politically almost disturbingly secular." Be that as it may, on January 16, 1961, just a few days before his inauguration, Kennedy invited the Reverend Billy Graham to Key Biscayne, Florida, for lunch and golf. In a subsequent press conference reported in the *New York Times*, Graham said, "Mr. Kennedy's victory had proved there was not as much religious prejudice as many had feared and probably had reduced forever the importance of the religious issue in American elections." In this latter instance Graham was wrong. The religious issue has remained a major component of national elections to this day and gives every indication of continuing to do so into the future.

Many today have forgotten the intensity of the religious issue of the 1960 presidential campaign. However, far more people have forgotten, and others have never even realized, that the religious issue of 1964 was as intense for moderate Protestants (comprising the so-called religious establishment) as the religious issue of 1960 was for fundamentalist Protestants. In 1964 the nation's leading moderate Protestant clergy and laymen were deeply concerned by Republican Barry Goldwater's lack of commitment to Christian social action. The mass media generally assumed that the 1964 religious issue could not arouse as much popular interest as the 1960 religious issue and therefore did not give it equal weight. This, however, was decidedly not the case within the media of the liberal Protestant establishment.

The anomaly of the heated opposition of moderate Protestants was that Goldwater, though never denying his Jewish origins, was proud of his association with Protestantism, especially with the Protestant Episcopal community. Yet, the moderate Protestant church establishment and Barry Goldwater represented two clearly different strands of American Protestantism.

The Protestant faith in which Josephine Williams Goldwater was reared and to which her husband, Baron, was converted from the Jewish faith of his forebears became in turn the faith in which their son Barry was raised. Barry Goldwater's Protestantism was also influenced and permeated by the post–Civil War business ethic. The self-made businessman became a symbol to many Americans in the 1870s and 1880s—a period of vast national and industrial expansion—especially in the West. Soon it became apparent that the successful businessman was exerting a great influence on numerous national institutions, including church organizations. Leaders of industry and finance were appointed to church boards, and new business methods and concepts of economic efficiency took hold within these organizations. Gradually, these ideas began to influence overall church philosophy, which came to emphasize free enterprise and political patriotism as twin pillars needed to uphold the "Christian faith." Many leaders of the great business organizations that emerged after the Civil War considered themselves devoted churchmen. Cyrus H. McCormick was a loyal Presbyterian, the financier Jay Cooke was an active Episcopalian, the meat-packing Swifts were committed Methodists, and John D. Rockefeller, who looked upon himself as a devout Baptist, also considered himself a "steward of the Lord," and declared his wealth to be really "God's gold."

The belief that Christians should be primarily concerned with social reform and economic improvement for the masses, as preached by the Social Gospel movement, conflicted with the idea that American Protestantism should be primarily concerned with the salvation of people's souls. In 1908, the General Conference of the Methodist Episcopal church adopted a very progressive social creed that called for the abolition of child labor, regulation of work conditions for women, reduction of work hours, "a living wage in every industry," and equitable division of the products of industry. This new commitment was soon adopted, almost verbatim, by the newly formed Federal Council of Churches of Christ in America (the predecessor of the National Council of the Churches of Christ). Social Gospel leaders had a great influence upon the minds of 20th-century Protestant thinkers. Walter Rauschenbusch, for example, who combined religious orthodoxy and a realistic, tough-minded approach to social problems (reflecting perhaps his education in New York's Hell's Kitchen), exerted a profound influence upon Reinhold Niebuhr, who, probably more than any other individual, molded and reflected the thinking of the progressive Protestant religious establishment of the mid-20th century.

In his writings, especially *The Nature and Destiny of Man,* published just prior to World War II, Niebuhr provided an articulate restatement of Christian faith amid the turmoil of the mid-20th century. His "neo-orthodoxy," concerned with intellectual, social, and moral issues, sought to create an independent Christian yardstick by which to evaluate and improve the economic and social scene.

Barry Goldwater, reared in his mother's early American Protestant tradition, was unaware of the depth of some Protestants' commitment to the Rauschenbusch-Niebuhr formula of social consciousness. He did not fully comprehend that an important and powerful element of American Protestantism had been influenced by many of the changes that the American economic and political order had undergone. The 1964 national political campaign was also to reveal the great authority and prestige that this progressive religious establishment retained within American society, and the considerable means for influencing political action at its disposal.

Protestant moderates began reacting almost as soon as the Republican National Convention ended, on July 17, 1964, with that final unforgettable Goldwater thrust at moderate opinion: "Extremism in the defense of liberty is no vice! Moderation in the pursuit of justice is no virtue!" It seemed to many that for the first time in this century, a national political convention had been taken over by a very conservative faction that sought to divide rather than to unite.

On September 9, 1964, *The Christian Century* ran a lead editorial that condemned Barry Goldwater's candidacy and unequivocally advocated the election of President Lyndon Johnson. Admitting that this was a rare departure from nonpartisanship, *The Christian Century* complained that the campaign had deprived the nation's citizens of those options that make "nonpartisanship viable." What churches and religious organizations and publications had espoused out of moral conviction in the areas of poverty, civil rights, and international relations, the editorial maintained, was now being denounced and attacked by the Republican presidential nominee. *The*

Christian Century went on to state that one need only compare the Episcopal church's proclamations of social and cultural issues with Barry Goldwater's expressed views to discover almost total disagreement.

Some of the most vociferous opposition to Senator Goldwater's presidential aspirations was to be heard from his own Episcopalian community. In mid-September, the Very Reverend Francis B. Sayre, Jr., dean of the Episcopal National Cathedral of Washington, D.C., delivered a sermon in which he said that the voters faced "a sterile choice" between, on the one hand, "a man of dangerous ignorance and devastating uncertainty," and, on the other, "a man whose public house is splendid in its every appearance but whose private lack of ethic must inevitably introduce termites at the very foundation." Sayre's not very subtle allusions to Barry Goldwater and Lyndon Johnson did not go unnoticed; he was, in addition to being a high-ranking Episcopalian clergyman, the grandson of Woodrow Wilson and a onetime confidant to the late John F. Kennedy. It was also well known that President Johnson, a member of the Disciples of Christ, nonetheless frequently accompanied his wife, Lady Bird, an Episcopalian, to services at Sayre's cathedral.

Meanwhile, another Episcopalian priest, the Reverend William Syndor, a former prison chaplain in Appalachia, criticized the Republican nominee at a Sunday service by stating, "When one listens to or reads Senator Goldwater, one finds that respect for God's law is ignored with conscienceless abandon." The rector's objection was expressed in a sermon delivered at the historic Christ Church of Alexandria, Virginia, where George Washington had been a vestryman and where Robert E. Lee had been confirmed. Shortly after Syndor's remarks, several people walked out of the church. Later, some parishioners asked to be removed from the communicants' list.

On October 5, 1964, *Christianity and Crisis,* whose editorial board was jointly chaired by Reinhold Niebuhr and John C. Bennett of the Union Theological Seminary, published a special election issue. The lead editorial on the first page stated: "We Oppose Senator Goldwater!" The periodical admitted that never before in its twenty-five-year history had it directly aligned itself with the presidential candidate of any political party. This departure, which it was hoped, the editors insisted, would never occur again, was based upon "the objective, unarguable conflict between his [Barry Goldwater's] record and the judgments of [many of] the Christian [Protestant] churches on most of the major issues of social ethics in our time." The editorial emphasized that a conflict existed between Goldwater's pronouncements and "the sizable body of ethical convictions that have been endorsed, after long processes of study and debate, by some of the major American denominations, by the National Council of Churches and by the World Council of Churches." The editorial also criticized Goldwater's positions relating to national defense, foreign-aid authorization, civil rights, and social and economic legislation, and insisted that Goldwater's "religion of national destiny" was an anachronism.

"The 1964 Religious Issue" was the title of another editorial in the October 1964 issue of *The Christian Century*. The editors observed that the issue had reached even more deeply into the campaign in 1964 than it had in 1960, and accused Goldwater of converting his nationalistic feelings into a "religious nationalism" and offering this up as the true religion of the modern world.

The anti-Goldwater religious bandwagon rolled on, as conspicuous at the end of the campaign as at the start by the quantity and quality of Episcopal establishment leaders involved. On October 14, an attack on Goldwater was issued and signed by 725 clergy and laymen, including 10 bishops of the Protestant Episcopal church. The statement, accusing the candidate of "a transparent exploitation of racialism," was signed by Episcopalians from forty-one states, and only 2 people who had been asked to sign had declined. Richard Nixon called a press conference after reading the statement and labeled the mounting attacks on the GOP candidate "the most vicious in political history." On October 28, just a week prior to the election, a statement entitled "Religion and the Goldwater Candidacy," signed by 80 clergymen in the Boston area, called on "all religious people to work for the defeat of Senator Goldwater in the presidential election." It was sponsored by the Committee Against Political Extremism, whose chairman was Canon James Breedon of St. Paul's Episcopal Church. Fissures continued to grow between liberal-minded clergy and generally more conservative church members. With the exception of the fundamentalist *Christianity Today*, a majority of the leading Protestant publications opposed Goldwater. When pressed by some angry Goldwater supporters, these publications would comment, as did the *United Church Herald*, that although the editorial-board members of a church publication had taken a particular position in a political campaign, they did not presume to speak for all the local churches and the vast membership of the entire denomination.

The election turned out to be a landslide of epic proportions, with Lyndon Johnson winning the electoral votes of every state in the Union except for Barry Goldwater's native Arizona (where the Republican nominee won a narrow majority) and five states of the Deep South. The ten states of the old Confederacy were the only regional group in the nation to give Goldwater a razor-thin percentage lead, 49.0% to 48.9%. Though this was the heart of the Bible Belt and it was apparent that many conservative evangelists had crossed party lines to vote for Johnson, it was also obvious that discontent with the president's civil rights position had been one of the prime causes for

Goldwater's majorities in Alabama, Georgia, Louisiana, Mississippi, and South Carolina. The election occurred shortly after passage of the monumental 1964 Civil Rights Act but before the full impact of its voting provisions, which would add to the political landscape of the South major black voter participation.

In other regions of the nation the president carved out a remarkable national consensus. For the first time since Franklin Roosevelt, a majority of white Protestants, almost 60%, voted for a Democratic candidate, a feat that no subsequent Democratic presidential candidate has been able to achieve.

THE MIXING OF RELIGION AND POLITICS IN RECENT PRESIDENTIAL ELECTIONS

If one were to look critically at religion and regional voting patterns for every presidential election from 1960 to 1992, one could better understand—even if one could not accept—the regional strategy of Harry Dent of South Carolina, architect of Richard Nixon's 1968 southern strategy and the mentor of Lee Atwater, who later became the chairman of the Republican National Committee. One could also understand how evangelists such as Pat Robertson and Jerry Falwell contributed to Ronald Reagan's religious strategy of the 1980 campaign. Both strategies were based upon the premise that Franklin Roosevelt's New Deal coalition, which had brought southern conservative white Protestants together with liberal Protestants, northern urban Catholics, progressive Jews, blacks, and other minorities, had come under great strain in the 1960s and was ready to crack. And so it did. With few exceptions, such as the 1964 Johnson landslide, Carter's 1976 victory, and Clinton's 1992 win, conservative southern Protestant and northern Roman Catholic support for Democratic presidential candidates has diminished. Among major religious groups, only Jewish voters remained loyal to the Democratic party. Republican presidential candidates, except for Barry Goldwater, have mostly held on to moderate Protestant support and even to liberal Protestant support, which has posed a major problem for most Democrats, who must win their party's nomination by courting liberal political constituencies and then hope to win a general election by attempting to move, most of the time unsuccessfully, to the center of the political spectrum.

As the pollster Louis Harris has noted, Barry Goldwater was viewed more as a radical than as a conservative, and this made it easier for white Protestants to break with their growing pattern of voting Republican in national elections. They would return to their former pattern by supporting a "moderate conservative," Richard Nixon, in his 1968 contest with Hubert Humphrey. Even though Richard Nixon was frequently seen in the company of his friend evangelist Billy Graham, the religious issue did not play the major role it had in the previous two elections. The Catholic vote basically held for New Deal liberal Hubert Humphrey; however, there were massive Protestant defections to the Republican, Richard Nixon, and the independent, George Wallace, who developed strength in his southern base. Protestants identifying with the Democratic party dropped by more than 20% from 1964 to 1968. Though Wallace votes came overwhelmingly from conservative Protestant Democrats, Nixon's votes came not only from liberal and moderate Protestants but also, to some degree, from conservative Protestants. The Protestant voting pattern in the 1972 Nixon-McGovern race was consistent with the 1968 election. George McGovern's terrible showing (he won only one state—Massachusetts) was due in large part to the Democrats' loss of much Catholic support, which dropped precipitously from 54% to 38% in four years. McGovern, a very liberal Democrat who was opposed to the Vietnam War, turned off conservative Democrats, especially Catholics, who had generally and consistently supported Democratic presidential candidates since the 1930s.

Jimmy Carter was the first Southern Baptist to be elected president.* He defeated President Gerald Ford in 1976 because he temporarily managed to put parts of the New Deal coalition together again, especially in his native South. The Democrats' largest voter increases occurred among two important parts of the old New Deal coalition: Catholics and conservative Protestants—especially the latter. One commentator, Paul Lopatto, wrote that "this represented a clear break with a political trend that had begun by 1964. . . . The decline of religiously based conflicts in 1976 played a large part in the success of the Democrats in reconstructing much of the old majority coalition."

Carter's close electoral victory over Ford was undoubtedly due in part to Carter's image as someone who could bring together moderate whites and blacks, who were now voting in large numbers. To the dismay of some northern liberals, Carter frequently spoke in spiritual terms, once berating himself for having "lusted" in his heart, but even he could not gain a majority of white Protestant support nationwide. A political anomaly to many, Carter was a self-proclaimed born-again Christian who said he believed in the Baptist tradition of separation between church and state. After Ronald Reagan narrowly lost the Republican presidential nomination to Gerald Ford in 1976, many of Reagan's fundamentalist backers either sat out the election in order to prepare for 1980 or voted for Jimmy Carter. Since Carter ultimately defeated Ford by only 2% of the national vote, Carter's

* Two previous American presidents, Republican Warren Harding and Democrat Harry Truman, though Baptists, were not Southern Baptists.

support among evangelicals had clearly been crucial—especially in his south-ern base. Nationally, Carter actually won a majority of white Baptist support (56%), although he lost the overall white Protestant vote to Ford. He also ran very strongly among blacks and Jews.

Jimmy Carter's 1976 coalition was short-lived. The 1980 Republican presidential candidate, Ronald Reagan, loosened Carter's southern regional base among evangelicals and conservative Protestants. He also caused large defections among Catholic voters and even conservative Jewish voters on a national level. Carter, however, held on to about 90% of the black vote, which is, of course, overwhelmingly Protestant. Region, race, and religion had clearly become important variables in presidential voting, and their significance has continued in all subsequent national elections.

FOREIGN-POLICY ISSUES AFFECT AMERICA'S RELIGIOUS COMMUNITIES

The debate in the late 1940s and early 1950s as to who was responsible for the loss of eastern Europe and China to communism and whether the Soviet Union could have gained the technology to develop the atomic and hydrogen bombs as quickly as it did without espionage became somewhat muted after the success of George Kennan's "containment" policy, the creation of the North Atlantic Treaty Organization (NATO), and the Marshall Plan. In addition, the censure in the U.S. Senate of Joseph McCarthy of Wisconsin also lessened, though temporarily, the hysteria over the world "Communist menace."

However, many Protestants, Roman Catholics, and Jews continued to be concerned by the Communist states' denial of religious freedom and their persecution of religious groups. American Jews set up a national network of organizations and demonstrated to free Soviet Jewry; American Roman Cath-olics marched on behalf of persecuted Catholic churches and their leaders, like József Cardinal Mindszenty in eastern Europe; Pentecostals, Baptists, and American evangelicals in general also demanded freedom for the perse-cuted Protestant minority behind the Iron Curtain. The fears of the "Com-munist monolith" increased again with Fidel Castro's successful revolution in Cuba in 1959, with the Bay of Pigs fiasco in 1961, and with the ensuing Cuban missile crisis in 1962. A new standoff developed between the two nuclear superpowers—the U.S.A. and the U.S.S.R. This changed in the mid- and late 1970s with the perception of further Communist advances into three major African nations: Angola, Mozambique, and Ethiopia, as well as the election of Chile's Salvador Allende, the first freely elected Marxist head of state. In Asia, Afghanistan came into the Soviet sphere of influence. Much more frightening to many Americans was that the "quarantine" of Cuba had begun to fail with the rise to power of the Soviet-supported Sandinista government in Nicaragua and the threat of Communist insurgents gaining control of El Salvador through civil war.

The Political and Religious Significance of Ronald Reagan's 1980 Victory

The 1964 Goldwater campaign brought to the surface a core of Protestant conservatism that would grow as it fine-tuned its message. It would also bring to the Republican party a growing number of socially conservative Catholics (they were later referred to as "Reagan Democrats"). Goldwater had realized that the future of a conservatively directed Republican party would depend on the party's ability to enlarge its northern Protestant support into the conservative Protestant South, which had been a Democratic bastion since Reconstruction. Ronald Reagan, who had nominated Goldwater at the 1964 Republican National Convention, would soon inherit the conservative mantle and would move to develop a coalition of essentially conservative political and religious groups. This would shift the political landscape to the right and bring about his election as president in 1980—he even defeated Jimmy Carter in most of Carter's southern base. In the process, the amiable, easygoing, former California governor and onetime head of the Screen Actors Guild would develop a persona (that had eluded Barry Goldwater) as a very conservative candidate who was decent and trustworthy. He would develop broad popular support for a conservative message that had been considered too radical in 1964 but would become the standard, at least for many white Americans, in the 1980s. Reagan's message consisted of tough talking in foreign affairs along with a strong defense posture. In domestic affairs it included deregulation of federal government agencies, lower taxes and incentives for private enterprise. And most important to many Americans, Reagan brought an upbeat vision of America's present and future mission. This, along with a social program emphasizing prayer in the public schools, choice in education, an anti-abortion stance, and "traditional" family values, moved the nation even further to the right. The alliance of the Protestant right and the political right was joined by many Roman Catholics fearful of the perceived power of the Communist states of the world.

Faced by Communist advances in Africa and Central America, numerous Protestants, Catholics, and Jews began to recognize a commonality of purpose. In many ways they used Ronald Reagan, who spoke against "the evil empire" of world communism, as much as he used them. In the process, Americans developed a new awareness and appreciation of the political strength of the largely conservative and newly motivated evangelical movement that was led by, among others, Pat Robertson and Jerry Falwell of the

Moral Majority. The 1980 presidential election, therefore, was a watershed in the merging of religion and politics in both domestic and foreign-policy issues.

When Ronald Reagan spoke in 1980 at a Dallas conference of evangelical and fundamentalist ministers, he assured them that he was a "creationist," revealing that he believed literally in the words of the Bible even if it meant a rejection of science's theory of evolution. He also told them that he endorsed their total agenda. According to Furio Colombo, author of *God in America,* Reagan was "espousing a position of true gospel-based Christianity . . . an end to church-state separation. . . . Only 20 years earlier, during the Kennedy-Nixon race, one of the two candidates had been forced to defend his Catholic origins by assuring the electorate that he would never allow American politics to be influenced in any way by his faith. In 1980, Reagan decided that he had to take the opposite oath." Reagan's two 1980 opponents, Jimmy Carter and John Anderson, also publicly espoused religious positions. Southern Baptist Jimmy Carter had referred to himself as "born again in Christ." John Anderson, who had been an evangelical preacher before being elected to Congress, also considered himself a born-again Christian. But the two eventually unsuccessful candidates had attempted to separate their religious beliefs from their political agendas, whereas Reagan blurred the difference in the direction of the Christian right.

Many Catholics, Jews, moderate Protestants, and some traditional evangelicals were uncomfortable with Reagan's stance. Yet he was able to win a large majority of the nation's Protestant votes, about half of Catholic voters, and more than a third of Jewish voters. Premeditated or not, the strong commitment from leaders of the Protestant right to support the State of Israel and their equally strong opposition to abortion rights have diffused some of the major fears in the traditional parts of both the Jewish and Catholic communities. Indeed, the nationally syndicated conservative columnist Cal Thomas, former vice president for communications of the Moral Majority, has said that evangelicals have tremendous love and concern for the Jewish community, and that there is no group of people more disposed to love them and the State of Israel then conservative Christians.

Some Orthodox Jewish organizations, led by Agudath Israel of America and, to a lesser extent, the Union of Orthodox Jewish Congregations of America, did come to accept some of the domestic-social-agenda items of the "Reagan Revolution" as a means of strengthening traditional family values. Nonetheless, the majority of American Jewish religious and human-relations organizations remained consistent in their support of the liberal agenda. However, a decade after Reagan's election, a prominent Jewish neoconservative leader, Irving Kristol, shocked some of his secular-humanist supporters when he wrote in the August 1991 issue of *Commentary* that "the real danger [to American Jewry] is not from a revived Christianity, which American Jews, if they are sensible, can cope with, but from an upsurge of anti-biblical barbarism that will challenge Christianity, Judaism and Western civilization altogether." He spoke of the passing of secular humanism and stated that "American Jews, alert to Christian anti-Semitism, are in danger of forgetting that it was the pagans—the Babylonians and the Romans—who destroyed the temples and imposed exile on the Jewish people."

Because evangelical leaders played a major role in Ronald Reagan's victory, it is important to understand their similarities and their differences. For example, Billy Graham, unlike his father-in-law, L. Nelson Bell, did not become publicly involved in the attempt by many conservative evangelicals and fundamentalists to defeat John F. Kennedy. Nor has he become publicly involved with conservative political movements or their candidates for elective office, as Pat Robertson and Jerry Falwell have. Graham did, however, play a major role in the 1950s and 1960s in moving many evangelicals away from the far right and bringing them and their conservative traditional values into mainstream America.

For almost half a century, Graham's evangelical crusades have taken him all over the United States and to over eighty countries around the world. In the process he has become America's best-known evangelist, reaching millions of people. Through the years, Graham has given spiritual guidance, in a nonpartisan manner, to leading public figures. He has also developed personal relationships with both Democratic and Republican presidents. He was particularly friendly with Richard Nixon but has also been close to Democrats Lyndon Johnson and Bill Clinton as well as Republicans Ronald Reagan and George Bush. He spent the last night of the Bush presidency in the White House as the guest of George and Barbara Bush. The following day, on January 20, 1993, he gave both the invocation and benediction at Bill Clinton's inauguration, which is exactly what he had done four years before at George Bush's inauguration. When he was asked by pro-life groups how he could possibly pray at the inauguration of a man who does not share the evangelist's anti-abortion stand, he responded, "I'm praying for the president, not for a party or a platform." Similarly, though he has called homosexual acts sinful, he has repeatedly warned against treating homosexuals as outcasts.

Probably more than anyone else, Billy Graham has been responsible for changing the way evangelicals are viewed by other Americans; and he has also continually supported coalitions with different groups to achieve common goals for what he believed to be the best interests of the nation. As a young man, and at a very early stage in the civil rights struggle, this Southern Baptist minister from North Carolina unequivocally and publicly condemned racism. Though his literal belief in the Bible never wavered, some of Graham's other opinions were open to change. In the 1940s and

1950s he railed against communism and the Soviet Union, which he said was "inspired, directed, and motivated by the Devil himself," but in the decade prior to the fall of the U.S.S.R. in 1991 he led several crusades to evangelize the Soviet people. Through the half century of his ministry, he has probably preached to more people than anyone else in human history, becoming, to many, the personification of American Protestantism. He has determinedly avoided wedding right-wing politics to his spiritual message, and even though the Billy Graham Evangelistic Association oversees millions of dollars, he has limited himself to a fixed salary that has not gone over $80,000 a year.

Jerry Falwell is different. An independent Baptist from Virginia, Falwell produces his own religious television program (originally called *The Old-Time Gospel Hour*). He has moved from the old Baptist tradition of political noninvolvement to massive political involvement. He established the Moral Majority in 1979 as a conservative political movement. Though most of the chairmen of state chapters were fundamentalist Protestants, he publicly espoused an ecumenical organization consisting not only of fundamentalists but also other Protestants, Catholics, Jews, and Mormons "united in returning America to moral sanity." He undertook a massive registration drive that greatly affected the 1980 presidential election. It is estimated that the Moral Majority church-by-church endeavor throughout the nation—and most especially in the South—registered an impressive 2 million to 3 million new voters. This was facilitated by the fact that conservative Protestant voters had developed misgivings about President Jimmy Carter for not pushing for school prayer and refusing to stop "federally funded abortions"; they were also incensed that he was pressing for the adoption of the Equal Rights Amendment to the Constitution. Evangelical and fundamentalist leaders buried their past differences and moved to support Ronald Reagan, who told a convention of evangelicals in Dallas during the 1980 campaign, "Religious America is awakening, perhaps just in time for our country's sake. . . . If you do not speak out your mind and cast your ballot, then who will speak and work for the ideals we cherish?" And they cast their ballots in 1980 in record numbers, driving from the White House a self-proclaimed born-again Christian whom many had supported four years before. *Commentary* magazine estimated that well over 60% of white Protestants cast their ballots for Ronald Reagan, including an even higher percentage of born-again Christians. A plurality of Catholic voters (49%) supported Reagan, while 42% supported Carter and 7% went for independent John Anderson. Also in 1980, for the first time in at least half a century, a Democratic presidential candidate did not receive an absolute majority of Jewish voters: According to a *New York Times*/CBS exit poll, Carter received 46% of the Jewish vote, Reagan 39% and Anderson 15%.

Reagan's reelection victory in 1984 against Walter Mondale was even more impressive. He won the votes of more than 80% of white evangelicals, 73% of white Protestants, and 55% percent of Catholics. Though a majority of Jews voted for Mondale, more than one third continued to support Reagan. Only the black vote, both Protestant and Catholic, held steady in large numbers for the Democratic candidate in 1984 (as Carter had done in 1980, Mondale won approximately 90%). Reagan had effectively broken the New Deal coalition.

In the battle throughout the South to register more voters, white evangelicals did even better than the blacks who were attempting to get out a large vote for Jesse Jackson. In the North Carolina 1984 presidential primaries, for example, an impressive black-voter registration drive on Jackson's behalf increased the black registration by almost 180,000, but this was bettered by an even greater increase of more than 300,000 new white voters, many of whom were evangelicals. This helped conservative Republican Senator Jesse Helms win reelection against popular white and black candidates such as Democratic Governor Jim Hunt in 1984 and Mayor Harvey Gant of Charlotte in 1990. The pattern was replicated in other southern states where a large black-voter registration increase was offset by an even larger white-Protestant-evangelical registration drive. The 1980 election was the modern turning point for evangelicals. What began in 1964 as an almost hopeless crusade ended in victory in 1980. Evangelicals supported the incumbent president, Ronald Reagan, with even greater numbers in 1984. In 1988 they supported, albeit with some misgivings, his anointed successor, George Bush.

GEORGE BUSH DEFEATS MICHAEL DUKAKIS IN THE 1988 PRESIDENTIAL ELECTION

In 1988, Vice President George Bush and his operatives, especially Lee Atwater, made maximum use of both a southern regional and a religious strategy. Previously Bush had been seen as the quintessential Episcopalian Brahmin candidate, the son of Wall Street banker and senator, Prescott Bush, of Connecticut, and owner of a summer home in Kennebunkport, Maine. During the presidential campaign George Bush was transformed into a southerner from Texas—his adopted state—and a very religious Christian who prayed regularly and was at home among evangelicals and ordinary folk. Michael Dukakis's northern liberal urban image appeared to play into Bush's hands, especially Dukakis's tardy response to questions dealing with the crimes of parolee Willie Horton and the hypothetical issue of how Dukakis would react if his own wife were raped.

According to CBS and ABC exit polls, George Bush was elected because he received the votes of 80% of born-again white Protestants and 60% of mainline Protestants, even though he failed to win among other religious groups. According to Albert Menendez of the Religious News Service, whose analyses of the election appeared in the *Washington Post,* evangelicals appeared to be less willing to vote for someone outside their religious tradition. As Menendez described it, "Dukakis's multicultural image—a Greek Orthodox Christian who attended a Quaker college and married a Jew in a Unitarian ceremony—may have appealed to religious liberals, but it turned off evangelicals."

The marriage between white Protestant voters and the Republican party had successfully come through a third consecutive presidential election, which had not happened since Herbert Hoover's victory over Al Smith in 1928. However, there were fissures appearing in the new coalition that Ronald Reagan had constructed that would lead to future problems for the G.O.P. For example, Bush ran about 8% to 10% behind Ronald Reagan among Catholic voters, barely gaining a majority of Catholics and actually running behind Dukakis in more than 60% of the 100 most heavily Catholic counties in the nation. Dukakis had apparently reached Catholic voters with his emphasis on economic and social-justice issues and the message that "Bush is not Reagan." Furthermore, although Jews had supported Republican presidential candidates with between 30% and 40% of their votes since 1972, in the 1988 election the Jewish vote for Bush was less than 30%. Dukakis also won over two thirds of the votes of people of other religions and those who said they were not members of any denomination.

The 1988 voter gap of 13% between Catholics and Protestants should have been an ominous sign for George Bush and his advisers. Even though Catholics as a group had achieved higher income and education levels than Protestants, they were still 13% less likely to vote for Bush than they'd been to vote for Reagan. These were clear indications that the Reagan coalition could be unlocked—but only if the Democrats were to nominate a moderate presidential candidate who could win back more Catholic and Jewish defectors and who could also cut into the Republican base support among white Protestant voters in the South and West.

RESULTS OF THE 1992 PRESIDENTIAL ELECTION

Bill Clinton won 43% of the total popular votes cast in the 1992 election, against 38% for George Bush and 19% for Ross Perot. In the electoral college, Clinton won 370 votes; Bush, 168. Bush's popular vote was even lower than Barry Goldwater's dismal showing of 39% in 1964. But Clinton did not do that well either. Fifty-seven percent of the voters did not vote for Clinton; his total was 3% lower than Michael Dukakis's poor showing of 46% in 1988. Ross Perot's candidacy diminished support for both major-party candidates.

Noting that Clinton's edge in the popular vote was just 5 points—the closest result since 1976—the *Economist* commented, "Had Mr. Bush won all the states in which he trailed Mr. Clinton by just four points, he would have had a bare majority (274 votes) in the electoral college." Voter Research and Surveys, a consortium of the four major television networks (ABC, NBC, CBS, and CNN), revealed that Clinton ran well ahead of Bush among Catholics, Jews, religious liberals, and religiously nonaffiliated voters. Clinton also made major inroads among mainline Protestant voters, running neck and neck with Bush among this group (each received about 38%), while Perot got 24%. Bush ran strongly among the 17% of the voters who identified themselves as born-again Christians, winning handily with 61% (20% fewer than in 1988) against Clinton's 23% and Perot's 15%, making this the incumbent president's best showing among any religious group. But in this important bloc of voters, Clinton received 5% more votes than Dukakis had four years before—and this in a three-man race. Bush's drop among born-again Christians could have been decisive in southern, western, and some midwestern states, especially in the ten states where Clinton's margin of victory was between 0.5% and 4% of the vote.

Bush also lost a sizable number of "Reagan Democrats" to his two opponents. The Catholic vote, which he won, 52% to 47%, over Dukakis in the 1988 election, now went 44% for Clinton, 36% for Bush, and 20% for Perot. Bush also suffered a major setback in the Jewish vote, dropping from 30% in 1988 to only 12% in 1992; 10% went to Perot, 78% to Clinton. The smallest change occurred in the black vote, which had gone overwhelmingly for Dukakis in 1988 and which Clinton won with 82% in 1992. Bush's support in the black community dropped from 12% in 1988 to 11% in 1992, while Perot received only 7%.

The most interesting voting bloc, however, was the large and diverse Protestant community, which constitutes 60% of the American voting population. In 1988, Bush won 66% of the white Protestant vote, to Dukakis's 33%. In 1992, white Protestant support for Bush dropped to 46% of voters, but he still had a plurality over Clinton, who received 33%, and Perot, who took 21%. Both Clinton and Perot cut deeply into the general Protestant vote. As noted above, only among evangelical Protestants did Bush win a clear majority. According to Voter Research Associates, even among those who attend religious services at least once a week Bush could not gain an absolute majority; he took only a plurality of 47% to Clinton's 35% and Perot's 15%. It would appear that even though southern Democrat Bill Clinton was part of a more moderate minority faction among Southern Baptists, he certainly had more appeal than the northern liberal Michael Dukakis.

A moderate Baptist publication, *Associated Baptist,* emphasized that the Clinton-Gore ticket was "the first all-Baptist ticket for the nation's highest office" and therefore in tune to some degree with Baptist and evangelical thinking. After the 1992 election, Albert Menendez of the Religious News Service reported that the ninety-six most heavily Southern Baptist counties, which went overwhelmingly Republican in 1988, supported Bush by only 46%, to Clinton's 40% and Perot's 14%. Whereas in 1988 Bush swept the entire South—every single southern or border state—in 1992 he won only seven of the eleven states of the former Confederacy, and the Clinton-Gore ticket won in eight of the fifteen southern and border states.

Bush's failure to achieve a landslide among Protestants, along with his inability to take a majority or even a plurality of Catholics, resulted in the loss of such states as Ohio, Michigan, Pennsylvania, Illinois, and Missouri. As it happened, Bush did best in the South, winning not only Texas and Florida but also three of the four most heavily Baptist states: Mississippi, Alabama, and North Carolina (Georgia went to Clinton). Clinton also won in such southern states as Arkansas, Tennessee, and Louisiana. The most heavily Roman Catholic states—Rhode Island, Massachusetts, Connecticut, and Louisiana—all went to Clinton. Actually, Clinton took all twelve of the nation's most heavily Catholic states, thereby surpassing Jimmy Carter's 1976 popularity with Catholics and doing almost as well in states with large Catholic voting populations as Lyndon Johnson had done in 1964.

In the states with the largest Methodist populations, two went for Bush (South Carolina and Kansas), and two went for Clinton (Delaware and Iowa). Similarly divided were upper midwestern states with large Lutheran populations, such as Minnesota and Wisconsin, which went for Clinton, and North and South Dakota, which went for Bush. In the states where Jews are numerous, including New York, California, New Jersey, Pennsylvania, Massachusetts, and Florida, all except the last went decisively for Clinton. In Florida, the larger Protestant population, along with Cuban American Republican voters, pushed the state into the Republican column.

In winning the 1992 election, Clinton held on to and even increased the Democratic share of the African American vote, and made major inroads with Catholic and Jewish voters. He and Perot also cut into the Republican base among Protestants in general: Bush won only a plurality of Protestant voters (46%) in 1992, compared to his majority of 66% in 1988. If Perot had not run in 1992, the election would have been closer, but Clinton still would have won; various polls indicated that the Perot vote would probably have shifted 10% to Bush and 9% to Clinton.

In 1992, the Democratic party made important inroads with voters whom Ronald Reagan had in the 1980s attempted to "lock up" permanently for the Republican party. But these were not changes that cannot be reversed. Republicans are still very strong among evangelicals, who now make up 20% of the population and are increasing. (What future impact will we see from Jerry Falwell's warning after the 1992 election that he would consider resurrecting his Moral Majority group if President Clinton moved too rapidly to enforce his "liberal" agenda on abortion and homosexual rights?) If a Republican candidate were to win a majority of Protestant voters and more than 50% of Catholic voters, as Reagan and Bush did in 1980, 1984, and 1988, and win at least one third of the Jewish vote, as they also did in those years, then 1996 would be quite different from 1992. If Republicans were to nominate a presidential candidate such as Jack Kemp, the self-described "bleeding-heart Lincoln conservative," who would attempt to win over more black, Catholic, and Jewish voters, then Republicans could conceivably return to the White House before the end of the decade. However, if President Clinton can hold on to these constituencies and win over most Perot voters, the results of 1992 could be a harbinger for the year 2000. The mid- and late 1990s will probably see the Democratic and Republican parties, and perhaps independents such as Ross Perot, competing for the evangelical vote while simultaneously seeking the support of moderate Protestants, Catholics, and Jews. In this light, the NSRI is important for what it reveals today and for what it implies about the future.

THE "REAGAN REVOLUTION" MOVES THE FEDERAL JUDICIARY TO THE RIGHT

One of the most important functions of the president of the United States is not usually discussed during the election campaign. It is the power to appoint people to the federal judiciary. One of the legacies of what has become known as the "Reagan Revolution" is that the Reagan-Bush administrations had appointed so many young conservative judges to sit on the federal district courts, circuit courts of appeals, and U.S. Supreme Court that their influence will be felt well into the 21st century. Indeed, the vast majority of the present members of the federal judiciary, including six of the justices now sitting on the U.S. Supreme Court, were appointed by presidents Reagan and Bush. The commitment of the Reagan-Bush administrations to conservative religious social priorities, including support for school prayer and limitations on a woman's right to have an abortion, has already brought about changes in public policy. The election of Bill Clinton in 1992 will initially have only minimal impact upon the federal judiciary. It will take at least two terms of Democratic administrations to move the judiciary back to the center.

U.S. SUPREME COURT DECISIONS MOVE MANY EVANGELICALS TO GREATER POLITICAL ACTIVITY

The National Association of Evangelicals (NAE)—the largest association of evangelicals—was established in 1942 to vigorously oppose modernity. Unlike some smaller groups of fundamentalists, the NAE decided to reach its objectives by "shunning all forms of bigotry, intolerance . . . hate and jealousy." Initially, the NAE was not much involved politically, devoting itself primarily to achieving and promoting personal salvation. However, the smaller and more right-wing American Council of Christian Churches (ACCC), which was organized the year before the NAE, attacked mainline churches directly for abandoning the literal truth of the Bible, and for becoming part of the "humanist heresy" through the adoption of the so-called Social Gospel, and for blinding themselves to what the ACCC considered to be a "world Communist conspiracy." Under the leadership of Carl McIntire, the ACCC became part of the anti-Communist crusade of the 1950s.

Eventually, three major Supreme Court decisions brought the NAE Evangelicals around to a broader mandate. The first was the 1963 *Schempp* decision, which banned Bible reading and prayer in America's public schools. The second was the 1971 *Lemon v. Kurtzman* decision, which prevented public funds going to nonpublic schools and set guidelines against violating the "no establishment" clause of the First Amendment to the Constitution. These guidelines included a three-part church-state test of the constitutionality of any law:

1. It must have "a secular purpose"
2. It must have a primary effect that neither "advances nor inhibits religion"
3. It must not foster an "excessive government entanglement" with religion

Finally, in 1973, the Supreme Court issued its famous *Roe v. Wade* decision on abortion, overturning a Texas law that made abortion a crime except to save a pregnant woman's life. By a vote of 7–2, the Court ruled that the constitutional right to privacy encompassed a woman's decision to terminate a pregnancy.

These three Court decisions and what evangelicals perceived as a general weakening of family values and a national increase in immorality, sexual permissiveness, drugs, and crime led many, including the National Association of Evangelicals, to greater political involvement.

Some nonevangelical traditionalist and neoconservative thinkers support an accommodationist approach to the church-state issue. They believe public life and American's institutions are enriched by acknowledging the country's religious traditions. The legal struggle between the strict separatists and the accommodationists was brought to a head by a Rhode Island legal case, *Lee v. Weisman,* that was heard by the Supreme Court in 1992. The case raised the question of whether even a "nondenominational" benediction can be given at a public-school commencement. In a close 5–4 decision in June 1992, the Court reaffirmed earlier decisions that prevented state-sponsored prayers by clergy at public-school commencements—a great disappointment to the Bush administration, which had urged the Court to develop a new standard that would give religion a more important role in public life. The majority in the Supreme Court, though rejecting aspects of the Bush administration's proposed new standards in *Lee v. Weisman,* did not foreclose a reexamination or perhaps even a reversal of *Lemon v. Kurtzman* in other situations. In this instance, the majority opinion very carefully noted the effect a reversal would have on irreligious schoolchildren who would have to sit through a clergyman's invocation and benediction at a school graduation. This, according to the opinion, breached the constitutional boundary between church and state. The Court was careful, however, not to extend its decision to other cases involving adults, and said, "A relentless and all-pervasive attempt to exclude religion from every aspect of public life could itself become inconsistent with the Constitution." Possible test cases of the limits of exclusion could include challenges to Hawaii's making Good Friday an official state holiday, Vermont's permitting Hanukkah menorahs in a public park, and the nationwide use of religious symbols on city seals and documents. The *Lee v. Weisman* decision also left open the possibility of a commencement prayer offered not by an adult clergyman but by a student volunteer. The decision might also have been different if the issue had been a personal, silent form of religious observance in the classroom rather than a recited prayer at a high-school commencement, which, the majority decision stressed, "is one of life's most significant occasions." These and similar issues might come before the Supreme Court in future years.

Less than a week after the Supreme Court's decision in *Lee v. Weisman,* a ruling in a major abortion case, *Planned Parenthood v. Casey,* left both pro-choice and pro-life groups unhappy by reaffirming what the Court called the "essence" of the constitutional right to an abortion while at the same time permitting four of the five restrictions to abortion that had been set by the Pennsylvania state legislature. The majority left little doubt that laws prohibiting most or all abortions are unconstitutional. At the same time, it ruled that states could impose some restrictions, such as parental or judicial consent to a teenager seeking an abortion, or a delay of twenty-four hours after a presentation in a medical office intended to change a woman's intentions. It also applied for the first time a new standard to the issue: Other restrictions could be enacted as long as they did not place an "undue burden" on the essential holding of *Roe v. Wade,* which should "be retained and once again reaffirmed."

The Supreme Court's decisions in 1992 on school prayer and abortion, which neither completely overthrew the previous decisions in the field nor affirmed them as they were, were victories for moderate conservatives. These rulings reaffirmed principles—both in the area of separation of church and state and in the area of a woman's right to an abortion—while at the same time allowing some accommodation and restrictions and opening the door to possible further changes.

WILL THE CONSERVATIVE ALLIANCE OUTLIVE THE SOVIET UNION?

In May 1992, after the collapse of the Soviet Union, the destruction of the Berlin Wall, the demise of the Communist regimes of Afghanistan, Angola, Mozambique, Nicaragua, and Ethiopia, and the end of the civil war in El Salvador, the former Soviet president Mikhail Gorbachev visited his onetime adversary and now friend the former U.S. president Ronald Reagan in Santa Barbara, California. That world politics had been turned upside down was evident in Gorbachev's public espousal of the values of a free society and a free-market economy when he received the Medal of Freedom at the Reagan Presidential Library. Later on this trip, history appeared to have come full circle when Gorbachev stood in front of a sculpture depicting the breakdown of the Berlin Wall and alongside the statue of Winston Churchill at the site where Churchill gave his "Iron Curtain" speech at Westminster College in Fulton, Missouri, in 1946. Newspapers headlined this event "Gorbachev Buries the Cold War."

Few would have dreamed a decade ago of the breakup of the Soviet Communist empire in the late 1980s and early 1990s. Except for the anti-Castro/Cuban American coalition, the anti-Communist religious lobbies— evangelical Protestants, Catholics, Jews, Eastern Orthodox—concerned with persecuted religious groups in eastern Europe attempted to redirect their energies, having achieved most of their goals. Conservatives could see that with the demise of what had been called "Godless communism," religion was again flourishing in eastern Europe, and even in the former Soviet Union. Furthermore, minorities such as Jews, Pentecostals, and evangelicals were free to emigrate to the West, and large numbers did—especially to the United States, Canada, and Israel. The key question for the future is what effect will this have on the conservative religious-political alliance that was forged in another decade and under different circumstances. For many years, the anti-Communist "crusade" was the cement that bound the American religious right and the political right together. But now a major political conservative like Pat Buchanan has split with other conservatives like Bob Dole, Jack Kemp, Dick Cheney, Dan Quayle, Phil Gramm, and William Bennett. Buchanan's "America First" theme not only conjures up the image of the extreme political rightists of the 1930s and their demand for isolationism at the start of Nazi and Fascist aggression in Europe and Africa; it also fractures the conservative movement, which is further split by Buchanan's statements espousing economic protectionism rather than free trade. The mid-1990s will surely witness a major test of the strength and endurance of the conservative religious-political coalition as a moderate Southern Baptist Democrat occupies the White House and his new attorney general commands the Justice Department. Will agreement on the domestic social agenda of school prayer, school choice, "traditional" family values, and limiting abortion rights be sufficient to hold disparate conservative groups together, especially with the changes brought about by the Clinton administration? What effect does all this have upon a new generation of moderate Democratic leaders—not only Bill Clinton and Al Gore but also Bill Bradley, Jay Rockefeller, Bob Graham, and Dick Gephardt—all of whom are potential presidential candidates and most of whom are from southern or border states?

THE EFFECT OF RELIGIOUS IDENTITY ON PARTY AFFILIATION

One of the popular criticisms of American politics is that there is a very constricted choice of party options compared with the range that exists in other multiparty Western democratic societies. Few other democratic countries offer a choice between just two main political parties. Given the enormous size of the United States and its large population, this limited choice means that a political-party label does not necessarily mean the same thing in Maine as it does in Alabama. As this chapter has illustrated, our two dominant parties are, in effect, coalitions, especially at the national level in presidential elections. Both parties have their liberal and conservative wings, though one (the Democratic party) has more liberals and the other (the Republican party) has more conservatives. The balance between liberal and conservative ideologies is the real locomotive of the American political process. Even this dualism is complicated by, for instance, the frequent crossover between economic and social liberalism. A person can support civil rights or choice regarding abortion but also believe in lower taxation and reduced government entitlements.

Conservative or liberal opinion does not automatically translate into support for the Republican or Democratic parties, except perhaps in recent presidential elections. On the local level there are liberal Republicans and conservative Democrats. The pattern of support is mediated by race, region, and, increasingly, gender. Nevertheless, religious identification is a factor in political-party preference. Every four years, journalists and political pundits, believing that religious tradition or culture affects voting patterns, show a renewed interest in the religious beliefs and opinions of both the electorate and the candidates. The NSRI reveals that the ideological line between Protestants and Catholics has blurred. The situation is no longer as simple as it once was, but nevertheless, Protestants were over 9% more likely to vote Republican in 1988 and 1992 than others, and regular Protestant churchgoers were 11%

more likely to vote Republican than those who identify but never attend.

Analysis of recent presidential campaigns has shown that partisan differences between Catholics and Protestants are marginal today. In the past the Catholic-Protestant division was explained by the Catholic concern with community and the Protestant emphasis on individualism. No doubt, conservative Protestant individualism does have a basis in Arminian theology, which claims that individuals, not groups, achieve salvation and that collectivities therefore cannot be "born again." Thus Catholics remain more likely than white Protestants to support an expanded role for government in the social and economic sphere to help the deprived. This contrast is especially true among the college-educated population: It is not that college-educated Catholics are particularly liberal—indeed, 38% are conservative—but that so many—48%, almost a majority—of college-educated white Protestants think of themselves as conservative.

Within Protestantism there are growing differences between the denominations, as Table 5-1 illustrates. Our "Fundamentalist" and "Born Again" respondents and the adherents of some of the smaller evangelical and fundamentalist denominations, such as the Wesleyan, Foursquare Gospel, and Christian Reformed churches, are highly supportive of the Republican party. The unexpected exception to this pattern is the Churches of Christ, the only Democratic party–oriented denomination in Table 5-1 that does not have a large ethnic-minority membership. A possible explanation is that denomination's strong presence in areas like rural Texas and Arkansas, where the Democratic party is still quite strong on the local level.

Adherents of the so-called mainline liberal Protestant churches—Episcopalians, Presbyterians, Methodists, Disciples of Christ, and members of the United Church of Christ—are more than 40% Republican, and only around 25% Democratic. This 15-point margin should not be unexpected to students of American history, for northeastern white Protestants have been the backbone of the Republican party since the Civil War. What is surprising is the wide discrepancy between the political views of the congregants and the official pronouncements of their denominations. This dissension may well account for the numerical decline of these denominations over the past few decades. Many critics in the pews believe that their churches have incorrectly embraced an all-loving, all-forbearing, all-forgiving God who overlooks all sin and welcomes anybody into the Kingdom of Heaven. They claim that this outlook has led to the adoption of a fashionable political agenda that casts Jesus and the Bible as the spiritual font for social and political liberalism. For example, the United Church of Christ General Synod Pronouncement of 1989 on economic issues was criticized in a published response by a lay member, W. Widdick Schroeder, for its "narrow, left-wing" stance on the political economy. Certainly the document appears to be out of line with

TABLE 5-1
THE PARTIES' STANDING BY PROTESTANT DENOMINATION
(IN PERCENT)

Republican Party–Oriented

DENOMINATION	REPUBLICAN	DEMOCRAT
Wesleyan	59	13
Christian Reformed	58	17
Foursquare Gospel	56	22
"Fundamentalist"	52	10
Evangelical/"Born Again"	46	20
Assemblies of God	46	23
Presbyterian	44	28
Brethren	43	27
UCC/Congregationalist	41	18
Episcopalian	44	23
Disciples of Christ	39	32
Nazarene	39	34
"Protestant"	37	29
Lutheran	37	26
Methodist	36	35
Christian Science	35	24

Democratic Party–Oriented

DENOMINATION	DEMOCRAT	REPUBLICAN
Church of God in Christ	66	4
7th-Day Adventist	44	23
Baptist	43	27
Churches of Christ	39	30
Pentecostal	38	27
Jehovah's Witness	6	3

the political opinions of the Congregationalist respondents to the NSRI. In many mainline denominations, seminary professors and national staff members, who tend to be more liberal, dominate the process of creating the church agenda. Similar tension can be seen in the United Methodist church, the nation's second-largest Protestant denomination, with 8.9 million members. In 1992, 1,000 elected delegates to the church's General Conference reaffirmed their opposition to homosexual behavior and overwhelmingly turned down a special committee's report that church teaching should be revised in this area. At the General Conference meeting, a reporter noted that "conservatism and suspicion of leadership had the edge." The conference also gave preliminary approval to moving its largest agency, the General Board of Global Ministries, away from New York City and its "negative" influences. This move away from the "liberal" and "unrepresentative" influence of the National Council of the Churches of Christ would follow the lead of the Presbyterian church, which in the 1980s decided to move its headquarters closer to its congregants by relocating to Kentucky.

THE IMPACT OF TELEVANGELISM

Throughout the 1992 presidential campaign there were constant allusions by candidates to Americans as a religious people and America as a religious nation with a special "mission." It made little difference whether the candidate was Episcopalian, Southern Baptist, Roman Catholic, or Greek Orthodox. This was not unusual. American political leaders since the birth of the country have used similar discourse. If we had closed our eyes and forgotten the year, we could have been in 1988, 1980, 1976, 1964, 1960, 1928, or even 1896, when Protestant fundamentalist and political populist William Jennings Bryan electrified voters in the prairie states and the South with his "Cross of Gold" Democratic National Convention address in the first of his three losing bids for the White House. The issues change, the names of the candidates are different, but the rhetoric is quite similar. Sometimes there is dissonance when religious prejudice is injected into a national political campaign, as in 1928, when Al Smith lost, or in 1960, when John F. Kennedy won. The underlying theme and religious rhetoric remain constant, however, and are intertwined with America's civil religion.

A new dimension has been added by the intimate and direct communication of television, especially cable TV. Religious groups recently began using this medium as a way of bringing their message directly into people's living rooms. In the 1970s and 1980s, televangelists like Jerry Falwell, Paul Crouch, Oral Roberts, Jim Bakker, James Robison, Jimmy Swaggart, and Pat Robertson became household names. In 1992 the head of the Christian Science church resigned after a bitter dispute involving his desire to build a cable TV channel and make it the church's primary ministry to the world. The late 1980s saw Jim Bakker and Jimmy Swaggart fall into disgrace, and Paul Crouch rise to the top rung of religious broadcasting. By the end of 1992, Crouch's Trinity Broadcasting Network had almost 290 stations, making it one of the largest sources of religious broadcasting in the world.

One of the salient leaders of the Christian right, who is also one of the best-known television evangelists, is the Reverend Pat Robertson, a graduate of Washington and Lee University and Yale Law School. He is the son of the late senator A. Willis Robertson of Virginia, a leading figure in the nation's political establishment and one of the most powerful men to serve in the U.S. Congress in the mid-20th century. Pat Robertson was a candidate for the Republican presidential nomination in 1988. He battled George Bush, Bob Dole, and Jack Kemp in several state primaries, even embarrassing Bush in the Iowa caucuses, where Robertson came in behind Dole but ahead of Bush. He later lost to Bush in South Carolina and shortly thereafter pulled out of the race. In 1992, after much prayer and soul searching, Pat Robertson, like Jerry Falwell, decided to support the president for reelection, primarily because of Bush's opposition to abortion and his commitment to school prayer and school choice.

Robertson founded the Christian Broadcasting Network (now the Family Channel) in 1977 as a showcase for his *700 Club,* an evangelical talk show. Soon he became the nation's most successful television evangelist. During the late 1980s and early 1990s, the Family Channel branched out from a strictly evangelical following, grew rapidly, and became an instrument for a wider audience interested in family entertainment; the channel now broadcasts reruns of such popular old TV serials as *Father Knows Best* and *The Waltons.* Eventually the Family Channel had as many viewers as MTV, the popular rock-video channel. According to the National Cable Television Association, the Family Channel is the tenth-largest cable TV operation in the nation, with 55 million household subscribers. Its successful management raised Robertson's stature as an astute businessman, and he has not only broadened his television ministry but also kept it free from the scandals that tripped up Jim Bakker and Jimmy Swaggart. In 1992, International Family Entertainment, the parent company of the Family Channel, began trading on the New York Stock Exchange and sold shares worth more than $150 million. The initial sale of the stock earned Robertson, already a wealthy man, more than $14 million.

Through the years Robertson has taken some controversial public positions, including his stance that the "no establishment" clause of the First Amendment applies only to Congress and not to the fifty states. He claimed that the clause "says nothing . . . about separation of church and state! Merely that Congress can't set up a national religion." He has also attacked the public schools as "agencies for the promotion of . . . the humanist religion" (which to him means atheism). He has also advocated the end of state support for public elementary and secondary education. In the realm of foreign affairs, he has predicted the approach of an Armageddon in the Middle East that will bring about the Second Coming.

Indications are that Pat Robertson will be a powerful force in the 1996 presidential election, and several Republican conservatives are already jock-eying for his support. He has formed the Christian Coalition to register new voters to increase pressure for the agenda of conservative evangelicals. The new organization may serve to aid Robertson should he decide to seek the Republican nomination himself in 1996. Indeed, in November 1992, build-ing from the ground up, fundamentalist Christian candidates, either loosely or directly aligned with Pat Robertson and the Christian Coalition, won almost 40% of the local elections they had targeted in such diverse states as Iowa, Oregon, Texas, Kansas, Florida, and California.

Ralph Reed, Jr., who directs the Christian Coalition, said these successes had placed numerous conservative Christians in positions that could serve as springboards for higher offices in 1996, if not sooner. He commented, "On the one hand, George Bush was going down to defeat. . . . On the other hand, the anecdotal evidence is that at school boards and at the state legis-lative level, we had big victories." Arthur Kropp, president of the liberal lobbying group People for the American Way, agreed, saying, "I think they've got to be pretty pleased with themselves. Right now the religious-right movement has a lot of political muscle. In the coming year they're going to have a lot of money." By 1993, Pat Robertson's Christian Coalition had a membership of 350,000 and over 700 affiliated chapters in all 50 states. It was in a strong position to raise much more than the $13 million it had acquired by 1992.

THE EFFECT OF RELIGION ON LEFT-RIGHT POLITICAL STANCE

The 1990 NSRI generated some important new information in response to the question "Which of the following best describes your usual stand on political issues?" This question was followed by a 5-point scale from very liberal to very conservative. Patterns emerge that correlate with the respon-dent's overall worldview or religious identification.

Table 5-2 shows the replies we received from a limited sample of the NSRI respondents within a restricted number of the larger religious groups. Among our six groups, only one, the Jews, showed a liberal plurality. In every other group, moderates outnumbered those to the left or right. Those adopting conservative stands outnumbered those advocating liberal or radical options. However, the large Catholic population had some internal variation. Data from the National Opinion Research Center (NORC) reveal that Hispanic- and Irish-origin Catholics are more liberal (their responses resemble the Jewish pattern) whereas Catholics from central, eastern, and southern Europe are more conservative.

The overall balance between liberal, moderate, and conservative opinion should not be surprising since we know that in the 1988 and 1992 general

TABLE 5-2

POLITICAL OUTLOOK BY RELIGIOUS GROUP

(IN PERCENT)

Which of the following best describes your usual stand on political issues?

RELIGION	VERY LIBERAL	LIBERAL	MODERATE	CONSERVATIVE	VERY CONSERVATIVE	DON'T KNOW	TOTAL
Jewish	9	34	33	17	2	5	100
Methodist	2	23	39	17	10	9	100
Catholic	3	21	36	28	6	6	100
Lutheran	2	18	42	30	2	6	100
Other Protestants	1	19	46	22	6	6	100
Baptist	1	16	39	25	8	11	100

elections, Republican candidates attempted to paint their opponents with the unpopular "L-word." And Democratic candidates in 1992 frequently referred to themselves as "moderates," "centrists," or "progressives." The *New York Times*/CBS poll for January 1991 showed that not only did more whites state that they were conservative rather than liberal, 31% versus 20%, but that this was also true for blacks, by 29% to 28%. Whereas there are, as we shall show, large differences in support for political parties by race, the actual ideological gap is much narrower. This explains why the Baptists in Table 5-2 are the most conservative group, yet they also have the largest proportion of black adherents. When it comes to issues such as belief in God or patriotism, the survey evidence shows that blacks and whites share similar cultural values. In May 1990 the Princeton Survey Research Associates' poll for the Los Angeles Times Mirror Syndicate showed that 92% of blacks and 87% of whites "never doubt the existence of God" and that 89% of whites and 87% of blacks agreed with the statement "I am very patriotic." We believe that this broad, religiously based consensus on cultural values at least partly accounts for the narrow spectrum of political choice offered by American party politics.

Religious identification is not the only factor associated with many people's position on the liberal-conservative spectrum. Survey data show that regular attendance at religious worship tends to pull people toward a more conservative outlook irrespective of whether they are Jewish, Catholic, or Baptist, and that the effect is even stronger for those who identify with a fundamentalist denomination. The reason for this is not too hard to divine: Attending worship regularly is in itself a traditional, or conservative, form of activity. On social issues, from premarital sex to living wills and euthanasia, the trend is clear. Even though Jews are more liberal than Protestants and Catholics, all those who regularly attend services—whether Catholic, Protestant, or Jew—are significantly less likely to support liberal positions than people who rarely go to services.

THE INVOLVEMENT OF EVANGELICAL CHURCHES IN THE POLITICAL PROCESS

Over the last three decades, there has been a growing alliance between the Republican party and evangelical Protestants, whose number has ranged from 30 million to 50 million people and who are primarily white. There are several umbrella evangelical groups, but the largest, the National Association of Evangelicals (NAE), represents 15 million people and has a largely conservative political agenda. Evangelicals encompass but do not necessarily include all fundamentalists, who represent the right wing of the movement and about one third of evangelicals. Fundamentalists believe in a literal interpretation of the Bible. Evangelicals, who have frequently had a personal and moving religious experience, emphasize the personhood of Jesus and consider proselytization to be very important. Their political agenda usually includes support for school prayer, school choice, and "traditional" family values. Many are involved in anti-abortion activities, frequently joining forces on this issue with Roman Catholics, though they have in the past criticized the American Catholic hierarchy and the papacy as well as Catholic teachings on salvation and the role of the Virgin Mary.

Evangelical Protestants now comprise more than 20% of the nation's population. According to A. James Reichly, they include "most Baptists and Disciples of Christ, many Methodists, Presbyterians and Lutherans and members of independent local evangelical churches." They tend to be "more rural, more southern, less affluent and less well educated" than the rest of the population. About one fifth of evangelicals are black. However, blacks are not usually designated as "fundamentalist" even though a sizable number of independent black churches are both theologically and doctrinally close to fundamentalist white Protestants. It is important to note that a much higher percentage of black evangelicals vote Democratic rather than Republican.

In the last generation, only two national Democrats—Jimmy Carter and Bill Clinton—have been able to break into this political pool and gather some support for their political ambitions. It is surely no coincidence that both men are Southern Baptists who feel at home using religious themes and preaching in Baptist churches, white and black.

The mission for many conservative evangelicals is nothing less than "the Christianization of America," as Paul Weyrich, a conservative Christian leader, put it. The new Christian right does not support the statement issued a generation ago by Protestant theologian Reinhold Niebuhr that "the tendency to claim God as an ally for our partisan values . . . is the source of all religious fanaticism." Jerry Falwell, leader of the now defunct Moral Majority and the more recent Liberty Federation, said during the 1980 presidential campaign, "I don't see how one can claim to be both a Christian and a liberal." Right-wing Christian voters are deeply committed to a conservative philosophy that they believe is based upon Christian faith and values. They consider themselves to have been instrumental in the 1980 election of Ronald Reagan and the defeat of three liberal senators, all of whom had sought the Democratic presidential nomination at one time—George McGovern in South Dakota, Frank Church in Idaho, and Birch Bayh in Indiana (who lost his seat to then Representative Dan Quayle in a bruising election battle).

The Importance of the Protestant Evangelical Vote

The increasing political involvement of evangelicals was the subject of a study, "Evangelicals in the Post-Reagan Era: An Analysis of Evangelical Voters in the 1988 Presidential Election," published in the *Journal for the Scientific Study of Religion* in 1992. The researchers, Corwin Smidt, a professor of political science at Calvin College in Grand Rapids, Michigan, and Paul Kellstedt, a graduate student in the Department of Political Science at the University of Iowa, concluded that a shift in the partisan identification of white evangelical voters toward the Republican party took place during the early 1980s and appeared to have solidified during Ronald Reagan's second term. It was most evident among younger evangelicals, and, as a result, Smidt and Kellstedt predicted that the trend's effects were likely to be felt in elections to come. They indicated that "previous conclusions concerning the relatively apolitical nature of evangelicals need to be reassessed" in light of the increased activism. They also detected "a growing divergence between the voting patterns of white evangelicals and white non-evangelicals, with white evangelicals being more likely to cast their ballots for the GOP presidential candidate." They speculated that "there might be a growing divergence between the political behavior of white evangelicals and non-evangelicals within the south. . . . As a result of this growing divergence, southern evangelicals seemingly have begun to reflect more closely the patterns evident among non-southern evangelicals than among southern non-evangelicals."

The alliance of conservative evangelicals with the Republican party has helped the religious group to achieve some of its social objectives and helped the political party to gather the votes needed to win a national election. It could take at least a decade, if not more, of moderate Democratic presidential administrations to reverse the conservative pattern that has been set in motion. In 1992, Bill Clinton attempted to win back some of the evangelicals, especially from his southern base, in order to create a "New South–New Generation" alliance among people of different races, regions, and religions. So far he has been only partly successful.

NON-PROTESTANT RELIGIONS AND PARTY AFFILIATION

The pattern of partisan politics among the non-Protestant Christian groups listed in Table 5-3 shows that the Mormons (who are not, according to themselves or self-acknowledged Protestants, a Protestant denomination) are firmly in the Republican camp. Politically, they resemble fundamentalist Protestants. This was not always so. Originally, Mormons were Democrats, but they were always hostile to the federal government, which had confiscated their lands and church property. In the 1890s, the government forced a two-party system on Utah as the price of statehood, but the two parties, the People's party and the Liberal party, were local and largely artificial. Later, the personal antagonism of Joseph P. Smith, president of the Mormon church in the 1930s, toward Franklin D. Roosevelt led the Mormons into the Republican camp. Nonetheless, their tradition makes Mormons suspicious of government, and so they favor reduced government interference in society rather than the New Deal or Great Society approach. Contemporary Republican calls to "get government off the backs of the people" resonate with the Mormons' history and their increasing self-perception as rugged western individuals. It is therefore not surprising that in 1992, Utah, with

TABLE 5-3

THE PARTIES' STANDING AMONG NON-PROTESTANT CHRISTIAN
DENOMINATIONS
(IN PERCENT)

DENOMINATION	REPUBLICAN	DEMOCRAT
Mormon	51	27
Eastern Orthodox	26	38
Catholic	27	38
Non-Hispanic White Catholics	34	29
Hispanic Catholics	23	43
Non-Hispanic Black Catholics	10	63

the highest percentage of Mormons, was the only one of the fifty states in which Bush ran first, Perot second, and Clinton last.

We have already observed that in presidential voting, the historic and overwhelming support for Democrats has largely disappeared from the nation's Catholic population. The blurred ideological line between Protestants and Catholics today reflects the great diversity among Protestant denominations and the loose ties between many Catholics and their church in matters of morality and politics. Nonetheless, Catholics are still more likely to be Democrats than Protestants are, by a margin of 7 percentage points. In other words, Catholicism is worth 7 percentage points to the Democratic party, and Protestantism 7 points to the Republicans. We found that this rule applies as well to the Hispanic population, two thirds of whom are Catholic and 23% of whom are Protestant. Nevertheless, we can see from Table 5-3 that there is variability among Catholics according to their ethnic origin. White Catholics now favor the Republicans over the Democrats. Among whites, the only remaining loyal bastion for the Democrats is Irish Americans, whose level of support, however, cannot compare with that of either Hispanic Americans or, certainly, black Catholics. Apart from Irish Americans, identification with the Democratic party among Catholics is usually strongest among the less educated, the less affluent, and older people.

Polling data show that, as a group, Catholics remain more likely than white Protestants to support an expanded role for government. This is in keeping with the stance of their church, which has never endorsed laissez-faire capitalism and has frequently advocated a communitarian view of society. This gap is particularly reflected among the middle class. National Opinion Research Center (NORC) data for the 1980s show that 34% of Catholic college graduates believe that government should do more to improve society, whereas only 16% of white Protestant college graduates hold that opinion. On other social issues, such as the death penalty, the Catholic hierarchy also takes liberal positions. While its economic and social positions are now to the left of many newly Republican middle-class Catholics, the church is regarded by its laity as too conservative on matters relating to sexuality and the family: divorce, contraception, abortion, homosexuality, and the role of women in the priesthood. In 1989, under the influence of a traditionalist Vatican, the National Conference of Catholic Bishops stated categorically that no Catholic can take a pro-choice stand when choice denotes abortion. This statement was supported by both John Cardinal O'Connor of New York and Joseph Cardinal Bernardin of Chicago. Yet many Catholic men and women seem unwilling to accept the bishops' authority. The American Catholic population is also divided on the issue of the ordination of women for the priesthood. This is only somewhat reflective of the feelings of America's Catholic bishops, a majority of whom are strongly opposed (as is the Vatican) to the ordination of women under any circumstances, while a minority would consider keeping the door ajar for future consideration and perhaps modification. After a decade of discussion, writing, and rewriting, the 1992 National Conference of Catholic Bishops could not secure a two-thirds vote to approve a pastoral letter that would have upheld now and forever traditional Catholic teaching in this area. A minority of bishops were concerned, as Bishop Kenny of Juneau said, about "the pain, the anger, and the growing alienation of some of the most loyal, learned, and active women and men in the church." A majority of bishops argued, as Auxiliary Bishop Vaughan of New York did, that the church's ban was "infallible" and "unchangeable." Bishop Vaughan went further in stating, "In the year 2,000, 20,000, and 2,000,000, there will still be a Catholic church and it will still have an all-male clergy. A woman priest is as impossible as for me to have a baby."

Writer Dennis Castillo, in an article in the magazine *America,* revealed another dimension to the ordination problem, and that is the diminishing number of priests: From a ratio in 1942 of 1 priest for every 617 American Catholics, the disparity ballooned to 1 priest for every 771 American Catholics in 1962, the time of Vatican Council II. During the next thirty years, the number of priests declined 6% while the Catholic community grew by 36%. In 1990, the National Conference of Catholic Bishops predicted that by the year 2005 there will be only one priest for every 2,200 parishioners. Similar problems have arisen in the decreasing number of nuns, both quantitatively and in relation to the overall American Catholic population.

Our NSRI and other poll data indicate that a gender gap exists politically among Catholics, as it does throughout American society. Catholic women favor the Democratic party by about 5% more than men do, largely because of the Democrats' apparent greater sympathy on social and women's issues. This is in spite of the fact that, as we shall discuss later, women in general are more religious than men and attend services more regularly.

GERALDINE FERRARO, ABORTION, AND THE CATHOLIC CHURCH

The 1984 presidential election became more than a footnote in American history with the selection of a woman, Representative Geraldine Ferraro of New York, by the Democratic party as its candidate for vice president. It was the first time that either of our major political parties had selected a woman for national office. The Walter Mondale–Geraldine Ferraro ticket was soon buffeted not only by charges of financial impropriety leveled against Ferraro's husband, but also by attacks on Ferraro herself by members of her own Catholic hierarchy. Ferraro, a leader of the women's movement and a believer in a woman's right to abortion, claimed that diversity of Catholic opinion on this issue was permissible. Not so, stated John Cardinal O'Connor, who publicly attacked Ferraro for what he called a distortion of Catholic teaching.

A subtler position on this controversial issue is taken by some other Catholic elected officials, including Governor Mario Cuomo of New York, who have sought to draw a line between an elected official's personal faith and beliefs and his or her public responsibility. Though these politicians believe that abortion might be wrong for them personally, they would not foreclose the possibility of the option for other Americans. Cuomo has stated, "You cannot stop abortion by prohibiting it. You can curtail abortions by helping men and women avoid unintended pregnancies." By contrast, Governor Robert Casey of Pennsylvania, one of the few prominent officials in the Democratic party who has taken an anti-abortion and pro-life position, does not differentiate between his personal belief and his public position. Casey's supporters were upset when he was not given time to speak at the 1992 Democratic Convention.

A dissonance developed within the Catholic community during the 1984 presidential campaign that was not unlike the conflict that occurred between clergy and some laity within the Episcopalian community in the 1964 presidential campaign. In both, some laypeople broke with church leaders on issues of importance: In 1964, the issue was the progressive agenda of the Social Gospel movement; in 1984, it was a woman's right to an abortion. In 1964, Episcopal church leaders accused Barry Goldwater of contravening their teachings; in 1984, Catholic church officials accused Geraldine Ferraro of contravening *their* teachings. Indeed, the Catholic hierarchy was utterly unified in its condemnation of Ferraro on the issue of abortion. Even a relatively progressive leader of the Catholic hierarchy, Cardinal Bernardin of Chicago, spoke of the sanctity of life as a "seamless garment," an opinion that would seem to cover opposition to abortion, the death penalty, and most wars. Cardinal Bernardin, Cardinal O'Connor, and other Catholic bishops have called for a "consistent ethic of life" that links rejection of abortion to opposition to euthanasia, capital punishment, and poverty.

The Mondale-Ferraro ticket, beset by numerous problems and opposed by a popular incumbent president, suffered a major defeat, winning the electoral votes of only Minnesota and the District of Columbia. Yet despite the loss, the Ferraro candidacy *did* reflect the growing Protestantization of Catholic laypeople, who were moving further away from the social positions of the American Catholic hierarchy. This shift had initially been revealed in John F. Kennedy's 1960 presidential campaign, but it did not reach its peak until the 1980s and early 1990s. It was perhaps best symbolized by the selection of Pamela J. Maraldo, a Roman Catholic, to succeed Faye W. Wattleton, a Protestant, as president of the Planned Parenthood Federation of America. At the time of her appointment in late 1992, Maraldo said, "Like most

Catholics, as shown by one national survey after another, I believe in the use of contraception and am pro-choice. I go to church on Sunday but do not subscribe to many of the basic tenets of the church. That does not mean I am any less a Catholic." A 1992 Gallup poll bore witness to Maraldo's feelings. The poll revealed that lay Catholics frequently take different positions from their bishops and the Vatican on such issues as artificial birth control, abortion, and the ordination of female priests, and corroborated other findings that Catholics below the age of thirty-five are more likely to favor change in traditional doctrines. The Gallup poll also found that though Pope John Paul II was personally very popular (84% of Catholic respondents professed admiration), his flock was not following his teachings. Bishop Raymond Boland of the Bishops' Communications Committee said that polls are of value at times but "extremely transient." He further said that "the church decides its doctrine on two thousand years of traditional teachings based on the Scriptures and the message of Our Lord Jesus Christ. We are not about to change it just because of the polls."

POLITICS AND THE AMERICAN JEWISH COMMUNITY

If in the past Catholics tended to be among the most loyal Democratic party supporters, today the evidence (see Table 5-4) suggests that non-Christians have taken on this role. Certainly, Republican Party support among these religious groups seems weak. The strongest Democratic group is Jews (though we should note that on Table 5-3, Eastern Orthodox adherents are similar in their political alignment). The Unitarians' figures are also similar to the Jews'. The explanation for this pattern may be in part due to the fact that Unitarians, Jews, and Eastern Orthodox Christians all tend to be more affluent and better educated than the average American, and more likely to reside in and around urban areas in the Northeast.

The political liberalism of American Jews has been much discussed in the academic and general literature on American politics. Since it is the Hebrew Bible that is the source of inspiration for much of conservative Christianity, the Jewish position appears to be a paradox. The reality is that under 10 percent of American Jews identify themselves as Orthodox Jews, the most traditional form of Judaism, which is usually associated with a conservative social and political outlook. In fact, the 1990 National Jewish Population Survey revealed a religiously less observant population. Only 13 percent of those Jews identifying themselves as "religious" agreed with the statement that "The Bible or Torah was the actual Word of God." What has happened is that, rather than traditional Jewish texts, American Jewry's domestic agenda has taken on many aspects of the universalist outlook of Reform Judaism. At the same time, humanists borrowed and reinterpreted a tradi-

Table 5-4

THE PARTIES' STANDING AMONG NON-CHRISTIAN RELIGIOUS GROUPS
(IN PERCENT)

Republican Party-Oriented

GROUP	REPUBLICAN	DEMOCRAT
Scientologist	41	23
"New Age"	36	22

Democratic Party-Oriented

DENOMINATION	DEMOCRAT	REPUBLICAN
Jewish	43	22
Unitarian	42	18
Hindu	36	24
Muslim	34	19
Buddhist	33	22
Agnostic	30	25
No Religion	27	21

tion of Jewish concern for building a good and just society. This has led to the development of an American Jewish "folk calendar" that emphasizes annual festivals concerned with liberation and freedom such as Passover, which recounts the exodus from slavery in Egypt, and Hanukkah, which is connected to national liberation and religious freedom in the Hellenic period. Such sentiments have been reinforced by memories of oppression in Europe. After the Holocaust and World War II, the Zionist national liberation movement, that lead to the creation of the State of Israel, was supported by a broad consensus of American Jewry.

American Jews have a political influence out of proportion to their numbers in society as both citizens and elected officials. There are a number of reasons for this. Partly it is their concentration in a number of politically influential states with some of the largest totals of electoral votes, such as New York, California, Florida, Illinois, Pennsylvania, and New Jersey. In addition, the educational and economic success of American Jews makes them a larger factor in the political arena. Jews are much more interested and involved in politics than most other Americans. Their rate of voter registration is 89% compared with 67% of the entire population. During the years 1988–90, 36% of Jewish households gave donations to a political campaign, mostly to Democratic candidates. These facts, plus a well-mobilized grass-roots communal structure, have led to the legend of the "strong Jewish lobby" that has served as a prototype for other groups in American society, such as Italian Americans and Arab Americans. The Jewish lobby works hard to influence both Congress and the White House to give aid and political support to Israel and to oppressed co-religionists in the former U.S.S.R., Ethiopia, and Arab countries.

Hindus, Buddhists, and Muslims (see Table 5-4) have similar patterns of party preference, favoring the Democrats by 12% to 14%. This suggests that they are alike demographically and in socioeconomic terms. Agnostics and religious "Nones" also have similar patterns, with about a 5% plurality favoring the Democrats. The slightly higher proportion of party preference among agnostics probably relates to their being, in the main, well-educated whites. The real surprise in Table 5-4 is that the followers of new religious movements, Scientologists and New Age adherents, are more likely to be Republicans than Democrats. In part the explanation is that many of them are middle-class white entrepreneurs, but perhaps the libertarian and individualistic ideas of the Republican party also appeal to them.

Who, then, are the political independents? First, they are the newcomers who have yet to acculturate to a democratic society. A majority of Taoist, Baha'i, and Shintoist adherents stated that they were political independents. As one might have expected, agnostics do not have strong views in this regard, and 43% of them are independents, as are 40% of Muslims, 37% of Unitarians, and 35% of Buddhists. A unique religious group is the Jehovah's Witnesses, who abhor politics in the same way they do blood transfusions and higher education. As Table 5-1 shows, only 9 percent aligned themselves with either of the two main political parties (16% refused even to answer the party-preference question).

RACE AND PARTY AFFILIATION

The current exception to the close correlation of Protestantism and Republicanism is among the African American population. Here we find the apparent paradox of theological conservatism and political liberalism. The most partisan Democratic party denomination in Table 5-1 is the black Church of God in Christ. Table 5-5 compares the white and African American party preference within denominational families or churches with a multiracial membership. The figures show quite clearly that there is a strong race factor in party alignment, and that it is not just a Protestant phenomenon, for it also appears among Catholics, Muslims, and religious "Nones." Class is only part of the white-black political differential. There are obvious cultural differences at work. African Americans make more use of the term "com-

TABLE 5-5

THE PARTIES' STANDING BY RELIGIOUS DENOMINATION: A COMPARISON OF
WHITE AND BLACK NON-HISPANIC ADHERENTS
(IN PERCENT)

DENOMINATION	WHITES		BLACKS	
	DEMOCRAT	REPUBLICAN	DEMOCRAT	REPUBLICAN
Holiness	38	24	70	8
Baptist	32	35	69	8
Pentecostal	29	38	62	7
Catholic	29	34	63	10
Methodist	28	41	75	7
7th-Day Adventist	27	34	67	5
"Protestant"	25	40	64	7
Muslim	26	31	49	5
No Religion	25	23	40	7

munity" in their discourse and are much more in favor of governmental interference in society on behalf of collectives. One can discern an espousal of their own social gospel, which combines a distrust of laissez-faire capitalism and a preference for a vaguely defined democratic or Christian socialism. Nevertheless, it is also blacks' perception that the current leadership of the national Republican party is unsympathetic to their civil rights agenda, which has caused them to favor the Democrats, especially since both their clergy and laity stress the incompatibility of Christianity and racial injustice. It is the Republicans' general skepticism about social engineering and collective solutions and their emphasis on individualism that has attracted increasing white support. However, here too we should not dismiss the religious factor in the process. A great deal of the attraction of the white middle class toward the Republican party is linked to the party's enthusiastic endorsement of values such as the Protestant ethic and the traditional family, as well as the Protestant emphasis on individual responsibility.

RELIGION, POLITICS, AND AFRICAN AMERICANS

It is interesting to note that the large community of African American fundamentalist churches and their memberships, though quite conservative on many theological and even social issues, did not, with few exceptions, join white Protestant evangelicals in their recent movement to the political right. Black Americans have always stressed the need for social justice and racial equality and have sought identification with a political party that also emphasized racial justice and inclusion. For more than sixty years, from Reconstruction to the advent of Franklin Roosevelt's New Deal, those who could vote voted Republican, while many of their white neighbors, especially in the South, voted Democratic. Martin Luther King, Jr., for instance, was raised in a Republican household and a fundamentalist Baptist environment; so were many of his contemporaries. In the last sixty years, however, African Americans have become an important component in the Democratic party coalition, and the political pattern of the past has been reversed: Blacks vote Democratic, and many of their white neighbors, particularly in the South, vote Republican, particularly in national elections. Ronald Reagan and George Bush received only about 10% of the black vote in the four presidential elections from 1980 to 1992. Even though several black conservative leaders accepted the Reagan-Bush agendas, as was notably revealed during the Clarence Thomas–Anita Hill Senate hearings, they represented only a small minority of black voters. The vast majority of blacks have continued to vote for Democratic candidates. The presence of Jesse Jackson as a candidate participant in the 1984 and 1988 races increased the number of black voters, but with or without Jackson, the percentage of black support remained constant for the Democratic presidential candidates during the 1980s and into the 1990s.

All recent major black elected officials, with the exception of Representative Gary Franks of Connecticut, are Democrats, including the first black to be elected governor of a state since Reconstruction—L. Douglas Wilder of Virginia—and the first black woman ever to be elected to the United States Senate—Carol Moseley Braun of Illinois. Indeed, the election to the House of Representatives of Republican Gary Franks in 1990 marked the first time that a black Republican had served in either house of Congress since the defeat of Senator Edward W. Brooke of Massachusetts by Paul Tsongas in 1978, and the first time there had been a black Republican in the House of Representatives since the 1930s.

Several prominent Democratic black elected officials are also Protestant ministers. These included such diverse political figures as Representative Floyd Flake of New York, former Georgia congressman and onetime Atlanta mayor Andrew Young, and the Reverend William H. Gray III, who has been a "preaching minister" at Bright Hope Baptist Church in Philadelphia since 1972, and who rose as a Democratic congressman to become House majority whip, the highest position ever achieved by an African American in Congress. Gray resigned from the House in 1991 to become president of the

United Negro College Fund, which supports black students and colleges. Many of these colleges were started by and are still linked to Protestant denominations. There are several white Protestant ministers in Congress, some with much prestige and seniority, like Senator John Danforth of Missouri, an Episcopalian priest, but a greater proportion are black. However, though there are numerous Catholics and a number of Jews in Congress, not one is a clergyman. The last Catholic priest to serve in Congress, Robert Drinan, Democrat of Massachusetts, was forced by his religious superiors to choose between elected office or the priesthood. He resigned from the House.

The 1990 NSRI has given us valuable insight into the relationship of religious and political affiliations. Religious leaders with a social agenda, politicians with a public agenda, and Americans in general might take note of this information and its implications, especially since it corroborates and explains the religious identification of the American people, which sets America apart from other modern democracies. Not all Americans today necessarily believe that "God has marked the American people as his chosen nation to finally lead in the redemption of the world," as Senator Albert Beveridge of Indiana remarked some ninety years ago. Yet they still want their leading political figures, especially the president of the United States, to express in a political context a new understanding of America's millennial hopes for this nation and the world.

In their presidential campaigns, Bill Clinton and Ronald Reagan understood what George Bush and Jimmy Carter did not—this need for the "vision thing," couched in inspirational and even evangelical language. President Clinton's "new convenant" is a continuation of the long political tradition of moving Americans to accept a political program with religious rhetoric that legitimizes a perceived common national purpose.

6

CULTURE WAR:
GENERATIONAL, GENDER, AND
FAMILY ISSUES

◆ ◆ ◆

Religions have always had a great deal to say about the human drama—the purpose of life, human sexuality, procreation, and death. Religious literature, particularly the Bible, is full of stories, parables, and teachings about family relationships. It also sets out the duties and responsibilities of individuals to one another according to age, gender, and kinship ties. Religious thinkers of the past assumed they were legislating to a relatively closed society where people lived in a stable relationship with their physical and social environments. They could not envisage the unprecedented social upheaval of the last few decades, particularly as regards the status of the family. The women's and gay liberation movements have made dramatic progress. Since the 1960s, divorce laws have been liberalized, abortion legalized, and the Pill introduced. Out-of-wedlock births now account for one in four of the national total, yet the number of abortions has tripled since 1970. Women's lives have undergone striking changes since they've increased their independence from men and marriage.

These developments inevitably have religious implications since they deal with the issues of what constitutes acceptable human behavior, an issue that has historically been the concern of organized religion. Most of these changes have run contrary to the religious prescriptions and norms of the traditional Judeo-Christian-Islamic consensus. The rapidity of these changes and the increasing break with past patterns of behavior inevitably disconcert serious believers in a life lived according to the social ethics of the Scriptures, who feel it incumbent on them to redirect society back onto its previous course.

The result is a battle for the hearts and minds of the American public between two sides variously labeled modernist and traditionalist, liberal and conservative, secular and religious.

Both sides in this increasingly polarized debate, which is now termed a "culture war," claim to represent the views of the conveniently silent majority of the American public. This chapter will examine the actual scorecard as American religion attempts to respond to the newly emerging social structure of the 1990s. The NSRI allows us the first opportunity to look in detail at how the various religious groups are faring in this new environment. We will discover which religious groups are most successful in attracting the loyalties of particular segments of the American population.

An obvious first question is how far the public's religious attitudes and behavior vary by age and sex. A 1991 Gallup poll that inquired into one key measurement—how important a role people say religion plays in their own lives—showed that women (66%) are far more likely than men (48%) to attach great importance to religion, and that men (18%) are more than twice as likely as women (8%) to say that it is not very important to them. Age differences are also significant. Less than half of those under age 30 (46%) say that religion is very important to them, whereas among those who are 50 and older, 70% consider religion of great importance in their lives. Behaviors such as membership in religious bodies and attendance at public worship reveal smaller gender and generational gaps than beliefs and attitudes. This finding leads to the conclusion that public religious display does not necessarily reflect inner devotion among contemporary Americans.

As regards church or synagogue membership, the older the person, the more likely he or she is to be a member. Of those under age 30, 60% claim membership, while 76% of those aged 50 and older say they are members. Women (72%) are more likely than men (64%) to be members. During a typical week in 1991, 42% of the adult population (46% of women and 39% of men) attended worship services at least once; only 35% of those younger than 30 attended church or synagogue, but 60% of those aged 70 to 79 did. One question we will explore is: Can we assume from this that people become more religious with age and that today's unchurched liberals are tomorrow's conservative church attenders, or is it that different generations of Americans really vary as a result of exposure to different life experiences and historic times?

GENDER DIFFERENCES

The lay and professional literature has consistently shown what ministers and parishioners have observed: that women are more likely than men to join religious organizations and participate actively. It appears that Christianity is especially associated with female spirituality. Adolescent girls exhibit stronger belief in the inerrancy of the Bible, and higher rates of participation in religious services. One explanation may be that women are more religious than men because of their different standing in society, reflecting a fundamental division of labor by sex. Religious and family spheres in the West were feminized and separated from the mainstream workplace activities, which were male-dominated. Another interpretation has it that men are less religious than women because of what psychologists refer to as sex-type personalities. In this view, being religious is consistent with a feminine orientation, which includes a religious experience of "otherness," a personal experience of "connectedness," and a sharing of the "We-ness" of a religious community. In the jargon of the men's movement, being religious is not conducive to maleness since it demands submission and is more left-brain-oriented.

Participation in churches has always been lower for men in all major Protestant and Catholic denominations in America. Historically, European Christianity, with its experience of feudal society and monarchy, has shown

chart 6-1

Profile of Religious Indentification:
Adult Males

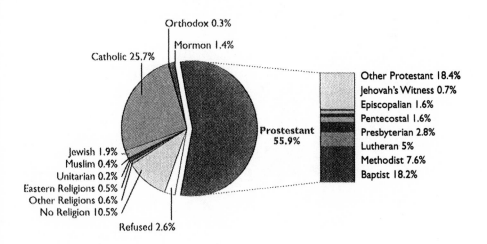

antipathy to maleness—the heroic, the hunter, the achiever, activism, and assertiveness. Its preferred definition of maleness has focused on fathering: either on the role of male as priest leading the flock in the ways of God or on the father as representative of Christ in the family and as head of the home. In America, as early as 1692, Cotton Mather wrote, "So still there are far more Godly women in the world than there are men; and our Church Communions give us a little demonstration of it." In Victorian times, women's organizations were catalysts for "benevolence" and reform in the community, and for the establishment of schools and churches. In contrast, when single men and their interests dominated, as on the frontier, the establishment of the local saloon took precedence.

The NSRI discovered that 87% of American males today define themselves as belonging to or believing in religion; 83% are Christians; 56% are Protestants of some kind. Analysis of the information in Table 6-1 shows a quarter are Catholic, almost a fifth are Baptists, and a tenth are Protestants (that is, define themselves as such regardless of denomination). As we might expect, the figures for women, provided in Table 6-2, are somewhat higher:

Chart 6-2

Profile of Religious Identification: Adult Females

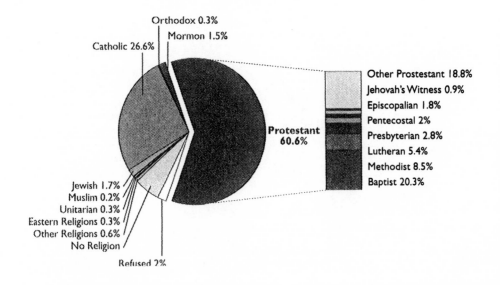

TABLE 6-1

PROFILE OF MALE RELIGIOUS IDENTIFICATION BY AGE

(In Percent)

RELIGION	AGE 18–24	AGE 25–44	AGE 45–64	AGE 65–74	AGE 75+
Roman Catholic	32.8	26.9	23.0	21.4	17.6
Baptist	18.2	18.2	19.7	16.8	15.6
Methodist	5.0	6.6	9.0	10.8	11.7
Lutheran	4.2	4.4	5.6	7.0	6.8
Presbyterian	1.8	2.2	3.6	4.4	5.1
Pentecostal	1.5	1.9	1.3	1.2	0.8
Episcopalian	1.2	1.4	1.9	2.0	2.7
7th-Day Adventist	0.2	0.4	0.3	0.5	0.4
Other Protestants	13.9	17.0	20.8	22.0	21.6
Mormon	1.4	1.4	1.4	1.3	1.0
Eastern Orthodox	0.2	0.2	0.3	0.4	0.4
Jehovah's Witness	0.7	0.7	0.7	0.6	0.4
Total Christian	**81.1**	**81.3**	**87.6**	**88.4**	**84.1**
Jewish	1.9	1.7	1.6	2.5	4.2
Muslim	0.9	0.6	0.1	0.0	0.0
Eastern Religions	0.9	0.7	0.4	0.1	0.1
Unitarian	0.2	0.2	0.3	0.2	0.3
Other Religions	0.5	0.7	0.6	0.6	0.3
None/Agnostic	12.8	12.7	7.3	6.0	9.0
No Answer	1.7	2.1	2.1	2.2	2.0
Total	**100**	**100**	**100**	**100**	**100**
Men of all Faiths by Age Group	15.2	44.9	25.7	9.1	5.0

92% identify with a religion; 89% are Christians; almost 61% of America's women are Protestants of some kind. As might have been expected, every Christian religious group contains more female than male adherents. An extreme example of the feminization of American Christianity is the African American community. The percentages of females among black adherents in the larger Christian denominations are 52% among Catholics, 56% among Episcopalians, 58% among Baptists, 60% among Methodists, 62% among Seventh-Day Adventists, 64% among Pentecostals, and 69% among Holiness sects.

TABLE 6-2

PROFILE OF FEMALE RELIGIOUS IDENTIFICATION BY AGE

(In Percent)

RELIGION	AGE 18–24	AGE 25–44	AGE 45–64	AGE 65–74	AGE 75+
Roman Catholic	34.2	27.7	25.5	23.1	18.5
Baptist	19.8	20.1	21.7	22.3	19.8
Methodist	5.8	7.2	9.6	11.3	13.9
Lutheran	3.7	5.4	5.8	6.0	6.7
Presbyterian	1.5	2.4	3.1	3.6	5.6
Pentecostal	2.0	2.5	1.7	1.4	1.2
Episcopalian	1.2	1.7	2.2	2.3	2.2
7th-Day Adventist	0.5	0.4	0.3	0.5	0.6
Other Protestants	15.2	17.4	20.0	20.2	22.2
Mormon	1.4	1.7	1.4	1.1	1.2
Eastern Orthodox	0.3	0.3	0.3	0.4	0.2
Jehovah's Witness	0.9	1.1	0.8	0.5	0.6
Total Christian	**86.5**	**87.9**	**92.4**	**92.7**	**92.7**
Jewish	1.6	1.6	1.4	1.9	2.4
Muslim	0.4	0.2	0.1	0.0	0.1
Eastern Religions	0.1	0.1	0.0	0.0	0.0
Unitarian	0.1	0.3	0.4	0.0	0.1
Other Religions	0.4	0.6	0.6	0.6	0.6
None/Agnostic	9.5	7.9	3.5	2.9	2.2
No Answer	1.4	1.4	1.6	1.9	1.8
Total	**100**	**100**	**100**	**100**	**100**
Women of all Faiths by Age Group	14.2	42.3	25.5	10.4	7.6

Non-Christian religions of America are the exceptions to this feminization pattern. Those who identify as Jews and as members of "other religions" have a slight male bias. Muslims, adherents of the Eastern religions, agnostics, and religious "Nones" have even more unbalanced sex ratios: almost two males for every female in each group. In contrast to the sex ratio among black Christians, only 36% of black Muslims and 40% of black religious "Nones" are women.

AGE PATTERNS

Age also makes a difference in the religious realm. The youngest respondents to the NSRI were aged 18 (born in 1972, during the Nixon presidency). The oldest respondents were in their late nineties (born in the mid-1890s, during the second term of Grover Cleveland). The world has undergone amazing change in the eight decades that separate our youngest and oldest respondents. The very elderly were born before the era of manned flight; the youngest take space travel for granted. In the 1890s, more Americans worked the land than any other occupation; by the 1970s America had more computer programmers than farmers. Technological change has affected society in fundamental ways. It changed people's relationship to natural and social environments: how they live, what they eat, how they move from place to place, how they spend their working and leisure hours, and how they relate to one another. Given the astonishing rate of technological change and its far-reaching nature, we should also expect dramatic change in how people see the world and their place in the universe, and, thus, in their religious outlook and identification.

The figures in Tables 6-1 and 6-2 show an unanticipated level of stability in religious identification across the generations. Whereas we might expect religious belief to have been undermined by the triumphs of science and modern technology, the change was only marginal. As Table 6-1 shows, the proportion of religious "Nones"—those of no religion and agnostics—among males under age 25 is only 12.8% while among those over 75 years of age, the proportion is even lower, 9%. The trend toward abandoning religious identification is predictable, but it is minimal. The generation gap is wider among women. Table 6-2 reveals that religious "Nones" comprise 9.5% of women under age 25 but only 2.2% of women over age 75. Among women, irreligion has increased slightly with every succeeding generation, but the largest gap is between women under 45 and those older. Among men, the pattern is similar except that the oldest age group, over 75, contains more "Nones" (9%) than those aged 65 to 74 (6%). Nevertheless there is little evidence, as shown in Tables 6-1 and 6-2, that Americans have abandoned religion during the course of the 20th century. In fact, as we shall see, though gender differences have narrowed recently, gender and marital status are better predictors of religious loyalty than is age.

Of course, it is reasonable to assume that the limited age differences we have identified are not really generational. Other studies have demonstrated that as individuals age and pass through different stages in the life cycle, they become more inclined to adopt a faith. Thus today's elderly are probably more religious than they were when they were fifty years younger. The current evidence on the younger generation suggests that the vast majority of America's elderly in the 21st century will identify religiously.

Do the younger and older generations differ in their level of identification with Christianity? Are the younger generation abandoning Christianity? Here again Tables 6-1 and 6-2 reveal an unexpectedly high level of stability in religious identification. Among the under-age-25 young-adult population, 86.5% of women and 81.1% of men identify with a Christian church or denomination. Among the oldest age group, those over age 75, the respective figures are 92.7% for women and 84.1% for men. These figures show that Christianity remains dominant and that the gender gap has narrowed among the young.

INTERGENERATIONAL DENOMINATIONAL CHANGE

Whereas Christianity has maintained its hold on the population, the pattern of denominational preference within it has changed over the course of this century. The overall trend is reflected among the larger Christian denominations by differences in their ability to attract varying age groups. This is apparent if we examine a revealing statistic, the median age, that is, the point that cuts the population of adherents into two halves according to age. The oldest median ages among our adult respondents were found among Presbyterians (48.2 years) and Methodists (48 years). Episcopalians (45.7) and Lutherans (45.4) were very similar on this score, while Baptists were slightly younger (44.1). The youngest denominations on this score, and so those with the greatest proportion of young-adult identifiers, were the Pentecostals (39.8 years), Catholics (40.1), and Mormons (41.6). The graying of the American mainline churches has been a documented trend for more than a decade. Observers have pointed out that white Protestants are older than black Protestants, and that liberal Protestants are older than conservative and fundamentalist Protestants.

These variations provide insight into which religious groups are "gaining" among the American population because they translate into very significant differences when we compare the populations aged under 25 with those over age 75. Female Methodists are 14% of the oldest cohort but only 6% of the youngest, indicating significant intergenerational losses. Similarly, Presbyterian loyalties account for 6% of the elderly females but only 2% of the younger cohort of women. Generational change has also negatively affected the Eastern Orthodox and Seventh-Day Adventist churches. The pattern of change is similar for both sexes across most religions except that, as we have observed, men are slightly less likely to provide a religious identification at any age. One significant exception is among Baptists: The same proportion of women (20%) is found among the oldest and youngest age groups, but among men the percentage increases from 16% among those over 75 years of age to 18% among those under age 25. A similar pattern of increasing attractiveness to young males is found for Pentecostals, where the proportion of males nearly doubles from 0.8% of the oldest age cohort to 1.5% among the youngest; and for Jehovah's Witnesses, up from 0.4% to 0.7%. Other religions that appear to be gaining, at least when comparing old to young men, are Islam and all the Eastern and alternative faiths. Jews and Unitarians, like mainline Protestants, appear to be losing ground.

The most important change over the generations has occurred among Catholics. Catholicism is more than twice as prevalent among the young than the very old. Identification with Catholicism accounts for 18% of males and 19% of females among those over 75 years of age. In contrast, Catholicism holds the religious loyalty of 33% of the males and 34% of the females under 25 years of age. In fact, the younger the age range, the higher the percentage of Catholics; and, therefore, the older the age group, the lower the percentage. At first sight this appears very good news for the Catholic church. Undoubtedly, some of the increase among the young is due to the high proportion of Catholics among recent immigrants, as we discussed earlier (immigrants tend to be young adults). Yet it is the low percentage among the elderly that is surprising. This is true even for the 65–74 age group, where Catholics account for 21% of the males and 23% of the females.

The NSRI results for older Catholic people (18%) are well below the proportion of Catholics found among the American population thirty-three years earlier in the March 1957 voluntary sample survey by the Bureau of the Census (25.7%). The question then was the same as the NSRI's: "What is your religion?" The median age of the Catholic respondents in 1957 was around 40, which means that the average person interviewed then would have been around 75 when interviewed for the NSRI. These figures suggest that around one 1957 Catholic in four no longer identified as such by the 1990s.

According to Gallup polls, Americans are more likely to stray from the Roman Catholic church than from any other major religious group. Considering the figures we have produced, we should not be surprised to find that these polls corroborate NSRI. They affirm that 31% of Americans say they were raised as Catholics, while 27% now identify with the church.

These findings for Catholics are significant because the results for our other elderly female respondents to the NSRI equate almost exactly with the 1957 figures for Baptists (19.7%), Methodists (14%), Lutherans (7.1%), Presbyterians (5.6%), and Jews (3.2%). In contrast to the Catholics, these religious groups seem to have been highly successful in retaining the loyalty of their adherents over more than three decades. Thus, it appears that the reason for the proportionate decline by Methodists, Jews, Presbyterians, and Lutherans within the total national population is not due to the loss of individuals through apostasy or religious switching as they grow older. The decline of these groups seems due to their inability to recruit sufficient numbers among the younger population born in the 1960s and 1970s.

The overall effects of change in religious identification within age groups vary, of course, according to the relative size of the population under consideration. For instance, among the total American population there are three times as many adult males under age 25 (15%) as over age 75 (5%), but only twice as many comparably aged young females (14%) as elderly ones (8%). These ratios reflect the different life expectancies of American men and women. Yet despite what is revealed about long-term trends by changes at either end of the age spectrum, what really affects the numbers today is what happens to the massive baby-boom generation born in the twenty years after World War II. This population comprises those aged 25–44, and accounts for 44.2% of adult males and 42.3% of adult females.

THE EFFECT OF THE POSTWAR BABY BOOM

Virtually without exception, all the nation's religions have been enlarged by Americans born between 1945 and 1965. Male baby boomers increased the ranks of all religions fairly evenly. They comprise the largest number of men in every religion—usually 2 out of 5. This ratio holds for Catholics, Baptists, Jews, Jehovah's Witnesses, Seventh-Day Adventists, Mormons, "No Religions," and many others. Only for the mainline Protestant denominations do males age 25 to 44 constitute a smaller than two-fifths proportion—men this age are only 1 of 3 male mainline Protestants. The few religions in which male boomers constitute *more* than two-fifths of the male adherents include Islam, Hinduism, Buddhism, Pentecostalism, and the alternative faiths. Recent immigration of young adults has created this pattern among the non-Christian religions. Males between the ages of 25 and 44 appear in a 3-out-of-5 ratio among male Muslims and in a greater than 1-in-2 ratio among men in the latter three religious groups.

Women baby boomers have had an even greater impact on religious patterns. Categories in which at least half of today's female respondents are baby boomers include Islam, Pentecostalism, Buddhism, Jehovah's Witnesses, New Age, Mormonism, and religious "Nones." This also holds true for Scientologists, Wiccans, and members of the smaller Protestant sects such as Charismatics, Holiness, Christian Reform, nondenomination, and

Wesleyan. Groups where female boomers comprise 2 out of 5 women include Catholics, Baptists, Seventh-Day Adventists, Lutherans, Orthodox Christians, Unitarians, other Protestants (that is, all the smaller Protestant groups taken as a whole), and adherents of the East Asian religions. Female boomers were less attracted to several mainstream religions, forming only a third of women Methodists, Presbyterians, Episcopalians, and Jews.

Extrapolating from figures on the baby-boom generation is problematic. The future prospects of smaller religious groups that derive the better part of their membership from female baby boomers can be seen either positively or negatively. If these women's attraction is only a generational fad, then the groups are not likely to last much beyond the current generation. On the other hand, as these young women raise families, their children increase the number of adherents. The future of these—and, in fact, all—religions largely depends, as we shall see, on the family status of their adherents and the relative success of the various religious groups in transmitting their beliefs to new generations.

MARITAL-STATUS PATTERNS

Marital status seems to affect the pattern of religious identification for both sexes. Being married and, even more so, being widowed appear to be associated with a greater likelihood of being religious and Christian, as Tables 6-3 and 6-4 demonstrate. Divorced, single, and separated males are considerably more likely to be religious "Nones" than married or widowed men. Among women, similar patterns emerge, except that single women are even more likely to be nonreligious (9.9%) than divorced women (7.9%). Also, the gap between widowed (2.7%) and single (never married) (9.8%) is greater for nonreligious women than for nonreligious men (8.5% for widowed and 13.8% for single).

These figures must be approached knowing that since the adult female population is larger than the male, discrepancies result. Since the female population contains so many more widowed, a higher proportion of men are of married or single status than women. The 1990 U.S. Census found five times as many widows as widowers in the United States: 11.5 million widows and 2.3 million widowers. As we might have expected, the religious profile of the widowed population in Tables 6-3 and 6-4 is very similar to the elderly population in Tables 6-1 and 6-2. Similarly, single status tends to correspond to the young-adult population.

Research studies have shown that in general the presence of a religious faith is associated with marital success. In other words, the family that prays together stays together. Clearly, the figures in Table 6-3 and 6-4 illustrate that being divorced is associated with lower levels of religious identification.

TABLE 6-3

MALE MARITAL STATUS BY RELIGION

(In Percent)

RELIGION	SINGLE	MAR-RIED	SEPA-RATED	DI-VORCED	WID-OWED
Roman Catholic	31.8	24.0	22.8	21.3	25.1
Baptist	17.2	18.2	27.7	19.7	19.1
Methodist	5.2	8.4	5.5	7.7	11.3
Lutheran	4.0	5.5	3.2	4.3	5.4
Presbyterian	2.1	3.2	2.1	2.0	3.2
Pentecostal	1.2	1.7	0.9	1.5	1.3
Episcopalian	1.4	1.7	1.1	1.7	1.6
7th-Day Adventist	0.2	0.4	1.2	0.3	0.1
Other Protestants	14.1	19.6	13.3	19.0	17.0
Mormon	1.0	1.6	0.8	1.2	0.8
Eastern Orthodox	0.3	0.3	0.1	0.2	0.3
Jehovah's Witness	0.6	0.7	1.2	0.7	0.5
Total Christian	**79.1**	**85.3**	**80.4**	**79.5**	**86.1**
Jewish	2.4	1.8	1.3	2.2	2.1
Muslim	0.8	0.3	1.0	0.4	0.0
Eastern Religions	0.8	0.4	1.6	0.4	0.3
Unitarian	0.2	0.2	0.3	0.5	0.2
Other Religions	0.8	0.5	1.6	0.8	0.2
None/Agnostic	13.8	9.0	12.2	14.4	8.5
No Answer	2.1	2.5	1.6	1.8	2.6
Total	**100**	**100**	**100**	**100**	**100**
Men of all Faiths by Marital Status	24.6	65.7	1.8	5.6	2.3

This might be either a cause or a result of the divorce. On the other hand, since divorced men and women have religious-identification profiles similar to those of single men and women, it might mean that they have merely returned to their old pre-marriage pattern. Yet many divorced people are parents, and this, as we will show, should tend to make them more susceptible to religious messages. Disillusion with marriage may make divorced people less religiously identifying just because marriage is so intimately associated with religion—from the marriage ceremony itself to the increased religious activity involved in family life.

TABLE 6-4

FEMALE MARITAL STATUS BY RELIGION

(In Percent)

RELIGION	SINGLE	MAR-RIED	SEPA-RATED	DI-VORCED	WID-OWED
Roman Catholic	32.5	26.9	24.1	21.8	21.1
Baptist	20.2	19.3	28.7	22.6	23.3
Methodist	6.4	8.7	6.3	7.7	12.0
Lutheran	3.9	6.0	2.5	5.2	5.4
Presbyterian	1.9	2.9	1.6	3.0	4.0
Pentecostal	1.6	2.0	3.8	2.4	1.8
Episcopalian	1.5	1.8	1.8	2.3	2.3
7th-Day Adventist	0.5	0.4	0.3	0.6	0.6
Other Protestants	14.8	19.2	17.3	19.2	19.7
Mormon	0.9	1.7	1.4	1.3	1.1
Eastern Orthodox	0.4	0.3	0.2	0.2	0.2
Jehovah's Witness	0.8	1.0	1.6	0.8	0.6
Total Christian	**85.4**	**90.0**	**89.4**	**87.1**	**92.2**
Jewish	1.9	1.6	0.8	1.5	1.9
Muslim	0.4	0.2	0.2	0.2	0.1
Eastern Religions	0.1	0.2	0.3	0.3	0.1
Unitarian	0.2	0.3	0.6	0.5	0.3
Other Religions	0.5	0.5	0.5	0.8	0.7
None/Agnostic	9.8	5.2	7.3	7.9	2.7
No Answer	1.7	2.0	0.9	1.7	2.0
Total	**100**	**100**	**100**	**100**	**100**
Women of all Faiths by Marital Status	18.5	59.1	2.4	8.1	11.9

Happily married couples are more likely than divorced couples to have had a religious wedding and to attend religious services regularly. The NSRI found that marriage rates are highest among white conservative denominations. For instance, 70% of adherents of the Churches of Christ, the Church of the Brethren, and the Assemblies of God are currently married (since there are more women than men in the total U.S. population, the proportion of currently married women is smaller than that of men: Two thirds of men and 59.1% of women are currently married). Mormon women have the nation's highest marriage rate, at 70%, among the major religions. Lutherans and Jehovah's Witnesses follow: Two thirds of their women are married. Most Protestant denominations have around 60% of their women currently married. Jews and Catholics have slightly lower rates: 57.2% for Jews, 59.3% for Roman Catholics. Particularly low rates are found among Seventh-Day Adventist women (48.9%) and Muslim women (47.8%). A low rate of marriage is also found among women who do not identify with any religion (50.5%). Those groups that have high rates of marriage for their women also tend to have women who marry at early ages. For instance, 48% of Mormon women under the age of 25 are married, as are more than 40% of the women of the Jehovah's Witnesses and Pentecostals. In contrast, we found that only 18% of Jewish and Presbyterian women and 23% of Catholic women married early.

Clearly, those religious groups that focus most energetically on traditional family values marry off their daughters earlier and in larger numbers than those groups that make allowances for modern feminist concerns such as advanced education and careers.

The highest marriage rates among males are found among the Eastern religions (77.1%), a category combining five Asian religions. More than three quarters of the male adherents are married. Another small group of males with a surprisingly high rate of marriage is the alternative-religion adherents (76.4%), including followers of New Age beliefs, Scientology, Ekankar, and Wiccan. These respondents, as we've said, tend to be young baby-boom males. Among the major religious groups, Mormons have the highest rate of marriage for men (75.6%). Most of the major Protestant denominations have marriage rates between 70% and 75%. Lower rates of marriage are found for Roman Catholics (61.2%) and Jews (59.9%), who are just ahead of the religious "Nones," of whom 56% are currently married. Again, Muslims have by far the lowest rates of marriage (41.6%). The reason for this is that a large proportion of this group is comprised of urban African American males who are part of a subculture indifferent to marriage. Indeed, many of the differences in marital status among the religions are due to the fact that marriage rates are higher for whites than for blacks because of age and social factors. For instance, 66.3% of white women are currently married, as compared to 44.4% of black women. Among religious groups to which blacks affiliate in significant numbers, the highest rates of marriage for blacks are found among Holiness adherents (57.3%), Pentecostals (56.4%), and Episcopalians (53.7%), while the lowest rates are found among Muslims (33.4%), and those of no religion (35.8%).

Though many religious groups discourage divorce, the only significant underrepresentation of divorced people irrespective of gender is among Catholics. This seems to show the tenacity of the Catholic proscription against divorce. On the other hand, Catholic rules are by no means universally accepted among Catholic identifiers. Analysis of the data reveals that 1 in 20 Catholic men and 1 in 14 Catholic women are currently divorced. This proportion is only 20% lower than the overall proportion among the aggregate of all Protestant groups, and exceeds that of Eastern Orthodox adherents.

These divorce figures do not represent actual rates of marriage breakup. This is because they are affected by the results of remarriage, which is more common for men than women. Overall, around 5–6% of the male population is currently divorced across most Protestant denominations, Jews, and Muslims. The Orthodox Christians and Catholics, as we mentioned, have below-average proportions of divorced men in their populations, while those of other religions and those of no religion have slightly higher percentages. As we suggested, more women (7–9%) than men in every religious group are currently divorced. Only the Eastern Orthodox and the Catholics have lower than 7% divorce rates (6.2% and 6.6% respectively). Seventh-Day Adventist women (10.7%) and women in the alternative or new religious movements (15.6%) have much higher percentages than males of the same groups, who have average scores. We cannot explain why this is so, but it is worthy of further investigation by the denominations themselves and by those interested in gender differences among religious groups.

The highest rate of men currently divorced is 12.1% among Unitarians, which exceeds the religious "Nones," of whom 7.6% are currently divorced. Among Unitarian females, 14.2% are also divorced. This figure again exceeds the "No Religion" group, in which 10.6% of women are divorced. It could well be that this religious group is attractive and welcoming to those who are already divorced, not that Unitarian Universalists are more likely to get divorced.

Table 6-3 shows that 1 in 4 men in America is single and has never been married. The proportion varies across religious groups from a low of around 17% for Methodists, Mormons, and Seventh-Day Adventists, to a high of 45% for those in the alternative religions and 48% for Muslims. Of religious "Nones," 32% are single.

Among all women (see Table 6-4), not even 1 in 5 is single. The smallest proportion of single females is found among Mormons (11.3%) and Presbyterians (12.5%). Above-average proportions occur among Jews (20.5%), Roman Catholics (22.4%), and Orthodox Christians (23.2%). Thirty percent of female adherents of Eastern religions and women of no religion are single, while the highest proportion of single women is found among Muslims (33.4%), many of whom are young African Americans. This is largely a mirror image of the marriage pattern described earlier.

MARRIAGE AS A RELIGIOUS INSTITUTION

Although marriage is still the living arrangement of choice, it is less common now than it was earlier in the century. Young people delay their first marriage, and those who divorce wait longer to remarry. The median age at first marriage increased by three years between 1970 and 1990 to 23.2 for women and 26.1 for men. Moreover, it is increasingly common for unmarried couples to live together. A 1988 National Center for Health Statistics study reported that one third of women age 15 to 44 said that they had cohabited at one point in their lives. The depression in marriage rates and increased cohabitation relate to social and economic changes. Growing numbers of men and women are getting bachelor's and advanced college degrees, and more women are pursuing careers. These trends have pushed up the age of marriage because people tend to wait until they complete their schooling or launch their careers before they settle down. There is also less social pressure to marry at a young age than there used to be. The result is that young people today are likely to experience a life cycle quite unlike that of their parents. Life expectancy has increased, so the life cycle has more stops along the way. In past eras, people stayed home until they married and then set up a new household that lasted until death. Today, there are more transitions as people form, dissolve, and re-form households and families.

The 1990 U.S. Census reported that for the first time in the history of the census the number of married couples heading households dipped below 50%. Meanwhile, divorce rates have flattened slightly in recent years but are still substantially higher than in the past. In 1988, approximately 19 per 1000 married couples got a divorce, compared to 14 per 1000 in 1970. Following the liberalization of divorce laws in the 1960s, divorce became more prevalent, more acceptable, and less of a barrier to remarriage. In fact, there is increasing marriage between divorced and single people, and in the 1990s, for the first time, significant numbers of divorced women are marrying first-time bridegrooms. Over the last few decades the mainline Protestant denominations have abandoned their barriers to church remarriage, and Conservative Judaism has eased the religious-divorce process for women. Even the Church of Jesus Christ of Latter-Day Saints, whose more formal temple ceremonies are "sealed through eternity," has made accommodations. The holdout has been the Catholic church, which has a commitment to "the indissolubility of marriage." Although Catholic couples can get civil divorce decrees, the Catholic church does not recognize the right of the state to dissolve a marriage. A divorced Catholic can still receive the sacraments, including communion, and Pope John Paul II has urged compassion for the church's divorced and remarried. Nevertheless, unless his or her marriage is negated by the church, a Catholic cannot remarry in a Catholic ceremony. If divorced Catholics remarry outside the church, they can continue to attend services but cannot formally receive sacraments. A Catholic can, however, seek to have a marriage bond severed by the church; the most common method is the annulment procedure which can take up to eighteen months. The petitioner usually needs to provide, to three members of a marital tribunal, dozens of pages of documentation, often including comments from witnesses and psychologists and answers to hundreds of questions, to develop a "history of the marriage." In 1990, according to the Canon Law Society of America, around 80% of received petitions were granted; 26,729 Catholic marriages were found invalid for "lack of form," and 525 were dissolved as a result of "Pauline privilege," which is to say that they involved someone who had not been baptized.

Although the ideal of a happy marriage is still treasured, the emphasis today is perhaps more on personal happiness than on the concept of marriage as set out in Judeo-Christian tradition. The "Quality of Life" Surveys conducted by the Institute for Social Research at the University of Michigan in 1971 and 1989 reflect this shift in attitude. Respondents rated having a "happy marriage" ahead of having an "interesting job" or a "large bank account" even "being in good health." Having a good marriage and family life ranked first in surveys of American high-school students throughout the 1970s and 1980s, and other surveys also indicate that having a good family life is the key to happiness. However, most respondents to these surveys admit that a bad marriage is highly detrimental to personal happiness and so accept the decline in the idea of marital permanence. The percentage of women asserting that parents who do not get along should split up rather than stay together for the sake of the children rose from 51% in 1962 to 82% in 1985. One in four children (16 million) lives with only one parent, usually the mother. Each year more than a million children are affected by their parents' separation or divorce, and at least one million more are born to unmarried mothers. Such data highlight the gap between Americans' professed family values and their real-life choices about family stability.

There is often a gap between people's personal experiences and their professed perception of national trends and overall social reality. Criticisms of the "American family" found by opinion surveys must be placed in context alongside similar criticisms of police brutality, congressional corruption, and rampant environmental pollution. The public maintains that all are common across the nation—except in their own neighborhood. According to the Massachusetts Mutual Survey on American family life, an overwhelming majority (85%) said that Americans value material things more than family. Yet the same people who hold a dim view of American family life express satisfaction with their own families. The same gap appears when people are asked about the state of marriage as an institution. Almost two thirds of the married respondents to the recent National Opinion Research Center (NORC) General Social Surveys rate their own marriage as "very happy" but see the institution as weaker.

THE DISAPPEARANCE OF THE
TRADITIONAL FAMILY

Recent socio-demographic trends of marrying later, having fewer children, and living longer have altered family life. The result is that both men and women spend less of their lives in family households than ever before. In 1970, 40.3% of Americans lived in so-called nuclear families, with children under 18. By 1990, that percentage fell to 26.3, and nearly a quarter of those are stepfamilies, also known as "blended families." This merging of two partial families into one occurs in numerous variations, depending on whose children move in and who has custody. As the traditional American nuclear family—Mom, Pop, and the kids—slowly disappears, new family formations quickly multiply, causing confusion among sociologists trying to define the family. How do you categorize women raising their own grand-children, as often occurs when an infant's mother has been damaged by drugs? According to the Census Bureau's rule, a family relationship is based on blood. Any household formations that do not fit this definition are lumped into the growing category of "nonfamily households." This category includes roommates of any type, and elderly Americans who band together for emo-tional and economic support. Gay and heterosexual cohabitators are trying to win benefits such as inheritance, child support, and health insurance that employers and courts have to date reserved for "families."

These demographic developments have major implications for American religion. In a society where fewer people marry and those that do have fewer kids, the notion of hanging around home on the weekends and, by extension, going to church, recedes. This is not a boon to conservative religious groups, who claim that there is an objective moral order based upon natural law, tradition, sacred scripture, or some combination of all three. This moral order describes, for instance, a certain family formation as a reflection of God's design for humankind. Conversely, it proscribes homosexuality, pre-marital sex, adultery, and close relative unions as violations of that design. Most religious groups assume that the responsibilities of parenthood include the transmission of values, assuring their continuity across generations. Ref-erences to "the decline of the family," long a staple comment of political and religious leaders, are now found in academic social-science literature. As Peter Berger suggested, there has been a secularization of consciousness so that "an increasing number of individuals . . . look upon the world and their own lives without the benefit of religious interpretations."

Until this century, most religions took the Genesis phrase "Be fruitful and multiply" as the essence of religious marriage. However, family size has fallen dramatically, especially in recent decades. The 1970s saw a decline in the desire for large families by all religious groups and a resulting fall in the birth rate. The number of parents wanting four children reached a new low. The Roman Catholic population adopted birth control, especially the Pill, despite the opposition of their church. It was not that Americans ceased to believe in the time-honored virtues of maintaining the family and raising children, it was just that it was harder for Americans to live by their beliefs: They did not have enough time and money. The 1990 U.S. Census showed that families had become smaller and that more mothers had joined fathers in the workplace. Almost 60% of women with at least one child under the age of 6 work, almost three quarters of those with children age 6 to 17 work, and 70% of employed mothers work full-time. Numerous surveys show that Americans still believe in family values and that traditional relationships among parents, children, and siblings are valued as the most important aspects of life. Families are seen as more consequential than work, recreation, or status. Yet America's family relations have changed dramatically.

Negative attitudes toward parenthood increased after World War II, according to the Mental Health Surveys, and values that emphasized material gain and individual achievement also increased. In more recent decades, it has become common wisdom to believe that growing materialism has undermined family values. When personal goals and family goals conflict, many people expressing strong support for family goals do not live up to them. The rift between word and deed is apparent. With time and money becoming interchangeable, everything outside the workplace becomes a hobby. Parenting has become a less respectable, less important activity in modern America.

People with religious commitment do appear to make economic and career sacrifices for their beliefs. Our data show that conservative Protestants have larger families than liberal Protestants, and other surveys show that antiabortion attitudes serve as the strongest predictor of desired fertility. Among Jews, who generally have below-average fertility patterns, the exception to the pattern is the Orthodox Jewish community, which in many ways resembles conservative Protestants in its family patterns. Women in conservative religious groups are likely to forgo education and high-status occupational roles. Time that might have been expended on study or a career outside the home is used for domestic labor, motherhood, and family duties, perpetuating a traditional family division of labor that distinguishes male roles from female roles.

A reader's survey in *Christianity Today*, the flagship of evangelical journalism, found that 88% of male respondents and 91% of female respondents either "strongly agree" or "agree" that the Bible affirms the principle of male leadership in the family, and 4 out of 10 would restrict women from becoming church elders or being ordained. In this scheme of things, women are likely to be homemakers or housewives. The traditional German expression states that the domain of women is *"Kinder, Kirche, Küche,"* that is, children, church, kitchen. We can observe in this instance the influence of religion on gender differentiation. Liberals and secularists assert that tradition creates a subordinate status for women; conservatives suggest that tradition reflects real gender differences and naturally prescribed roles. The role of women as helpmate and mother is clearly set out in the Book of Genesis, and is partly restated, and elaborated upon, in the New Testament in Ephesians 5:22–24 and I Timothy 2:12. Religious conservatives thus oppose new definitions of the place of women in modern society. They resist the new role of the working woman which has altered marital decision making, sex-role attitudes, and expectations about childbearing and child rearing, which have in turn led to declining family size. They believe that modern trends have directly contributed to higher rates of divorce and to other social problems like juvenile delinquency.

By contrast, some liberal religious positions embrace societal change. Unitarian Universalism was once known as a haven for starchy humanists and well-heeled liberals. Universalists believed in the salvation by God for all people, and Unitarians held to the unity of God. The two denominations merged in 1961, and their legacy has been one of the most theologically diverse and socially active strains of religion in America. Today, its openness and outreach is changing to include homosexuals, Buddhists, neopagans, and other alternative-society seekers, through the sect's call for religious freedom, tolerance, social justice, spirituality, democracy, and world peace, and its assertion of the interdependence of all creation. This ideology represents the views of many well-educated cosmopolitan people on a range of life-style issues—openness to different family forms, deep antiauthoritarianism, and egalitarian sex roles. It has a clear niche on the religious left. In 1970 the Unitarian Universalist Association began ordaining gays and lesbians, in 1984 it started blessing gay unions, and in 1985 it eliminated sexist and patriarchal language from its statement of faith.

THE GAY COMMUNITY

One social trend that has emerged into public view over the last two decades has been the gay life-style. Homosexuality in modern American society has both demographic and religious implications. Yet gays are a largely undocumented group in terms of standard data collection such as the U.S. Census.

Apart from the 1948 Kinsey Institute study, there are few reliable estimates on the proportion of the population that is gay. The Kinsey study suggested that around 4% of men age 16 to 55 were exclusively homosexual and that another 6% had been homosexual for at least three years. This meant that 10% of the male population was homosexual at one time or another. Women who were exclusively lesbian accounted for 2% to 3% of the female population, while another 2% to 3% had been in a lesbian relationship for at least three years. In April 1993, a major study was released by the Batelle Human Affairs Research Centers in Seattle, claiming that homosexual men comprise only 1% to 2% of the male population. It is probable that around 4 or 5 % of American adults are predominantly gay, but the actual size of the population is unknown. As a result, we have no real idea of the extent to which marriage and fertility patterns have been affected by this sector of the population.

If we were to repeat the NSRI in the future, a question on sexual preference would probably be included to fill another important gap in our knowledge about American society. Since so many gays have now come out of the closet, we are more aware of their geographical location; many live in San Francisco and Manhattan. In addition, market surveys of self-identified gay men and lesbians who subscribe to life-style magazines have revealed the group's social attributes. Compared to average Americans, gays are more middle-class. They have received three more years of education, are 50% more likely to have attended college, and earn above-average incomes. Their median ages are 37 for men and 35 for women.

Though the gay community may be an attractive market for businesses, it is problematic for many religious organizations because the Judeo-Christian tradition has historically regarded homosexuality as sin. It is severely sanctioned in the Hebrew Scriptures (Leviticus 18:22) and condemned in the New Testament (Romans 1:26–27). Even social aspects of the gay life-style such as transvestism are described as "abhorrent to the Lord" (Deuteronomy 22:5). These strictures lead traditionalists in all major religious groups— Protestants, Catholics, Jews, and Muslims—to condemn the increasing gender ambiguity of modern society as moral decay and chaos. Extremists regard the apparent growth of homosexuality as both a sign and a symptom of the approach of "Endtimes" and of the inexorable degradation that will precede the rise of the Antichrist and the Apocalypse.

Yet it is also true that not since pre-Christian Hellenistic times has homosexuality been as accepted by civil society as it is today. In 1991 a New York judge approved the adoption of a 6-year-old boy by his biological mother's lesbian partner, and the Lotus computer company announced that gay employees' companions would be eligible for the same benefits as spouses. Many states have repealed their anti-homosexuality laws, and some have now passed gay rights laws that prohibit discrimination based on sexual orientation.

This new tolerance of homosexuals has not gone unchallenged from religious opponents, as we noted earlier in connection with the New York Saint Patrick's Day Parade. That was a Catholic response, but conservative Protestants have been no more accepting. In fact, they have regarded anti-discriminatory legislation as threats to their own First Amendment rights to say, do, and act what they believe. A San Francisco church was sued when it fired its homosexual organist, though it eventually won the case. In order to clarify the situation, one small conservative denomination, the Orthodox Presbyterian church, tried to obtain a federal court order in New Jersey nullifying the state's gay rights law. They failed in this, but they were able to obtain a promise from the state attorney general that they would not be prosecuted for their anti-homosexual stand. If their church tenets pronounced homosexuality a sin, they were assured, they could legally refuse to hire gays even for secular positions. Some evangelical Protestant groups were in the forefront of the successful 1992 campaign to repeal homosexual rights in Colorado, which in turn has led supporters of gay rights to an economic boycott of that state.

Whereas Catholic priests and Orthodox Jewish rabbis have made clear that they will never compromise on the homosexual issue, other denominations have been racked by debates between their conservative and liberal wings over whether or not to welcome gays and lesbians. In 1992, the United Methodist church's General Conference set aside the conclusions of a special committee and rejected recommended revisions of church teachings. The church attempted to end a twenty-year controversy over social ethics by reaffirming the principle declaring homosexual behavior "incompatible with Christian teaching." Also in 1992, two churches that accepted homosexuals were ousted from both the North Carolina and Southern Baptist conventions. One church, in Raleigh, had blessed the union of two gay men; the other, in Chapel Hill, had licensed a gay divinity student to preach. This ouster was an unusual move because of the traditional Baptist principle of congregational autonomy. The powerful Southern Baptists strongly approved a change in their by-laws mandating the ouster of any church that "acts to affirm, approve or endorse homosexual behavior" as "contrary to the Bible on human sexuality and the sanctity of the family."

That same year, the Rabbinical Assembly of Conservative rabbis was bitterly divided over whether to assist a gay Conservative Jewish congregation in New York's Greenwich Village in its search for a rabbi. Yet the more liberal Jewish denominations have come to terms with homosexuality. Reform Judaism's Central Conference of American Rabbis voted to ordain gays, and many of its members bless gay and lesbian unions. As we mentioned earlier, Unitarians have completely accepted gays on their own terms. The

Beacon Press, which is connected with the Unitarian Universalist Association, has earned a reputation as the publisher of controversial, avant-garde, gay-oriented books. Quakers, too, have been in the forefront of publicly blessing homosexual relationships, and according to their publication *A Friendly Letter,* gay Quaker weddings are now "conducted strictly by the book." In the light of these developments it is worth noting that gay marriage may be a radical union for most straight people, but it might also be deemed a conservative notion for many gays.

The movement of gay issues into the religious forum in the 1990s seems to reflect a return to religion within the gay community. Traditionally, gays have been on the leading edge of secular humanism. As our data show, young single people tend be more irreligious than other Americans, and though we have no data as such on the gay community, our finding that San Francisco, which has a large gay population, was the most secular city in the nation gives us some indication of gays' lack of religious identification. However, gays and lesbians now seem to be moving back toward the mainstream, and they have begun to petition for acceptance in moderate denominations. In part this interest in religion might be a very American search for societal respectability through religious affiliation, but there is no doubt that the traumatic psychological effects of the AIDS epidemic among gay men has had some influence.

THE INFLUENCE OF PARENTING

Statistical evidence supports the existence of a link between the nuclear family and religious participation. The birth of a child often leads to a baptism, christening, circumcision, or naming ceremony. All evidence suggests that married people increase their religious participation and often join churches, synagogues, or temples if and when they have children of school age. Social commentators postulate that people are willing to invest time and money into organizations that offer them something in return. When children are in the home, the church can offer more to people and demand more in return. This appears to suggest that parents' concern for the moral and social welfare of their children leads them to religion. Children have long been the object of religious benevolence, and their religious education has been a prime concern for religious bodies. Not only do children provide their parents with an incentive for attending services, but the moral and social welfare of the children becomes an institutional mission that strengthens the organization and increases the level of parental involvement. Beyond their historically explicit purpose, which was to offer an alternative to the public schools, Catholic schools have also tended to involve the children's parents in the life of the parish, provide evangelical outreach, and encourage all parishioners to increase their level of support and commitment. Protestants developed effective Sunday-school programs for the religious socialization of their children. Sunday schools require the support of a religious organization and promote the outreach and development of the church.

It is worth noting that most faiths have a ritual passage for adolescents between the ages of 12 and 16. Historically, family rituals surrounding confirmation have provided long-term ties between the individual young person and his or her family and the religious body. The importance of these life-cycle activities led synagogues in America to become more egalitarian, emphasizing both bar mitzvah (for boys) and bat mitzvah (for girls) ceremonies. From the perspective of the religious body, such rites of passage are of debatable value, since polarization seems to occur among adolescents immediately afterward; most feel they have "graduated" and disappear from the life of the congregation. Because teenagers and young adults are a problem for American religion, American religion has in turn become more child-centered. But the appeal of child-centered religion in a society where the traditional family comprises a declining proportion of the population is problematic. As a result, consistent religious socialization and religious activity will decline as a normative family erodes. In this scenario, religious disaffiliation may rise to new heights in the United States just as it has in Great Britain, Canada, and Australia.

It is not just that parenting encourages religion. Strong religious belief is associated with parenting. Although we have no fertility data as such in the NSRI, we can gain some idea of the differences among religious groups by comparing the average number of children per woman aged 18 to 44 among our various respondents. There were 2.2 children for each Mormon woman, which was precisely double the number for each Jewish or nonreligious woman. Pentacostals and Jehovah's Witnesses also had high ratios of children per woman (1.6 and 1.8 respectively). The ratio for Catholics was 1.3 children per woman. According to other studies, although Catholic fertility has fallen quite dramatically in recent decades, it still predicts the degree of Catholic devotion. For example, Catholic schooling or frequency of communion is closely linked to high birth rates. The high Mormon figure is due to their temple-centered culture. Mormons interpret all activities in the context of the ultimate Mormon goal: preserving the family into eternity. Therefore, the heavily Mormon state of Utah has a fertility rate almost double that of the national average.

BABY-BOOM RELIGION

The baby boom that began after World War II and crested in the late 1950s constitutes the largest generation of newborns (75 million) ever produced in

America. As they matured from the late 1960s through the 1980s, boomers strove for personal freedom and individual fulfillment, and distrusted tradition and history. They married later, fostered feminism, and accepted high divorce rates.

One of the most important features of the religious outlook of baby boomers is "religious privatization," a concept that explains the cultural shift to individualism within this generation. It encourages personal needs and interests in the shaping of religious commitment and ideology. As a result, religious insight is increasingly based on personal experience, and the church becomes a means to meeting personal objectives. When faith is a personal affair, ties to institutionalized religion are reduced.

Another important key to understanding baby boomers, and modern Americans as a whole, is to gain insight into their adoption of "cultural egalitarianism" as a creed. They increasingly question all authority, hierarchy, and domination. They show less loyalty to denomination and congregation, and are less likely to acknowledge the church as the source of religious insight or its authority on matters of religious truth and doctrine. It is as if they have collectively imbibed George Bernard Shaw's statement that "every profession is a conspiracy against the laity." This is a particular problem for those hierarchially organized Protestant denominations, such as the Episcopalians, Lutherans, and Methodists, who can no longer expect their laity, as the old adage says, to "shut up, sit up, and pay up." The clergy have responded by dispensing as far as possible with their clerical collars and other robes of office, opening up their ranks to women, and adapting their once-powerful role as pastors into that of enablers, facilitators, and managers of communities of the faithful.

The corrosive effect of modernity on the religious leadership of a historically aloof ordained ministry is even more of a concern for the Catholic church, whose parishioners were always expected "to pray, pay, and obey." The period of Vatican II inaugurated a reconceptualization of the church and the traditional view of the "good Catholic." The role of individual conscience increased, while the authority of the traditional hierarchy was reduced. Yet once the floodgates were opened, they became very difficult to shut. Even Catholic women, traditionally the most loyal followers, now question a priest's right to interfere in their private lives. Surveys of younger white Catholic women report that they have a much more liberal definition of "good Catholic" than their mothers and grandmothers did. You can still be a good Catholic if you divorce and remarry, according to 81%, while 68% say that you can be a good Catholic without obeying the church's dictates on abortion. Even more threatening, in some ways, to traditional authority is that 95% of Catholic women want the laity to partake in making doctrine, and a majority favor the ordination of women priests.

The problem of authority and discipline is a particularly modern American

Catholic issue. In Europe, most people with anti-hierarchial attitudes would have the good grace to leave the Catholic church. However, as the NSRI and other recent surveys demonstrate, America's Catholic dissenters and "nominals," as they are called by the church, identify themselves proudly as Catholics. Many even attend mass as they continue to disagree with the pope and their priest. They appreciate and remain loyal to what Andrew Greeley has described as the "Catholic imagination"—the nonrational and noncognitive side that pervades the Catholic sacraments and liturgy—but they reject much of the ideology that underpins it. Increased belief in individual conscience and reduced guilt and obligation among younger Catholics can be interpreted only as a form of Protestantization and assimilation, the direct consequence of the modernization and Americanization of this college-educated generation. Assailed in its role as interpreter of truth and tradition and facing a critical shortage of priests and candidates for seminaries, it is no wonder that the hierarchy of the Catholic church in America has developed a pervasive sense of siege.

MARKET SEGMENTATION AND
RELIGIOUS SHOPPING

As we have seen, baby boomers were socialized very differently from preceding generations. They were the first generation largely reared in prosperity and by television, and they were, apparently, the best-educated. As they grew up, their whims and needs dominated the marketplace of American capitalism. In general, boomers are seen as consumers, as could be expected for a group raised on a diet of television advertising and Madison Avenue hype. Most baby boomers became suburban householders and parents, but the number of dropouts, mostly in urban, trendsetting states, was more numerous than in previous generations. This suggests that there is a widening cultural gulf between conformist, churched baby boomers and a growing minority of their unconventional, unchurched peers. The former are more likely to be parents than the latter, though even they find parenting difficult, having often spent many years of adult life free and single. Surely, a major cause of the 1990s baby-boom return to religion is the family cycle.

Baby boomers have largely conformed to what sociologists of the 1950s called "ingrained routine religious behavior." That is, children attended church with their parents and absorbed the particular brand of religion offered there, avoided church while sowing wild oats during their late teens and twenties, married, matured, had a family, and, having returned to their senses, came back to church with their little ones in tow. The 1990s are the baby boom's family years. More than 60% of households headed by baby boomers now contain children, and those who once lived for "sex, drugs, and rock 'n' roll" now want to protect their children from these threats to the "American family." As today's parents, they are the main target for missionizing by the country's religious bodies.

Tracking the baby boomers' market is important to almost anyone in business for one simple reason: The baby boom is the most economically powerful generation in U.S. history. Marketers are most interested in the young professionals, or "yuppies," especially the educated, affluent two-earner families. Marketers tell us that those baby boomers who have settled down seem to like the suburbs even more than their parents did. They are heavily concentrated in the metropolitan areas that surround major cities like Los Angeles, New York, Boston, Washington, D.C., and Chicago, as well as the new boom cities of recent decades such as Orlando, Dallas, Seattle, and Atlanta. In the society that has arisen in these areas, everything—including religion—competes for scarce resources such as time and money. As we have noted, the erosion of traditional authority combined with the acceleration of individualism has tended to transform religion into a personal consumer item.

In recent years, then, some churches and ministers have responded by becoming more businesslike in their attention to social trends as a guide to successful recruitment, outreach, and missionary activities. This has been especially true among evangelical Protestants, who have often hired polling organizations to provide them with marketplace data. The evangelicals saw a major opportunity in America's demographic changes—in the emergence of a large population of elderly people and, especially, in the baby boom. They had obviously read the sociologist Ernst Troeltsch, who suggested that if a religion wants to grow, it needs "cultural fit" and a willingness to accommodate to the needs of its market. Early on, evangelicals realized that as baby boomers aged, church membership would grow and religion would take a more important place in their lives. By 1990, Gallup polls revealed that the proportion of American adults who described their faith in evangelical terms had reached 38%.

In the 1990s, a large element of the baby-boom generation is experiencing a resurgence of religious involvement as they seek stable and more lasting kinds of values, especially for their children. What is different and attractive about this population to religious entrepreneurs, or "church planters," as they're often called, is that most boomers do not follow the traditional pattern of having a "home" church, but, rather, attend different churches on an "as-needed" basis. Though, as the NSRI shows, the vast majority of baby boomers continue to identify with a religious tradition, they also treat practice, belief, and behavior as optional items that, in turn, are available in an endless array of old and new forms. Thus, although they may still profess loyalty to a denominational label, they are really religious shoppers, and many of them are currently walking up and down the aisles. A 1991 local poll by *The Bergen Record* of New Jersey found that 43% of Protestants, 36% of Jews, and 24% of Catholics said they looked at other churches, synagogues, and parishes before settling down with the one they now attend. Boomers in particular appear to set about finding a spiritual home with all the diligence of savvy consumers making a major appliance purchase. Many people no longer choose on the basis of ideology, theology, or tradition. Instead, they seek diversity, an expanded menu, and like-minded peers. This is a particular problem for the Catholic church because canon law directs members of the flock to attend the church within a prescribed geographical distance of their home. Other findings suggest that baby boomers are less likely to be motivated by guilt and that they will fill the collection plate, tithe, or give *tzedakah* (charity) only if they see a value return to such giving. Right behavior, such as not being a hypocrite, takes precedence over correct doctrine and denominational teaching.

CHILD-CENTERED RELIGION

As we've said, the focus of the baby boomers' interest in religion is their children even more than their own spiritual needs. As the birth rate has risen to new heights, a reflection of the sheer volume of women of fertile age at present in the U.S. population, religious interest has increased. This trend means that a larger proportion of the American population will be involved with religion during most of the 1990s, lending an aura of success and higher morale to the clergy. As a result, Sunday and religious schools are filling up, and special services are being designed around children and young families. Even those parents who do not themselves attend weekly services make sure their children do. As we mentioned earlier, they appear to want to provide their children with the rites of passage that marked their own sense of belonging to a religious community, be it baptism, circumcision, first communion, bar or bat mitzvah, or confirmation. It could well be that these milestones are now treasured because the shift away from religious teaching or involvement in public schools means that the only place children will learn about Moses or Jesus Christ or even cultural standbys such as Bible stories or Christmas carols is in a religious or home setting.

In an era of clear and increasing separation of church and state, religious and spiritual matters are increasingly regarded as personal or individual attributes. Thus parental influences and responsibility are particularly strong in the religious realm, since the common influences of schooling and peer group, which supplement socialization of children as they mature beyond the confines of the family, are largely absent in the area of religious socialization of children.

Most modern parents claim that they look to religion as an ally in instilling morals and values in a society that often emphasizes individual gain or superficiality. In this unique postmodern world, where for the first time since the term was coined "nuclear families" are a minority, parents perceive threats to their mission. Many are concerned that they do not have control over their children's lives, and they seek a community that supports them in protecting children from society's evils, such as drugs, gangs, teenage pregnancy, and loss of academic motivation. Many agree that grave problems in U.S. culture can be traced to the decline of the family. As a result, *pro-family* is a new buzzword that describes a whole range of crusades, from the fight against television violence to the campaign against too-explicit sex education. A pro-family stance has been taken by some leading Democrats as well as Republicans, as is evidenced by Tipper Gore's book, *Raising PG Kids in an X-Rated Society*. Indeed, the current vice president's wife and Susan Baker, wife of the former secretary of state James Baker, formed and led a group in the 1980s that sought self-regulation in the record industry to protect children from violence, obscenity, and pornography.

Certainly the widely perceived loss of faith in the public schools as agents of positive socialization into respectable society has propelled the pro-family movement, as well as the general return to religion. The question for organized American religion is whether it will be able to sustain a connection with the baby boomers once their children are grown. Boomers start their families later and finish earlier. The window of opportunity for organized religion is limited because today's parents have fewer children. New styles of religious organization geared to the evolving nature of contemporary America's socio-demographic realities will be required.

THE NEW-TIME RELIGION—MEGA-CHURCHES

Religiously, baby boomers are more likely than members of previous generations to look for avenues that help make sense of their lives. The opportunities available to these inhabitants of the "global village" for religious and spiritual exploration have multiplied. Religious groups that have been successful among the baby boomers have been those that meet the desire for a "user-friendly" and anti-bureaucratic, anti-apathetic, and noninstitutional environment. The most prosperous religious organizations today are those that realize that this generation does not feel comfortable with traditional services full of rituals that are largely incomprehensible to irregular worshipers and are performed by robed clergy in august buildings. Baby boomers tend to value emotional expression, participatory worship, and music. Rock bands, dramatic sketches, and a fast pace characterize the new breed of

Sunday service. Contemporary music is especially associated with the Assemblies of God, the largest Pentecostal movement. Rather than offer traditional sermons based upon theological learning, the Assemblies have emphasized experience, feelings, therapeutic values, ambience, warmth, fellowship, and nonjudgmentalism. Also satisfying to this new market is a low-key, conversational sermon—TV style—with nontraditional oratory, which can address business and political as well as spiritual issues. This trend has not been good news for Episcopalian, Lutheran, Orthodox, and Catholic churches, nor for attendance at Conservative synagogues.

Some of the most successful churches are so-called mega-churches, which are part of a growth strategy associated with a new evangelical style and expanded attention to personal issues such as divorce or drug use. They tend to offer communion-free, nonliturgical worship services with "something for everyone." Already, there are more than 5,000 such congregations nationwide, each with a membership in excess of 5,000 persons. The model for many is Willow Creek Community Church in South Barrington, Illinois, a Chicago suburb, which attracts 14,000 people to its entertaining weekend services and 6,000 to its more religious Wednesday-evening services. Willow Creek understands the demographics of market segmentation by age and marital status, the factors that are the focus of this chapter. The brochure given to visitors describes a range of programs for children, teenagers, older singles, adults, elderly people, and those in the midst of a personal crisis. The social and prayer-group offerings for singles include "Prime time," for 18- to 32-year-olds; "Focus," for baby boomers age 32 to 40-something; "Quest," for older singles; and "Grasp," for single-parent families.

Another mega-church is the First Baptist of Orlando, Florida. There, latecomers can catch the start of services from outdoor speakers as they enter the enormous sanctuary from Walt Disney World–style parking lots named "Peace," "Joy," and "Love." Newcomers have their own parking lot, where they can seek information on Sunday school and services at Welcome Centers A or B. Like other mega-churches, First Baptist of Orlando features charismatic ministers, orchestra-accompanied choirs, and well-known Christian performing artists attracted by a multimillion-dollar budget. The sanctuaries are so large that people come precisely because they like the anonymity. The wide offerings range from dance troupes to couples' conferences. It appears that the mega-church meets the needs of the modern American family unit and the various stages of the individual life cycle—single, newly wed, and so on through the widowed. Its members find the appropriate activities for the phases they traverse.

As we have noted, most mainline Protestant churches contain a largely elderly laity, wedded to tradition, who demand a familiar, more sacramental, and liturgical form of worship. Thus denominations such as the Luther-

ans have found it difficult to respond to the innovation-seeking segment of
the religious marketplace. Their problem is that their liturgical approach
tends to be seen as a "closed process" difficult for outsiders to understand.
One mainline response is not to try to adapt by merging current membership
with newcomers but, as in the case of the United Church of Christ, to begin
a program of establishing baby-boomer mega-churches from scratch.

The mega-church is to the old-style chapel what the suburban shopping
mall is to the small stores on Main Street—a replacement. The mega-church
is geared to the realities of modern American patterns of living, recreation,
and social relations. Nostalgia for walking to the old stone cold steepled
neighborhood church will fleetingly revive every time the family drives past
it on the way to the parking lot of their regional religious theme park.

THE RISE OF THE INTERFAITH HOUSEHOLD

We have discovered a paradox. Though an initial demographic analysis of the
NSRI findings suggests that there is a remarkable level of continuity in
America's religious life, the level of societal change the nation has undergone
over the past few decades means that everything is in a state of flux and that
all our conclusions are subject to revision. There are few certainties in this
new post-industrial world, and there is indeed a feeling of apprehension
among many religious leaders that "everything nailed down is coming loose."
This is true even for the religious identification of the nuclear family. We
have seen that the baby-boom parents of the 1990s are now the backbone of
organized American religion, but we have yet to consider the impact of one
enormously important and complicating trend of the 1970s and 1980s—
interfaith and interdenominational marriage.

An individual's movement from one religious faith or denomination to
another, commonly known as conversion, is called "switching" by sociologists seeking a more objective term; the movement to the religious "None"
category is still called by its traditional name: "apostasy." Modern America
is unique for the sheer volume of religious switching that goes on among the
populace and the relatively low level of apostasy. Various polls suggest that
somewhere in the range of 25% to 30% of the American public switch
denominations in their lifetime. Some acquire the habit and go on to become
"multiple switchers." Of course, those who change religion tend to be people
who take religion seriously, since change is an active experience. The largest
reasons for religious change, in descending order of importance, are marriage
with someone of a different religious background, shift in religious stance or
belief, and migration to a new geographical community. Most changes to
achieve religious consensus in the home usually occur at the time of mar-

riage, at the birth of the first child, or when children reach school age. The push toward religious homogeneity is rooted in the American belief that religious differences between husband and wife are not good either for the marriage or for the children of the marriage. Moreover, it is simpler and more convenient for everyone in the family to belong to the same religious group.

A number of factors have contributed to the loss of traditional religious boundaries in social interaction. Among these are social trends we have already mentioned such as secularization, the rise of individualism, the diminishing influence of parents on children, the suburbanization of Catholics, and an issue we will deal with in the next chapter, the declining status gap between major religious groups. Nevertheless, the traditional social norm of marrying within one's own group, known as endogamy, continues to influence the majority of adherents. Despite the evidence that religious involvement has become more privatized and isolated from other spheres of life, the close connection between religious and family life has been maintained. Results of the 1987 National Survey of Families and Households indicate that 78% of currently married people were married in a church. Because religious groups are geographically concentrated and people socialize locally, this increases the probability of association with potential marriage partners of the same religious preference. Moreover, socioeconomic and ethnic factors, which are associated with religion, come into play during mate

TABLE 6-5

PERCENTAGE OF RESPONDENTS LIVING IN MULTI-ADULT HOUSEHOLDS IN WHICH ALL ADULTS ARE OF THE SAME RELIGIOUS IDENTIFICATION*

RELIGIOUS GROUP	PERCENTAGE	RELIGIOUS GROUP	PERCENTAGE
Hindu	94.5	Presbyterian	73.1
Assemblies of God	87.0	Unitarian	71.5
Baptist	85.0	Mormon	70.1
Pentecostal	84.1	Jehovah's Witness	69.1
Church of Christ	83.6	Jewish	68.7
Nazarene	80.6	Episcopalian	68.2
Holiness	79.6	Eastern Orthodox	68.1
Catholic	78.6	7th-Day Adventist	67.9
Congregationalist	78.2	No Religion	67.3
Methodist	77.2	Agnostic	61.2
Evangelical	77.2	Muslim	59.6
Lutheran	74.7	Buddhist	42.6

* Includes only groups with more than 100 respondents.

selection. Though rates of same-faith marriage between people of the same religion have declined, they are still high. However, different religious groups have fared very differently on this statistic over recent decades.

Switching occurs most often between denominations similar in social class composition. In part this is because people marry mostly within their own social class. In addition, it appears that people cognitively map similarities and differences between denominations—in other words, they place the various religious groups in some kind of order of compatibility. They then use their mapping system when choosing spouses and switching denominations. This is because religious distance is very closely associated with social distance.

A 1992 Gallup poll reported that the "winners" in this switching process in recent years have been the small Protestant denominations. One of the biggest losers has been the Catholic church, which attracted only 1 in 11 of the switchers. Sociologist Milton Rokeach suggested, in his 1960 work, *The Open and Closed Mind,* that switchers moving between Christian denominations usually change to a denomination only one or two steps away from their own in terms of liturgy and theology. His "R-order" formula is Catholic, Episcopalian, Lutheran, Presbyterian, Methodist, and Baptist. The first three share the liturgical tradition, with communion the focal point of the service; the latter three share the sermon-centered liturgies of the Reformation. In this model, the Catholic "losses" can be explained because this church is disadvantaged by lying at one extreme on Rokeach's theological scale. Probably more important than theological factors in contributing to the decline is the increasing number of young Catholics living in more open social environments. The suburbanization process for Catholics has entailed the movement of people out of small homogeneous communities and a decline in Catholic school enrollment. Both have resulted in greater opportunities for young Catholics to socialize with people from different religious backgrounds.

It is doubtful that small religious groups can survive for long periods without a high rate of same-faith marriage. The weakness in smaller groups is the sheer difficulty of finding compatible mates from within a restricted "marriage market." However, smaller religious groups can maintain a sense of cohesion, identity, and belonging that is impossible in very large groups. To achieve high rates of marriage within the religious group, random choice of marriage partners must be curtailed. Nowadays this seems to require that the group have a relatively high level of education, a balanced sex ratio, and a regional and ethnic concentration. At the individual level, factors such as a preference for ideological and cultural consensus and social pressure from parents assist same-faith marriage. Parents sometimes act as matchmakers, and when children are recalcitrant, parents may even threaten to withhold support in the early years of marriage.

Until the 1950s religiously mixed marriages seemed more uncommon than they actually were because of the tendency for one spouse to switch and align with the other. Sociologist Gerhard Lenski found in the 1950s that the more Americanized the individual, in terms of generations of the family born in this country, the greater the probability that there would be a mixed marriage. It was also probable that a mixed marriage would lead to the conversion of one partner so that religious unity would be established within the nuclear family. Since the nation was at that time religiously divided along regional and class lines, there were still relatively few Catholic-Protestant marriages and little interdenominational marriage among regionally concentrated Protestant groups such as Baptists and Lutherans. In 1957, the proportion of the U.S. population currently married to a member of the same denomination was 94% for Jews, 88% for Catholics, 83% for Baptists, and 81% each for Lutherans, Methodists, and Presbyterians.

The 1968 University of Chicago studies of 1961 alumni showed that the same-denomination marriage rates were all in the same 80% + range as the 1957 Census Bureau survey. However, the proportion of alumni in which marriage took place between people whose *original* denomination was the same was found to be much lower: in the range of only 15% to 35% for most Protestant denominations, and 75% for Catholics. In other words, in approximately 60% of Protestant marriages and 11% of Catholic marriages, one partner had converted. These results suggested that the tendency to seek denominational homogeneity in marriage had not weakened. It was clear that denominational homogeneity was maintained by Catholics and Jews mostly by the process of marrying within the group, whereas it was maintained by other religious groups largely through considerable amounts of denominational switching.

By the 1990s, all the social trends we have discussed so far, especially the innovative spirit of young people, had begun to erode this pattern of religious homogeneity in both marriage and the home. As adults marry later in life (the average age in the 1990s is 26 for men and 24 for women), parental influence over children's marriage decisions has diminished. Today's couples have more economic independence than the teenage bride and groom of the 1950s. In addition, the individualism in our society conflicts with the notion that third parties should interfere in a couple's marriage decision. With people increasingly assertive concerning their own experiences and ideas, one would naturally expect them to be less willing to give up their own religious identity. Moreover, in these pluralistic times, we would expect partners to be more respectful and, therefore, more tolerant of their spouses' religious differences. In addition, the ecumenical atmosphere generated by religious bodies has created an acceptable milieu for religious compromises. Nevertheless, there is research to show that interfaith marriages are more subject to divorce than same-faith marriages.

Because denominational switching often occurs in connection with marriage, some institutional opposition to interfaith marriage is understandable. However, this stance entails the risk of losing current members and possibly a new generation to a competing religious institution. Under these conditions religious institutions today have an incentive to be lenient in their denunciation of intermarriage if they wish to hold on to the increasing number of interfaith households.

INTERMARRIAGE: WHO'S MARRYING WHOM?

Theories of secularization suggest that the trend of interfaith marriage will grow in the future. In the process of industrialization and urbanization, religious beliefs have become less important in governing people's lives. Thus, as members of religious groups become less devoted to their own religion, it can be expected that the social boundaries between them will decline. Similarly, as we have noticed, the social norms against interfaith marriage will also wane. As marriage choices become individualized and religious boundaries weaken, traditional American "communal" religion is being transformed into an "associational" religion.

We decided to investigate religious homogeneity and heterogeneity in the household in the NSRI. Given the problems of new family formations, we decided not just to investigate married couples, but to inquire about the religion of other adults in the home. Of course, the vast majority of other adults were spouses, but the data in Table 6-5 do include adult children, relatives, significant others, and, in small numbers, roommates. This is the most comprehensive data yet available on the pattern of religious difference within American homes. The data revealed that 78.2%, or 117 million, of the 150 million American adults who live in households containing more than one adult reside in religiously homogeneous households. In other words, 21.8%, or 33 million, of American adults live in households where at least one adult has a different religious identification.

The most religiously homogeneous households in America are inhabited by smaller Eastern religious immigrant groups and conservative Protestant denominations. Whereas Baptists have the same level of religious homogeneity as they had in 1957, small declines have been recorded for mainline Protestant denominations. Methodists have fallen by 4%, Lutherans by 6%, and Presbyterians by 7%. The most surprising change is that the most homogeneous groups in 1957, the Jews and Catholics, have suffered much more erosion. The percentage of Catholics living in religiously homogeneous households has fallen 9%, to 79%, while that of Jews has fallen 25%, to 69%. A number of other groups, such as Jehovah's Witnesses (73%

homogeneous households) and Mormons (72% homogeneous households) seem to lack the high levels of religious conformity in the home that would be expected. The Unitarians (71%), Episcopalians (68%), Eastern Orthodox adherents (68%), Quakers (67%), Seventh-Day Adventists (70%), agnostics (61%), and people of no religion (67%) all have homogeneity in around two thirds of their households. The major religion with the lowest rate of homogeneity is the Buddhists (43%). Low proportions were also found among most of the new alternative religions, but since the numbers of respondents for these groups were small, we cannot conclusively consider this a trend.

We can learn a good deal about the changing pattern of social relationships in this country by viewing in detail the patterns of interfaith and interdenominational cohabitation among seven religious groups representing a variety of patterns.

CATHOLICS, EPISCOPALIANS, AND JEWS

Roughly 1 in 4 Americans is Catholic, and 2 in 4 are Protestants of some kind. It is not surprising, then, that when Catholics marry outside their faith, most marry partners from Protestant denominations. It is a significant social development that 22% of our Catholic respondents lived with an adult of another faith. This means that there are 6.5 million adult Catholics living with non-Catholics. About 13.5% of Catholics live with members of Protestant groups (4% with Baptists, 2.5% with Methodists, 2% with Lutherans, 1% each with Presbyterians and Episcopalians). About 4.8% live with adults of no religion or agnostics, 0.4% live with Jews, and 0.2% live with members of other religions. These figures suggest that there are currently around 4.8 million Catholic-Protestant households in the United States, 1.3 million Catholic–religious "None" households, and 250,000 Catholic-Jewish households.

Both Jews and Catholics have only recently experienced a rapid rise in interfaith marriages. If marriage is increasing based upon random choice, then we would expect Jews, as a smaller population, to intermarry more than Catholics. About 11% of adult Jews live with Protestants of various denominations, 12% live with Catholics, 7.5% live with religions "Nones," 0.5% live with Unitarians, and 0.5% live with adherents of other religions. It is possible that most of the religious "Nones" are in fact ethnic or secular Jews. Thus the rate of intermarriage, in Jewish terms, is lower than it appears. In fact, the Council of Jewish Federations' 1990 National Jewish Population Survey reported that on this basis, 72% of married Jews are married to somebody who is of the Jewish religion or of Jewish ethnic origin, rather than the NSRI rate of 69%.

Most households involving intermarried Catholics and Jews remain mixed because the members of these two quasi-ethnic groups are less likely to switch religions, viewing the religious differentiation between their own group and other religious groups as greater than, for instance, the differences among various Protestant denominations. As a result, Jews and Catholics are more likely to abstain from any religious identification than they are to adopt another religious position. This explains the high proportion of "cultural" secular Jews and secularized Italian Americans. The ties to community through language, folklore, custom, and solidarity groups make it extremely difficult for them to completely abandon their community of origin.

Episcopalians represent a prime example of a liberal mainline Protestant group of high prestige and social status. Of course the highest proportion (27%) of intermarried Episcopalians wed members of other Protestant denominations, but the second highest proportion (10%) marry Catholics. On theological grounds this is perhaps unsurprising for, as "Anglo-Catholics," Episcopalians lie on Milton Rokeach's "R-order" continuum of denominational similarity between Catholics and other mainline Protestant denominations. Half of Episcopalians who do not live with other Episcopalians live with some other type of Protestant. More specifically, 16% of adult Episcopalians live with "Protestants," 4% each with Baptists or Methodists, 2% with Presbyterians, and 1% with Lutherans. Ten percent of Episcopalians live with Catholics, 5% with religious "Nones," and 1% with non-Christians.

The high concentration of Jewish, Catholic, and Episcopalian populations in the Northeast has surely contributed to the increase in intermarriage among these three religious groups. An additional factor is the increasing social homogeneity of these populations as the Catholics and Jews have begun to achieve the same educational and class attainment, an occurrence that will be discussed in the next chapter.

MORMONS, JEHOVAH'S WITNESSES, AND BUDDHISTS

In light of their strict theologically defined, community-oriented religions, Mormons and Jehovah's Witnesses display much-higher-than-expected levels of interfaith cohabitation and intermarriage. They also appear to reside with adults of no religion to an unexpectedly great extent. Geography may be the explanation. Mormonism concentrates in the western United States, the heartland of irreligion, and Jehovah's Witnesses are thinly spread throughout the country. The largest proportion (13%) of Jehovah's Witnesses who live with nonadherents live with religious "Nones." Six percent live with Baptists, and 4% with Catholics. The Mormon pattern is slightly different. Seventeen percent of Mormons live with Protestants (4% with Baptists, 2% with Methodists, 2% with Lutherans, 9% with members of other Protestant denominations), 8.5% live with religious "Nones," and 5% live with Catholics.

Buddhists, like Mormons, are clustered in the West. Ethnically they are a mixed group, comprised of both white and Asian Americans. They exhibit the highest rates of intermarriage of any religious group cited in Table 6-5 as well as the highest rate of intermarriage with religious "Nones" (21%). Presumably, theology contributes to this pattern. Buddhists' open-minded, non–Judeo-Christian perspectives do not antagonize members of other religions, and they themselves are not offended by irreligious views. Among those Buddhists who do live with non-Buddhist religious identifiers, 9% live with Catholics, 25% live with Protestants (4% with Baptists, 2% with Episcopalians), 2% live with Jews, and 3% live with members of other non-Christian religions.

ASSEMBLIES OF GOD: AN EXAMPLE OF HOMOGENEITY

As discussed in Chapter 3, homogeneous Protestant communities are particularly located in the South and in rural areas. For instance, the Assemblies of God draw 49% of their members from the South and 37% from rural areas outside the South. Thus the Assemblies of God are second only to Hindus in household homogamy, having a rate of 87%. Among the small minority of this denomination that live with nonidentifiers, 3% live with Catholics, 3% with Baptists, 1.5% with Methodists, 1% with religious "Nones," 0.5% with Orthodox Christians, and the rest with members of other Protestant denominations. Their regional pattern of settlement largely explains the low percentages living with Catholics, since only 7% of Assemblies of God adherents live in the heavily Catholic Northeast.

THE JEWISH COMMUNITY—FACING THE CHALLENGE OF INTERFAITH MARRIAGE

We noted earlier that there has been a rapid change in the rate of religious mixing by American Jews. The NSRI figures largely corroborate the findings of the 1990 National Jewish Population Study (NJPS). The discrepancies between the two studies are caused by different methods of analysis. In the NSRI we classified Jews as people who stated that Judaism was their current religion. The NJPS, on the other hand, as a Jewish community–sponsored study, worked with the modern Jewish frame of reference, which considers Judaism a cultural as much as a religious identity. This has also been the customary approach used by the sociologists of American Jewry. The NJPS concluded that among Jews by birth, only 11% of those who married before 1965 were married to somebody who was not born Jewish. This figure rose to 57% for those married after 1985. The number married to Jews by choice (converts to Judaism) was 2% for those marrying before 1965 and 4% for those marrying after 1985. The findings of the NJPS also suggested that there were around 200,000 people born or raised as Jews who now identified with another religion, and a similar number of born Gentiles who had converted to Judaism.

Religious switching by Jews to other religions is not, historically, unusual, but Gentiles converting to Judaism is. Jewish renunciation was a major trend in 19th-century Europe. Since the rise of Christianity and Islam, Judaism has not been a missionizing religion, and it lacks experience in this endeavor. As a result, large-scale conversions of Gentiles to Judaism has been practically unknown for 1500 years. In fact, it appears that of all the Gentiles who have converted to Judaism in the past 1500 years, the majority are living in the United States today. According to the NJPS results, two thirds of Jews by choice (and, for that matter, two thirds of those born Jewish who now follow other religions) are married women in the 30-to-50 age group. In the past, the mandatory ordeal of circumcision for male converts was considered the prime reason why Gentile men married to Jewish women failed to convert to Judaism. However, today we see that the Jewish husbands of intermarried Gentile women are just as unlikely to convert; it is always the wife who is more likely to adjust her religion. Thus, the data now confirm the literature claiming that the search for marital consensus on religion is the motivating factor for religious switching and that women are more concerned about this than are men.

The evidence of the NJPS also showed that Jews by choice are especially serious about their new faith. They demonstrate above-average rates of Jewish behavior and practices, and 99% of their children are being raised in Judaism. It may also be significant that converts to Judaism resemble born Jews in their high level of education and high-status occupational patterns; thus, the differences between the spouses' religious upbringings are offset by their similarities in class and educational background. Converts are readily assimilated into American Jewry.

A small group such as American Jews is, as we have stated, vulnerable to demographic erosion if interfaith marriage without conversion of the non-Jewish spouse becomes a significant trend. Jews have shown a particular sensitivity to this issue because of their history of oppression and the catastrophic losses they suffered during the Holocaust. Traditional elements in the Jewish community have lamented the recent trend toward intermarriage and have called for increased efforts to prevent it by enhancing Jewish identity through better religious education. Some more progressive elements have seen the trend as an opportunity for outreach and conversion.

There is an asymmetry in the effects of interfaith marriages because of the size of the various groups. Whereas, as we have seen, the 250,000 Catholic-Jewish households are of no statistical or social significance for American Catholics, this number represents a considerable proportion of the American

Jewish population. Thus the recent departure from a long history of intra-group Jewish marriage, evidenced by the fact that half the American Jews who married in the last decade have chosen somebody who was not born or raised Jewish, was regarded with great interest when the news was released in 1991 after the National Jewish Population Survey. The major American media all carried stories on this assimilation trend.

The propensity to intermarry was found to be closely linked to the intensity of Jewish practices, religious education, and beliefs of the individual. These also correlate closely with the denominational background of the Jewish people involved. The more traditional the upbringing, the less likely the person is to intermarry at all; if an intermarriage *does* occur, that person is more likely to have a converted spouse. In recent years there has been growing differentiation among the Jewish denominations as to their involvement in interfaith marriages. For marriages after 1985, 24% of those raised in the Orthodox Jewish denomination married somebody who was not Jewish, as compared to 52% of those in the less rigid but still traditional Conservative denomination, and 66% of those raised in the liberal Reform Jewish denomination. The gap in the proportion who married non-Jews has widened between the Orthodox and Reform Jewish denominations, from 7% in the period prior to 1975, to 16% in the period 1975–84, to an enormous 43% in the most recent period.

The interfaith aspect of these marriages and the attempts by couples to integrate the religious festivals of Judaism and Christianity, especially Chanukah and Christmas, draw considerable attention from the media, especially at holiday times. One indication that this religious merging is not simply a trend manufactured by surveys is that the Hallmark company has begun to issue cards and other products geared to the interfaith family. Among interfaith Christian-Jewish families where both parents identify with their own religion, 78% celebrate religious festivals of both faiths.

Another issue that has piqued general interest is the upbringing of the 770,000 children being raised in mixed households. It was found that 35% of the children were being brought up with no religion. Now, this may pose no problem for the secular-Jew–lapsed-Catholic couple. It is widely held that most of these irreligious children are part of the Jewish cultural sphere since, historically, Jews have often tended toward secularization. In the European Jewish experience, religious "Nones" in cosmopolitan settings—in France, the *laïque;* in central Europe, the *Konfessionslos* population—were indeed more Jewish than Christian. However, the actual religious balance in modern America does not favor Judaism. Only 25% of children in Jewish-Gentile homes are being raised as religious Jews, while 40% are being raised as Christians or in other non-Judaic religions. Some among these 40% do eventually evidence residual Jewish behaviors, but the asymmetrical relationship between Christianity and Judaism means that while Jewish practices do not usually undermine Christian faith, the opposite is not true. For instance, going to a synagogue and reading the psalms and other Old Testament prayers is not a barrier to a Christian, but participation in Christian worship is incompatible with Jewish belief. The 25% of children of intermarried Jews being raised Judaically means that the future potential Jewish population is halved; 50% would be necessary to maintain the balance.

The complications of intermarriage and its relationship to changing household-formation patterns are demonstrated by the fact that a considerable number of Jewish-Christian marriages are second marriages for one or both partners. This means, among other things, that under different custody agreements, siblings may have to be raised in different denominations or faiths. There is a growing trend in American society whereby religious identity no longer automatically binds the family. As a result, religion has become less of a common family or household attribute and more of an individual characteristic.

INTERIM REPORT CARD

Little evidence can be found in the NSRI data for a generation gap based upon religious identification. The data on the diversity of religious opinion and the religious marketplace show that every age group is highly segmented and that there is a certain level of tenacity in denominational ties. True, there is a tendency for the highly influential baby-boom generation, which has been generally characterized by its reputation for social rebellion, cultural innovation, and secularization, to exhibit greater social tolerance and weaker denominational loyalties than their elders and to borrow more from different religious and cultural traditions. Yet the baby-boom generation also contains significant numbers of religious traditionalists who have contributed to the recent growth of conservative religious groups. As Marilyn Quayle, wife of the former vice president, reminded the 1992 Republican National Convention, "Not everyone demonstrated, dropped out, took drugs, joined the sexual revolution, or dodged the draft."

Rather than being a generational battle, the culture war over gender and family issues involves a clash of values that divides *within* generations. It pits believers in personal autonomy and rights-based individualism against communitarians and traditionalists who advocate the common good and take issue with the unencumbered sovereignty of the individual. The battle is also between conformity and pluralism. Conservatives argue that no society can maintain itself without a certain consensus and that religion should be the agent for integrating values and securing this consensus. Their progressive opponents claim that American society is too disparate for close social control and that the real need is for an ideology of harmony that recognizes diversity and legitimizes difference. There is great polarization of opinion among the young in a conflict often pictured as a clash between the Christian right and secular humanism. However, there is still much more of a continuum than a divide among the population.

In between these two groups of articulate idealists stand the vast majority of Americans—the realists, most of whom likely share traditional religious concerns about the moral vacuum in society and the disintegration of the family. They may harbor a nostalgia for past certainties and a more cohesive society, but they also realize that their world allows little room for moral absolutes. They acknowledge that the religious traditionalists—supported by most sociological and psychological research—are correct when they argue that an intact family, including fathers who are present in the life and growth of their children, and maximum contact between mothers and their young offspring, is the best guarantor of an individual's happiness and health and society's best bet against disorder. However, they realize that we live in an imperfect world. Many mothers must work outside the home, and some parents are abusive and irresponsible. Thus latchkey children, divorce, and single parenthood are inevitable features of the modern social landscape. The same moral dilemma applies to abortion. Some women who would not countenance it for themselves believe that they cannot deprive other women of the choices in our tragically imperfect world where AIDS, incest, and rape are not as uncommon as was once imagined.

Issues of gender and family will persist on religious, social, and political agendas well into the 21st century. Advances in biomedical technology relating to areas such as sex-typing, the creation of artificial life, and the definitions of death and parenthood may well increase the philosophical and practical challenges to traditional religion. The debate on gender and family issues will escalate as society confronts these and other fundamental questions.

THE RELIGIOUS PECKING ORDER

◆ ◆ ◆

Religious organizations are part and parcel of the American social and economic system. Local congregations and national denominational bodies are buyers, sellers, employers, investors, and property owners. In recent years they have grown in organizational sophistication and efficiency and have become imitative of the modern business corporation. They spend vast amounts of money: for example, around $2 billion annually on new church construction. The Roman Catholic church alone operates 730 hospitals in the United States. These ties between organized religion and the economy largely arise from the charitable and stewardship activities of local congregations. Americans are charitable people and direct much of their generosity toward religion. Religious organizations receive the bulk of the $90 billion of philanthropic contributions annually. In fact, the majority of individual donations, as opposed to corporate and foundation giving, go to religious charities. This is no doubt because local houses of worship provide significant social and welfare services and often act as community centers; in addition to religious services and traditional life-cycle rituals, they offer a variety of services and programs to their members, and sometimes to noncongregants, such as day care, nurseries, meals for shut-ins, homeless shelters, youth activities, programs for the elderly, and cultural or leisure events.

Houses of worship are part of what is variously termed the independent, voluntary, or nonprofit sector of society, yet in practice they work in a competitive environment in their struggle for souls. Along with every other center of voluntary activity, they must compete for the time, attention, and resources of the public. Practicalities require them to attract high-income people who have high rates of participation in all types of voluntary activity. In this goal they are quite successful, for the rich are well represented and involved in religious organizations as members of boards of trustees and in other leadership roles. This involvement in organizational aspects of religion tends to suggest that the middle and upper classes discharge their religion through ancillary or public-service activities, while the lower-status person tends to a more private religion, oriented more to devotion and prayer.

SOCIAL PRESTIGE AND RELIGIOUS IDENTIFICATION

The pattern of interaction between social status and religious outlook extends beyond the micro-, or congregational level. A relationship between social position and religion is found in most Western societies, whereby those who have done best in society generally are those most likely to be committed to religion. The respectable members of society, the middle class, attend church as part of their life-style. America differs from most other such countries in that urban working-class people are also religious. This may be the reason why secularized political movements—such as socialism, communism, and the anti-clerical left-wing groups that turned these classes against religion in other Western societies—have never been particularly strong in the United States.

In America, social class differentiates religious denominations. Historically, certain religious denominations in America have had higher social status than others. Those with the highest social status have been the mainline liberal churches associated with the oldest wave of immigrants from Britain, such as the Episcopalians, the Presbyterians, and the Congregationalists, a pattern that was first recognized by H. Richard Niebuhr in his 1929 book, *The Social Sources of Denominationalism*. According to the American Institute of Public Opinion in 1945, the proportion of members of the upper class within various religious groups, defined in terms of male occupations, was 24% each for Episcopalian and Congregational adherents, 22% each for Presbyterians and Jews, 13% for Methodists, 9% for Catholics, and 8% for Baptists. Surveys of trade-union memberships from the same period revealed a mirror-image class hierarchy. Only 12% to 14% of Presbyterians, Episcopalians, Congregationalists, and Methodists belonged to trade unions, compared with 20% Lutherans, 23% of Jews, and 28% of Catholics.

The religious identification of the 111 justices appointed to the U.S. Supreme Court since 1790 illustrates this pattern of prestige in American society. Only successful, professional lawyers are recruited for the post of

Supreme Court justice, so the figures are by no means representative of the distribution of religion in the nation. Only 9 Catholics, 4 Baptists, 4 Methodists, 2 Lutherans, and 1 religious "None" have ever been appointed. In contrast, there is a marked overrepresentation (given their numbers in the population) of Episcopalians (36), Presbyterians (19), Unitarians (8), and Jews (5).

Social studies of small California towns in the 1940s found that businessmen and the occupational elite tended to be Congregationalists and Methodists, while manual workers identified with the Church of the Nazarene or the Assemblies of God. This pattern is not just a historical vestige; it also operates in the modern business world. A 1976 survey of Fortune 500 CEOs reported overrepresentation of Episcopalians, Presbyterians, and Congregationalists, and underrepresentation of Baptists and Catholics. Methodists, Lutherans, and Jews were roughly in proportion to their percentage in the population.

It has been said that the U.S. Senate is the most exclusive male club in the country. In the 101st Congress (1989–91), there were significant differences between the religious profile of the senators and the American electorate as a whole. The pattern is by now almost predictable. One fifth of the Senators were Episcopalians, ten times their proportion in the general population. The other overrepresented group were Unitarians (3%), Congregationalists/ United Church of Christ adherents (5%), Jews (8%), and Mormons (3%). As we might have expected, all the other religious groups were underrepresented.

We can already see that denominational membership is not randomly distributed across social strata. Religious identification is often a badge of social standing. The process by which this happens is well known. A local religious congregation is not just a collection of people who pray together; it is a neighborhood-based surrogate community with similarities of occupation and life-style among the membership. The individual members choose a particular congregation on the basis of their own compatibility with its other members, that is, the social atmosphere and the belief that they will "fit in" and make friends. This feeling is of course modulated by their ethnic background and residential choice.

The link between certain religions and high social prestige in a society as open as the United States is not just a matter of birth and family connections. Religious mobility follows social mobility. Upwardly mobile individuals seek to join denominations with high social status, primarily the liberal Protestant denominations like the Episcopalian and Presbyterian churches. The voluntaristic nature of American religion encourages people to "shop around," increasing the likelihood that changes in affiliation coincide with changes in social standing. This status-transmission theory also works in reverse; persons who cannot socially keep up or fit in with the rest of the denomination will move to a congregation of a more compatible class. This often entails switching from a mainline denomination to a more conservative church or to one of the smaller fundamentalist sects.

THE PROTESTANT ETHIC

We have now seen in numerous ways that religion is not only part of people's inner lives, but that it also affects their social outlook and prospects. What precise role does religious identification play in economics and the social order? A leading German sociologist, Max Weber, stipulated in a controversial 1903 essay on the Protestant work ethic *The Protestant Ethic and the Spirit of Capitalism* that the doctrine and devotionalism of socio-religious groups affected the economic behavior of their adherents. He maintained that a religion supplies a distinctive worldview and cultural values that influence its adherents. This creates a particular bias concerning what is important and worth seeking in one's life, which, in turn, can affect economic attainment and social status in the wider society. In modern American society, differences among various religious teachings are important because they apparently induce distinctly differing reactions among people who are subjected to the same experiences. One of the results is the social-prestige differences we have described.

Weber asserted that Protestantism was the locomotive of capitalism. The Weberian school maintains that Puritanism and its evangelical offshoots created a morality that inspired individualism, activism, and pragmatism, and encouraged perseverance and personal effort among its followers. The Calvinist spiritual goal of personal achievement of grace oriented such Protestants toward adopting the goal of personal achievement in economic life as well.

In many ways, structural changes in the economy during this century have had an impact on the Protestant ethic. Large-scale corporations and international conglomerates have displaced small business. The glorification of consumption and readily available credit have undermined thrift and the belief in deferred gratification. Through advertising, corporations have largely taken over the traditional role of religion. In this consumer society, they now determine the correct way to behave and what conformity to group norms means. Enjoyment through consumption has almost become an obligation for Americans. This is a contentious issue for conservative religious sects, and lies at the heart of their hostility to modernizing social and economic trends. They look back with nostalgia to a less-complicated small-town society close to the original Puritan model.

The conservative view of the traditional Protestant ethic is based not only on the value placed on virtues, but also on the judgment of vices. For instance, conservatives still hold to the Victorian attitude that associated poverty with laziness and alcohol (drugs have since been added to the equation). This can create an anomaly, as most fundamentalists and evangelicals also hold to the American business creed, which espouses the value of competition, the dignity of work, the right of the individual in the marketplace, the desirability of material possessions, and the willingness to take risks. Yet they condemn much of the major corporations' material output (along with welfare, government regulations, and labor unions). In recent years they have been particularly upset by the advertising of major corporations in the fast-expanding media; clothing, equipment, leisure, and travel industries, which has engendered a hedonistic "fun" morality hostile to traditional Puritan ethics.

THE DECREASING SOCIAL GAP BETWEEN CATHOLICS AND PROTESTANTS

Max Weber claimed that Protestants were more likely than Catholics to rise rapidly in the economic world because Protestants were more entrepreneurial and business-oriented and so more successful in the competition for economic advancement. He could point to Catholic teaching to support him, for in the late 19th century the Vatican favored a guildlike economic system that was neither socialism nor capitalism. This was espoused by Pope Leo XIII in 1891 when he issued *Rerum Novarum,* which affirmed the right of private property as part of natural law. But the pope's encyclical also condemned capitalism for putting a terrible burden on the working classes, and for mistreating them to the point where they were only somewhat better off than slaves; and it urged society to control property for the common good. The rich were considered to be only custodians of their wealth, and the poor, Pope Leo declared, had the right to share it. Social needs had to be the major area of concern for Roman Catholics.

Echoes of the Protestant-Catholic values gap were found in a 1950s Detroit-area study, in which sociologist Gerhard Lenski reported that "working-class Protestants had an affinity for middle-class economic values, while middle-class Catholics had an affinity for working-class values." Lenski also suggested that a Catholic anti-intellectualism and an overemphasis on family life disadvantaged American Catholics in the marketplace. Lenski, following the German economic historian Werner Sombart, contentiously suggested that everything Max Weber had ascribed to Puritanism could also be ascribed to some degree to Judaism, since Weber envisioned Puritanism

as a modified form of Judaism and an important source in the development
of capitalism. Distinguishing Jews and white Protestants from Catholics and
black Protestants, Lenski found that the former two identified with "individualistic, competitive patterns of thought and action linked with the
middle class and historically associated with the Protestant ethic or its secular counterpart, the spirit of capitalism." In contrast, the latter groups were
associated more with "the collectivistic, security-oriented working-class patterns of action, historically opposed to the Protestant ethic."

Various polls conducted before and just after World War II showed that
except in the South, American Protestants were twice as likely as American
Catholics to be found in the upper class. In recent decades, however, the
older established white Catholic groups have undergone *"embourgeoisement"* to
a considerable degree. Although late 1980s National Opinion Research Center (NORC) surveys showed that Catholics (24%) were still more likely than
white Protestants (17%) to live in union households, the groups' occupational situation has changed a great deal. Equal proportions of Catholics and
white Protestants were in professional (19%) and managerial and administrative occupations (19–21%). In fact, Irish Catholics (46%) and northern
European Catholics (41%) were more likely than white Protestants to be in
professional and managerial occupations.

White Catholics are now very much a part of the established American
middle class and upper-middle class. When one looks only at white Catholics, it appears that a social revolution has occurred since the 1950s. They
have become better educated and socially and economically more integrated
into suburban society. As a result, the overall situation for Catholics has
improved considerably since Lenski's studies. However, the growing proportion of Hispanics and blacks among the Catholic population negatively
affects the current figures on the social standing of the Catholic community
(see Tables 7-1A–E). For instance, the median Catholic household income
drops from $29,100 for white Catholics to $23,900 for Hispanic Catholics
and $21,000 for black Catholics. The consequences of the disappearing social
gap have been, among other results, a major restructuring of traditional
political loyalties, a rising level of Catholic-Protestant intermarriage, and a
loosening of the ethnic bonds and hostility within the white population in
America. It is evidence of the melting pot at work.

THE DATA ON SOCIAL STANDING

The "Protestant ethic" has been absorbed into American values. Contemporary America places considerable emphasis on meritocracy, by which occupations and roles are assigned according to qualifications, such as college

diplomas. The 18th-century Scottish free-market economist Adam Smith suggested that "an instructed and an intelligent people . . . are always more decent and orderly than an ignorant and stupid one." The extension of this in the meritocratic atmosphere of the modern United States, according to Will Herberg, is that "the American believes in progress, in self-improvement and quite fanatically in education." In the spirit of the free market, America also respects and values hard work; people who work full-time are considered more acceptable than, for instance, unemployed people who receive welfare. Property and home ownership are, as we have suggested, a symbol of a participating and taxpaying member of society with a stake in the "system." Finally, in a free-market society with open careers and opportunities, financial success is both a tangible and a symbolic token of personal accomplishment.

The NSRI has provided us with the opportunity to inquire in considerable detail into the actual relationship of social-class factors and the pattern of religious identification. We do this by comparing a range of social indicators relating to the Protestant ethic. The four indicators we have chosen are the pattern of employment, the extent of home ownership, the level of education, and the level of household income. In Tables 7-1A–E we have assembled data on these four social variables relating to the thirty largest religious groups in this society. We list the religious groups according to their rank-order position on these four variables and finally on their overall aggregate score. In this manner we should obtain an overall picture of the relative social standing of the religious groups in the country today. Of course, every religious group contains a variety of people from all status groups. Although the differences between some denominations are small, clear rankings do emerge.

The first position is held by Unitarian Universalists, a group with a long history of high status in this society. Theirs is a very liberal religion, both in theological and social outlook.

The second position is held by the Disciples of Christ, one of the smaller mainstream Protestant denominations founded as part of the mid-19th-century movement to restore New Testament faith and practice as well as to establish Christian unity. It has often been viewed as the typical American denomination because of its frontier beginnings and emphasis on Christian living rather than theology and creeds. Ronald Reagan and several other U.S. presidents were raised in this faith. Geographically, the church is a slice of Middle America, but its core strength lies with middle-class urban members. It has lost conservative members in the past through schisms due to its acceptance of evolutionary theory and its desire to address current social issues. This group posed a problem for us as statisticians because it is also known as the Christian Church. The number of respondents to the NSRI

TABLE 7-1A

EDUCATIONAL RANKING BY RELIGIOUS GROUP

RELIGIOUS GROUP	PERCENT COLLEGE GRADUATES
Unitarian	49.5
Hindu	47.0
Jewish	46.7
NRMs *	40.6
Disciples of Christ	39.3
Episcopalian	39.2
Agnostic	36.3
Presbyterian	33.8
Congregationalist	33.7
Buddhist	33.4
Christian Science	33.1
Eastern Orthodox	31.6
Muslim	30.4
No Religion	23.6
"Protestant"	22.1
"Evangelical"	21.5
Methodist	21.1
Catholic	20.0
Mormon	19.2
Lutheran	18.0
7th-Day Adventist	17.9
"Christian"	16.0
Churches of Christ	14.6
Assemblies of God	13.7
Nazarene	12.5
Brethren	11.4
Baptist	10.4
Pentecostal	6.9
Holiness	5.0
Jehovah's Witnesses	4.7

* New Religious Movements

who self-identified as Disciples is much lower than the claimed membership figure of 1 million. Many adherents probably described themselves as "Christians," a group that does not rank high on our status list. Thus it may well be that this situation has created slight biases toward an exaggerated "upmarket image" for the Disciples.

TABLE 7-1B

EMPLOYMENT RANKING BY RELIGIOUS GROUP

RELIGIOUS GROUP	PERCENT WORKING FULL-TIME
Hindu	64.1
Agnostic	63.5
NRMs	63.4
Muslim	62.5
No Religion	60.5
Buddhist	59.4
Disciples of Christ	55.4
Eastern Orthodox	55.1
Catholic	54.3
Pentecostal	52.8
Unitarian	52.7
Episcopalian	52.6
Baptist	52.3
"Christian"	51.8
Jewish	50.1
Lutheran	50.0
Holiness	49.9
Mormon	49.9
Congregationalist	49.7
Methodist	49.6
"Protestant"	49.3
Presbyterian	48.8
Assemblies of God	48.8
Nazarene	48.5
Churches of Christ	47.2
"Evangelical"	47.0
Brethren	46.2
7th-Day Adventist	46.0
Jehovah's Witnesses	44.1
Christian Science	40.1

The third position is held by agnostics. As we might have expected, the social standing of the group is high, reflecting the fact that the term *agnostic* is likely to be used only by reasonably well educated people. The next two positions are held by Congregationalists and Episcopalians, two of the historically high-status Protestant "establishment" denominations. Then follow adherents of the Eastern Orthodox church and of Judaism. Both groups are

TABLE 7-1C

INCOME RANKING BY RELIGIOUS GROUP

RELIGIOUS GROUP	MEDIAN ANNUAL HOUSEHOLD INCOME
Jewish	$36.7 K
Unitarian	$34.8 K
Agnostic	$33.3 K
Episcopalian	$33.0 K
Eastern Orthodox	$31.5 K
Congregationalist	$30.4 K
Presbyterian	$29.0 K
Disciples of Christ	$28.8 K
Buddhist	$28.5 K
Hindu	$27.8 K
Catholic	$27.7 K
NRMs	$27.5 K
No Religion	$27.3 K
Churches of Christ	$26.6 K
Lutheran	$25.9 K
Christian Science	$25.8 K
Mormon	$25.7 K
"Protestant"	$25.7 K
Methodist	$25.1 K
Muslim	$24.7 K
7th-Day Adventist	$22.7 K
Assemblies of God	$22.2 K
"Evangelical"	$21.9 K
Nazarene	$21.6 K
Jehovah's Witnesses	$20.9 K
"Christian"	$20.7 K
Baptist	$20.6 K
Pentecostal	$19.4 K
Brethren	$18.5 K
Holiness	$13.7 K

urban, middle-class populations and are increasingly prominent in political and cultural life. After them are the Presbyterians, traditionally a high-status group, usually ranking just below Episcopalians.

The high standing of Hindus and Buddhists, mirroring the current high standing of the Asian population in general, which has apparently imbibed liberally of the Protestant ethic, is socially significant for the future of

TABLE 7-1D

PROPERTY OWNERSHIP RANKING BY RELIGIOUS GROUP

RELIGIOUS GROUP	PERCENT OWNING THEIR HOME
Brethren	81.4
Congregationalist	80.9
Churches of Christ	78.1
Presbyterian	76.9
Lutheran	76.5
"Protestant"	75.4
Methodist	75.2
Assemblies of God	75.1
Mormon	74.0
Unitarian	73.2
Eastern Orthodox	72.7
Disciples of Christ	72.3
Nazarene	71.2
Episcopalian	70.6
"Evangelical"	69.7
Catholic	69.3
Christian Science	69.0
Baptist	66.6
"Christian"	63.7
Jewish	61.7
Pentecostal	60.8
No Religion	60.6
Agnostic	59.7
Jehovah's Witnesses	59.1
7th-Day Adventist	54.6
Holiness	53.7
NRMs	53.4
Buddhist	50.6
Hindu	47.1
Muslim	43.3

American society. Ironically, Eastern religions in their natural environment in Asia have tended to stress passivity, detachment from the world, and contemplation of the inner being, to the detriment of economic development. As suggested in Chapter 4, U.S. government policy and preference have skewed the Asian immigrant population by admitting mainly the most "American" Asians. It is noteworthy that the 1990 U.S. Census reported

TABLE 7-1E

AGGREGATE SOCIAL-STATUS RANKING ON "PROTESTANT ETHIC" VARIABLES
BY RELIGIOUS GROUP

RELIGIOUS GROUP	RANK ORDER
Unitarian	1
Disciples of Christ	2
Agnostic	3
Congregationalist	4
Episcopalian	5
Eastern Orthodox	6
Jewish	7
Presbyterian	8
Hindu	9
NRMs	10
Buddhist	11
No Religion	12
Catholic	13
Lutheran	14
"Protestant"	15
Methodist	16
Mormon	17
Churches of Christ	18
Muslim	19
Assemblies of God	20
Christian Science	21
"Evangelical"	22
Brethren	23
"Christian"	24
Nazarene	25
Baptist	26
Pentecostal	27
7th-Day Adventist	28
Holiness	29
Jehovah's Witnesses	30

that, overall, Asian median household incomes exceeded white incomes by over $5,000 a year.

The relatively high social-status position of what we call here the New Religious Movements (NRMs), with their countercultural outlook, may seem somewhat paradoxical, yet it fits the common stereotype of these groups as being largely made up of young, white, educated, urban, middle-class people. The social-standing figures demonstrate that Catholics, Lutherans, Methodists, and Mormons have a middle-range social standing, and that the lowest ranks are held by the Protestant sects.

Though Mormons, Seventh-Day Adventists, Black Muslim sects, Jehovah's Witnesses, and Holiness sects all claim to revere the Protestant ethic, these groups do not appear to be doing very well, at least according to our scale. The biggest surprise is the poor showing of the Mormons, whose own surveys show higher socioeconomic performance. However, their surveys are mailed to members, resulting in an element of self-selection. Data from the U.S. Bureau of Economic Analysis on personal income per capita by state support our findings: In 1989, according to this indicator, Mormon-majority Utah was ranked number 46, and Idaho, which contains a Mormon plurality, stood at number 40.

In the light of what we discovered about the relationship between religion and politics in Chapter 5, our results (Tables 7-1A–E) are paradoxical. In the religious divide between conservatives and liberals, the higher social-status groups tend to be concentrated at the liberal end of the spectrum. The successful adherents of liberal and secular groups also appear to be more amenable to economic and social reform and welfare-state ideas. In contrast, the strongest supporters of the Republican party and the free-enterprise system are the theologically conservative evangelical and fundamentalist groups, whose followers do not tend to be very successful economically.

Since religion in general is increasingly associated with lower-middle-class families, conservative Protestantism is flourishing proportionately. The less-well-off classes tend to be found at the conservative end of the religious spectrum because people facing uncertainty and instability in their lives, whether social or economic, look toward religious groups with more structure and fewer interpretative options—that is, toward the fundamentalist denominations. It has been suggested that the middle and upper classes like to "do their religion and attend worship services" while the lower classes are more inclined to "feel it." This accounts for the fact that expressive religions such as Pentecostalism are regarded as a "haven for the dispossessed." In this formulation, certain religions can be seen as channels for lower-class frustration. There is still a strong correlation between religion and social respectability, as we see in the fact that the mostly male urban underclass is among the least religious groups in American society.

THE SECTS

Understanding the beliefs of the millennialist groups and "revolutionist" sects that want to reform human values and behavior will explain their social outlook as well as their low ranking on our social-status scale. A sect is a dissenting religious group that seeks to preserve its spiritual purity by remaining apart from the world. Its members believe in a moral truth that is unchanging, universal, and divinely sanctioned. A sect frequently exercises close control over its members and their personal lives. A prime example of such a closed community is the Seventh-Day Adventist. Its members can be born in an Adventist hospital, educated in Adventist schools from kindergarten to university, work in Adventist institutions, buy Adventist food, live in Adventist communities, and end their days in Adventist retirement centers.

Sectarians reject much of the current economic system along with mainstream ideas of religious respectability as part of their general withdrawal from what they consider to be a corrupt and complacent world. Many sectarians have responded to their poverty by denouncing what the economy withheld from them and by clinging to Calvinism. Their beliefs teach them that human beings are weak, sinful, and hopeless before God. Asceticism is their lot and hard work their only bulwark against escape through pleasures they cannot, in any event, afford. Sects teach an otherworldly religion and usually reject drinking, gambling, dancing, attending amusements, and conspicuous consumption. This asceticism and work discipline tend to make their members desirable employees. Sectarians are often anti-union but stress ideas like "A fair day's work for a fair day's pay" and "Honesty is the best policy." They believe in actively rejecting the greed and values of the consumer society. The Amish farmer, for example, will disadvantage himself rather than buy on credit. Jehovah's Witnesses accept low pay because they see consumer culture as false and evil. The Holiness sects, which began in the late 1800s, teach that the only real problem is sin, which can be overcome by an encounter with God. A search for perfection and sanctification orients sectarians to a personalized idea of right conduct and individual achievement within their own nonmaterial value system.

OTHER FACTORS INFLUENCING SOCIAL RANKING

The internal composition of the religious groups affects all four social variables in Tables 7-1A–E. Race and gender have a major impact, and factors such as age and the number of generations of the respondent's family that have lived in this country affect the figures as well. As we saw in Chapter 6, the role and status of women varies considerably according to their theology and social outlook. We will discuss the importance of the gender factor in some detail later in this chapter. As regards race, religious groups with a large black constituency are affected by the disadvantaged situation of blacks in society. For instance, only 48.9% of black households own their own home, while 74.0% of whites do. Black income is considerably lower than white. Yet, blacks are more likely to be working full-time.

INCOME

In the 1980s a new trend arose with the growth of a leisure industry geared to the health-conscious baby-boom/yuppie generation. More people than ever before spent their weekends pursuing recreational activities with high entry costs, such as tennis, skiing, sailing, golf, and horseback riding. As a result, upper-middle-class people, especially those without young children, were less likely to be involved in religious activities. A pattern emerged of membership and attendance at religious services that was negatively associated with income: 60% of all income groups below $100,000 reported membership in religious groups, compared with 49% of those among the very wealthy; 28% to 35% of households with an income below $50,000 reported weekly attendance, while fewer than 20% of those with an income of $50,000 and above reported attending services weekly.

Income appears to differentiate religious groups across a wide range. Since the top income range for the NSRI was simply "over $75,000," it is not possible to give an accurate figure for average income. Instead, we have reported the median income—that is, the total household annual income that divides the group into two halves. On this scale, the highest household incomes are found among Jews, followed by Unitarians, agnostics, Episcopalians, Eastern Orthodox adherents, and Congregationalists. It is curious that the NSRI survey, an anonymous telephone poll, reported median incomes slightly lower than those reported by the 1990 U.S. Census, which were obtained on a personal basis. However, this does not alter the overall ranking of the religious groups.

As with most social indicators, race affects the results. Asian and white incomes are much higher than black and Hispanic incomes in the United States. Thus, any religious group's average is affected by the proportion of its members who are black and Hispanic. For some groups this factor is of considerable importance. White Catholic median income, at $29,100, would lie above that of Presbyterians if minorities were excluded. Episcopalian median income would be $1,000 higher, more than for agnostics, if whites were the only group included. For Baptists, white median income is $22,900, while black income is $17,100. The gap is even wider for Methodists, with $26,500 for whites and $18,200 for blacks; for "No Religion" respondents, with $28,400 for whites and $19,600 for blacks; and for Muslims, $33,000 for whites and $19,500 for blacks.

Household size also affects real income. For the reasons stated above, we do not have a precise per capita income. Nevertheless, we know that for

many of the high-income groups, household size is comparatively low; therefore, the real difference between Jews, Unitarians, agnostics, and Episcopalians as compared to Brethren, Baptists, Pentecostalists, and Holiness
adherents is actually wider than it appears.

The way we collect the data allows for more differentiation among Protestants than other groups. We have seen that there are significant income
differences among Catholics according to race and ethnicity, but even among
white Catholics incomes are finely graded at the parish level. Income differences among Jews used to show that Reform Jews had the highest and
Orthodox Jews the lowest. These differences, though narrowed recently,
persist because traditional Jews make economic sacrifices to observe the
Sabbath and other religious holidays and are also slightly less likely than
liberal Jews to seek higher education.

Home Ownership

Home ownership is a desirable goal in American society. It provides a secure
investment, social standing in the community, and a sense of belonging.
Owning your own home is not directly affected by income; it appears to be
more closely related to age, area of residence, and religious affiliation, though
the last factor may be strongly connected to the first two. Since it is linked
to thrift, home ownership may be thought to have some ties to the Protestant
ethic. It could also be that property ownership is attractive to those seeking
social status who are not able to obtain it professionally or by other forms of
consumption. Protestant groups have the highest rates of home ownership
(see Table 7-1D), particularly those groups that are attractive to the elderly
and residents of rural areas, such as the Brethren (81.4%), Congregationalists (80.9%), Churches of Christ adherents (78.1%), Presbyterians (76.9%),
Lutherans (76.5%), and Methodists (75.2%). In part this is because many
urban dwellers, especially in the large metropolitan centers, are renters. This
is particularly true for Jews, agnostics, and members of the NRMs, all of
whom have surprisingly low rates of home ownership (61.7%, 59.7%, and
53.4%, respectively) and are concentrated in cities. Also, it is mainly the
non-Christian groups such as Buddhists, Hindus, and Muslims, groups that
rank high in terms of education, full-time employment, and income, that
have the lowest rates of home ownership. This seems to suggest that they are
not yet fully participating members of American society, which considers
owning one's own home as the achievement of the American dream. More
predictably, sects with low overall social status, such as the Jehovah's Witnesses, Seventh-Day Adventists, and Holiness, also have low rates of home
ownership.

FULL-TIME WORK

Rank order of groups in terms of those who are currently employed full-time shows that non-Christians, such as Hindus (64.1%), agnostics (63.5%), members of the NRMs (63.4%), "No Religion" respondents (60.5%), and Buddhists (59.4%), are found at the top. The relative youth of these populations explains the lack of retired persons among them. Nevertheless, they score higher than youthful Christian groups such as Pentecostals and Baptists. The difference is that although the non-Christians have higher proportions of adults who are students, this is more than compensated for by the fact that they have more females who are in the work force. As we discussed in Chapter 6, conservative Christians have more female homemakers in their ranks. This, in turn, results in fewer economically active adults.

THE RELIGIOUS REPERCUSSIONS OF COLLEGE EDUCATION

According to the latest Gallup polls, in an average week 42% of American adults attend religious services, but among college graduates the rate is 46%. Overall, 68% of Americans claim to currently belong to a church. College graduates (71%) are slightly more likely to belong to a church. The American educated classes are obviously not alienated from religion. The 1991 UCLA study "The American Freshman" reported that 29% were professed born-again Christians and that 83% had attended a religious service during the past year. Yet there are some paradoxes here. Controlling for other factors, highly educated parents are less likely to instill in their children a reverence for the Scriptures. Better-educated parents do not expect their children to attend church as frequently, and do not imbue their children with strong beliefs in the Bible.

Table 7-1A shows that percentages of college graduates vary widely from group to group. The range spans from under 7% for the Protestant sects such as Jehovah's Witnesses (4.7%), Holiness (5%), and Pentecostals (6.9%), to over 40% among non-Christian groups such as Unitarian-Universalists (49.5%), Hindus (47%), Jews (46.7%), and members of the NRMs (40.6%). The highest-ranked Christians are in the mainline liberal churches: Disciples of Christ (39.3%), Episcopalians (39.2%), Presbyterians (33.8%) and Congregationalists (33.7%).

Mainline Protestants do well academically largely because the prestige institutions within the American educational system are "their system." Until the 20th century, higher education in America was cast in a Protestant light. It was founded by Protestants, and its intellectual and moral coloration was heavily tinted with Calvinism. Few historians of higher education would deny that the old-time college was a stepchild of Protestant churches. Most college presidents, trustees, and faculty members were ministers whose appointments depended on their beliefs. Right up to World War II, religion was still prominent in the colleges and entered the curriculum as moral philosophy that attempted to integrate the entire course of study and instill a common set of social values. Most studies have shown that the differences in occupation and income between groups in American society are largely due to differences in education. However, certain nominally mainline Protestant or Christian preparatory schools and private colleges have served a social rather than religious purpose. Elite networks and valuable contacts begin in these settings. This kind of socializing is also important in achieving success in many areas of economic life.

Exception to the Protestant attention to higher secular education is found among fundamentalist Protestants. It is not just a matter of social status. They tend to be highly anti-intellectual and hostile to formal secular education.

The ranking of certain groups' educational achievements is not random. Jews, for example, do well in measures of education because of a general orientation arising from Jewish intellectual traditions. They place high value on education, sacrifice to obtain it, and persevere once they enter the system. The exceptions are significant elements in the Orthodox community, including the Hasidim, who are similar to the Protestant fundamentalist sects in their disdain for secular education.

In recent years, education factors have been found to be partly responsible for apostasy in mainline religion and conversion to NRMs. A high proportion of NRM adherents are college graduates, attracted to the new ideas projected by these cults. Only those with a certain level of education, and thus a certain degree of sophistication, explore new forms of spirituality, meditation, and Eastern philosophies. NRMs have therefore found many more followers among the materially advantaged than among the lower-class members of modern society.

Changes in the educational levels of the general population in recent years appear to account for much of the variance in biblical beliefs over time. The current proportion of biblical literalists is 32%, only half of what it was in 1963, when 65% of Americans said they believed in the absolute truth of all words in the Bible and that it represented the actual word of God. Belief in inerrancy is most likely to be found among people who did not complete high school (58%), and least likely among college graduates (29%).

Higher education has not dramatically eroded the religious loyalties of Catholics. Almost 61% of Catholic college graduates still attend mass every week. Although only 10% of Catholic college students attend the nation's

239 Catholic colleges and universities, the relative standing of their schools has improved over the last two decades; institutions like the University of Notre Dame and Georgetown University are now highly regarded. However, Catholic schools may encounter problems if they follow the trend of Protestant-founded universities. Most of the universities founded under Protestant auspices went from denominational to generic Christianity, then to vaguely defined religious values, and, finally, to total secularism. Catholic universities seem to be headed in the same direction.

The 1991 UCLA study of college freshmen indicates intergenerational rates of loss among the educated classes according to religious group. Students were asked for their own religious identification and that of their mothers. When we compare the actual numbers of replies between the generations, we find that there were nearly twice as many "No Religion" students as "No Religion" mothers, and 10% more "Other Religion" students than "Other Religion" mothers. This suggests an erosion of religious belief between the generations. However, not all religions were affected in the same way. There were 2% *more* Baptist students than Baptist mothers, equal numbers of students and mothers (i.e., no loss) for Muslims, Mormons, Quakers, and Eastern Orthodox members. Some groups were diminished: The proportion of students who were of the same religion as their mothers was 93% for Catholics, 91% for Lutherans, 88% for Methodists, 84% for Episcopalians, 83% for Jews, 81% for Presbyterians, 75% for Seventh-Day Adventists, and only 50% for Buddhists. This is further evidence that Buddhism is being eroded by intergenerational change faster than any other religion in America.

RELIGIOUS SCHOOLS AND THEIR SOCIAL IMPLICATIONS

Parochial schools propound a clear worldview based upon religious doctrine to which, presumably, both the teachers and the students' parents subscribe, and these schools tend to have a more traditional view of education than contemporary public schools. Their preference for uniforms symbolizes their disciplinary demands and pressures for conformity. The educational results they obtain should be higher than public schools, not just because of their ideology and policies but because they can both select and expel students. As private schools requiring fees, they tend to have mostly middle-class students, and their scholarship students are, obviously, pre-selected.

Historically, the overwhelming majority of parochial schools in the United States were in urban areas and associated with the Catholic church. This picture has changed in recent decades as a result of the suburbanization of the Catholic population. Between 1965 and 1985, the number of Catholic schools fell 28%, and enrollment dropped 46%. According to church statistics, only 28% of Catholic children in grades 1 to 8 currently attend Catholic schools. Only 16% of Catholic high-school students are in Catholic schools. Yet Catholic schools continue to enroll more than 50% of all private-school students. In 1992 there were approximately 2,550,000 students attending 8,508 Catholic parochial schools: The 7,239 elementary schools had 1,964,000 students, and the 1,269 high schools had approximately 587,000 children. This is a major decrease from the almost 5,000,000 students in Catholic parochial schools in the early 1960s, but the number of students attending these schools appears to have stabilized in recent years. Indeed, Catholic-school enrollment in elementary and/or secondary schools has recently increased in thirty-five states. The future appears to be even brighter, since Catholic pre-school enrollment tripled between 1982 and 1992. Although some of these students may not continue their education in Catholic schools, some will. Two other factors are notable: The percentage of minority students attending Catholic schools more than doubled between 1970–71 and 1991–92, from 10.8% to 23%, and non-Catholics came to represent 12% of Catholic-school enrollment. This minority increase is particularly noticeable in major urban areas, such as New York, where black Protestants use the Catholic schools as a means of upward mobility. For example, black Protestants comprise approximately 75% of the children attending Catholic schools in Harlem.

Recent surveys have shown that Catholic schools have had a stronger impact on their students' lives than was thought during the 1970s, although not necessarily in the direction of greater orthodoxy. A survey of Catholic high-school students from the late 1980s that was reported in *U.S. Catholic* showed a high rate of dissent. Although 82% wanted to be Catholics all their lives, only 13% agreed with the church condemnation of birth control; 19% thought all sexual activity belongs only in marriage; 22% agreed that women cannot be priests; 45% called abortion a sin; 47% thought homosexual activity a sin; 49% said the continued development of nuclear arms is immoral; 44% said Virgin Birth is an essential Catholic doctrine, and 70% said the same for the Resurrection.

In the years of Catholic-school decline, 1965–85, non-Catholic religiously affiliated schools grew 149%. Total enrollment in parochial schools not related to the Roman Catholic church increased from 1,028,000 in 1981 to 1,715,000 in 1988, according to the U.S. Department of Education. The school enrollment figures suggest that a pluralistic and secular America, as represented by its public schools, has become a more comfortable place to live for most American Catholics since the 1960s. For evangelicals, however, the U.S. environment has become significantly more hostile. Evangelical schools are growing rapidly because evangelicals believe that nonsecular education is the only way to preserve their distinct religious identity into the next generation. Christian schools see themselves as an extension of the church or an extension of the family. The evangelical Association of Christian Schools International, headquartered in California, claims 2,778 member schools. Another 1,200 schools belong to the American Association of Christian Schools International, headquartered in Virginia, which has a more fundamentalist orientation.

Christian colleges range from fully accredited, well-equipped institutions to Bible colleges run out of church basements. Eighty thousand full-time students attend the 81 member schools of the Coalition of Christian Colleges; another 40,000 are enrolled in 600 Bible colleges, according to the American Association of Bible Colleges. Educating a new generation has become a top priority of many evangelical leaders. Jerry Falwell dropped his involvement in politics to focus on Liberty University. Pat Robertson has also followed this path. Over two thirds of the Christian Broadcasting Network's revenue goes to Regent University in Virginia Beach, Virginia.

Jewish parochial schools, usually known as Hebrew day schools or yeshivas, have also grown rapidly in the last decade. For example, in the six-year period between the 1982–83 and the 1988–89 school years, the student population of these schools grew from 103,000 to 168,000; the number of schools increased from 445 to 530. The vast majority of these schools are Orthodox (68%), but a growing number are Conservative (15%) and communal (nondenominational) schools (14.5%). The number of Reform Hebrew day schools is still nominal (2.5%), but that is to be expected as Reform Judaism is deeply committed to the public schools of America. The anomaly is that while Jewish day-school enrollment has risen rapidly, enrollment has dropped in Jewish supplementary afternoon or Sunday schools for those attending public school. These educational figures reflect the polarization that is occurring among American Jews between a religiously devoted minority and an increasingly secularized majority.

RELIGION, RACE, AND EDUCATIONAL ATTAINMENT

We have suggested that religious groups are social and cultural groups as well. No clearer proof of this can be provided than the data on the educational attainment of non-Hispanic whites and blacks in Table 7-2. The NSRI educational attainment results were slightly more favorable than the U.S. Census with regard to blacks, but the NSRI and census figures for non-

TABLE 7-2

EDUCATIONAL ATTAINMENT OF NON-HISPANIC WHITES AND BLACKS FOR
SELECTED RELIGIOUS GROUPS

Percentage of High-School Graduates (Age 18+) and College Graduates (Age 25+)

RELIGIOUS GROUP	WHITE		BLACK	
	HIGH-SCHOOL GRADUATE	COLLEGE GRADUATE	HIGH-SCHOOL GRADUATE	COLLEGE GRADUATE
Episcopalian	92.7	41.9	90.4	40.5
Muslim	87.9	57.9	73.8	22.6
Presbyterian	87.4	35.6	77.5	36.9
Catholic	84.5	23.4	83.2	21.4
Methodist	82.1	22.6	69.7	17.2
"No Religion"	81.7	27.8	80.5	18.7
Lutheran	81.0	18.9	86.6	20.5
"Protestant"	80.3	22.8	81.9	23.7
"Christian"	78.8	17.7	78.8	21.3
Jehovah's Witnesses	67.6	4.4	82.6	7.6
Baptist	66.9	11.3	67.8	11.4
Seventh-Day Adventist	65.0	16.8	81.9	23.7
Pentecostal	61.1	6.3	69.7	9.1
Holiness	39.5	3.7	51.1	6.3
U.S. All Religions	80.9	22.5	72.0	15.2

Hispanic whites are almost identical. These figures, which relate to religious groups where the NSRI contributed a sufficient sample of both races for statistical accuracy, suggest that religious identification in the United States is a better predictor of educational achievement than is race. We have seen that the educational gap between blacks and whites within the same religious group is much smaller than the chasm between the two races for the national population as a whole. For example, including both sexes, 93% of white and 90% of black Episcopalians have completed high school, and 42% of white and 41% of black Episcopalians are college graduates. Presbyterians and Catholics, whether white or black, also have very similar, invariably high educational attainments. On the other end of the spectrum, white and black Baptists have similar educational achievements, both at lower levels than Episcopalians, Presbyterians, and Catholics. In contrast, one can discern different educational levels among the more socially segregated Methodists and Muslims, where whites outperform blacks. Blacks, on the other hand, outperform whites among those groups with low levels of educational attainment, such as Pentecostals, Holiness adherents, and Jehovah's Witnesses. A more extreme example of this pattern are the Seventh-Day

Adventists, for whom the white-black differential is strikingly weighted toward blacks (17% higher for high-school graduation, and 7% higher for college graduation). The black Seventh-Day Adventist scores are very similar to black Catholic scores. This may well be a reflection of the fact that the Adventist church, too, has a well-developed system of parochial schools.

Whereas black Episcopalians are a small elite, only 250,000 or so people, black Catholics form a much larger population and now account for 9% of all African Americans. This makes the Catholic figures more salient. If one examines black Catholic educational achievement more closely, some noteworthy results are revealed by the NSRI. More black Catholics are graduates from high school and college than are blacks in general. They are roughly equal in educational attainment to other Catholics and greater than the overall American average regardless of race. Furthermore, proportionately fewer black Catholics drop out of high school compared with either the total black population or the overall white population. It appears that black Catholics are 40% more likely to graduate from college than other black Americans. In the 40-to-59-year-old group, 26% of black Catholics, 25% of white Catholics, 24% of all whites, and 15% of all blacks are college graduates. Though we have no quotable statistics, an analysis of parochial-school enrollment figures by race suggests that a majority of black Catholics attended parochial schools. Moreover, increasing numbers of African Americans seek a Catholic parochial-school education for their children, even while they themselves remain Protestants.

THE SOCIOECONOMIC POSITION OF WOMEN

In traditional religious households, women derive their social and economic status through marriage and husbands. Conservative religious beliefs perpetuate traditional gender roles, assigning women to the home and men to the work force. Study and work outside the home is forgone in order to concentrate on motherhood and family duties. Thus, groups that stress traditional divisions of labor tend to limit the socioeconomic opportunities of their female members, thereby lowering the group's average social status.

Although modern society encourages women to study into their adult years, to work outside the home, and, as we have noted previously, to have fewer children, what usually motivates women to go to work is economic pressure, which often leaves no other choice but to seek an extra income. This need has increasingly forced the majority of American women into the work force. Labor-force participation tends to foster liberal views, since women with greater involvement outside the home are more likely to desire roles that conservative theology usually reserves for men. This has important long-term implications for American religion since, up to now, women have been the backbone of their respective denominations.

GENDER INEQUALITY AND EDUCATION

As educational levels have risen nationwide over the past few decades, gender equality in educational attainment has reached new heights. Nevertheless, in most religious groups in the United States, men are still more likely than women to have completed high school. As Table 7-3 shows, females have reached higher educational levels than males only in the Eastern non-Christian religions and the "No Religion" group. The Episcopalian ratio is almost equal, indicating very slight gender differences. The most inegalitarian groups are the Pentecostals and Jehovah's Witnesses, where men are respectively 21% and 14% more likely than women to have completed schooling beyond the secondary level. The gender gap with regard to college graduation is wider than for high-school completion, but the overall pattern follows the ranking in Table 7-1A.

When we looked at the percentages of students among women age 18 to 24, we found that Jewish women received the highest level of investment in adult education. Thirty-three percent of young Jewish women were students. The second-highest group was the Mormons, where 23% of women in this age group were students. Presbyterians followed with 19%. Most other groups had 13% to 16% of their young females as students, the exception

TABLE 7-3

GENDER INEQUALITY IN EDUCATION:
MALE/FEMALE RATIO IN POST-SECONDARY-SCHOOL EDUCATION

RELIGIOUS IDENTIFICATION	M/F RATIO
Eastern Religions	0.89
"No Religion"	0.97
Episcopalian	1.01
Mormon	1.04
Eastern Orthodox	1.04
Jewish	1.09
Lutheran	1.12
Catholic	1.13
Jehovah's Witnesses	1.14
Presbyterian	1.15
Baptist	1.15
Pentecostal	1.21

being the Jehovah's Witnesses, only 4% of whose women were students, reflecting their aversion to higher education for both sexes. This rejection of higher education becomes even clearer because, as we shall see, Jehovah's Witnesses have high rates of high-school graduation irrespective of sex or race. The Mormons, too, evidence a slight variation in their educational pattern; they do not deny higher education to their females and are closer to egalitarian religious groups on this indicator than they are to other sects. Yet, if their young women are not students, they are married housewives.

GENDER INEQUALITY AND EMPLOYMENT

Once education is completed, women face the options of homemaking, part-time work, and full-time career. The data in Table 7-4, showing labor-force participation for women age 25 to 44, derive from several competing forces, not just religious orientation. Economic needs, the burden of young children at home, the availability of child care, as well as the labor market all affect the pattern of employment. Economic necessity generally encourages high rates of labor-force participation, especially for unmarried women. Thus we find that the variation in economic-activity rates among religious groups is rather narrow, less than 25%. Today, the vast majority of women in the prime childbearing years are economically active. The range among

TABLE 7-4

EMPLOYMENT STATUS BY RELIGIOUS GROUP IDENTIFICATION
FOR WOMEN AGE 25–44

(In Percent)

RELIGIOUS IDENTIFICATION	HOME-MAKER	PART-TIME	FULL-TIME	STUDENT	OTHER	TOTAL
"No Religion"	15.9	14.7	65.3	2.4	1.7	100.0
Episcopalian	16.0	17.9	63.0	2.0	1.1	100.0
Methodist	16.4	15.7	65.6	1.6	0.8	100.0
Jewish	17.5	16.4	61.1	2.9	2.0	100.0
Presbyterian	18.0	15.3	63.3	2.7	0.8	100.0
Baptist	18.0	11.9	65.9	1.7	2.5	100.0
Catholic	19.7	17.6	59.6	1.7	1.4	100.0
Lutheran	20.0	20.1	58.2	1.1	0.6	100.0
Pentecostal	27.2	14.2	54.7	1.6	2.3	100.0
Mormon	30.0	23.6	42.4	2.6	1.3	100.0
Jehovah's Witnesses	32.6	24.5	37.7	2.8	2.4	100.0

the denominations is from 62% to 82% of women currently in the part-time or full-time work force. The lowest rates of full-time workers are found among Jehovah's Witnesses (38%) and Mormons (42%). Most groups are in the range of 55% to 63%. The highest rates are found among "No Religion" respondents (65%), Baptists (66%), and Methodists (66%). The figures for the latter two groups reflect the greater number of full-time working women among the African American population.

Religious differences have a greater effect on variations in full-time employment rates between men and women than they do on education. Table 7-5 indicates that the ratio among Jehovah's Witnesses and Mormons is more than 2 to 1. There are 1.9 men working full-time for every 1 woman among Pentecostals. For most other groups the ratio is between 1.5 and 1.7. The lowest ratio, and so the greatest employment equality, is found amongst Eastern Orthodox adherents, where it is 1.3. This is probably due to the occupational structure of ethnic groups within the Orthodox church such as the Greeks, who are very much involved in small family businesses, particularly in the catering and restaurant industry.

Once again, the religious denominations fall along a liberal-conservative continuum with regard to women's socioeconomic attainment. In the interest of clarity, we have restricted the analyses in Tables 7-3–7-5 to a few selected religious groups illustrative of the broad theological cross section in American society. Two major clusters appear at either end of the spectrum. The first cluster includes the sects, such as Jehovah's Witnesses, Mormons,

TABLE 7-5

GENDER INEQUALITY IN THE WORK FORCE:
MALE/FEMALE RATIO IN FULL-TIME EMPLOYMENT

RELIGIOUS IDENTIFICATION	M/F RATIO
Eastern Orthodox	1.34
"No Religion"	1.50
Episcopalian	1.53
Eastern Religions	1.56
Jewish	1.64
Baptist	1.64
Catholic	1.65
Lutheran	1.68
Presbyterian	1.72
Pentecostal	1.87
Mormon	2.19
Jehovah's Witnesses	2.25

and Pentecostals. The opposite extreme includes moderates and liberals, comprised of the non-Christian groups, the Episcopalians, and the Eastern Orthodox. In effect, this pattern mirrors the status rankings in Table 7-1E. This is easily explained, for the liberal religious groups are more likely to have dual-earner rather than single-earner households. Over time, economic advantage is transferred to the next generation, which, in turn, can attain higher levels of education and economic prosperity. This analysis suggests that the observed social-status ranking of America's religious denominations is unlikely to change. Max Weber's theory seems to be verified by the NSRI data; different religious doctrines in contemporary America have visible and tangible consequences for adherents' social outlooks and economic behaviors.

CONCLUSION

◆ ◆ ◆

Religion took very different directions in the United States and France in the aftermath of their revolutions. The new American nation encouraged people to exercise religious liberty, and opposed favoritism for any particular church; the new French republic was hostile to religion in general. The First Amendment to the U.S. Constitution prohibited any law "respecting the establishment of religion" or "prohibiting the free exercise thereof." It not only created what Thomas Jefferson called a "wall of separation between church and state," but also encouraged exercise of religious beliefs without any interference from the state or state support of one denomination over another. Some claim that religious liberty arose in the United States because the first Congress, which adopted the Bill of Rights, really had little choice due to the large and diverse number of denominations spread throughout the thirteen newly formed states. If there was to be an American nation, there could not be a national church. Whatever the reason, it is important to note that religious liberty did arise in the United States and that it was prescribed by the Constitution.

The First Amendment to the Constitution is probably the most important contribution America has made to the history of religion. And it has made this contribution to religious freedom with an undoubtedly Protestant accent, brought about by Protestant sectarianism and the strongly held Protestant concept of the importance of individual conscience. Without state or tax support, churches in America have been existing, and sometimes flourishing, with private contributions, and have been stimulated periodically by revivalism and evangelism.

This has produced a uniquely American religious experience for most people. Catholicism in America is not the mirror image of Catholicism in Ireland, Italy, or Poland. Judaism in America is not the mirror image of Judaism in Israel. Islam in America is not the mirror image of Islam in Saudi Arabia. To some degree, all faiths in America have been Protestantized. Protestant groups such as Baptists, Methodists, Lutherans, Episcopalians, and Presbyterians have in turn been Americanized, and they are not the exact reflections of these denominations in other countries. And still other religious groups—Mormons, Seventh-Day Adventists, Jehovah's Witnesses, Unitarians, and Disciples of Christ, among many others—have germinated and evolved from the American experience. America has been a greenhouse for religious formation, adaptation, and change.

Belonging to a state and belonging to a church have been considered one and the same thing since 380 A.D., when the emperor Theodosius the Great blended political and religious loyalty together by making Christianity the official church of the Roman Empire. He then proceeded to persecute the pagan sects just as they had previously persecuted the early Christians. This eventually led to Catholic states' persecution of Jews and, after the Reformation, of Protestants. This continued with persecution of Catholics as well as Protestant dissenters by Protestant states, and persecution of Jews by Catholic and Protestant states alike. To find an even partial precedent for the American experience of religious liberty, one has to go well back in history, perhaps to before Constantine the Great's era (306–37), when people voluntarily joined and supported their churches. But even this is not an accurate parallel, because America was and is comprised of great ethnic and racial diversity, and religion has become a powerful and unifying factor in bringing different peoples together. Religion and religious groups have also been recast and re-created in the United States, developing, in the process, a particular American taste and a distinctly Protestant flavor. Here, all religions both compete and coalesce with an American civil religion, which blends together the sacred and the secular in an attempt to give the United States a special mission in the world. Thus, in 1789 President George Washington authorized the nation's first Thanksgiving Day by saying that it is the duty of all Americans "to acknowledge the Providence of Almighty God, to obey His will, to be grateful for His benefits, and humbly to implore His protection and favor." And in 1863, in the middle of the Civil War, President Abraham Lincoln made Thanksgiving a permanent national holiday and thereby a primary fixture in our nation's civil religion.

An outstanding feature of America today is that the vast majority of people identify with a religion. This feeling is almost universal, yet it exists within a secular framework, an outer shell of secular values. For what we have witnessed in the latter part of the 20th century is the growing secularization of a self-described religious people.

In other nations, in countries as different as Italy and Algeria, the tension between religion and secularism is more pronounced than it is in the United States, where secularism and religion regularly use and redefine each other. Religion in the United States frequently sanctifies the goals of a basically secular society, and the secular society affects and influences the very meaning of religious identification and association. It is therefore not surprising that America appears to be growing more secular precisely at a time when religious identification is highly pronounced.

Liberty has become a major cornerstone of religion and individual religious identification in America. Americans today are more religiously identified and more religiously committed than the people of any other Western nation. Yet, as pollsters George Gallup, Jr., and Sarah Jones recently revealed, 7 out of 10 Americans believe that one can be religious without attending church. Similarly, 8 out of 10 Americans say that a person's religious beliefs should be decided independent of organized religion. Furthermore, America's religious liberty has brought about an increase in denominational switching. Fewer than half of American adults say they have always been members of their current denomination.

All this has led to a growing civil religion, which enhances secular values and uses sacred symbols and sacred days to advance the national mission. As early as the 1950s, the writer Will Herberg described this aspect of what we call American exceptionalism. He related that when the Italian socialist and writer Ignazio Silone was asked the most important date in history, he replied, "The twenty-fifth of December in the year Zero." When thirty distinguished Americans answered that same question, first place went to Columbus's discovery of America; the birth of Jesus tied for fourteenth place with the Wright brothers' first plane flight and the discovery of the X ray.

These questions were asked almost forty years ago, long before the quincentennial celebration of Columbus's discovery. During those four decades the rate of change has accelerated for all humans. Political, social, economic, and societal change has turned the world upside down, from the advent of space exploration to the demise of the Soviet Union to undreamed-of lifestyles and moral codes. Yet, amid talk of moral pluralism, 8 in 10 Americans agree, "mostly" or "completely," that absolute standards of good and evil apply universally, and 94% would welcome stronger family ties. Is it any wonder that in 1992, for the first time in American history, the presidential race witnessed Republican and Democratic candidates battling over who could best strengthen "family values" and become the instrument of change to preserve "basic values"? But the two men had different ideas about the meaning of these terms. Republicans tended to stress traditional two-parent families, discipline, abstinence, faithfulness, a notion of right and wrong. Democrats, also acknowledging the importance of families, were more likely to see families as evolving with different life-styles, and to see the need for society and government to accommodate all these changes honestly and forthrightly.

The resurgence of religion in American society is due in part to cultural divisions that are increasingly evident. Politics is in large part a function of culture, and at the heart of American culture is religion. The escalation of religious references in public debate relates to the most troubling social issues of our time: abortion, euthanasia, medical and biological ethics, sexuality, patriotism, church-state relations, public education, and the moral status of the family. In many if not most of our religious denominations, cultural liberals and cultural conservatives have become divided over values, over whether to return to traditional behavior patterns or to adapt to changing behavior patterns. Ultimately, decisions are based upon personal determination of morality and life-styles. What may follow is the growth of religious identification, revivalism, evangelism, or, as frequently happens in America, spin-offs out of, as well as splits within, denominations. This relates to the ambivalent response to authority that has been a theme of this book. Americans are suspicious of authority and hostile to hierarchy. Yet most religions require a hierarchical structure as well as an authoritative revelation.

As we have noted, there is considerable debate today about multiculturalism and the questions it raises on the value of transmitting "Western culture" to another generation of Americans. Such a debate inevitably involves religion because Christianity, especially Protestantism, is so integrally linked to the historical development of American society. As this becomes more obvious, the present cultural divide could become further exacerbated before there is an accommodation in the body politic. A countercurrent leading to a possible accommodation among some groups is that as African Americans and southern whites reject their subordinate status in American society, they will become increasingly aware of their common Protestant Christian culture. This possibility arises because religion still has an influence on regional culture, especially in the South. In fact, the growth of Evangelicalism nationally is bringing about a "southernization" of American religion.

Religious identification does not split the generations as one might expect; on the contrary, it actually reveals a broad intergenerational continuity. Even more crucially, religious identification does not divide the nation's population on ethnic/racial lines, but rather cuts across the divisions to unite Americans. Religion also stratifies society along life-style choices and social classes and greatly affects education.

The general climate of uncertainty can unnerve the public. Not only societal values and norms but even such mundane issues as what people work at and how they play have undergone vast and accelerating changes in the modern period. Where once it was unacceptable, it is not uncommon now for an individual to make three or four career changes in the course of his or her lifetime. Often the result is a sense of disorder and drift in people's lives, which sometimes motivates a search for a deeper, more meaningful, and, perhaps, unchanging reality. This could explain why there exists a growing minority searching beyond the civil religion and beyond a loose identification with religion for a spiritual base, and questioning the direction of a basically secular society. The need to create order out of chaos in their personal lives has motivated a growing number of Americans to adopt traditional values or fundamentalist beliefs.

There are, however, countervailing trends in society that tend to undermine the movement toward more traditional religious beliefs. Many of these are brought about by economic forces that encourage migration from established communities and rural areas, thus undermining local communities and traditional family networks. The economic and social pressures for women and mothers to join the work force also serve to weaken conservative religious tendencies. The competitive economic environment gives rise to a constant search for innovation and attention in the marketing of goods and services. This leads major corporations to pursue commercial advertising that challenges social taboos and traditional mores. Depictions of violence and sexuality have become commonplace in the media. Youthful challenges to authority are glorified in film and music. These commercial forces often influence the movement toward social and spiritual experimentation and the breakdown of traditional values.

These opposing forces create the paradoxical nature of American religion, to which we have often referred. There appears to be a collective schizophrenia whereby the public says one thing, with apparent sincerity, in answer to public-opinion polls and acts quite differently. The modern and the traditional become both seductive and repulsive simultaneously. America's market-oriented religion bears a similarity to the rest of society in its hopeful and optimistic tone and its unwillingness to face certain uncomfortable realities.

With increased life span and the development of increasingly effective medicines, there is a refusal to face the reality of decay and death. Whereas in traditional societies elders were a source of wisdom and taught people how to live, in today's American society they are considered by many to be outdated and out of touch with current reality. They are frequently shunted aside in an uncritical celebration of the new and the young and an emphasis on appearing youthful. Few weekly sermons in contemporary America focus upon death—and hellfire and damnation are unpopular themes for an increasingly sophisticated audience. Modern religion seems to have lost touch with its roots, which were historically linked to death and the preparation for death. In the past, religion not only supported the social system and provided for a moral and ethical base to society, but it also helped to explain the purpose of life and the individual's own mortality. Complex and yet moving rituals surrounding death gave social and psychological consolation for the inevitable loss of loved ones. In a society where the thought of personal mortality is avoided, religion, regardless of strong identification, will continue to play a less profound role in a person's life.

Considering the rapid changes of the past century, few if any can predict what a National Survey of Religious Identification will reveal a century or even a decade from now. Predictions are not always wise or safe. Yet our expectations are that religious interest will rise during the 1990s as we approach a new millennium with all its hopes and fears for the future. This is made more likely by the recent near-total collapse of world communism, an upheaval that has led many religious and even not-so-religious people to believe that they are living in a unique but uncertain period of history. Many factors will influence the survival and appeal of today's American religious groups and the rise of new forms of religion. Among these are the continuation and perhaps even the acceleration of the Protestantization of American society, the incidence and effects of intermarriage, conversion, and secularization, as well as unimagined technological developments. The important thing to realize is that religion in America is dynamic, creative, and relevant, continuously changing and developing.

APPENDIX:
RELIGIOUS STATISTICS

◆ ◆ ◆

THE METHODOLOGY OF THE NATIONAL
SURVEY OF RELIGIOUS IDENTIFICATION (NSRI)

Perhaps our most important innovation as an academically based project was our decision to use a commercial market-research firm and its omnibus market-research survey for our data collection. In recent years the commercial polling organizations have made rapid strides and large-scale investment in both computerized equipment and quality-control interviewing techniques. We chose an industry leader, the ICR Survey Research Group of Media, Pennsylvania, which operates the twice weekly EXCEL national representative sample survey directed at 1,000 households. In effect, this involved purchasing time for a question to be included in the survey alongside a variety of other constantly changing questions on topics as varied as cable TV use, preference for consumer items, and social or political issues. Our question was included in 113 rounds over 56 weeks in the period April 1989–April 1990.

In any type of research it is important that the topic and the questions be introduced appropriately and do not appear too intrusive or threatening. We chose the multipurpose questionnaire because we believed we would gain better results than if we merely called up the general public and asked them to participate in a purely religious survey. Our question in the multipurpose context often appeared appropriate when it was positioned alongside others on life-style, attitudes, food preferences, or public policy issues. As a result, once a respondent agreed to be interviewed, the actual refusal rate to our religious question was a very low 2.3%.

In addition to easing religious answers from the respondent, the multi-question, census-like format supplied us with detailed socio-demographic information. This book has organized a wealth of information alongside religious identification. For example, the respondent's age, sex, race, marital status, education, and political-party affiliation allowed us to see the relationship among religion and ethnicity, politics and life-style. Household characteristics such as income, family size, and geographical location provided the opportunity to analyze religious identification in light of social status, residency, and economics. The unique value of the NSRI was appreciated by the authors of the study *Churches and Church Membership in the United States in 1990,* who used this data source to obtain the first estimates of black Baptists by county throughout the nation.

One of the negatives of using commercial market research was that the response rate was lower than most social surveys would usually receive. Even after four attempts to contact respondents, the cooperation rate was only 50%. However, this did not pose a problem because we intended to carry out a massive number of interviews. We also had the benefit of access to the latest weighting and other statistical techniques, which allowed our statistician, Dale Kulp, the president of the Marketing System Group in Philadelphia, to weight, or recalculate, our findings in proportion to the current profile of the known composition of U.S. households and the total population. This kind of adjustment is necessary because, despite all our best efforts to obtain a representative sample, the experience of interviewing the American public shows that certain types of people are more reluctant than others to participate in surveys. Elderly women, especially those living alone, and inner-city residents are particularly hard to interview, whereas young families, especially in small towns in the Midwest, are highly cooperative. Therefore, it is necessary to adjust the raw figures accordingly. The weighting also took into account the probabilities of disproportionate household selection due to the number of separate telephone lines in the home.

The most important technical innovation that made this mammoth task possible was the use of ICR's Computer-Assisted Telephone Interviewing (CATI) system. The computer randomly chose telephone numbers across the United States in proportion to the number of residential telephone lines. This technique, known as Random Digit Dialing (RDD), creates a geographically representative sample. We used the GENYSYS system to create 113 individual national samples. Basically, GENYSYS chooses an area code, then a telephone exchange, and then the first two digits of a four-digit suffix. Then the computer randomly dials the last two numbers. In this manner a sample frame with very fine geographical stratification is created. The respondent within the household was a randomly chosen adult picked according to who had the last birthday.

The NSRI is much more accurate and detailed as to geographical distribution than any previous survey because of the number of interviews that took place within each state. For instance, there were 5,168 completed interviews in Michigan, and even small or sparsely populated states such as Vermont and Idaho had 297 and 531 interviews respectively within a carefully structured scientific sampling design.

The best way to test and corroborate the validity of the results is in a small state with a stable population. Rhode Island is an obvious choice since its population totals almost exactly 1 million, which makes translation of percentages into real numbers very easy. The NSRI reported that Rhode Island was 61.7% percent Catholic; that's about 617,000 people. The number used by well-informed diocesan researchers, using a comparison of parish and state demographic data, was 624,000 in 1989. This is a remarkable level of precision, considering that there were only 810 NSRI interviews in the state.

Nationally, the sheer number of interviews and careful research design resulted in a high level of precision. Nevertheless, an error factor was created. Standard error estimates for our overall national sample show that we can be 95% confident that the figures we obtained have an error margin, plus or minus, of less than 0.2%. This means, for example, that we are more than 95% certain that the figure for Catholics is in the range of 26.0% to 26.4% for the U.S. population. We must admit, however, that for a small group such as Unitarians, whom we found constitute 0.3% of the American population, the actual figure could be subject to greater proportionate fluctuation, even though the standard error for Unitarians is much less than 0.2%.

SOURCES OF POSSIBLE INACCURACY

Nearly every data collection concerning religion in America has had to face enormous problems of defining its terms and categories. This is due to the dynamic nature of religion in America and constant schisms and unions within Protestant denominations. New religions arise and others fade away. Navigating the complex byways of the ever-changing religious scene is fraught with difficulties. For instance, at the time of the Korean War, the Department of Defense listed 40 denominations under the general heading of Protestant chaplaincy, while today 260 groups are authorized.

Being asked to state their religion in a few words over a telephone is a problem for many people since they may find it difficult to classify their local church according to recognized denominational labels. In what denomination should we place "Christian Free-will Baptist Church of Christ?" How should we expect someone who attends the "First Church of Christ (Congregational)" to know that he is really a member of the United Church of

Christ? In addition, some local congregations are members of more than one denomination (for instance, of both the main Presbyterian and Methodist bodies).

The medium of communication, the telephone, has its restrictions. It is very likely that our Mennonite total does not include the estimated 90,000 Old Order Amish who do not possess telephones. It is also possible that our methodology tended to undercount groups that live in communal settings. Such a lapse was suggested to us by the Baha'i religious organization, which operates several collective settlements in the Carolinas and claims 110,000 adherents nationwide, as a partial reason for the undercount in the NSRI (we found only 28,000). It is also likely that many recent immigrants from Iran, with their experience of persecution, were reluctant to reveal their Baha'i faith in a telephone interview.

As we explained earlier, the range of miscount for small groups of 200,000 or fewer adherents could be proportionately very large. Quite possibly, the NSRI underestimated many small groups and overinflated others.

Our weighting system, which adjusted for race and inner-city dwelling, could not compensate for characteristics that were neither geographic nor demographic in nature. We had no ability to contact the homeless or the institutionalized population. Our reliance on interviewing in English may have led to underestimates of religious groups containing high proportions of recent immigrants. It is also possible, as mentioned above, that recent immigrants from societies with deep religious hostilities were reluctant to reveal their religion. Other foreign-origin religious groups probably went into the "miscellaneous" category under "Other Religions" since they gave unclear or complicated answers. For instance, "Sunni" or "Brahmin" might not always have been correctly categorized by our interviewers under the Muslim or Hindu designation. However, there are other sources of information that allow us to test and adjust our findings.

When our Muslim figure appeared much lower than some estimates ranging from 2 million to 6 million people; we looked to the U.S. Census as well as other sources to check our accuracy. Without much evidence or objective scientific measurement, some scholars, media people, and Muslim community representatives claimed that adherents to Islam had grown enormously in the last few years as a result of massive immigration from the Middle East. The 1990 census found that only 1,067,000 people (0.4% of the U.S. population) reported their ancestry as "Arab" or from an Arab nation. Even before the census figures were available, the Princeton Religious Research Center, utilizing accumulated Gallup polls, attempted to verify our findings. "Where Are the Muslims in the United States?" an article in the September 1991 issue of the center's publication, *Emerging Trends,* reported that their findings almost corroborated our own—only 0.2% nationally—

and concluded that enthusiastic supporters have in the past few years greatly exaggerated the number of Muslims. Nevertheless, we believe that there are specific research design factors, which we explained in Chapter 4, that resulted in an undercount; the Muslim population is probably around 0.5% of the U.S. population, and not the initial NSRI figure of 0.3%

THE NATIONAL FINDINGS

Although the NSRI does not profess to be a census of religious affiliation or denominational membership from the perspective of students of religion, it is valuable to know that in 1990 the public favored denominational and church names over theological terms in their replies. They provided generic brands of religion and denominational family names. It appears that the replies reflected people's perceived faith loyalty and background, the rootage of their faith rather than any actual current membership. For instance, few Lutherans provided their church's exact name, and hardly any Jews made a distinction between the denominational brands of Orthodox, Conservative, Reform, or Reconstructionist Judaism. One explanation is that in the context of the interview situation they gave "social" rather than "theological" answers.

A CANADIAN PARALLEL

There are obvious discrepancies between the NSRI findings and the membership figures of religious groups, which might have been predicted as the very construct of the term *member* means different things in different denominations. For most of the mainstream Protestant denominations, the Unitarians, and the Jehovah's Witnesses, the NSRI count exceeds that of the denominations for reasons we have discussed before. For a few, such as the Church of the Nazarene and the Seventh-Day Adventists, our numbers for adult adherents replicate the denomination's own figures. "Undercounted" groups with large claimed memberships include Muslims, Jews, Mormons, and the Eastern Orthodox churches, the United Church of Christ, the Church of God in Christ, and the Disciples of Christ. More discrepancies were found for smaller groups such as most of the non-Christian Eastern religions, the Christian Reformed Church, the International Church of the Foursquare Gospel, the Salvation Army, as well as many of the New Religious Movements (NRMs), such as New Age believers.

There are clear and readily available explanations for these trends. The best parallel source of corroboration lies with our near neighbor Canada. The Canadian census has long asked the same religious question as the NSRI did. In addition, Canadian churches' membership statistics appear alongside those of U.S. denominations in the *Yearbook of American and Canadian Churches,* produced for many years through the personal efforts of Constant H. Jacquet, Jr., of the National Council of Churches.

In 1991, Professor Marc Mentzer of the University of Saskatchewan tested the validity of the church-provided membership data by comparing them with the self-reported data on religion from the Canadian census. In an article in the *Journal for the Scientific Study of Religion* he produced a very interesting ratio, between the number of adherents reported in the Canadian census and those reported by the denominations. His main finding was for the mainstream Protestant groups: For every adherent the denomination was aware of, there was another person who identified with that tradition but was not on the church roll. One of the highest ratios was in the order of over 3 to 1, for the Unitarians. This is very similar to the proportion found in the NSRI. Officially, American Unitarian-Universalist Association claim 182,000 members, though NSRI found 502,000 identifiers.

The Protestant ratio of roughly 2 identifiers for every 1 member also applied to Canadian Jehovah's Witnesses. Similarly, in the United States, the claimed current membership figure for the Jehovah's Witnesses was around 830,000 people, whereas the NSRI discovered 1.38 million identifiers. Many of these are probably "regular visitors" who are in the process of becoming members. Though not officially members yet, they are often already active in evangelistic work. In addition, there may be people who self-identified as Jehovah's Witnesses who have been dropped from the official rolls.

Among those groups that claimed more members than were actually reported in the Canadian census were the Mormons, with a ratio of only 0.82. Other cases where the census reported fewer adherents than the denomination claimed were even more troubling, since the bias is expected to run in the other direction. Professor Mentzer explained that some adherents, such as those of the highly decentralized conservative denominations, have a very poor sense of denominational identity. He also found the tendency of some conservative Protestants to use the term *Christian* to mean *evangelical Protestant* and to use the category "Pentecostal" rather than to name a specific church.

The most extreme tendency to overestimate the number of adherents was found among the Eastern Orthodox churches, with the exception of the Greek Orthodox. Several reported membership that was twenty times what the Canadian census showed. This is unexpected; since their ethnicity and religion are so closely intertwined, one would expect Orthodox adherents to have a strong sense of identity. Again, the American situation with the NSRI exactly replicates the Canadian situation using their census. While NSRI figures estimate 0.5 million adult Orthodox adherents, the various Orthodox churches in the United States, counting as adherents anyone whom they baptize and anyone who admits to an ethnic or national heritage associated with an Orthodox church irrespective of that individual's current religious identification, claim 3.5 million members. It appears that this ethnic, ceremonial-focused religion is losing touch with the younger generations of North Americans.

Interestingly enough, in Canada two groups, Catholics and Jews, use the census as their official membership counts, so that the *Yearbook* and the census report tally exactly.

RELIGIOUS "NONES"

The main findings of the NSRI were mentioned earlier, in Chapter 1, and they are set out in detail in Table 1-2. Only a small minority (7.5%) stated that they had no religion. Another 0.7% were agnostics or humanists who probably should be included in the category known to sociologists of religion as religious "Nones." It is also possible that many of the refusals to respond to the question (2.3%) fall into this category. Nevertheless, our figures are very close to those collected by other recent surveys. The latest Gallup polls suggest that 1 in 11 Americans has no religion.

Since the 1950s were considered the recent high point of organized religion, the 1957 Bureau of the Census sample found lower figures for religious "Nones"; 0.9% refused to report, and 2.7% were either atheists or agnostics. There were few mentions of the term *atheist* in the survey. It seems that the term *atheist* is still unpopular today, possibly because it was associated with "atheistic communism" during the Cold War. The contacts we have had with the organized chapters of American Atheists suggested that these nonbelievers perceived themselves as an oppressed group. As one told us, "The worst thing you can be in this country is an atheist. . . . Everything else is excusable." The terms *agnostic, humanist,* and *freethinker* are more socially acceptable. Certainly, America is different from other Western countries in this regard. The 1986 Australian census of religious affiliation reported that 12% refused to answer and 13% reported no religion. In Canada, the governmental 1990 General Social Survey also reported that 12% of adults had no religion. The contrast with western Europeans is even stronger. In the Netherlands, 22% of the population reported no religion in the 1971 census, while recent surveys have found that this figure has risen to over 30%.

CHRISTIAN GROUPS

It is important to state that the NSRI designation of Christianity is broad-based and relates to what the actual religious group claims to be. As a result, we have included some of the smaller, controversial sects that do not include trinitarian beliefs. Their inclusion may annoy some theologians but is appropriate for this book, which is about religion in society rather than theology.

Based upon an estimated total adult U.S. population of over 175 million, the NSRI found that more than 151 million, comprising 86.2% of the population, provided a religious preference related to some form of Christianity.

"PROTESTANTS"

This is obviously a very mixed collection of people of whom we know little except that they are neither Catholic, religious "Nones," or of any non-Christian religion. We have therefore made limited use of this category in our tabulations and analyses.

The term *Protestant* does have theological meaning related to the belief in the Bible as a source of truth and right and to the concept of "the priesthood of all believers." We have often used the term *Protestant* without quotation marks to describe those Christian groups that are neither Catholic nor Orthodox. This covers four types of Protestants: the Lutherans; the Calvinist, or Reformed, tradition; the Episcopalians; and the independent, radical, or free type, which is predominant in the United States. The last group consists of Baptists, Methodists, Congregationalists, and sectarians, who stress the individual's direct approach to God, the church as an intimate fellowship of believers, and, frequently, the separation of church and state. Many Protestants do not identify themselves as members of a national denomination, but instead see themselves simply as members of a particular church. Paradoxically, this leads them to answer "Protestant" when asked their religion.

Despite our best efforts to press them to supply an actual denomination or church, 9.7% maintained that their religion was "Protestant." This total was larger than for any other of the forty-three Christian categories, except Catholic or Baptist.

"CHRISTIANS"

As we can observe from Table 1-1 in Chapter 1, "Christians" total 8 million and comprise 4.5% of the population. It might be thought that this is a generic or even residual category for people who are even less sure of what they are than are "Protestants." However, the facts are otherwise. Several churches have the word *Christian* in their titles. The best-known originate from the Christian Church (Disciples of Christ), which was founded in the 1830s. In 1906 a schism produced the Churches of Christ, and another in

1968 produced the Christian Churches and Churches of Christ. In addition there are the Christian and Missionary Alliance, the Christian Reformed church, the Christian Congregation, the Christian Methodist Episcopal church, the Christian Catholic church, the Christian Union, and the Christian Church of North America. Additional groups are listed in J. Gordon Melton's *Encyclopedia of American Religions*.

Anyone associated with the above-mentioned Protestant denominations could legitimately respond "Christian" if asked his or her religious identification. An obvious consequence was the deflation of specific denominational replies. Another complication arose for the Disciples of Christ, a strongly ecumenical group whose adherents may also have simply called themselves "Protestant." No doubt others with just vaguely Christian sentiments but no recent ties with a particular church also stated that they were "Christian." We also have some evidence to suggest that members of less well-known churches, such as the various Armenian churches, transdenominational churches, and nondenominational churches, provided this reply.

LUTHERANS

This term relates to the original Protestant church founded by Martin Luther in 1517. Though there have been mergers in recent years, three main and seven minor Lutheran groups remain. The largest is the Evangelical Lutheran Church in America, with a claimed membership of 5.2 million. The next two largest are the Lutheran Church–Missouri Synod, which claims 2.6 million members, and the Wisconsin Evangelical Lutheran Synod, with 420,000 adherents.

According to the NSRI, Lutherans are the fourth-largest denominational group in the United States, accounting for 5.2% of the adult population. Very few respondents made a distinction as to the type of Lutheran they were, even though there are significant differences between the larger liberal church and the two conservative churches.

BAPTISTS

Baptists, accounting for 19.4% of the population, are the second-largest denomination in the country. They account for one third of U.S. Protestants. All Baptists share the ritual of adult baptism by immersion but no overlying creed. They are a very mixed group (see Table A-1). There are a number of Baptist groupings, the largest of which, the Southern Baptist Convention, is the biggest Protestant denomination in the United States. The Southern Baptist Convention is a national organization comprised of 15 million current adult members—twice the number than in 1950. The term *Southern*

TABLE A-1

MAJOR COMPONENTS OF THE BAPTIST AND METHODIST
DENOMINATIONAL FAMILIES

BAPTISTS	METHODISTS
Southern Baptist Convention	United Methodist Church
National Baptist Convention of America	Africa Methodist Episcopal Church
National Baptist Convention U.S.A.	Africa Methodist Episcopal Zion Church
American Baptist Churches U.S.A.	Christian Methodist Episcopal Church
Baptist Bible Fellowship	Free Methodist Church
General Association of Regular Baptist Churches	
Baptist Missionary Association	
American Baptist Association	
Conservative Baptist Association of America	
Progressive National Baptist Convention	
National Association of Free Will Baptists	
Liberty Baptist Fellowship	
Baptist General Conference	
Seventh Day Baptist	
General Association of General Baptists	

Baptist does not simply apply to any Baptist who happens to live in the South. It is also true that there are numerous independent Baptist chapels and churches unconnected with any denomination.

The NSRI reported more Baptists than most membership figures, which suggests that since baptism is a voluntary act and membership requires a further step, many who are baptized may not have gone the additional step of joining a congregation.

METHODISTS

This is the second largest Protestant denominational family, accounting for 8% of the U.S. population. The reported memberships of Methodist churches have shown a considerable decline since the 1950s, and the NSRI reflects this trend. Even so, some leaders of the United Methodist church were skeptical of the NSRI's numbers, regarding them as inflated. However, they did not allow for the fact that the NSRI includes the historic black churches under the category "Methodist" (see Table A-1). It is also to be expected that a denominational family that has recently lost members so rapidly will have a lot of nominal, or unchurched, people who still identify with this religious tradition.

The NSRI found that many of those who are no longer on the rolls, the "nominals," maintain their traditional religious loyalty. They still return for family life-cycle events such as baptisms, weddings, and funerals. They are obviously not sufficiently alienated to drop the denominational identification, which they regard as part of their family tradition or social or ethnic heritage. This was summarized by one reaction to our survey from a United Methodist church minister quoted in the *Chicago Tribune,* "In my fifteen years as a pastor in Iowa, I probably conducted half my funerals for non-churched people. I've never seen them in church and they weren't listed as members. But when they died, their obituaries said they were Methodists."

MAINLINE PROTESTANT DENOMINATIONS

Terms such as *mainline, mainstream, old-line,* and *central tradition* are used a great deal in the literature about American religion. They relate to the country's religious and cultural center, which were the faiths held by the majority of Americans at the time of the Revolution. Even today, these faiths are nationally visible and prominent, partly due to their leadership of the National Council of the Churches of Christ in the U.S.A. Having a culturally rational tradition, they include strong elements of theological liberalism and reach out to the secular culture into which they are integrated.

Mainline groups include the Episcopalians, the Presbyterians, the Congregationalists (now the United Church of Christ), and, as some have recently suggested, the United Methodist Church, the liberal Lutherans, and the Disciples of Christ. These churches have been in relative decline for most of the last century, and most have lost a quarter of their memberships since the 1960s. As was mentioned for Methodists, family tradition and ethnic heritage cause many nonmembers to maintain a religious identification with these denominations.

As we said earlier, the Canadian pattern was directly reflected in the NSRI. The Episcopal church, which has 1.7 million fully confirmed members on its current roll, had nearly twice as many, over 3 million, appear on the NSRI. The Presbyterian Church (U.S.A.) and two smaller Presbyterian bodies together claim 3.1 million members, whereas the NSRI found nearly 5 million.

The conservative nature of the American public as far as religious denominations is concerned is shown in the respondents' treatment of the United Church of Christ. Even after careful checking of our responses, we found this denomination severely undercounted. It appears that a plurality of their members are still loyal to the historic Pilgrim brand name, "Congregational," much to the annoyance of the Cleveland-based denominational leadership. In part this is because many UCC churches in New England and the West have retained the word *Congregational* in their name.

EVANGELICALS

As a theological term, *Evangelicalism* includes five major religious traditions: the Baptists, the Holiness-Pentecostals, the Anabaptists, the Reformed, and the independents-fundamentalists. As we have noted, our respondents tended to provide specific church answers rather than theological or ideological ones. Most of the respondents who replied "Evangelical" were probably members of churches such as the Evangelical Free Church of America or possibly the Evangelical Congregational church. We doubt that many belonged to the Lutheran groups that have the word *Evangelical* in their church titles. It is possible, however, that some members of the former Evangelical and Reformed church of German and Swiss origin, which merged into the United Church of Christ in 1957, gave this reply, further lowering the UCC total.

The National Association of Evangelicals, the conservative alternative organization to the National Council of the Churches of Christ in the U.S.A., consists of over fifty denominations, 42,000 local congregations, 4.3 million communicants. It includes churches in the European Free, Holiness, Pentecostal, and Reformed traditions (see Table A-2), which stress the constancy of the Bible.

PENTECOSTALISM

This is a particular religious tradition "for saints who believe in the baptism with the Holy Ghost." It emphasizes religious experiences and can involve the paranormal. For example, the initial witness of the spirit is speaking in tongues, or glossolalia. Pentecostalism arose in the United States in the 1890s, and its largest body, the Assemblies of God, began in 1914.

Many respondents who belong to the Assemblies, which claims a membership approaching 2 million, identified themselves as Pentecostal in the NSRI. This reluctance to specifically identify may have been a result of the recent scandals involving televangelists Jim Bakker and Jimmy Swaggart. In addition, many of this denomination's congregations are known by titles such as "Cavalry Temple," so that the denominational affiliation is not that obvious to some members.

HOLINESS

The term *Holiness* refers to denominations that have a common belief in "entire sanctification," which teaches that believers can achieve a state of perfection in this life. Aside from this essential teaching, Holiness denominations hold much in common and overlap with other evangelical groups (see Table A-2). The main division in Holiness groups is between Pentecostals and non-Pentecostals. In social terms, they are also divided between white, black, and racially integrated churches. There are many small, independent churches and denominations within this category.

CHARISMATIC

This is not a denomination, but a highly heterogeneous movement. It is usually seen as a profoundly American form of religion. There are many forms of charismatic Christianity, ranging from associations of Roman Catholic priests to small independent house churches, large mega-churches, and even local Episcopalian congregations that have "gone charismatic." Essentially, charismatic belief involves "gifts of the spirit" and the presence of the supernatural in this world. It can involve divine healing and is often linked to Pentecostalism. There are networks of independent charismatic churches, including Oral Roberts's Charismatic Bible Ministries, and the Vineyard Fellowships.

FUNDAMENTALIST

This is one of the few theological terms that does not appear in any denominational title. Fundamentalists are a subgroup within Evangelicalism. If people were to be asked directly whether they were fundamentalists, obviously a far higher proportion would agree than actually answered with this term in the NSRI. Many individual denominations regard themselves as fundamentalist because of their dependence on personal revelation from the Holy Spirit and their belief in the literal truth, or inerrancy, of the biblical Scriptures. They are noted for the utilization of these beliefs in the shaping of their lives. The church takes a central position in the lives of its core members. They have separatist inclinations that include abstention from alcoholic beverages, smoking, attending movies, or mixing much with non-fundamentalists.

CHURCHES OF GOD

This category provides yet another problem of terminology, but it is deliberate. At least seven major denominations, mostly in the Holiness or Pen-

TABLE A-2

MAJOR DENOMINATIONAL COMPONENTS OF THREE PROTESTANT THEOLOGICAL
GROUPINGS

NATIONAL ASSOCIATION OF EVANGELICALS	HOLINESS TRADITION	PENTECOSTAL
Assemblies of God	Church of God in Christ	Assemblies of God
Church of the Nazarene	Church of God (Cleveland, Tennessee)	Int'l Pentecostal Holiness Church
Church of God (Cleveland, Tennessee)	Church of the Nazarene	Church of God (Cleveland, Tennessee)
Christian Reformed Church	Int'l Pentecostal Holiness Church	Open Bible Standard Churches
Presbyterian Church in America	Christian and Missionary Alliance	Pentecostal Church of God
Conservative Baptist Association of America	Wesleyan Church	United Pentecostal Church, International
Christian and Missionary Alliance	Free Methodist	Pentecostal Assemblies of the World
Int'l Church of the Foursquare Gospel	Salvation Army	Int'l Church of the Foursquare Gospel
Wesleyan Church	Church of God of Prophecy	
Baptist General Conference		
Int'l Pentecosal Holiness Church		
Free Methodist		
Church of God (World Headquarters)		
Evangelical Free Church of America		
Salvation Army		

tecostal tradition, claim this title because they wanted to re-create the original New Testament church.

APOSTOLIC, BRETHREN, MISSIONARY, CHURCH OF AMERICA

These designations reflect a mixture of groups with a wide variety of theological backgrounds that use these terms in their local denominational titles. Unfortunately, they are such a mixed bag that they have little analytical value.

MORMONS

The term *Mormon* is another name for the Church of Jesus Christ of Latter-Day Saints. Fifty-five percent of the LDS identifiers describe themselves as Mormon. The main LDS church and the smaller Mormon offshoots, such as the Reorganized Church, claim just under 4 million adherents. NSRI results suggest that this is an overestimate and that there are only 2.5 million adult adherents. One would be concerned about these figures if the Canadian data did not suggest that Mormons tend to overestimate their numbers; the church has a good knowledge of those entering but knows much less about those leaving the fold. As Mormonism is a rapidly growing religious movement, Mormon adherents are constantly moving in and out of the denomination. For instance, a study in Utah in the early 1980s found that for every 5 converts, 2 left the church. Those who leave do not have deeply embedded ties and are therefore unlikely to retain the kind of nominal loyalty, seen in lapsed Catholics and Episcopalians.

THE CATHOLIC DATA

Obviously, the term *Catholic* includes not only the Latin-rites Roman Catholic church but those Eastern-rites churches such as the Ukrainians and the Maronites and the other Middle Eastern churches that pledge their allegiance to the pope.

DETERMINING WHO IS A CATHOLIC

As with other religious groups, the problems associated with any attempt to tabulate the number of Catholics are largely those of definition. The number of estimated Catholics can be greater or smaller depending on the criteria used to measure the size of the population. The first step in understanding any count of the Catholic population involves learning the definition of membership underlying the count.

One method is an organizational census; the number of Catholics in a given jurisdiction is defined by the management of the parish and published annually in *The Official Catholic Directory*. The shortcoming of the organizational definition is that there are no specific criteria offered to qualify the estimates of the Catholic population. If a pastor determines that there are 1,000 Catholics in his parish, then the organizational-based estimate reflects that statistic.

The data from the NSRI is an alternative approach in which the delineating factor is an individual's wish to identify with Catholicism. Gallup surveys also employ the inclusive standard of measurement of self-definition; a Catholic is a person who says he or she is a Catholic.

COMPARISON OF GALLUP AND NSRI RESULTS

It appears that many more Americans identify themselves as Catholic than register in some fashion as a member in the Catholic church. Perhaps the most commonly quoted statistic about the size of the Catholic population is that Catholics comprise 28% of the American population. The source of this estimate is the Gallup research on religious percentages, which is based on smaller and less representative samples than the NSRI. Gallup reports that about 20% of this group say they are not church members. This "nominal" portion of the Catholic population probably measures about 4% to 6% of the total American population, or about 8 million adult Catholics in the broad sense of the term.

The NSRI is unique in that it involves a national representative sample of 29,600 Catholic respondents including 900 African Americans, 600 Asian Americans, and over 3000 Hispanic Americans. The most scientifically precise and valid data from the NSRI relate to the Catholic population because of the vast size of this Catholic sample. The demographic data associated with the NSRI research would describe both nominal and registered Catholics. As we have seen, our figure for 1990 (26.2%) is very close to that obtained in March 1957 (25.7%), using exactly the same question.

The difference between the two survey-based estimates of the Catholic preference is 1.7%. This percentage translates into a variation of 4,078,760, not an inconsiderable sum. The 1.7% variation, however, is well within the 3% margin of error typical of samples used for the Gallup survey.

JEWS

The NSRI question "What is your religion?" is very much a modern, Western concept. Historically, most Jews have never thought to separate Judaism as a religion from their ethnic or national culture. For many Jews, Judaism is much more of a family, or communitarian experience than a personal faith. Many secular Jews attend and celebrate home rituals, such as the Passover Seder meal, with their religiously observant relatives. which outsiders might interpret as a religious act.

The distinction between "Jewish" and "Judaic" populations is, like the existence of Jewish religious denominations, very much a modern and mainly American phenomenon. This trend reflects the influence of American pluralism and accounts for the difference between the NSRI figures (1.8%) and those normally reported for the Jewish population of the United States (2.2%). The NSRI nonspecific question on religious identification does not identify the secular ethnic 20% of the population, which is regarded by the organized Jewish community as part of its core.

A differently worded question would probably have evoked the loyalty of this additional 0.4% of the American population, who reported themselves as religious "Nones." Such a question is used by the National Opinion Research Center (NORC) in their annual General Social Survey and asks, "What is your religious preference: Is it Protestant, Catholic, Jewish, some other religion, or no religion?"

NEW AGE

Since this is not a religious group as such, the small numbers who reported this as their religion are not surprising. Probably only the most committed are included here. Many who have had a spiritual experience beyond the confines of traditional definitions of religion in the groups in which they were raised would, if asked directly, admit to New Age beliefs. However, they maintain their traditional religious identification in the context of the NSRI. Thus a Methodist with some New Age beliefs or views likely identified as a Methodist in our survey.

Religious groups can be organized by belief, life-style, rituals, institutionalization, and government structure. They can also be divided between imported and home-grown traditions, between democratized, centralized, and authoritarian systems, and between priestly and lay-led groups. Christian baptism divides between "sprinklers" and those who adopt immersion. Another possible division is between those groups with a U.S. majority, such as Quakers, Baptists, Unitarians, and Conservative and Reform Jews, and those faiths with large constituencies abroad, such as Catholics, Episcopalians, Lutherans, Muslims, and Orthodox Jews. All of these factors account for the appeal of particular denominations to particular people at particular times. The NSRI is valuable because it allows us to tease out these variations and subtleties in relation to contemporary American social life.

For the reader who wishes to learn more about complex issues such as a taxonomy of religions, or the origins, governance, and detailed beliefs of the nation's religious groups, a vast literature exists to inform you. The place to begin your studies is with our bibliography.

BIBLIOGRAPHY (BY CHAPTER)

◆ ◆ ◆

CHAPTER 1: INTRODUCTION

Brickman, William W., and Stanley Lehrer, eds. *Religion, Government and Education.* New York: Society for the Advancement of Education, 1961.

Coalter, Milton J., John M. Mulder, and Louis B. Weeks, eds. *The Organizational Revolution: Presbyterians and American Denominationalism.* Louisville: Westminster/John Knox Press, 1992.

Gallup, George, Jr., and Sarah Jones. *A Hundred Questions and Answers: Religion in America.* Princeton: Princeton Religion Research Center, 1989.

Jacquet, Constant H., Jr., and Alice M. Jones. *Yearbook of American and Canadian Churches.* Nashville: Abingdon Press, 1991.

Lenski, Gerhard. *The Religious Factor.* Garden City, N.Y.: Doubleday, 1963.

Rosten, Leo. *A Guide to the Religions of America.* New York: Simon and Schuster, 1955.

CHAPTER 2: RELIGION IN AMERICAN CULTURE: A HISTORICAL OVERVIEW

Ahlstrom, Sydney E. *A Religious History of the American People.* New Haven: Yale University Press, 1972.

Catton, Bruce. *This Hallowed Ground.* Garden City, N.Y.: Doubleday, 1956.

Coalter, Milton J., John M. Mulder, and Louis B. Weeks, eds. *The Organizational Revolution: Presbyterians and American Denominationalism.* Louisville: Westminster/John Knox Press, 1992.

Commager, Henry Steele. *The American Mind.* New Haven: Yale University Press, 1950.

Cowing, Cedric B. *The Great Awakening and the American Revolution.* Chicago: Rand McNally, 1971.

Degler, Carl N., ed. *Pivotal Interpretations of American History.* 2 vols. New York: Harper and Row, 1966.

Frazier, E. Franklin. *The Negro Church in America,* 10th ed. New York: Schocken Books, 1974.

Gaustad, Edwin Scott. *Historical Atlas of Religion in America.* New York: Harper and Row, 1962.

Handlin, Oscar. *Adventure in Freedom.* New York: McGraw-Hill, 1954.

Hennesey, James, S.J. *American Catholics: A History of the Roman Catholic Community in the United States.* New York: Oxford University Press, 1981.

Herberg, Will. *Protestant, Catholic, Jew.* Garden City, N.Y.: Doubleday, 1955.

Kammen, Michael. *People of Paradox.* New York: Knopf, 1972.

Lincoln, C. Eric. *The Black Church Since Frazier.* New York: Schocken Books, 1974.

———. *Race, Religion, and the Continuing American Dilemma.* New York: Hill and Wang, 1984.

Lincoln, C. Eric, and Lawrence H. Mamiya. *The Black Church in the African American Experience.* Durham, N.C.: Duke University Press, 1990.

Marcus, Jacob R. *Studies in American Jewish History.* Cincinnati: Hebrew Union College Press, 1969.

Maynard, Theodore. *The Story of American Catholicism.* 2 vols. Garden City, N.Y.: Doubleday Image, 1941.

Miller, Perry. *New England Mind from Colony to Province.* Cambridge, Mass.: Harvard University Press, 1953.

Morison, Samuel Eliot. *The Oxford History of the American People.* New York: Oxford University Press, 1965.

Niebuhr, Reinhold. *The Nature and Destiny of Man: A Christian Interpretation.* New York: Scribners, 1949.

———. *Pious and Secular America.* New York: Scribners, 1958.

Sklare, Marshall. *American Jews.* New York: Random House, 1971.

Stevens-Arroyo, Anthony M. *Prophets Denied Honor: An Anthology on the Hispanic Church.* New York: Orbis Books, Maryknoll, 1980.

Tyler, Alice Felt. *Freedom's Ferment: Phases of American Social History to 1860.* Freeport, N.Y.: Books for Libraries Press, 1944.

CHAPTER 3: GEOGRAPHY IS DESTINY

Bruce, Steve. *Pray TV: Televangelism in America.* New York: Routledge, 1990.

Carter, Lewis F. *Charisma and Control in Rajneeshpuram: The Role of Shared Values in the Creation of a Community.* New York: Cambridge University Press, 1990.

Clarke, Clifford J. "The Bible Belt Thesis: An Empirical Test of the Hypothesis of Clergy Overrepresentation, 1890–1930." *Journal for the Scientific Study of Religion* 29: 210–25 (1990).

Egerton, John. *The Americanization of Dixie: The Southernization of America.* New York: Harper and Row, 1974.

Finke, Roger. "Demographics of Religious Participation: An Ecological Approach, 1850–1971." *Journal for the Scientific Study of Religion* 28: 45–58 (1989).

Finke, Roger, and Rodney Stark. "How the Upstart Sects Won America: 1776–1850." *Journal for the Scientific Study of Religion* 28: 27–44 (1989).

Frankel, Sandra Sizer. *California's Spiritual Frontiers: Religious Alternatives in Anglo-Protestantism, 1850–1910.* Berkeley, Calif.: University of California Press, 1988.

Gordon, James S. *The Golden Guru: The Strange Journey of Bhagwan Shree Rajneesh.* Lexington, Mass.: Stephen Green Press, 1987.

Johnson, Curtis D. *Islands of Holiness: Rural Religion in Upstate New York, 1790–1860.* Ithaca, N.Y.: Cornell University Press, 1989.

Kraybill, Donald B. *The Riddle of Amish Culture.* Baltimore: Johns Hopkins University Press, 1989.

Meinig, D. W. "The Mormon Culture Region: Strategies and Patterns in the Geography of the American West." *Annals of the Association of American Geographers* 55: 191–220 (1960).

Stump, R. W. "Regional Divergence in Religious Affiliation in the United States." *Sociological Analysis* 45: 283–99 (1984).

Quinn, Bernard, et al. *Churches and Church Membership in the United States, 1980.* Washington, D.C.: Glenmary Research Center, 1982.

Shibley, Mark A. "The Southernization of American Religion: Testing a Hypothesis." *Sociological Analysis* 52: 159–174 (1991).

Young, Robert. "The Protestant Heritage and the Spirit of Gun Ownership." *Journal for the Scientific Study of Religion* 28: 300–309 (1989).

Zelinsky, Wilbur. *The Cultural Geography of the United States.* Englewood Cliffs, N.J.: Prentice-Hall, 1973.

CHAPTER 4: FROM THE ETHNIC FACTOR TO THE NEW AGE

Alba, Richard. *Ethnic Identity: The Transformation of White America.* New Haven: Yale University Press, 1990.

Albanese, Catherine L. *Nature Religion from the Algonkian Indians to the New Age.* Chicago: Chicago University Press, 1990.

Allen, James P., and Eugene Turner. *We the People: An Atlas of America's Ethnic Diversity.* New York: Macmillan, 1988.

Bean, Frank D., and Marta Tienda. *The Hispanic Population of the United States.* New York: Russell Sage Foundation, 1987.

Brown, Karen McCarthy. *Mama Lola: A Vodou Priestess in Brooklyn.* Berkeley, Calif.: University of California Press, 1991.

Choldin, Harvey. "Statistics and Politics: The 'Hispanic Issue' in the 1980 Census." *Demography* 23: 403–18 (1986).

Cox, Harvey. *Turning East.* New York: Simon and Schuster, 1977.

Davis, Cyprian. *The History of Black Catholics in the United States.* New York: Crossroad, 1990.

Dobyns, Henry F. *The Number Became Thinned: Native American Population Dynamics in Eastern North America.* Knoxville: University of Tennessee Press, 1983.

Durkheim, Emile. *The Elementary Forms of Religious Life.* Translated by Joseph W. Train. Glencoe, Il.: Free Press of Glencoe, 1948.

Gans, Herbert J. "Symbolic Ethnicity: The Future of Ethnic Groups and Cultures in America." In Herbert J. Gans, ed. *On the Making of Americans: Essays in Honor of David Reisman.* Philadelphia: University of Pennsylvania Press, 1979.

Glazer, Nathan, and Daniel Moynihan. *Beyond the Melting Pot.* Cambridge, Mass.: MIT Press, 1972.

Gonzalez, Robert, and Michael LaVelle. *The Hispanic Catholic in the U.S.* New York: Northeastern Pastoral Center, 1988.

Grayson, James Huntley. *Early Buddhism and Christianity in Korea: A Study in the Explanation of Religion.* Leiden: Brill, 1985.

Greeley, Andrew M. *The Denominational Society.* Glenview, Il.: Scott, Foresman, 1972.

———. *That Most Distressful Nation: The Taming of the American Irish.* Chicago: Quadrangle Books, 1973.

Hammond, Phillip, and David Bromley, eds. *The Future of New Religious Movements.* Macon, Ga.: Mercer University Press, 1987.

Hurh, Won Moo, and Kwang Chung Kim. "Religious Participation of Korean Immigrants in the United States." *Journal for the Scientific Study of Religion* 29: 19–34 (1990).

Kosmin, Barry A., et al. *Highlights of the CJF 1990 National Jewish Population Survey.* New York: Council of Jewish Federations, 1991.

Lieberson, Stanley. "Unhyphenated Whites in the United States." *Ethnic and Racial Studies* 8: 159–180 (1985).

Lieberson, Stanley, and Mary C. Walters. *From Many Strands: Ethnic and Racial Groups in Contemporary America.* New York: Russell Sage Foundation, 1988.

Martin, David. *Tongues of Fire: The Explosion of Protestantism in Latin America.* Oxford: Blackwell, 1990.

Myers, Ronald E., Hie-Won Tie, and Richard S. Hann. *Social Organization of Church-Based Screening.* Cheltenham, Pa.: Fox Chase Cancer Center, 1991.

Palinkas, Lawrence A. *Rhetoric and Religious Experience: The Discourse of Immigrant Chinese Churches.* Fairfax, Va.: George Mason University Press, 1989.

Porterfield, Amanda. "Witchcraft and the Colonization of Algonquin and Iroquois Cultures." *Religion and American Culture* 2: 103–24 (1992).

Progressions, 4 (1), 1992 [The Black Church in America].

Religion Watch (newsletter), 1985–92.

Spickard, James V. "Experiencing Religious Rituals: A Schutzian Analysis of Navajo Ceremonies." *Sociological Analysis* 52: 191–204 (1991).

Stillson, Judah. *Hare Krishna and the Counterculture.* New York: Wiley, 1974.

Williams, Raymond Brady. *Religions of Immigrants from India and Pakistan.* Cambridge: Cambridge University Press, 1988.

Zogby, John. *Arab America Today.* Washington, D.C.: Arab American Institute, 1990.

CHAPTER 5: THE POLITICS OF RELIGION AND THE RELIGION OF POLITICS

Castillo, Dennis. "The Origin of the Priest Shortage: 1942–1992." *America* (24 October 1992).

Chidesper, David. *Patterns of Power: Religion and Politics in American Culture.* Englewood Cliffs, N.J.: Prentice-Hall, 1988.

Colombo, Furio. *God in America: Religion and Politics in the United States.* Translated by Kristin Jarrat. New York: Columbia University Press, 1985.

Duke, James T., and Johnson, Barry L. "Religious Affiliation and Congressional Representation." *Journal for the Scientific Study of Religion,* 31: 324–29 (1992).

Fuchs, Lawrence H. *John F. Kennedy and American Catholicism.* New York: Meredith Press, 1967.

George, Carol V. *God's Salesman.* New York: Oxford University Press, 1992.

Greeley, Andrew M. *Religious Changes in America.* Cambridge, Mass.: Harvard University Press, 1989.

Greenawalt, Ken. *Religious Convictions and Political Choice.* New York: Oxford University Press, 1988.

Herberg, Will. *Protestant, Catholic, Jew.* Garden City, N.Y.: Doubleday, 1955.

Hertzke, Alan D. *Representing God in Washington.* Knoxville: University of Tennessee Press, 1988.

Johnson, Stephen D., and Joseph B. Tamney, eds. *The Political Role of Religion in the United States.* Boulder, Colo.: Westview Press, 1986.

Krinsky, Fred. *The Politics of Religion in America.* Beverly Hills, Calif.: Glencoe Press, 1968.

———. *Democracy and Complexity: Who Governs the Governors?* Beverly Hills, Calif.: Glencoe Press, 1968.

Lachman, Seymour P. "Barry Goldwater and the 1964 Religious Issue." *A Journal of Church and State* 10 (Autumn 1968): 389–404.

Lopatto, Paul. *Religion and the Presidential Election.* New York: Praeger, 1985.

Martin, William. *Billy Graham: A Prophet With Honor.* New York: William Morrow & Co., 1991.

Roof, Wade Clark, ed. *Religion in American Today,* the Annals of the American Academy of Political and Social Science, vol. 480 (July 1985). Beverly Hills, Calif.: Sage, 1985.

Smidt, Corwin, and Paul Kellstedt. "Evangelicals in the Post-Reagan Era: An Analysis of Evangelical Voters in the 1988 Presidential Election." *Journal for the Scientific Study of Religion* 31: 330–38 (1992).

Taft, Charles P., and Bruce L. Felknor. *Prejudice and Politics.* New York: Anti-Defamation League, 1960.

CHAPTER 6: CULTURE WAR: GENERATIONAL, GENDER, AND FAMILY ISSUES

Babchuk, Nicholas, and Hugh Witt. "R-Order and Religious Switching." *Journal for the Scientific Study of Religion* 29: 246–54 (1990).

D'Antonio, W. V., and J. Aldous. *Families and Religions: Conflicts and Change in Modern Society.* Beverly Hills, Calif.: Sage, 1983.

D'Antonio, William, James Davidson, Dean Hoge, and Ruth Wallace. *American Catholic Laity in a Changing World.* Kansas City: Sheed and Ward, 1989.

Daly, M. *The Church and the Second Sex*. Boston: Beacon Press, 1985.

Ellison, Christopher G., and Darren E. Sherkat. "Patterns of Religious Mobility Among Black Americans." *The Sociological Quarterly* 31: 551–68 (1990).

Heaton, T. B., and M. Cornwall. "Religious Group Variation in the Socioeconomic Status and Family Behavior of Women." *Journal for the Scientific Study of Religion* 28: 283–99 (1989).

Heaton, Tim B. "Religious Group Characteristics, Endogamy, and Interfaith Marriages." *Sociological Analysis* 51: 363–76 (1990).

Jacquet, Constant H., Jr. *Women Ministers in 1986 and 1977: A Ten-Year View*. New York: National Council of Churches of Christ, 1988.

Kalmijn, Matthius. "Shifting Boundaries: Trends in Religious and Educational Homogamy." *American Sociological Review* 56: 786–800 (1991).

Mosher, W., L. Williams, and D. Johnson. "Religion and Fertility in the United States: New Patterns," *Demography* 29: 199–214 (1992).

Perrin, Robin D. "American Religion in the Post-Aquarian Age: Values and Demographic Factors in Church Growth and Decline." *Journal for the Scientific Study of Religion* 28: 75–89 (1989).

Rokeach, Milton. *The Open and Closed Mind*. New York: Basic Books, 1960.

Roof, Wade Clark, and William McKinney. *American Mainline Religion*. New Brunswick, N.J.: Rutgers University Press, 1987.

Roof, Wade Clark. "Multiple Religious Switching: A Research Note." *Journal for the Scientific Study of Religion* 28: 530–35 (1989).

Roozen, David A., William McKinney, and Wayne Thompson. "The 'Big Chill' Generation Warms to Worship." *Review of Religious Research* 31: 314–22 (1990).

Stark, Rodney, and Charles Glock. *American Piety: The Nature of Religious Commitment*. Berkeley, Calif.: University of California Press, 1968.

Thornton, A. "Reciprocal Influences of Family and Religion in a Changing World." *Journal of Family and Marriage* 47: 381–94 (1985).

Wuthnow, Robert. *The Restructuring of American Religion: Society and Faith Since World War II*. Princeton: Princeton University Press, 1988.

CHAPTER 7: THE RELIGIOUS PECKING ORDER

Berger, Peter, Brigitte Berger, and Hansfried Kellner. *The Homeless Mind*. New York: Random House, 1973.

Berger, Peter L. *The Sacred Canopy: Elements of a Sociological Theory of Religion*. Garden City, N.Y.: Doubleday, 1967.

Bull, Malcom. "The Seventh-Day Adventists: Heretics of American Civil Religion." *Sociological Analysis*. 50: 177–87 (1989).

Hodgkinson, V., and M. Weitzman. *Giving and Volunteering in the United States*. Washington, D.C.: Independent Sector, 1988.

Kosmin, Barry A., Ariela Keysar, and Nava Lerer. "Secular Education and the Religious Profile of Contemporary Black and White Americans." *Journal for the Scientific Study of Religion* 31: 523–32 (1992).

Lazerwitz, Bernard. "A Comparison of Major United States Religious Groups." *Journal of the American Statistics Association* 56: 574–78 (1961).

Niebuhr, H. Richard. *The Social Sources of Denominationalism*. Hamden, Conn.: Shoestring Press, 1954.

Pope, Liston, "Religious and Class Structure." *Annals of the American Academy of Political and Social Sciences* 256: 84–91 (1948).

Princeton Religion Research Center. Princeton, N.J. *Religion in America 1991*.

Princeton Religion Research Center. *Emerging Trends*, Volumes: 1–15 (1977–92).

Sorokin, Pitirim. *Social Mobility*. New York: Harper, 1927.

Sweet, William. "The Protestant Churches." *Annals of the American Academy of Political and Social Sciences* 256: 49–50 (1948).

The Roper Center. *The Public Perspective* 2 (1990–92).

Weber, Max. *The Protestant Ethic and the Spirit of Capitalism*. Translated by Talcott Parsons. New York: Charles Scribner's Sons. 1958.

Wuthnow, R., and Virginia Hodgkinson & Associates. *Faith and Philanthropy in America*. San Francisco: Jossey-Bass, 1990.

APPENDIX: Religious Statistics

Association of Statisticians of American Religious Bodies. *Churches and Church Membership in the United States 1990*. Atlanta: Glenmary Research Center, 1992.

Bruce, Steve. *A House Divided: Protestantism, Schism and Secularization*. New York: Routledge, 1990.

Bull, Malcolm, and Keith Lockhart. *Seeking Sanctuary: Seventh-Day Adventism and the American Dream*. San Francisco: Harper and Row, 1989.

Corbett, Julia Mitchell. *Religion in America*. Englewood Cliffs, N.J.: Prentice-Hall, 1990.

Current Population Reports. *Religion Reported by the Civilian Population of the United States: March 1957*, series P-20, no. 79. Washington, D.C.: Bureau of the Census, 1958.

D'Antonio, William, James Davidson, Dean Hoge, and Ruth Wallace. *American Catholic Laity in a Changing Church*. Kansas City: Sheed and Ward, 1989.

Eisinga, Rob, and Albert Felling. "Church Membership in the Netherlands 1960–1987," *Journal for the Scientific Study of Religion* 29: 108–12 (1990).

Ethridge, F. Maurice. "Under-Reported Churches in Middle Tennessee: A Research Note." *Journal for the Scientific Study of Religion* 28: 518–29 (1989).

Greeley, Andrew. *The American Catholic*. New York: Basic Books, 1977.

Melton, J. Gordon. *The Encyclopedia of American Religions*, 2nd ed. Detroit: Gale, 1987.

Mentzer, Marc S. "The Validity of Denominational Membership Data in Canada." *Sociological Analysis* 52: 293–99 (1991).

Poloma, Margaret M., and Brian F. Pendleton. "Religious Experiences, Evangelism, and Institutional Growth Within the Assemblies of God." *Journal for the Scientific Study of Religion* 28: 415–31 (1989).

Rosenberg, Ellen M. *The Southern Baptists: A Subculture in Transition*. Knoxville: University of Tennessee Press, 1989.

Stark, Rodney. "The Reliability of Historical United States Census Data on Religion." *Sociological Analysis* 53: 91–95 (1992).

$$\Omega$$

INDEX

◆ ◆ ◆